Cult and Controversy:

The Worship of the Eucharist Outside Mass

Studies in the Reformed Rites
of the Catholic Church,
Volume IV

Nathan Mitchell, osb

Cult and Controversy:

The Worship
of the Eucharist Outside Mass

Pueblo Publishing Company

New York

Design: Frank Kacmarcik

Scriptural pericopes quoted from the Revised
Standard Version.

Exerpts from "East Coker" and "Little Gidding" by
T.S. Eliot are reprinted from his volume FOUR
QUARTETS by permission of Harcourt Brace
Jovanovich, Inc.; copyright 1943 by T.S. Eliot;
renewed 1971 by Esme Valerie Eliot.

Exerpts from the English translation of *The Rite of
Holy Communion and Worship of the Eucharist Outside
Mass*, © 1974, International Committee on English in
the Liturgy, Inc. All rights reserved.

Printed in the United States of America.

ISBN: 0-916134-50-4

For My Parents

Acknowledgment

It is an author's happy task to acknowledge those whose behind-the-scenes work makes the production of a book possible. To Aidan Kavanagh, General Editor of this Series, I am grateful both for his inspiration as a teacher and his guidance throughout the process of this book's birth. Mrs. Shirley Risinger, who typed the manuscript, deserves particular credit for her patience and skill in deciphering the author's hieroglyphics. Brother René Bouillon painstakingly photocopied the manuscript; to him much gratitude is due. Finally, a word of thanks to all those, known and unknown, whose prayer and good humor made it possible for me to complete the work.

Nathan Mitchell, osb
St. Meinrad Archabbey
Eastertide, 1981

Contents

History of the Cult of the Eucharist Outside Mass

Abbreviations

Corpus Christianorum	*Corpus Christianorum.* Series Latina. Turnhout: Brepols, 1953–present.
CSEL	*Corpus Scriptorum Ecclesiasticorum Latinorum.* Edited by the Vienna Academy. Vienna: 1866–present.
DACL	*Dictionnaire d'archéologie chrétienne et de liturgie.* Edited by F. Cabrol, H. Leclercq and H.I. Marrou. 15 Volumes. Paris: 1907–1953.
DS	H. Denzinger and A. Schönmetzer, eds. *Enchridion Symbolorum, Definitionum et Declarationum.* 33rd edition. Rome: Herder, 1965.
Dictionnaire de spiritualité	*Dictionnaire de spiritualité ascétique et mystique.* Doctrine et Histoire. Edited by M. Viller *et al.* Paris: Beauchesne, 1937–present.
Mansi	J.D. Mansi, ed. *Sacrorum Conciliorum nova et amplissima Collectio.* 31 volumes. Florence and Venice: 1757-1798. Reprinted and continued by L. Petit and J.B. Martin (to 53 volumes). Paris: 1889–1927.
MGH	*Monumenta Germaniae Historica.* Berlin: 1826–present.
PG	*Patrologia Graeca.* Edited by J.P. Migne. 161 volumes. Paris: 1857–1866.
PL	*Patrologia Latina.* Edited by J.P. Migne. 217 volumes, with 4 volumes of indices. Paris: 1878–1890.

History of the Cult
of the Eucharist Outside Mass

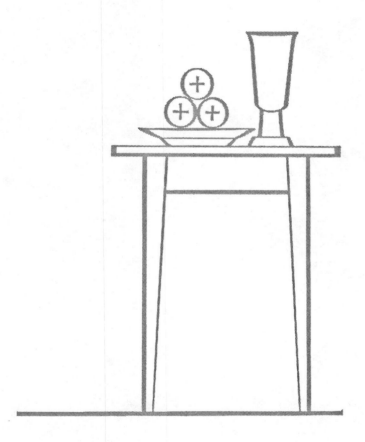

Introduction

"At the heart of it all is the eucharistic action, a thing of an absolute simplicity—the taking, blessing, breaking and giving of bread and the taking, blessing and giving of a cup of wine, as these were first done with their new meaning by a young Jew before and after supper with His friends on the night before He died. . . . He had told His friends to do this henceforward with the new meaning 'for the *anamnesis*' of Him, and they have done it always since."[1]

With these words Gregory Dix brought his remarkable study *The Shape of the Liturgy* to a conclusion. After nearly 800 pages of description, analysis, and historical research, Dix ended where he had begun: with the words and actions of Jesus "on the night before he died." That a liturgist might conclude with an explicit eucharistic theme is not surprising. Perhaps more startling, however, is what we find at the end of the second volume of Edward Schillebeeckx's recent and monumental christology. Under the subtitle "Eucharistic Thanksgiving," Schillebeeckx writes:

"And we remember
how he, who loved us so much,
and was one with you, his good Father,
in the last night of his life on earth,
took bread in his holy hands,
blessed, broke and shared it
at table with his friends, saying:
'This is my body for you.'

And what he did filled his heart:
he also took the cup at the table

gave thanks, praised you, Father, and said:
'Drink this cup, all of you, with me. . . .'"[2]

Dix the liturgist and Schillebeeckx the systematic
theologian find common ground in the eucharistic
words and deeds of Jesus. And this is altogether appropriate, for it reminds us that doctrine is first of all doxology, that faith is first rooted in the gestures and utterances of worship.

If this is so, however, how can one explain the evolution, within the Catholic tradition, of a cult of the
eucharist *outside* Mass? How did the eucharistic
action—a thing, as Dix says, "of an absolute
simplicity"—give way to a pattern of devotion quite independent of "taking, blessing, breaking, giving?" To
put the question another way, how did the eucharistic
action become a eucharistic *object*?

The first part of this book attempts to deal with these
questions. It is my conviction that the emergence of a
eucharistic cult outside Mass can be explained only by
careful attention to the evolution of the liturgy itself.
This does not mean that other matters—theological controversy, social and economic factors, religious movements of dissent and reform—failed to play a role in the
development of eucharistic devotion. Theological debate certainly contributed to the perhaps exaggerated
attention to the eucharistic species popularly (if not always accurately) identified with medieval Latin piety.
And social change in medieval Europe, especially the
movement toward an urban-centered economy as the
old feudal system waned, was definitely a contributing
factor in the appearance of feasts like Corpus Christi,
with its pattern of procession, exposition of the sacrament, and Benediction.

When all is said and done, however, the liturgy itself is
the primary source of those eucharistic customs now
regulated by the 1973 rites for "Holy Communion and
Worship of the Eucharist Outside Mass."[3] Many of

4

these customs, such as communion for the ill or for those absent from the Sunday assembly, reach back to the earliest generations of Christians. For the eucharist, as both "holy meal" and "sacred food," rather quickly gained independence from its original setting in a *full* meal where other foods were shared in common. Chapter One will explore how and when the eucharistic action and the eucharistic food were disengaged from the communal acts of dining. Chapter Two will show how, as a result of this disengagement, a new interpretation of eucharistic activity could emerge: the ancient human symbols of dining together were reinterpreted as *ritual drama,* vivid symbolic reenactments of Jesus' life, death, and resurrection. And from ritual drama it is a relatively short step to the dramatic allegorizations of the eucharistic liturgy proposed by early medieval commentators like Amalarius of Metz.

Chapters Three and Four offer detailed discussions of the medieval eucharistic debates that helped create the atmosphere within which cultic devotion flourished. Although they often deal with questions that contemporary theology would consider tangential at best, they are important because they represent the earliest efforts to treat the eucharist systematically, apart from its immediate liturgical context. Thus, for example, the ninth-century quarrel between the monks Paschasius Radbertus and Ratramnus illustrates some of the problems that arise when eucharistic *interpretation* is cut loose from eucharistic *action*. Similarly, the Berengarian controversy (eleventh century) and the early scholastic debates about the moment of consecration (twelfth century) eventually led to alterations in the liturgy itself: e.g., the use of the sacrament as a processional object in the liturgy of Holy Week, and the elevation of the species after the Lord's words in the eucharistic prayer.

The often complicated distinctions that these medieval disputants elaborated will strike many modern readers as banal, perhaps even absurd. But they reveal something crucial. Speculation of the sort engaged in by Paschasius Radbertus, Ratramnus, Berengarius, Lanfranc and others was possible precisely because the primitive liturgical genre—symbolic transactions of dining centered on bread broken and cup shared—had gradually been transformed into a genre of another order, a mystical reenactment of the events by which Jesus offered himself on the cross. This shift of liturgical genres could perhaps be compared in effect and consequence to what happens when a poem, say, Dante's *Divine Comedy*, is "translated" into narrative prose. In liturgy, as in literature, change of genre or form produces change of content and meaning. The integrity of art depends on unity of form and content, genre and meaning; that is why one cannot "translate" Picasso's "Guernica" into some other medium like glass or stone without altering its meaning. Something similar happened when the eucharistic action, disengaged from a community's meal, was "translated" into the genre or form for ritual drama. When Theodore of Mopsuestia (+ 428) describes the deacons who bear the gifts to the altar as pallbearers who carry Jesus to his place of burial, we are faced with a decisive shift of liturgical genre, and a concomitant shift in meaning and interpretation.[4] The table has become a tomb; the people's servants (deacons) have become Jesus' pallbearers; the actions of eating and drinking have become part of the ritual drama in which Jesus once more dies and rises in mystery. The change of genre, holy meal to ritual drama, symbolic action to dramatic allegory, implies a significant alteration of content, meaning, and interpretation.

To say this is not to dispute the legitimacy of change or development in the forms or meanings of worship. Worship changes because people do. And as Gregory Dix insisted, the fundamental shape of the eucharist has survived: we still take, bless, break, and give bread and cup. The point here is simply that these ritual verbs (to take, bless, break, give), when inserted into a new

6

liturgical genre (drama instead of meal, allegory instead of symbol), absorb different meanings and inspire different interpretations. Sometimes these meanings and interpretations may come into conflict with one another. This happened, surely, when the ancient symbols of dining together, obviously intended as invitations to *eat* and *drink* at the eucharist, gave way to "ocular communion"—the desire to *see* the host. The bodily symbolism of ingestion and nourishment was all but overpowered by the visual symbolism of "gazing at the Beloved."[5] The consequences of this conflict between types of eucharistic symbolism (and corresponding types of interpretation) will be evident in our discussion of medieval eucharistic cult outside Mass (Chapter Four).

The four chapters of Part One thus provide an historical synopsis of eucharistic cult outside Mass—what made it possible, and what promoted its growth and popularity. Our attention in these chapters will focus almost exclusively on the western (Latin) churches, since it is in these that the customs liturgically regulated by the reforms following the Second Vatican Council originated.[6] Some customs common to both eastern and western churches, such as eucharistic reservation, are discussed only incidentally here.[7] Other practices such as visits to the Blessed Sacrament, processions, Benediction, exposition, the Forty Hours Devotion, eucharistic congresses are discussed in greater detail, since the 1973 document on "Holy Communion and Worship of the Eucharist Outside Mass" deals explicitly with them.

Unquestionably, the liturgical reforms mandated by the Second Vatican Council represent a return to the primitive liturgical genre of a holy meal eaten and drunk in celebration of the Risen One, present among his people in word and sacrament. This return does not disqualify those cultic customs that have for centuries been associated with eucharistic devotion in its Roman Catholic expression, such as processions, exposition, Benediction, and prayer in the presence of the sacrament. Nevertheless, the conscious return to the ancient genre of holy meal and sacred food necessitates changes in both pastoral practice and theological interpretation. These changes will be discussed in greater detail in Part Two of this book.

Perhaps some lines from T.S. Eliot's "Little Gidding" may form an appropriate conclusion to these introductory remarks:

"What we call the beginning is often the end
And to make an end is to make a beginning.
The end is where we start from. . . .

We shall not cease from exploration
And the end of all our exploring
Will be to arrive where we started
And know the place for the first time."[8]

The eucharistic experience of the Christian community ends where it begins and begins where it ends, in the actions of taking, blessing, breaking, and giving "as these were first done with their new meaning by a young Jew before and after supper with His friends on the night before He died." Even the most highly elaborated forms of eucharistic cult outside Mass—the Forty Hours Devotion, for example—have as their ultimate purpose to help us "arrive where we started/And know the place for the first time." Christian life begins and ends at the table: the table of the baptismal eucharist, the table of the farewell meal of a Christian in the liturgy of death and burial. We begin to live and we begin to die in that corporate assembly among whom Jesus Christ eats and drinks now that he is risen from the dead.

NOTES

1. Gregory Dix, *The Shape of the Liturgy* (Westminster: Dacre Press, 1945), pp. 743-744.

2. Edward Schillebeeckx, *Christ*, translated by John Bowden (New York: Seabury Press, 1980), p. 749.

3. For the text of the new rites for "Holy Communion and Worship of the Eucharist Outside Mass," see *The Rites* (2 vols.; New York: Pueblo Publishing Company, 1976-1980), I, pp. 449-512.

4. See Theodore of Mopsuestia, *Baptismal Homily*, IV; in Edward Yarnold, *The Awe-Inspiring Rites of Initiation* (Slough: St. Paul Publications, 1971), pp. 211-237.

5. In the final chapter of this book we shall return to this conflict between types of symbolism in the eucharist: visual vs. acoustic, ingestive vs. intellectual.

6. Some customs, such as communion of the ill and dying, are obviously common to both eastern and western churches; others, such as exposition of the eucharistic species in a monstrance, are western innovations.

7. The question of eucharistic reservation has been studied rather extensively in the twentieth century. Among the most recent historical studies is Otto Nussbaum's *Die Aufbewahrung der Eucharistie* (Theophaneia, 29; Bonn: Hanstein, 1979). In English, the following studies are still valuable: W.H. Freestone, *The Sacrament Reserved* (Alcuin Club Collections, XXI; London: A.R. Mowbray and Co., 1917); Gregory Dix, *A Detection of Aumbries* (Westminster: Dacre Press, 1954); Archdale A. King and Cyril E. Pocknee, *Eucharistic Reservation in the Western Church* (London, 1965).

8. T.S. Eliot, *The Complete Poems and Plays, 1909-1950* (New York: Harcourt, Brace and World, 1971), pp. 144, 145.

Chapter One

Holy Meal and Sacred Food

INTRODUCTION
Nearly every student of Christian worship is familiar
with Justin Martyr's celebrated description of the
eucharist at Rome about the year 150 A.D. As an
apologist, Justin was anxious to explain the "new wis-
dom" of Christianity to both pagan and Jewish
readerships, and his account of the Sunday celebration
remains among the most primitive ones we possess.
After describing the gifts of bread and wine brought by
the people to the "one who presides" at the liturgy,
Justin continues:

"He takes them and offers prayers, glorifying the Father
of all things through the name of the Son and the Holy
Spirit; and he utters a lengthy thanksgiving because the
Father has judged us worthy of these gifts. When the
prayer of thanksgiving is ended, all the people present
give their assent with an Amen. . . . When the president
has given thanks and the people have all signified their
assent, those whom we call deacons distribute the bread
and the wine and water, over which the thanksgiving
has been spoken, to each of those present; they also
carry them to those who are absent."[1]

Justin's description is important not only because of its
great antiquity and its tantalizing references to liturgical
ministry (who is the "one who presides"?), but also because it witnesses to a custom of long duration in the
church: the taking of communion to those unable to
attend the eucharistic assembly. Indeed, our very first
literary encounter with this custom occurs in Justin's
First Apology. The *Didache*, a short manual of Christian
cult and catechesis that appeared some decades before
Justin's work, describes baptismal initiation and Sunday

eucharist, but never mentions the custom of carrying communion to the absent faithful.[2]

The ritual pattern described by Justin Martyr is, of course, entirely familiar: a "Liturgy of the Word" is followed by a "Liturgy of the Table"[3] and communion is then taken by deacons to "those who are absent." Presumably these absent ones are the sick of the community or those whose work prevented their attending the Sunday synaxis.[4] In any case, Justin's report is significant because it provides the earliest evidence for a distribution of the eucharist *outside* the immediate celebration of the liturgy itself. At the same time, however, the intimate connection between Sunday worship and communion outside Mass is evident: the deacons appear to proceed directly from the assembly to the distribution of the gifts to those absent. Justin makes no mention of any cultic ceremonial that accompanied the deacons' ministry.

Less than a century later, however, another Roman document—the *Apostolic Tradition* of Hippolytus (ca. 215 A.D.)—clearly witnesses to a private reservation of the eucharist in the homes of Christians. The author of this work, whose exact identity is still debated by scholars, explains that the eucharist, taken home, should be eaten before ordinary food is consumed:[5]

"Let every one of the faithful take steps to receive the eucharist before he eats anything else. For if he receives in faith, even if some deadly thing is given him, after that it shall not overpower him.

"Let every one take care that no unbeliever eats of the eucharist, nor any mouse or other animal, and that none of it falls and is lost. For it is the body of Christ, to be eaten by believers, and not to be despised."[6]

As commentators have often noted, the custom referred to by Hippolytus apparently involves communion at home on weekdays, when the eucharistic liturgy was not customarily celebrated.[7] This domestic ritual did not involve the presence of any ordained minister, although it did include reception of both bread and cup. For in the section that immediately follows Hippolytus's advice about the careful reservation of the eucharistic bread we read:

"For having blessed [the cup] in the name of God, you received as it were the antitype of the blood of Christ. Therefore do not pour any out, as though you despised it, lest an alien spirit lick it up. You will be guilty of the blood, as one who despises the price with which he has been bought."[8]

It is possible, as Geoffrey Cuming has suggested, that the communicant "blessed" the cup by dropping a small portion of the eucharistic bread into it—a custom we will meet again in our discussion of the Roman liturgy of the presanctified.[9] But whatever may have been the precise ritual, it seems clear that Hippolytus refers to a custom familiarly known and practiced by Christians at Rome in the early third century. And since Hippolytus describes the actual celebration of eucharist only in specific contexts—the ordination of bishops on Sunday, the initiation of Christians at Easter—it may reasonably be presumed that Christians took the eucharist home with them from the Sunday liturgy and kept it for communion during the week.

Much more could be said about the sacrament reserved at home in the *Apostolic Tradition,* but for the present it is sufficient to note that this domestic ritual for communion was known elsewhere in Latin Christianity during the third century. In Cyprian's North African community of Carthage, for example, Christians were accustomed to taking the eucharist home, where it was kept in a small receptacle. In his work on *The Lapsed* (persons who had faltered in faith during the Decian persecutions of 250–251 A.D.), Cyprian offers this anecdote: "There was a woman who with impure hands tried to open the locket in which she was keeping Our Lord's holy body, but fire flared up from it and she was too terrified to touch it."[10]

Cyprian's story is, clearly, a hyperbolic admonition against approaching the eucharist unworthily. The larger context of the work suggests that Cyprian's pastoral attention was directed toward repentance and reconciliation as the appropriate conditions for eucharistic communion—whether that communion is received at home or in the liturgical assembly itself.[11] It may also be noted that Cyprian, like Hippolytus in the *Apostolic Tradition*, sometimes speaks of the eucharist as though it were a kind of talisman that protects the worthy but exposes the sinner.[12]

Unlike Hippolytus, however, Cyprian alludes to celebrations of the eucharist on weekdays in addition to Sundays. In his correspondence, much of it written under the pressure of persecution and the threat of martyrdom, Cyprian appeals to a military metaphor to describe the courage Christians need; at the same time, he seems to speak of a daily celebration of the eucharist:

"A severer and fiercer combat is now threatening for which, with an incorrupt faith and robust courage, the soldiers of Christ ought to prepare themselves, considering, therefore, that they daily drink the Chalice of the Blood of Christ so that they themselves may also be able to shed their blood for Christ."[13]

It is possible, of course, that Cyprian is here referring not to a daily eucharist liturgy, but to the custom of receiving communion daily (under both species) at home—a practice already noted in the *Apostolic Tradition* of Hippolytus. From other sources, however, we know that some Latin Christian communities in North Africa celebrated liturgy on "stational days" during the week in addition to Sundays. This custom is spoken of by Tertullian (ca. 160–225) in his treatise *On Prayer*:

"with regard to the station days, many do not think that there should be any attendance at the prayers of sacrifice, because the station should be ended when the Lord's Body is received. Has the Eucharist, then, dispensed with a duty vowed to God, or does it place upon us a great obligation to God? Will not your station be more solemn if you stand at the altar of God?"[14]

The station days, probably Wednesdays and Fridays, were devoted to prayer and fasting, and seem also to have included a celebration of the eucharist. Tertullian's treatise indicates that some Christians had scruples about attending the liturgy and receiving communion on a day devoted to penance on the principle that penitential fasting and eucharistic feasting are incompatible. The scrupulous felt they had no choice but to absent themselves from the eucharistic assembly, since to attend and not to receive the Lord's Body was unthinkable. Tertullian, however, recommends an alternative: those who fear that receiving communion will break the stational fast may carry the eucharist home with them and receive it after the fast has ended. That way, scrupulous persons may fulfill both principles: participation in the liturgy and abstention from food until after sundown, the hour at which the fasts customarily ended.[15]

Somewhat indirectly, then, Tertullian bears witness to a North African custom of celebrating the liturgy on other days besides Sunday. Since it is probable that Tertullian was connected with the church at Carthage—and since Cyprian later became bishop of that church—it is possible that *Letter* 58, with its allusion to "daily drinking the Chalice of the Blood of Christ," may refer to a regular pattern of celebrating eucharist on weekdays. One should remember, however, that Cyprian wrote under conditions of extraordinary political pressure, and that what was done in a time of persecution was not necessarily the norm for other periods of the community's life.

The material cited from sources like Hippolytus, Tertullian, and Cyprian does, however, reveal several important points about eucharistic practice in third-century Latin Christianity:

First, the custom of reserving the eucharist for use by Christians in their own homes had developed by at least the early third century in Rome, if the testimony of Hippolytus's *Apostolic Tradition* is to be believed. This domestic form of reservation involved neither ordained ministers nor official rites.

Writers like Tertullian and Cyprian seem to indicate that the principle "Lord's Supper on the Lord's Day" had in some churches given rise to greater frequency of celebration. Stational liturgies on Wednesday and Friday, as they are described in Tertullian's treatise *On Prayer*, appear to include a celebration of eucharist.

At least some theologians of the period did not consider it inappropriate for a Christian to "fast" from the eucharist while participating in the liturgy, and to reserve the sacrament for private consumption at home later. This was, in fact, Tertullian's recommendation to Christians scrupulous about the conflict between stational fasting and eucharistic feasting.

The authors examined thus far affirm that the eucharist, whether received at the liturgy or consumed privately at home, is to be regarded reverently as the body and blood of the Lord. But there are indications, too, that the eucharist is regarded as doing something more than effecting communion between believer and Christ, believer and church. It has apotropaic powers that protect Christians from danger (Hippolytus); it also provides a kind of folkloric remedy against sinners and deceivers in the church (Cyprian).

Finally, the reception of eucharist at home seems to have involved the twofold action of eating and drinking, even though it is probable that the faithful carried only consecrated bread away from the community's celebration.[16] The practical difficulty of reserving eucharistic wine at home may have prompted Hippolytus's solution in the *Apostolic Tradition*: the individual is instructed to bless a cup of unconsecrated wine as part of the domestic ritual for communion.

These details derived from the literature of second- and third-century Latin Christianity reveal the emergence of two patterns destined for a long history in the eucharistic repertoire of the West. The first of these patterns involves the disengagement of holy communion from public liturgy. The second involves the extension of Lord's Supper beyond Lord's Day. Taken together, these patterns gradually contributed to a shift in understanding about the relation between Sunday, eucharistic *liturgy*, and eucharistic *communion*. Once holy food (communion) becomes independent of sacred meal (liturgical action), the basic conditions are established for both communion outside Mass and, eventually, a cult of the eucharist outside Mass.

This chapter will explore the two patterns of disengagement named above. We will see how, at a fairly early period, the eucharistic liturgy achieved independence from its originating context in a community's meal. We will also see how the ancient connection between Sunday and eucharist was obscured by a multiplication of Masses on other days of the week.

PATTERN ONE: THE DISENGAGEMENT OF COMMUNION FROM THE LITURGY
The first pattern reveals the beginnings of a disassociation between participation in the liturgy and the act of eucharistic communion, between sharing the community's meal in public and consuming what remains of the meal at home. Although the *norm* clearly remained eating and drinking at the community's meal, the quasi-private and devotional consumption of the eucharist at home was considered neither extraordinary nor inap-

16

propriate in the third century. Only after Christianity became a licit religion in the Empire during the fourth century did church leaders begin inveighing against the custom of taking the eucharist home. For example, St. Jerome, ever vigilant against abuses and errors, complained that some Roman Christians who were otherwise barred from public communion felt no scruple about consuming the eucharist in the privacy of their own houses. With typical acerbity, Jerome wrote: "What is not allowed in church is not allowed at home. Nothing is hidden from God, and even darkness is light in his presence. Let each one examine himself and then approach the body of Christ. . . ."[17]

The portion of Jerome's letter just cited refers to a very specific situation: that of married persons who had not abstained from sexual intercourse in preparation for eucharistic communion. Failure to observe such abstinence was considered sufficient reason for barring a couple from communion at the liturgy, and Jerome argued that what is prohibited in public is prohibited in private, too. In light of today's theology of Christian marriage, Jerome's response may seem ludicrous. But given his affection for ascetic ideals, the argument is intelligible even if unconvincing. It should be noted, further, that Jerome did not reject communion at home in principle; he objected instead to the double standard of forbidding it in one place (church), while allowing it in another (home).

In a roundabout way, then, Jerome attests to a custom that was still familiar in the late fourth century: the domestic ritual of communion at home. Nor is Jerome the only prominent ecclesiastic who knew about the endurance of this custom. His contemporary, St. Basil of Caesarea (+ 379), also speaks of it:

"All the solitaries in the deserts, where there is no priest, keep the communion by them and partake of it by themselves. At Alexandria too, and in Egypt, each

17

one of the laity, for the most part, keeps the communion at home, and whenever he wishes partakes of it himself. For after the priest has completed the sacrifice and distributed it, he who then received it in its entirety . . . must believe that he duly takes and receives it from the hand that first gave it. For even in the church, when the priest distributes each portion, he who receives takes it into his complete control, and lifts it to his mouth with his own hand. It comes to the same thing, whether one or many portions at a time are received from the priest."[18]

Quite clearly, Basil regards communion at home as simply an extension of the public liturgy in church; postponing the consumption of some of the bread until a later time is quite inconsequential, since one still "takes and receives it from the hand that first gave it." Clearly, too, Basil does not restrict this custom of communion at home to males. Both of his examples—solitaries in the desert, lay persons at liturgy—obviously include both men and women.

There is reliable evidence that the custom of taking the eucharist home for communion during the week continued until the seventh or eighth centuries, though the practice declined after the fourth century.[19] Nor was this pattern restricted to places like Rome and North Africa, as Basil's letter shows. Local church councils sometimes objected to the custom, but the objection itself proves that the practice still appealed to many Christians. Occasionally, the conciliar objections were perhaps aimed less at the custom than at heretical communities who might have adopted it. This was probably the situation at a Council which met at Saragossa (Spain), ca. 379–381. The council fathers met to discuss and condemn the errors of the Priscillianists, a sect that seems to have promoted Gnostic or Manichaean ideas about the humanity of Christ and about the human body as Satan's evil creation. Included among the council's condemnations was the following: "If anyone is found guilty of not consuming *in church* the eucharist he has received, let him be anathema.[20] Although it is impossible to reconstruct the exact historical situation, it is at least plausible that the Council was worried about what might happen to the eucharist if it were carried home by lay persons, e.g., it might fall into the hands of Priscillianist sectarians. It is also possible that the Council prohibited the custom as a test of orthodoxy useful in distinguishing orthodox Christians from heretical sectarians.[21] In any case, it is clear that this Council's primary concern was to condemn a heresy, not to prohibit a popular eucharistic custom.

It has been suggested that the custom of communion at home developed during a period when the church's existence in the Roman Empire was threatened, at least periodically, by political opponents and persecution.[22] Historically, this is true enough. But the possiblity, and sometimes the actual fact, of persecution does not explain fully the pattern under discussion here. The question remains: *why* did customs like communion at home develop in the first place? How does one account for this disassociation between sacred food and holy meal?

Some answers to these questions may emerge if we examine the principal states in the liturgical evolution of the eucharist. As exegetes have noted, such an evolution is already discernible in the eucharistic traditions of the New Testament.[23] In the paragraphs that follow, four principal stages of that evolution will be studied.

Stage One: Eucharist as Meal
It is admitted by virtually all New Testament scholars today that the earliest Christian eucharist was in fact a complete meal, one that was closely associated with Jesus' own historical ministry of table-fellowship. As Norman Perrin has argued,[24] the *meal* provided Christians with the connecting link between their own experience of Easter faith and the historical career of Jesus:

19

"The central feature of the message of Jesus is . . . the challenge of the forgiveness of sins and the offer of the possibility of a new kind of relationship with God and with one's fellow man. This was symbolized by a table-fellowship which celebrated the present joy and anticipated the future consummation; a table-fellowship of such joy and gladness that it survived the crucifixion and provided the focal point for the community life of the earliest Christians, and was the most direct link between that community life and the pre-Easter fellowship of Jesus and his disciples."[25]

The symbolism of this primitive eucharistic meal was thus rich in meaning. On the one hand it was eschatological: the meal signaled the presence of God's kingdom which reigns even before it has fully arrived. On the other hand the meal was reconciliatory: it signaled the forgiveness of sins and the possibility of new relationship with God and others. Such dual symbolism makes the meal's connection with both Jesus' ministry and the events of Easter much clearer. For as Schillebeeckx has observed, Easter means more in the New Testament than simply what God did by vindicating Jesus out of his death; it also includes the disciples' own process of conversion.[26] It must be remembered that at the crucial moment of Jesus' trial and death, the disciples failed, fled, and abandoned their Master, a point strongly emphasized in the theology of Mark's gospel.[27] Yet we also know that at some point after Jesus' death these same disciples returned, regrouped, and inaugurated a ministry of preaching. What happened in this interval between Jesus' death and the disciples' regathering? Schillebeeckx answers this question in a word: "Easter."[28] But an important qualification must be added immediately: Easter is not to be confused simply with the resurrection of Jesus (an event which the New Testament never describes). Rather, it is an experience by the disciples of renewed salvation and forgiveness offered them by the Crucified One who now shows himself alive and risen.[29] What the disciples experienced at Easter was thus not the resurrection of Jesus as such (they did not directly witness this event), but rather conversion, forgiveness, and salvation offered at the gracious initiative of Jesus the Risen One.[30]

In the New Testament Easter is an *ensemble of events* that includes God's act of raising Jesus (never directly described); the disciples' experience of conversion, forgiveness, and commissioning for ministry; and Jesus' gracious manifestation of himself as the Crucified and Risen One (narrated in the Easter appearance stories). That the meals shared by the disciples should have played a central role in this process is not surprising. For in his historical career Jesus used the ministry of the table as a central feature in his proclamation of God's forgiveness. In light of Easter, the same offer Jesus made in his ministry was now accepted by the disciples: namely, forgiveness.[31]

The connecting link between Jesus' ministry and the community's meals after Easter, spoken of by Norman Perrin, is now reasonably clear: what Jesus offered through table-fellowship was *forgiveness*; what the Risen One offers disciples through their experience of conversion is *forgiveness*. In both cases, the experience of forgiveness can only be thought of as *grace*, a free gift given at *another's* (Jesus') initiative.

At the earliest stage in the evolution of the eucharist, therefore, the community's meal, its eucharist, is intimately connected with both Jesus' historical ministry and with the ensemble of events known as Easter. These two sources of the eucharistic tradition focus on a common experience: conversion and forgiveness offered at Jesus' gracious initiative. For these reasons, it would not have been important to the earliest believers to distinguish, rigorously, between a eucharistic meal and an ordinary community meal. Whenever the community of believers assembled to break bread, it experienced the

21

presence of the Risen One who offers "forgiveness of sins" (see Acts 10.34-43).

Stage Two: Eucharist at the End of a Meal
It seems rather clear from evidence in the New Testament, however, that the identity between eucharist and complete meal was short-lived. The earliest New Testament material that deals with the Lord's Supper, found in Paul's First Letter to the Corinthians, indicates that only a couple of decades after Jesus' death, the relation between eucharist and complete meal had begun to shift.

The precise historical situation at Corinth during this time (the 50s) remains a disputed question among biblical exegetes; it is difficult to say who was doing what to whom in that quarrelsome community. In any case, there were abuses of both a practical and (from Paul's point of view) a doctrinal nature. At the level of practical action, Paul condemns members of the Corinthian community who humiliated the poor by refusing to wait until they arrived in order to eat and drink (1 Cor 11.17-33). As Willi Marxsen observes, Paul's comments imply that at Corinth the pattern of celebrating was a community meal, followed by the "Lord's Supper" as a kind of "sacramental appendix or conclusion to the ordinary meal."[32] This would mean, of course, that the actions of blessing bread and cup no longer frame the complete meal, as they did in Stage One. It would mean, too, that the practical abuses Paul condemns are connected with the meal that *precedes* the sacramental appendix known as the Lord's Supper.

If Marxsen's interpretation is accurate, then it is possible to be a bit clearer about the Corinthian situation. Paul is actually dealing with two distinct but closely related problems: at the practical (ethical) level, there were conflicts between rich and poor involving the community meal; at the doctrinal level, there were mistaken interpretations of the meaning of the Lord's Supper (the

22

sacramental appendix at the conclusion of the meal).
Paul's response to each of these problems is
straightforward. As far as the meal is concerned, Paul's
directions are "Wait until everyone has arrived" (1 Cor
11.33). As far as interpretations of the Lord's Supper are
concerned, Paul issues a theological corrective: the Supper proclaims the death of Jesus (1 Cor 11.26). Doctri-
nally, Paul appears to be reacting against certain sacramental enthusiasts at Corinth who claimed that believers already participate in the full life of the resurrection
through actions like baptism and the eucharist.[33] Paul
reacts to this by affirming some aspects of the enthusiasts' position and denying others. True, he admits,
baptism and the Supper do give believers a real participation in Christ; but it is a participation primarily in
Jesus' *death*. The consummation of resurrection life remains, for Paul, a future reality; hence believers participate in Christ only by letting the power of that future lay
claim to their lives in the present. As Leander Keck remarks: "To live by participation in what is not yet fully
here is to live by anticipatory participation; it is to claim
the life of the future ahead of time and so get out of step
with the present. Participation accents the present ac-
cessibility of the future; anticipation accents the futurity
of that in which one participates. Participation emphasizes the already, anticipation the not yet."[34]

Paul's pastoral concerns for the Corinthian Christians
are thus simultaneously ethical and theological. The two
problems—abusive treatment of the poor at the meal,
mistaken notions about the meaning of the Lord's
Supper—converge on a single point: recognition of the
body of the Lord. As Keck notes one may infer that for
Paul "the body of Christ is not only *on* the table but also
at the table."[35] Although by Paul's time the Supper may
have shifted its location slightly (it is now an appendix
at the conclusion of a meal), the deep connection between the community's meal-sharing and its Supper-
sharing remains clear.

Stage Three: Eucharist as an Independent Rite

At what point did the eucharist become an independent rite which neither framed a meal (Stage One) nor came as a cultic conclusion to a meal (Stage Two)? A precise answer to this question is impossible. For one thing, a movement toward ritual independence for the eucharist would not necessarily have occurred in all Christian communities at the same time. Some communities, for example, may have retained the primitive custom of framing the meal with the blessings over bread and cup long after other churches had abandoned it. Chapters 9 and 10 of the *Didache*, for instance, may reflect the primitive practice of Stage One, even though the document must have been compiled some decades after Paul wrote to the Corinthians (who seem to have adopted the more evolved practices outlined in Stage Two). It is fairly clear that by Justin's time (ca. 150 A.D.), the Roman community's eucharist is an independent rite, and it may be that a similarly independent rite is reflected some decades earlier in the letters of Ignatius of Antioch (+ ca. 107). In any case, within a hundred years after Paul's correspondence with Corinth, ritually independent eucharists are known in many if not all Christian churches.

How did this independence evolve? Willi Marxsen has suggested that the phenomenon is already evident in the eucharistic traditions of the synoptic gospels. The earliest of these, Mark, already seems to reflect an independent "sacramental meal."[36] That may be why the Markan version of Jesus' eucharistic words omits the phrase "after Supper," whereas in Paul's quotation of the tradition the phrase is still present:

Paul: "For I received from the Lord what I also delivered to you, that the Lord Jesus on the night when he was betrayed took bread, and when he had given thanks, he broke it, and said, 'This is my body which is for you. Do this in remembrance of me.' In the same way also the cup, *after supper*, saying . . ." (1 Cor 11.23-25).

24

Mark: "And as they were eating, he took bread, and blessed, and broke it, and gave it to them, and said, 'Take; this is my body.' And he took a cup, and when he had given thanks . . ." (Mark 14.22-23).

It is Marxsen's conviction that in Mark's gospel the meal has disappeared altogether.[37] The eucharist is now an independent liturgical rite that makes the meal itself "superfluous."[38] Not only has the relation between community meal and Lord's Supper shifted, but there has also been a corresponding shift in the interpretation of the Supper. In the Markan redaction, Marxsen argues, we see an emphasis that is more specifically "eucharistic" than Paul's more broadly "ecclesiological" concerns. Paul was preoccupied about recognizing the body, i.e., about relations among church members and about their participation in Jesus' death, which establishes a new covenant-community. But Mark seems more intent on the *contents* of the bread and the cup. His version of Jesus' words "harmonizes" the two formulas so as to make it clear that the body and blood are those of Jesus:

Paul:
Bread = Body ("This is my body which is for you.")
Cup = Covenant ("This *cup is the new covenant* in my blood.")
Mark:
Bread = Body ("Take; this is my body.")
Cup = Blood ("*This is my blood* of the covenant.")

This comparison helps show Paul's ecclesiological concerns in contrast to Mark's more explicitly eucharistic ones. Paul quotes a tradition that emphasizes a new community that has entered into a new covenant sealed by the sharing of a meal; both bread and people can be called "Body of Christ." But in Mark's hands, the tradition modulates into a new key: the contents of the bread and cup are Jesus, the One who gave himself for sinners. As Marxsen observes:

"Body and blood (that is to say, the whole man) now belong together with bread and wine. The 'elements' make their appearance. The presence of the Lord is attached to this food. But the meal, which originally stood in the center of the meal of the new covenant, is now robbed of its significance. Hence it is only a logical development that the meal as such is dropped."[39]

If Marxsen's analysis of these texts is accepted, then the emergence of the eucharist as an independent liturgical rite, separate from any meal, occurred at an early period in Christian history. Moreover, this ritual independence is closely connected with a specific theological interpretation of the Lord's Supper: "the presence of the Lord is attached to this food." Obviously, this does not mean that Mark, for example, was an early proponent of transubstantiation or that he was attempting to trace a theory of "real presence." These are questions of a later period and cannot be projected back onto the New Testament material.

What can be said, however, is this. In the New Testament there seems to be a shift from eucharist as all or part of a meal to eucharist as an independent rite; from emphasis on the act of community dining to emphasis on the food itself. At the risk of oversimplifying a complicated problem, these shifts could be expressed as follows. Paul represents a tradition that stresses the community and its new covenant relationship with the Lord. The meal seals and ratifies this covenant, and in the context of that meal the Lord is experienced as powerfully present "eating and drinking along with his people." Mark (as interpreted by Marxsen) represents a tradition that stresses the food itself as the community's point of contact with the Crucified One. The covenant motif has receded a bit into the background, as seems to be evident when one compares Mark's version of the words over the cup with that of Paul's. In sum, one

tradition emphasizes community–covenant–
covenant-meal; the other emphasizes community–
food–body and blood of Christ.

Stage Four: Eucharistic Food
Although not all exegetes would agree with Marxsen's
analysis of eucharistic traditions in the New Testament,
one thing is clear: by the second century, the eucharist
has become ritually independent of the meal.[40]
Marxsen's interpretation, in my opinion, helps us
understand how and why this happened. Once the
connection is made between "food" and "presence of
the Lord," then Christians can "make contact" with the
Lord even if they are unable to be present at the assembly's celebration. This is what we see going on in Justin
Martyr's description of Sunday worship at Rome in the
mid-second century. Those who cannot attend the
community's meal (now an independent eucharistic
rite) can still receive the food hallowed at that meal
through prayer and thanksgiving. And this food, Justin
informs us, "becomes the flesh and blood of the incarnate Jesus, in order to nourish and transform our flesh
and blood."[41] In short, the inability to make contact
with the celebrating community does not prevent Christians from making contact with Jesus through the "food
over which thanksgiving has been spoken."

The connection between food and presence of the Lord
helps explain the custom of communion at home discussed in the works of Hippolytus, Tertullian, and Cyprian. Since the food is the point of contact with the Lord,
and since this food derives ultimately from the community's action of prayer and thanksgiving, it is rather inconsequential whether the reception of that food happens "all at once" or "in stages." (This was, we have
seen, Basil's defense for the propriety of eucharist reserved and consumed at home by lay persons). For similar reasons, Tertullian can recommend that the scrupulous postpone their reception of the eucharist until after

the fasting has ended on stational days. Neither post-
ponement nor "prolonging" reception (through communion at home) prevent the Christian from making
contact with the Lord's presence through food blessed
at the assembly's liturgy.

It should be pointed out, however, that none of the
sources we have examined thus far speak of any special
cult attached to the eucharist carried to those absent
from the liturgy or reserved at home for consumption on
weekdays. Although writers like Hippolytus insist on
reverence in communicating oneself, there are no references to signs of cultic distinction attached to the
eucharistic food (e.g., lights, incense, processions, or
other ceremonial gestures of adoration). Among these
early writers, the eucharist is food to be eaten, not a
cultic object to be adored.

These four stages in the liturgical evolution of the
eucharist help to explain why Pattern One—the disengagement of eucharistic communion from the immediate context of public worship—emerged among
Christians. Originally, this disengagement seems to
have occurred for two reasons: 1) a gradual shift away
from emphasis on "community–covenant meal" toward
emphasis on "food–presence of Christ"; 2) a desire to
make this presence available to those absent from the
liturgy (Justin Martyr), combined with a desire to pro-
long (or postpone) the contact with the Lord which this
food makes possible (Hippolytus, Tertullian). After the
eucharist achieved ritual independence as a sacramental
meal, the connection between "food" and "presence of
Christ" became more prominent. Still, throughout this
period (until the end of the fourth century), the origin of
this eucharistic food in the community's liturgical action
of prayer and thanksgiving is constantly affirmed. Basil,
we have seen, reminds his readers that whether they
receive in church or at home, they still "take and receive
from the hand that first gave it."[42] And even Jerome's
comments about persons barred from public commun-

ion testify, indirectly, to the community's worship as the originating source for communion received privately.

PATTERN TWO: DISENGAGEMENT OF LORD'S SUPPER FROM LORD'S DAY

Stage One: Celebrations on Days Other Than Sunday
The occasional disengagement of eucharistic communion from the immediate context of liturgical action began at a period in the church's life when the ordinary rhythm for celebrating the Lord's Supper was once a week, on Sunday. The Lord's Supper on the Lord's Day: this seems to be the norm presupposed by early writers like Justin Martyr and Hippolytus. But we have seen, too, that by the early third century some churches—especially in the region of North Africa around Carthage—developed the custom of celebrating eucharist on certain weekdays as well. These celebrations during the week were sometimes attached to penitential station days (Tertullian), sometimes to the cult of the martyrs (Cyprian).

The custom of celebrating the anniversaries of martyrs with a community eucharist is clearly attested in the letters of Cyprian written during the Decian persecution. In a short letter to his presbyters and deacons Cyprian requests that careful note be made of the days on which the martyrs die so that their anniversaries can be celebrated:

"take note of the days on which they die that we may be able to celebrate their commemorations among the memorials of the martyrs. . . . And, for their commemorations, let there be celebrated here by us Oblations and Sacrifices which, with protection of the Lord, we shall celebrate soon with you."[43]

In another letter written to his clergy and people during the same period, Cyprian indicates that these commemorative celebrations of the martyrs were held annually: "We offer Sacrifices for them always, as you remember, as often as we celebrate the passions and days of the martyrs with an annual commemoration ."[44]

Although the vocabulary of sacrifice could also refer to prayer (the "sacrifice of praise"), these references are almost certainly to the eucharist. Cyprian's experience as a pastor during a period of persecution led him frequently to speak of the connections between martyrdom, Jesus' passion, and the eucharist as sacrifice:

"we find that the Chalice which the Lord offered was mixed and what He called Blood had been wine. Whence it appears that the Blood of Christ is not offered if wine is lacking in the Chalice and that the Sacrifice of the Lord is not celebrated . . . unless the Oblation and our Sacrifice correspond to the Passion. . . ."[45]

A little later in the same letter Cyprian associates the blood of Christ, present in "the very Sacrament of the Passion," with the blood of the martyrs. Whoever is ashamed to drink Christ's blood, Cyprian argues, will also blush to shed blood for Christ: "For how can we who blush to drink the Blood of Christ shed our blood for Christ?"[46]

By the middle of the third century, therefore, it had become customary in some sectors of Latin Christianity to celebrate eucharist in memory of the martyrs on the anniversary of their death (dies natalis, their "birthday" into everlasting life).[47] It also seems likely that during the same century the custom of celebrating eucharist on the occasion of any Christian's death arose. Tertullian hints at this custom indirectly by referring to Christians who celebrate the eucharist on the anniversaries of relatives or loved ones. In his treatise On Monogamy, Tertullian relates a story about a wife who annually celebrated the eucharist on the anniversary of her husband's falling asleep:

"To be sure, she prays for his soul. She asks that, during

30

the interval, he may find rest and that he may share in the first resurrection. She offers the Sacrifice each year on the anniversary of his falling asleep. If she fails to do this, she has indeed divorced him as far as it lies in her power to do so."[48]

The context of Tertullian's comments is a discussion of the marriage bond among Christians, which is, in the author's rigorist opinion, "stronger than death." (Tertullian opposed remarriage by a Christian after the death of a spouse, since he argued that the relationship between man and wife is not severed when one of them dies.) It is interesting that Tertullian considers the "anniversary eucharist" for a dead spouse as quasi-obligatory; failure to do this is tantamount to an act of divorce.

Although Tertullian does not explicitly enumerate the eucharist as an element among the rites of Christian burial, it can be plausibly inferred that the custom existed in his time.[49] Certainly by the fourth century Latin Christianity is familiar with the practice. In his *Confessions*, Augustine notes that when his mother Monica was buried, the eucharist was offered at the graveside:

"Lo, when her body was carried away, we went out, and we returned without tears. Not even in those prayers we poured forth to you when the sacrifice of our redemption was offered up in her behalf, with the corpse already placed beside the grave before being lowered into it, as is the custom of that place, not even during those prayers did I shed tears."[50]

This custom of offering eucharist at the graveside in fourth-century Italy should not be confused with another custom spoken of by Augustine: the practice of the *refrigerium* ("refreshment"). Essentially, the *refrigeria* were private funeral feasts provided by families for dead relatives.[51] Since they were private familial commemorations, the *refrigeria* were not easily controlled by the

31

clergy and this sometimes created pastoral difficulties. The growth of the cult of the martyrs in North Africa led to a proliferation of such feasts which, although they did not involve offering the eucharist, had a quasi-liturgical character. What bothered the clergy were the pagan origins of this custom, and it is probable that the "graveside eucharist," mentioned by Augustine in connection with Monica's burial, represents an attempt to control the practice by substituting a Christian rite for a pagan one.[52] In any case, Monica's North African roots would have made her familiar with the *refrigeria* and we know she was still devoted to the custom (much to Ambrose's chagrin) while she and Augustine were living in northern Italy.[53] Ambrose eventually forbade these celebrations, and later Augustine, in his career at Hippo, also attempted to regulate them by insisting that "refreshment" was better served by giving to the poor.[54]

The custom of celebrating eucharist at the liturgy of Christian burial may, then, have resulted from a desire to avoid pagan rites on such occasions. Funeral customs are, after all, deeply embedded in the cumulative psychological history of a people; they are not easily changed. Early church leaders frequently admonished Christians against burial practices that reflect a pagan perception of death and its consequences. Tertullian, for example, paints a sarcastic picture of what he considers an excessive use of aromatic spices by Christians in burying their dead: "we do not buy incense, [but] if the Arabians complain, let the people of Saba know that their more precious and costly merchandise is expended as largely in the burying of Christians as in the fumigating of gods."[55]

There is a double irony here: Tertullian chides the Arabian merchants who complain that their sales have dropped since Christians appeared on the scene; but he also pokes fun at the funereal excesses of some Christians.

32

The texts we have been examining indicate that the emergent custom of celebrating eucharist at burial was part of a larger battle to wean Christians away from pagan practices. It was a case, perhaps, of ritual substitution: unacceptable customs were countered by substituting acceptable ones including the Lord's Supper celebrated at graveside.

To sum up, the first four centuries of Christian history reveal that the norm of weekly eucharist—the Lord's Supper on the Lord's Day—was rather quickly altered by occasional celebrations that occurred on other days of the week. These celebrations, votive and less public than the full assembly's Sunday worship, were associated with specific circumstances of Christian life:

1) Some were attached to days of prayer and penance, as were the Wednesday and Friday station-days mentioned by Tertullian;
2) At other times, eucharist was connected with the cult of the martyrs, especially in North Africa. Martyred heroes and heroines of the community were remembered with annual "sacrifices" on the day of their death;
3) Finally, the eucharist became part of the liturgy of Christian burial. By the fourth century, and perhaps earlier, a concerted effort was being made by pastors and church leaders to substitute the eucharist at graveside for pagan *refrigeria*.

These developments indicate that the exclusive connection between Sunday and eucharist was being altered. Sunday remained, of course, *the* central day for Christian assembly, but its uniqueness was imperiled by the multiplication of eucharistic liturgies on other days for other occasions. In short, the eucharist was gradually being disengaged from its unique relation to Sunday, the original feast day, the weekly remembering of the events of Easter. This disengagement helped create an atmosphere that led to a second stage of development: the multiplication of eucharistic liturgies on a single day.

Stage Two: Multiplication of Masses on a Single Day
It seems reasonably evident, then, that by the fourth
century in the Latin West, the ancient rhythm of Lord's
Supper on the Lord's Day had become somewhat
obscured by a multiplication of eucharistic liturgies on
other days for other purposes—the annual commemoration of martyrs, the anniversaries of other Christians
who had died, the liturgy of burial. As Christianity expanded under imperial patronage during the fourth and
fifth centuries, a new phenomenon appeared: the multiplication of Masses on a single day.

This phenomenon probably had its roots in pastoral
necessity. As the church grew larger in great urban centers like Rome, it became increasingly difficult to accommodate all the members of the local community at a
single celebration. This was already a pastoral problem
by the middle of the fifth century, when Leo I was
bishop of Rome (440–461). In a letter written to Dioscorus, Bishop of Alexandria, Leo speaks at some length
about the repetition of the eucharist on days when large
numbers of people were expected:

"Whenever any more solemn festival indicates a larger
concourse of people and such crowds of the faithful
come together that a basilica cannot hold all of them at
once, the offering of the sacrifice should unquestionably
be repeated. Otherwise, with only those who came first
admitted to this sacrifice, the others who came later may
seem rejected. Yet it is quite in keeping with devotion
and reason to have a later repetition of the sacrifice as
often as a new group of people is present to fill the
basilica being used. On the contrary, if the custom of
having but one Mass is kept and only those who came
early in the day can offer the sacrifice, then, of necessity,
some part of the people will be deprived of their religious devotion."[56]

The repetition of Mass recommended by Leo is clearly
intended to meet a pastoral need. In making the rec-

ommendation, however, Leo seems to be aware of another (and more ancient) custom: having but one Mass on a given day. He defends the newer practice as consistent with both devotion and reason, though he makes no effort to trace it back to "ecclesiastical custom" or "apostolic authority," as he does with other issues discussed in the same letter to Dioscorus (e.g., ordination of presbyters and deacons).

It is important not to confuse Leo's comments about "repeating the sacrifice" to accommodate large crowds on more solemn festivals with another practice: the celebration of the eucharist in several different churches in the same city on the same day. In Rome, this latter practice gave rise to the *fermentum*, a fragment of consecrated bread sent from the pope's liturgy to the churches where presbyters were presiding at the eucharist. The fragment was placed in the chalice at the presbyters' Masses in order to signify the unity of *all* who were celebrating eucharist, even though they could not all be assembled in one church. Use of the *fermentum* in Rome was certainly known at the beginning of the fifth century. In his letter to Bishop Decentius of Gubbio, Innocent I (bishop of Rome, 401–417) explicitly mentions it:

"On Sunday the presbyters at the *tituli* are not able to join us because of the people entrusted to their care; the *fermentum* consecrated by us is therefore sent to them by acolytes, so that they [the presbyters] will not consider themselves separated from communion with us, especially on that day [Sunday]. The *fermentum* is not, however, sent to the rural churches, because sacraments should not be carried such great distances. . . ."[57]

Among other things, Innocent's letter reveals that a kind of parish system had already begun to emerge in a large metropolitan area like Rome. It is not clear whether the presbyters who served the *tituli* (major urban churches) in Innocent's time were resident pastors of a congregation, but it is clear that the Christian community in Rome had grown too large to be easily accommodated at the bishop's church. If we put the information from Innocent's letter together with Leo's remarks to Dioscorus, a picture of eucharistic practices in fifth-century Rome begins to appear.

1) On Sundays, eucharist is celebrated in the bishop's church and in major urban churches (*tituli*) served by presbyters. Unity of celebration is signified by use of the *fermentum*. The eucharist is also celebrated in rural communities (*parochiae*) but the *fermentum* is not sent to them.[58]

2) On more solemn festivals, the eucharist is celebrated in the bishop's church and, if the crowds are large, "the offering of the sacrifice . . . should be repeated." Leo does not specify what these festivals were, but in the fifth century they might have included days like Christmas, Easter, Pentecost, and the anniversaries of martyrs prominent in the Roman community (e.g., Peter and Paul).

3) It seems probable that eucharist was celebrated in connection with the liturgy of Christian burial. These occasions may have been more "private" in character, especially if the rite was celebrated at graveside.

4) It is difficult to determine whether fifth-century Rome was familiar with daily celebrations of the eucharist, even though such a custom seems already to have existed in some North African churches during Cyprian's time (third century). Innocent's letter to Decentius suggests that certain fast days (Friday, Saturday) are inappropriate for celebrating the mysteries. The ecclesiastical historian Socrates (ca. 380–450) mentions that while "all the churches in the world" celebrate the holy mysteries on Saturday each week, the Alexandrians and the Romans "following an ancient tradition" do *not*.[59] It seems probable, then, that the custom of daily eucharist developed only later in the Roman church.

36

Although the information provided by Innocent and Leo indicates a trend toward "multiplication of Masses on a single day," it is also evident that the trend represents an effort to meet the pastoral needs of an expanding community in a large urban environment. None of the sources we have examined thus far speak of repeating the eucharist simply to satisfy the personal devotion of presiders or people who wish to attend the liturgy more frequently.

With the passage of time, however, personal devotion as a motive for repeating the eucharistic celebration several times a day entered the picture. An interesting canon from the Twelfth Council of Toledo (ca. 681) admonishes presbyters who celebrate several times a day that they must communicate at each liturgy: "When certain priests celebrate several times in a single day, they delay communicating until the final celebration. For the future, anyone who does this will be excommunicated for a year, for each communion that he did not receive. Every priest should communicate whenever he offers the holy sacrifice."[60]

While it is possible that this canon deals with prebyters who repeat the celebration for pastoral reasons, it is more likely that devotional motives are involved in the repetition. There is evidence that eucharistic celebrations of a private and devotional character had already developed by the seventh and eighth centuries, especially in Frankish territory.[61] Almost certainly, too, these private Masses, celebrated for the sake of devotion, were popular among monastic clergy, whose numbers increased dramatically during the seventh, eighth, and ninth centuries.[62]

The impact of private Masses on the development of eucharistic cult and devotion will be discussed more fully in the third chapter of this book. For the present, it is sufficient to note that the original motive for multiplying Masses on a single day was pastoral, not personal or

37

devotional. The practices described by Innocent and Leo in the fifth century are aimed at satisfying the legitimate needs of Christians living in a large city.

SUMMARY
Before entering upon a more detailed discussion of the development of eucharistic cult and devotions in later centuries, it will be useful to summarize some of the principal points contained in this chapter.

During the first five centuries of the Christian era, two patterns emerge that result in a certain disengagement of the eucharist from its original setting, the liturgical assembly on Sunday. The first of these is the separation of eucharistic communion from its immediate context in the liturgy itself. This has already begun to occur by the middle of the second century, when Justin Martyr speaks of taking the eucharist to members of the community who are absent from the Sunday celebration. By the early third century, the domestic ritual of weekday communion at home has developed, as we know from reading Hippolytus's description of it in the *Apostolic Tradition*. Neither of these customs is abusive; indeed, both intend to strengthen the individual Christian's relationship to the Sunday assembly and its worship.

The second form of disengagement involves a gradual loosening of the intimate bond between Lord's Supper and Lord's Day. This loosening develops in two different directions during the early centuries of the church's life. On the one hand, a custom of celebrating the eucharist on days of the week other than Sunday develops in some communities, especially those of North Africa, where evidence for celebrating eucharist on station days and on the anniversaries of martyrs is fairly strong. On the other hand, the increasing size of Christian communities in large cities like Rome leads to a multiplication of Masses on the same day, either by "repeating the sacrifice" in the same church or by celebrating simultaneously in several different churches. Again, these practices develop as responses to pastoral need.

Finally, our synopsis of the liturgical evolution of the eucharist shows that at a very primitive period—probably in the New Testament era—the Lord's Supper achieved ritual independence from its original context of a community's meal. When this happens, the full action of the meal was rendered superfluous and the "presence of the Lord" came to be more directly attached to the food itself, the ritual elements of bread and wine. A shift occurred from emphasis on *community dining* to an emphasis on *ritual food*.

All three of these points are important for understanding how a cult of the eucharist outside Mass could develop in later centuries. The process of disengagement did not stop; it intensified, and the eucharistic elements came to be regarded as worthy of cultic distinction in their own right, independent of their originating source in the liturgical assembly. In the three chapters that follow, we will trace this process as it unfolds under the influence of liturgical change and theological debate.

NOTES

1. See Justin Martyr, *First Apology*, Chapter 65, in Rordorf *et al.*, *The Eucharist of the Early Christians*, translated by Matthew J. O'Connell (New York: Pueblo Publishing Company, 1978), p. 72.

2. See Maxwell Staniforth, trans., *Early Christian Writings* (Baltimore: Penguin Books, 1968), pp. 227-235, for a convenient translation of the *Didache*.

3. Justin Martyr, *First Apology*, 67, translation in Rordorf, p. 73.

4. Sunday did not become an official day of rest until about 321 A.D., when the Emperor Constantine legislated abstention from ordinary work and business for Christians living in urban areas; farmers, however, were exempted from this rule.

5. See Jean Michael Hanssens, *La Liturgie d'Hippolyte* (Rome: Pontificium Institutum Orientalium Studiorum, 1959). Hanssens has denied that the "Hippolytus" associated with the *Apostolic Tradition* was a "Roman" from Rome (see pp. 290-291). He feels there is perhaps surer proof that Hippolytus was Alexandrian and that he may have spent a good deal of time in Rome, especially in the late second and early third centuries (see pp. 291-301). See further, Geoffrey J. Cuming, trans., *Hippolytus: A Text for Students* (Grove Liturgical Study No. 8; Bramcote, Nottinghamshire: Grove Books, 1976), pp. 3-7.

6. *Apostolic Tradition*, 36-37, translation in Cuming, p. 27.

7. See Cuming, note on *Apostolic Tradition*, 37, p. 27.

8. *Apostolic Tradition*, 38, translation in Cuming, p. 28.

9. See Cuming, note on *Apostolic Tradition*, 37, p. 27.

10. St. Cyprian, *The Lapsed; The Unity of the Catholic Church*, translated by Maurice Bevenot (Ancient Christian Writers, No. 25; Westminster, Md.: The Newman Press, 1957), p. 34. The Latin word which Bevenot translates "locket" is *arcam*; it may also be translated "box" or "vessel" (literally, "ark").

11. Earlier in Section 26 of *The Lapsed*, Cyprian speaks of a girl whose secret sin was revealed when she collapsed in convulsions after attempting to receive the eucharist at the liturgy. See Bevenot's translation, pp. 33-34.

12. In the medieval period the eucharist was sometimes used in "ordeals" as a way to discern which party in a dispute was telling the truth.

13. St. Cyprian, *Letter* 58.1, in *St. Cyprian: Letters 1-81*, translated by Rose Bernard Donna (Fathers of the Church, Vol. 51; Washington, D.C.: The Catholic University of America Press, 1964), p. 163.

14. Tertullian, *On Prayer* 19.1-3 in *Tertullain: Disciplinary, Moral and Ascetical Works*, translated by Rudolph Arbesmann *et al.* (Fathers of the Church, Vol. 40; New York: Fathers of the Church, 1959), p. 174.

15. Tertullian, *On Prayer* 19.4, translation in Arbesmann *et al.*, pp. 174-175.

16. See W.H. Freestone, *The Sacrament Reserved* (Alcuin Club Collections, Vol. XXI; London: A.R. Mowbray and Company, 1917), pp. 44-45.

17. St. Jerome, Letter 49 (*Apologeticum ad Pammachium*), text in Isidore Hilberg, ed., *Sancti Eusebii Hieronymi Epistulae* (CSEL, Vol. 54; Vienna: F. Tempsky, 1910), p. 377; author's translation.

18. St. Basil, *Letter 93*, translated in Freestone, p. 41.

19. See Freestone, pp. 40-44.

20. Latin text of the conciliar decree in Charles Joseph Hefele and Henri Leclercq, *Histoire des Conciles* (11 vols.; Paris: Letouzey et Ané, 1907-1952), Vol. I/1, 98.7.

21. On the use of liturgical customs as a "test of orthodoxy" against heterodox sectarians, see Luke Eberle, trans., *The Rule of the Master* (Kalamazoo, Mich.: Cistercian Publications, 1977), p. 216, note 27.

22. See Freestone, pp. 44-45.

23. See Willi Marxsen, *The Beginnings of Christology*, translated by Paul Achtemeier and Lorenz Nieting (Philadelphia: Fortress Press, 1979), pp. 88-122 ("The Lord's Supper as a Christological Problem").

24. See Norman Perrin, *Rediscovering the Teaching of Jesus* (New York: Harper and Row, 1967), pp. 102-108.

25. Perrin, p. 107.

26. See Edward Schillebeeckx, *Jesus*, translated by H. Hoskins (New York: Seabury Press, 1979), pp. 320-397.

27. See Paul Achtemeier, *Mark* (Proclamation Commentaries; Philadelphia: Fortress Press, 1975), pp. 92-100.

28. See Schillebeeckx, p. 331.

29. Ibid., p. 390.

30. The collection of appearance stories in the New Testament points to precisely this experience of conversion and forgiveness on the part of the disciples. At the same time, these stories serve to legitimate the missionary ministry of the con-

verted disciples. See Reginald Fuller, *The Formation of the Resurrection Narratives* (New York: Macmillan, 1971).

31. See Perrin, pp. 107-108: "we are justified in seeing this table-fellowship as the central feature of the ministry of Jesus; an anticipatory sitting at table in the Kingdom of God and a very real celebration of present joy and challenge."

32. See Marxsen, p. 93.

33. See Leander Keck, *Paul and His Letters* (Proclamation Commentaries; Philadelphia: Fortress Press, 1979), pp. 63-64.

34. Ibid., p. 81; see pp. 78-81 for fuller discussion by Keck.

35. Ibid., p. 64.

36. See Marxsen, p. 93.

37. Ibid., pp. 94-95.

38. Ibid., p. 95.

39. Ibid., p. 110.

40. For a different interpretation of the relation between Paul's and Mark's texts, see Keck, pp. 62-63.

41. See Justin Martyr, *First Apology*, 66, translation in Rordorf, p. 72.

42. St. Basil, *Letter 93*, translated in Freestone, p. 41.

43. St. Cyprian, *Letter 12*, in *St. Cyprian: Letters*, translated by Rose Bernard Donna (see note 13, above), pp. 35, 36.

44. St. Cyprian, *Letter 39*, translated in Donna, p. 100.

45. St. Cyprian, *Letter 63.9*, translated in Donna, p. 208.

46. St. Cyprian, *Letter 63.15*, translated in Donna, p. 213.

47. See Geoffrey Rowell, *The Liturgy of Christian Burial* (Alcuin Club Collections, no. 59; London: SPCK, 1977), p. 19.

48. See Tertullian, *On Monogamy*, in *Treatises on Marriage and Remarriage*, translated by William P. Le Saint (Ancient Christian Writers, Vol. 13; Westminster, Md.: The Newman Press, 1951), pp. 91-92.

49. See Rowell, pp. 19-20.

42

50. St. Augustine, *Confessions*, Book 9, Chapter 12, in John K. Ryan, trans., *The Confessions of St. Augustine* (New York: Doubleday Image Books, 1960), pp. 225-226. See the comments on this passage in James White, *Introduction to Christian Worship* (Nashville: Abingdon, 1980), pp. 263-264.

51. See Rowell, p. 11.

52. Ibid.

53. See St. Augustine, *Confessions*, Book 6, Chapter 2, translated in Ryan, pp. 134-135.

54. See Rowell, p. 11.

55. See Tertullian, *Apology*, Chapter 42, translated in Rowell, p. 20. I have slightly altered Rowell's translation here.

56. See St. Leo I, *Letter 9*, in *St. Leo the Great: Letters*, translated by Edmund Hunt (Fathers of the Church, Vol. 34; New York: Fathers of the Church, 1957), pp. 35-36.

57. Text of Innocent's letter in PL 20:556-557; author's translation.

58. It is possible that these rural churches were served by resident ministers, deacons, or presbyters. See H. Leclercq, "Paroisses rurales," DACL 13/2, cols. 2198-2235.

59. See Socrates, *Ecclesiastical History*, Book 5, Chapter 22; Greek text in PG 67:636; English translation in Socrates, *Ecclesiastical History*, (The Greek Ecclesiastical Historians, Vol. 3; London: Samuel Bagster, 1844), p. 406.

60. See Hefele-Leclercq, Vol. 3/1, p. 544; author's translation.

61. See A.-G. Martimort, ed., *The Church at Prayer: The Eucharist*; English translation edited by Austin Flannery and Vincent Ryan, translated by Damian Smyth et al. (New York: Herder and Herder, 1973), p. 67.

62. See Theodor Klauser, *A Short History of the Western Liturgy*, 2nd edition, translated by John Halliburton (New York: Oxford University Press, 1979), pp. 101-108. The question has been studied in detail by Otto Nussbaum, *Kloster, Priestermönch und Privatmesse* (Theophaneia, no. 14; Bonn: P. Hanstein, 1961).

Chapter Two

Communal Symbol and Ritual Drama

INTRODUCTION
In a commentary on Psalm 98 (99) delivered to the
people of Carthage, St. Augustine once offered the following remarks:

"He [Jesus] took earth from the earth; because flesh is of
the earth, he took flesh from the flesh of Mary. And
because he walked here in this flesh, he also gave us this
flesh to eat for our salvation. But no one eats this flesh
unless he has first adored it. . . . Not only do we not sin
by adoring, but we would sin if we did not adore. . . . 'It
is the spirit that gives life; the flesh profits nothing.'
When, therefore, you bow to the earth and prostrate,
you do not gaze upon the ground; rather, you adore the
Holy One whose footstool the earth is. . . .

"He himself instructs us and says, 'It is the spirit that
gives life; the flesh profits nothing: the words I have
spoken to you are spirit and life.'"[1]

The larger context of Augustine's remarks suggests that
he was referring in this passage to a popular custom
among North African Christians: the custom of rev-
erencing the eucharistic elements during the liturgy,
probably at the time of communion.[2] Augustine defended the custom by relating it to a verse of the psalm
he was commenting on: "Extol the Lord our God, and
worship at his footstool: Holy is he!" (Ps 98.5). By weav-
ing together the psalm verses with passages from the
sixth chapter of John's gospel, Augustine developed a
short catechesis on the eucharist. He reminds the people
that while the custom of bowing and prostrating is
praiseworthy, it must not be interpreted in a "fleshy"
sense. For the sacrament of the eucharist, Augustine

44

urged, must be understood "spiritually." In order to make his point more vigorously, he puts these words on Jesus' lips:

"Understand what I have said spiritually. You will not eat this body that you see, nor will you drink the blood that will be shed by those who will crucify me. A sacrament is what I have given to you: understood spiritually, it will give you life. Even if it is necessary to celebrate [this sacrament] visibly, it should be understood invisibly."[3]

Quite clearly, Augustine was attempting to forestall any "cannibalistic" interpretation of the eucharist: Christians eat and drink the Lord's risen body and blood in a *sacrament*; they do not (to borrow a graphic image Augustine uses elsewhere) eat flesh from a "butcher shop."[4] In this brief eucharistic catechesis, therefore, Augustine was concerned to explain two things: the legitimacy of reverential gestures toward the eucharist in the liturgy, and the importance of understanding the eucharist "spiritually" (i.e., *sacramentally*).

Nor was Augustine alone in insisting upon reverence toward the sacramental species at communion time. Other Christian bishops of the late fourth and early fifth centuries indicate that gestures of reverence accompanied the reception of communion. Among the more famous descriptions of eucharistic communion from this period is the following one attributed to St. Cyril of Jerusalem (+ ca. 386):

"Make your left hand a throne for your right, because your right is going to receive the King; make a hollow of your palm and receive the body of Christ, saying after it: 'Amen!' . . . Then, after you have partaken of the body of Christ, come forward to the chalice of His blood, not with upstretched hands, but bending forward in the manner of one who worships and reverences; sanctify yourself by partaking also of the blood of Christ and answer: 'Amen!'"[5]

Cyril also mentions that it was customary for Christians to "sanctify" their bodily senses with the Lord's body and blood: "While the moisture from His blood is still on your lips, touch it with your hands and sanctify your eyes, forehead, and other senses."[6] This custom of "hallowing" one's own body with the sacramental elements may strike modern readers as bizarre, but it represents continuity with a tradition that regarded the eucharist not only as spiritual food but also as a protective talisman against danger and illness.

Both Augustine in the West and Cyril in the East attest to popular gestures of reverence and adoration toward the eucharistic elements. But it must be noted that these gestures occur *within the celebration of the liturgy itself*. The bowings and prostrations, the hallowing of the senses with the eucharistic species, are devotional customs that emerge *within* the larger framework of a community's worship. And indeed, until roughly the Carolingian period (late eighth and early ninth centuries) there seems to be little evidence for a devotional cult of the eucharist outside the liturgical context.[7] Not until eucharistic controversies arise among Carolingian theologians like Paschasius Radbertus and Ratramnus (both ninth-century monks of the Abbey of Corbie) do we find reliable evidence for an extra-liturgical cult of the blessed sacrament.

In this chapter, then, we will explore the emergence of devotional and ritual gestures toward the eucharist as these develop within the framework of public worship. The first of these gestures involves the elevation of the consecrated gifts when the people are invited to communion; the second concerns the ritual of preparing the gifts of bread and wine at the "offertory"; and the third develops in connection with the "fraction" (bread-breaking) rites. Our exploration of these ritual customs will reveal a gradual but decisive shift in liturgical sensibility during the late fourth to the seventh centuries. Gradually, the sense of the eucharist as an ensemble of

46

communal symbols is replaced by a sense of the eucharist as ritual drama interpreted allegorically. As eucharistic reception declines—John Chrysostom already complains about it in the late fourth centuy—mystical interpretations of the liturgy arise. These allegorical, mystical and dramatic reinterpretations of the eucharist mark an important step in the evolution toward a cult of the eucharist independent of Mass.

SHOWING THE PEOPLE THE BODY OF THE LORD
"Come, people, celebrate the holy and undying mystery—the offering. Approach with fear and faith. With clean hands let us grasp the fruit of repentance: for the Lamb of God is offered in sacrifice to the Father on our behalf. Let us adore and glorify him alone, and with the angels let us sing: Alleluia!"[8]

This ancient invitation to communion, used in the Gallican and Ambrosian liturgies, seems to provide indirect evidence for a custom of lifting the eucharistic elements and showing them to the people.[9] This sort of "elevation" of the elements, not to be confused with the elevation of bread and cup during the eucharistic prayer, may in fact have developed as early as the fourth century.[10] In a biography of St. Euverte a fourth-century bishop of Orleans, for instance, we find the following:

"At the time when the heavenly bread was broken, when according to priestly custom he [Euverte] lifted his hands to offer God the victim for a third time, a shining cloud appeared over his head; just then, a hand with outstretched fingers emerged from the cloud to bless the offerings."[11]

Even though one must allow for hagiographical hyperbole in this text, there is no reason to doubt that the liturgical customs mentioned by its author are authentic.[12] The text also holds special interest because of its reference to "offering God the victim for a *third* time." This detail suggests that elevating the gifts may have occurred at three points in the liturgy—probably at the "offertory," at the conclusion of the eucharistic prayer, and at the bread breaking when the people were invited to communion. We know, for example, that in the sixth-century Gallican rite commented upon by Germanus, bishop of Paris, the eucharistic gifts were solemnly lifted and carried to the altar at the offertory. We know, too, that in the Ordo Romanus Primus (OR I), a description of the papal liturgy compiled by an anonymous writer about the year 700 A.D., the consecrated gifts were lifted at the end of the eucharistic prayer:

"When he [the pope or another bishop] has said 'Through him, with him. . . .,' the archdeacon lifts the chalice, with its veil, by the handles and holds it, raising it toward the pope. The pope then touches the side of the chalice with the offerings, and says 'Through him, with him' up to 'forever and ever.' He next puts the offerings in their place and the archdeacon puts the chalice near them."[13]

It would seem, then, that the custom referred to in Euverte's biography is at least as old, perhaps older, than the elevations at the offertory and at the end of the eucharistic prayer mentioned by Germanus of Paris and the OR I. There is evidence, moreover, that in the liturgies of the eastern churches the gifts were shown to the people for their veneration just before communion. St. Maximus the Confessor (ca. 580–662), in his commentary on the works of Pseudo-Dionysius, explicitly alludes to this custom:

"He [Christ] revealed divine gifts and favors, that these might accomplish forgiveness of sins and entrance into everlasting life. And these gifts are mystical in nature. This is demonstrated when the holy gifts are first shown to our eyes, then covered after the prayers; and they remain covered until communion-time. . . . Then the priest lifts them [uncovered], and says 'Holy things for the holy. . . .'"[14]

48

These words of invitation, with their accompanying gesture of lifting the gifts, are familiar from their incorporation at a later period, into the Byzantine liturgy of St. John Chrysostom.[15]

The texts cited in the preceding paragraphs indicate that during the fourth, fifth, and sixth centuries, the custom of lifting the gifts and showing them to the people just before communion was rather well-established in churches of both East and West. This gesture of elevation was ordinarily accompanied, it seems, by words of invitation: "Holy things for the holy"; "Approach with fear and faith." The primary significance of the gesture is obvious: it is a ritual invitation to share the gifts by eating and drinking. Was the gesture also intended as an invitation to reverence or adore the consecrated elements? It is possible, especially in light of Augustine's remarks about "adoring the Lord's flesh" before eating it. For as we shall see in the section that follows, such eucharistic customs easily lent themselves to mystical and allegorical interpretation, as well as to ritual expansion and development.

THE EUCHARISTIC DRAMA:
CHRIST'S PASSION, DEATH, AND BURIAL
In our discussion of the custom of showing the gifts to the people we noted that in the fourth to the sixth centuries, gestures of elevation occur at three points in the eucharistic liturgy: at the offertory, at the doxology of the eucharistic prayer, and at the breaking of bread just before communion. Of these three, the last may well have been the first to develop. Nevertheless, there is also early evidence for lifting the gifts in connection with their preparation on the altar at the offertory.

Theodore of Mopsuestia, who spent time as a presbyter in Antioch during the 380s, appeals directly to the Lord's passion, death, and burial in his allegorical interpretation of the liturgy.[16] In his fourth *Baptismal Homily*, Theodore comments on the offertory rite:

"They bring up the bread and place it on the holy altar to complete the representation of the passion. So from now on we should consider that Christ has already undergone the passion and is now placed on the altar as if in a tomb. That is why some of the deacons spread cloths on the altar which remind us of winding-sheets, while others after the body is laid on the altar stand on either side and fan the air above the sacred body and prevent anything from settling on it. . . . This shows us the importance of the body on the altar; for it is the custom among the great ones of this world that at their funerals . . . attendants fan the body as it is carried on its bier. The same practice must be observed now that the sacred, dread and incorruptible body submits to being laid out on the altar, soon to rise again with an immortal nature."[17]

As Theodore interprets it, the liturgy of the eucharist, from offertory to communion rite, is a ritual allegory that reenacts the events of Jesus' passion, death, burial, and resurrection. The consequences of such an interpretation are far-reaching. In the text cited above, for example, the deacons' actions—spreading cloths on the altar—are no longer regarded as "setting the table for the community's meal," but as "preparing Jesus' body for burial." Similarly, the practical gesture of fanning the bread and wine (to keep insects off the food) have been transformed into allegorical rites pertaining to Jesus' "funeral." Theodore thus interprets the eucharist as a ritual allegory that culminates during the epiclesis of the eucharistic prayer, in Jesus' resurrection.[18]

A similar interpretation has made its way into the *Expositio Antiquae Liturgiae Gallicanae*, commonly attributed to St. Germanus of Paris (ca. 496–576), where there occurs a description of the ritual of bringing the gifts of bread and wine to the altar:

"The song which is sung when the offerings are brought forth originated in this way: The Lord commanded

Moses to make silver trumpets which the levites sounded when the victim was offered. This was a sign that let the people know when the offering was being made: all bowed down, adoring the Lord. . . . Now, however, the Body of the Lord is carried to the altar accompanied not with trumpets but with spiritual voices. The church sings the great and marvelous deeds of Christ with sweet melody."[19]

The *Expositio* goes on to describe the vessels used for bringing up the gifts, and adds a mystical interpretation of their significance:

"The Body of the Lord is borne in 'towers,' because the Lord's tomb was hewn out of rock in the likeness of a tower. Within it is the bier on which the Lord's Body rested. But since the King of Glory rose in triumph, Christ's blood is offered in a special chalice; for the Lord himself used such a vessel to consecrate the mystery of the eucharist, when he said: 'This is the chalice of my blood—the mystery of faith—which will be shed for many unto the remission of sins.'"[20]

When, at the offertory, the gifts are brought forward in "towers" (an ancient eucharistic vessel made of wood, stone, or precious metals), the people are invited to re- member Jesus' burial: "because the Lord's tomb was hewn out of rock in the likeness of a tower."[21] State- ments like this one signal an important shift in liturgical sensibility: the communal symbols of eating and drink- ing a meal with the Risen Lord are slowly being trans- formed into a ritual drama designed to edify and instruct people in the meaning of Jesus' passion and death. To put it another way, the ancient symbols of eating and drinking a meal of sacred food are becoming allegories that remind people about Jesus' cross and burial. Some additional comments about this point are in order.

Symbols, it must be remembered, are not objects; they are actions—verbs, not nouns. Every symbol involves the human subject in a transaction, an interaction, be-

51

tween "self" and "other." The result of this transaction is disclosure, revelation: the "other" reveals itself as present and powerful for the human subject. Luke's story of the disciples on the road to Emmaus (Luke 24) is a good illustration of how symbols operate. The disciples are walking along sadly, when they encounter an "other," a stranger whose identity is hidden. They continue the journey, walking with the stranger and talking about their disappointment over Jesus' death. The stranger offers them instruction; he discloses the meaning of biblical texts that refer to the need for God's servant to suffer and die. When they reach an inn at nightfall, the disciples and the stranger sit together for a meal: "and they recognized the Lord Jesus in the breaking of the bread." It is important to realize that the entire encounter between Jesus and disciples is a symbol: the disclosure of an "other" who is present and powerful, who is recognized through actions of eating and drinking. Note, too, that this symbolic transaction is fraught with multiple meanings and ambiguous experiences of hiddenness and revelation. Such is the character of all symbols: they have more than one meaning, and they are intensely ambiguous. Finally, as Luke's story suggests, symbols yield up their meanings only when we start living in them, acting and moving about in them.[22]

Symbols thus put us in touch with reality by exposing us to the ambiguous richness of an "other" whom we encounter in the symbolic action. The strategy of symbols is an ambiguous one: we are led deeper into the complexity of what *is* and what is *real*. For this reason, symbols do not explain; they tantalize, tease the human imagination into new ways of seeing, knowing, being and having.

Allegory, on the other hand, strives to explain what actions and objects mean. In so doing, it tends to reduce the inherent ambiguity of persons, things, and events by assigning one meaning to each action or object. John

Bunyan's classic *Pilgrim's Progress* is a well-known example of allegorical interpretation applied to the Christian life. "Christian," Bunyan's hero, meets temptation in the form of "Wordly-Wiseman," help in the form of "Evangelist" and "Good-Will," grace on the "Delectable Mountains." In all this Bunyan's intentions are allegorical: he exhorts and explains, urges his readers to accept the cross and glory of a Christian life intensely lived. Allegory thus employs a strategy of reduction: it seeks to limit and control ambiguity so that meaning can be clearly grasped; it reduces complexity by assigning one meaning to each person, event, action, or object. In the gospel of Mark, for instance, Jesus' parable of the sower and the seed (Mark 4.3-8) has been subjected to allegorical interpretation (see Mark 4.10-20); the editor of the gospel pictures Jesus explaining the story to uncomprehending disciples. In fact, however, parables, like symbols, do not explain; they challenge and confront us with their strange notions about virtue and vice, their explosive suggestions about how God acts in the world.[23] The gospel editor has reinterpreted Jesus' story allegorically in order, probably, to support his own theological position and to serve the pastoral and catechetical needs of the church for which the document was written.

The movement from symbol to allegory is thus a movement from ambiguity to clarity, from multiple meaning to single meaning, from revelation to explanation. The ambiguous strategy of symbols provokes action; the reductive strategy of allegory provokes passivity. Whereas symbols require one to search and struggle for meaning, allegories explain meaning.[24]

To speak of a shift in liturgical sensibility from communal symbols to allegorical drama is thus to speak of an understanding of eucharist different from that held by the earliest generations of Christians. In Chapter One we noted a shift from emphasis on meal to emphasis on sacred food; here we notice a more emphatic and far-reaching change. During the period under discussion in this chapter, a shift in liturgical sensibility occurs at the more basic level of root metaphors.[25] Two such metaphors are table and sacrifice (or oblation).

As we saw in Chapter One, the table as a root metaphor of the new relation that exists between God and world in Jesus traces its origins back to Jesus' historical ministry and the Easter experience of the earliest Christians. If one were to unpack the root metaphor of table, one could say that it discloses the radical identity of Jesus' followers: gathered at table, these believers recognize themselves as new people of a new covenant, as people who eat and drink with the Risen One. The table metaphor generated primary symbols: Lord's Supper and Lord's Day, actions that disclosed an "other," ritual gestures that revealed how Christians were different from those who had not experienced Easter.

But in the allegorical interpretations of Theodore of Mopsuestia and Germanus, table has become tomb. And this shift of root metaphor eventually produces a very different attitude toward the eucharist. Table, after all, is a fact of our immediate everyday experience; it signals something we can do now (gather, eat and drink, share food with others). Tables are distinctively ours; they are familiar places in the present where we can engage in communal actions. But tomb is a different matter; we experience it as something that belongs to someone else, as a familiar yet alien object. A tomb may very well excite psychological reactions of recognition, fear, admiration, but it remains a monument to something and someone past. In short, table provokes action in the present; tomb evokes the remembrance of things and people past.

The interpretation of the eucharist as an allegorical drama that evokes the past by ritually reenacting the death and burial of Jesus thus serves to distance people from the immediate actions appropriate to a table (gathering, making a meal, sharing food). Symbols are becoming allegories, verbs are becoming nouns, actions are becoming objects. One is invited to contemplate the drama that unfolds through the gestures of ritual actors (liturgical ministers), and one is encouraged to participate by personally meeting the drama's triumphant hero in the act of communion. The table metaphor emphasizes what we are doing together now; the tomb metaphor emphasizes what someone else did for us in a sacred past.

Something similar happens with regard to the root metaphor of sacrifice. An extremely archaic metaphor, sacrifice was used by early Christians both in their interpretations of Jesus' death and in their understanding of eucharist. [26] But it is one thing to say that eucharist is a "sacrifice of praise and thanksgiving" done by Christians as the memorial of Jesus dead and rising! It is quite another to say that the eucharist is *Jesus'* sacrifice, ritually rehearsed in a liturgical drama witnessed by Christians. In the first case, sacrifice is a symbolic action in which Christians themselves are the central agents; in the second, sacrifice is an allegorical drama at which Christians are present as participant witnesses.

Once again the shift in liturgical sensibility is evident. In a drama that rehearses historical events like Jesus' death and burial, someone must assume the role of the hero. Increasingly during this period, that someone is the priest (bishop or presbyter). He is the one, after all, who speaks Jesus' lines in the drama, and from the fourth century onward these lines ("This is my body; this is my blood") assume increasing importance in the dramatic mysteries of the eucharist. One need only listen for a moment to Ambrose:

"at the consecration this bread becomes the body of Christ. Let us reason this out. How can something which is bread be the body of Christ? Well, by what words is the consecration effected, and whose words are they? The words of the Lord Jesus. All that is said before are the words of the priest. . . . But when the moment comes for bringing the most holy sacrament into being, the priest does not use his own words any longer: he uses the words of Christ. Therefore, it is Christ's word that brings this sacrament into being."[27]

Ambrose's theological conviction about the power of the words of Jesus was destined for a long and influential history in the West. For the present, however, it is sufficient to notice that his understanding of the "words of consecration" represents a new emphasis. If at an earlier stage in the liturgical evolution of the eucharist concern about the Lord's presence shifts from common meal to sacred food, with Ambrose the concern shifts to the *words of the Word*. In the context of a ritual drama, these words take on added significance: they represent the climactic point of change, the central dramatic moment that divides what went before from what comes after.

We can summarize this section of our chapter by noting that allegorical interpretations by writers like Germanus and Theodore witness to an important shift in the understanding of the eucharist. Ancient communal symbols (table, the actions of eating and drinking) are in process of transformation into dramatic allegories (tomb, the passion and triumph of a hero). As earlier the eucharist achieved ritual independence from meal, so now the holy elements have begun to achieve dramatic independence from the ancient symbolic rhythm of the liturgy (taking, blessing, breaking, eating, drinking). The eucharist is not only blessed and consumed, it is also reverenced, greeted, acclaimed and adored.

GESTURES OF REVERENCE IN THE LITURGY
One of the earliest descriptions of eucharistic ceremonial in the Roman Church, OR I, is also one of the first to describe ceremonial gestures of reverence toward the eucharist within the celebration of the liturgy. After outlining the bishop's journey to the church where Mass is

to be celebrated, the author of OR I lists procedures for vesting the ministers in the sacristy. That done, he continues with details of the ceremonies that accompanied the entrance procession of ministers into the church proper. The bishop enters the assembly accompanied by two assisting deacons; subdeacons and acolytes carry incense and candles (traditional signs of honor and rank in the ancient Roman world) before him, while the choir sings an introit psalm. Then, upon arriving at the altar,

"two acolytes approach, holding open pyxes that contain the Holy Elements. The subdeacon takes the pyxes . . . and shows the Holy Elements to the bishop and assisting deacon. Then the bishop and deacon reverence the Holy Elements with bowed heads, and check to see if there are too many fragments—in which case some of them are to be returned to the sacristy."[28]

This brief eucharistic ceremony at the beginning of the liturgy in OR I is known as the *Sancta* (Holy Elements). It reflects a custom which involved saving a portion of the eucharist consecrated at a previous Mass celebrated by the bishop for use in his next liturgy. At a point shortly before the communion of the Mass, some of this reserved portion was dropped into the chalice, probably as a sign of the unity and continuity of all eucharistic celebrations presided over by the bishop. The *Sancta* rite should not be confused with the rite of the *fermentum*. As we have seen in Chapter One, the *fermentum*, a small portion of eucharistic bread sent from the bishop's Mass to other churches where presbyters presided at liturgy on the same day, signified the unity of the eucharist, even when it was not possible for all the Christians of a city to assemble in one spot for its celebration.

In actual fact, the manuscript tradition of OR I witnesses to the existence of both the *Sancta* and *fermentum* ceremonies:[29]

Before breaking the bread, at the words "May the peace of the Lord be always with you," a portion of the *Sancta* reserved from a previous Mass and reverenced by the bishop during the entrance procession, is dropped into the chalice.[30] *After* the bread has been broken, a particle of the loaf consecrated by the bishop at *this* Mass is dropped into the chalice.[31]

One can easily see that both these rituals amount to the same thing: the dropping of a small portion of eucharistic bread into the chalice shortly before the communion. The only difference seems to be that the first portion of bread was consecrated at a *previous* liturgy, while the second was consecrated at the *present* celebration. The question naturally arises: why this doubling up of rituals that appear to signify the same thing (unity and continuity of the eucharist)?

To answer this question, one must note that despite their ritual similarities, these two eucharistic ceremonies, the *Sancta* and *fermentum*, have different origins that reflect different pastoral purposes.

The *Sancta* ritual is actually a miniature liturgy of the presanctified. At Rome, it seems to have originated in situations where the pope, who ordinarily presided at the liturgy on important days at the stational churches (e.g., St. Mary Major, St. John Lateran, St. Peter's) was unable to be present because of illness or some other urgent reason. In such circumstances, another principal celebrant, preferably a bishop, was chosen to preside in the pope's absence. In order to show, however, that this liturgy was in communion with previous Masses actually celebrated by the pope, a fragment of eucharistic bread consecrated at an earlier papal Mass was dropped into the chalice at the words "May the peace of the Lord be always with you." It became customary, in fact, to reserve for this purpose portions of the eucharist (*Sancta*) from papal Masses celebrated on certain days—Holy Thursday, the Easter Vigil, Easter Sunday, Pentecost, Christmas.[32] These reserved *Sancta* were then used in the miniature liturgy of the presanctified described above, on occasions when someone other than the pope was celebrating the stational liturgy at one of Rome's major churches. In effect, the *Sancta* ceremony was a species of the ancient *fermentum* rite, designed to signify eucharistic unity with the bishop of Rome when he was unable to preside at the liturgy.

The *fermentum* rite, however, originated because of pastoral circumstances that developed as the Christian community expanded in large urban centers. Since the entire local church could no longer be accommodated in a single place, several liturgies had to be celebrated in different churches on the same day. To those liturgies presided over by presbyters, a portion of bread, the *fermentum*, from the bishop's Mass was brought in order to signify eucharistic unity.

Both *Sancta* and *fermentum* ceremonies developed, therefore, as ritual metaphors of unity in pastoral situations where something central to the integrity of eucharistic liturgy was missing. For in the ancient church, as is well known, three things were usually considered normative for the integrity of the eucharist: the gathered assembly of all people in the local church; the presidency of the bishop, assisted by other ministers; and the actions of praise and thanksgiving over gifts of bread and wine. This, at least, was the vision of eucharistic integrity promoted by early Christian writers like Ignatius of Antioch.[33] Thus, when one of these central elements was missing—e.g., when the bishop of the place could not preside—some ritual sign of unity with him was needed. In a sense, both *Sancta* and *fermentum* served as stand-ins, ritual surrogates for an absent presider (the bishop).

OR I includes both these rituals probably because by the eighth and ninth centuries, when the document was compiled and circulated, the earlier significance of the rites was no longer widely grasped. For outside the immediate environs of Rome and its liturgies the original meaning of *Sancta* and *fermentum* were easily misunderstood. This misunderstanding is evident in works written by non-Roman liturgists like Amalarius of Metz (ca. 780–850). Although he wrote during the period when documents like OR I had begun circulating in churches outside Rome, Amalarius seems to have been confused about the exact meaning of rites like the *fermentum*. In a letter to Abbot Hilduin, he elected to interpret the rite in an accommodated allegorical fashion:

"Fermentum is the gift of charity. It takes but a little of its leaven to bind the hearts of many into a body. For charity is far-reaching, and can unite the hearts of all the faithful by its bonds. The gospel indicates this in the story of the woman who hid the leaven in three measures of flour until all was leavened. That woman is the apostolic person, the church, who shows her love for her 'leaven' [i.e., her clergy] so that all can be moved to true love by her example."[34]

Elsewhere, Amalarius offers a christological interpretation of the rite in which the celebrant drops a particle of consecrated bread into the chalice:

"Why does the priest drop the bread into the wine while making the sign of the cross when he says 'May the peace of the Lord be always with you?' In order to show that the soul of Christ returns to his body—and that peace is thus effected not only in heaven but also on earth.

"What does it mean to mix the bread with the wine? [It means] that Christ's soul returns to his body."[35]

Such allegorical interpretations, written about a century after OR I had appeared, indicate once more the shift in liturgical sensibility mentioned earlier in this chapter. The *fermentum* rite, originally a sign of communion with the bishop even when he was unable to be present at every liturgy, has now become a christological allegory.[36] The pastoral origins of the rite—the effort to express the full integrity of eucharist even when one of its central elements (the bishop as presider) was missing—has now become a sacred ritual drama that portrays the events of Jesus' life, passion, death, and resurrection.[37]

This movement toward allegorical and dramatic interpretations of ritual represents an important stage in the evolution of a cult of the eucharist outside Mass. The liturgy gradually ceases to be an action done in common; it becomes a series of scenes to be watched while one meditates on the events of Jesus' life. Eventually, the eucharistic elements themselves become part of the stage props: they can be separated from their immediate liturgical environment in the Mass and deployed for other purposes. If, at an earlier stage of liturgical history, the act of eucharistic communion was sometimes disengaged from the action of the worshiping community, now the sacramental elements are becoming props in a drama that will eventually achieve independence from the liturgy altogether. The eventual use of the eucharist as an independent object of ritual drama will be discussed in Chapters Three and Four; for the present it is sufficient to note that allegorical interpretations of rites like the *Sancta* and *fermentum* helped pave the way for this development.

SUMMARY

To sum up, a decisive shift in liturgical sensibility appears in the fourth century. At that time we begin to notice important changes in both ritual action and ritual interpretation. Gestures of reverence and adoration emerge at the point in the Mass when the people are invited to communion—and these gestures are commented upon by pastoral leaders like St. Augustine. Increasingly, the eucharist is interpreted as ritual drama, the remembrance of things past, the solemn rehearsal of events in Jesus' life, death, and resurrection. Writers like Theodore of Mopsuestia regard the altar not so much as a table but as a tomb where Jesus is laid and then resurrected through the liturgical action. Finally, we can begin to notice the appearance of ceremonial gestures of reverence toward the reserved eucharist as it is used within the celebration of the liturgy (the *Sancta* and *fermentum* rites). The pastoral origins of these rites fade from consciousness, and writers like Amalarius (in the ninth century) reinterpret them in allegorical style. In short, the communal symbols of gathering at table to eat and drink with thanksgiving have become ritual dramas of watching at Jesus' tomb while the priest pronounces sacred words that confect a sacrament.

NOTES

1. St. Augustine, *Enarrationes in Psalmos* 98.9, edited by Eligius Dekkers and Johannes Fraipont, *Corpus Christianorum*, Vol. 39, pp. 1385-1386.

2. See the commentary in E. Bertaud, "Dévotion eucharistique" in *Dictionnaire de Spiritualité*, IV/2, col. 1623.

3. St. Augustine, *Enarrationes in Psalmos* 98.9, edited by Dekkers and Fraipont, p. 1386.

4. See St. Augustine, *Commentary on John*, 27.5, PL 35, col. 1617.

5. St. Cyril of Jerusalem, *Catecheses* 22.21-22, translated in Paul W. Harkins, *St. John Chrysostom, Baptismal Instructions* (Ancient Christian Writers, no. 31; Westminster, Md.: The Newman Press, 1963), p. 330.

6. Ibid.

7. See Bertaud, "Dévotion eucharistique," *Dictionnaire de Spiritualité*, IV/2, col. 1623.

8. Fernand Cabrol, *Le Livre de la Prière antique* (Paris: Libraire Religieuse H. Oudin, 1900), p. 542.

9. The elevation of the host during the institution narrative is a much later development that did not appear in the West until the end of the twelfth century; this point will be discussed in Chapter Four.

10. See Fernand Cabrol, "Elevation," DACL IV/2, col. 2661.

11. See *Acta Sanctorum*, September, III, edited by J. Stiltingo *et al.* (Rome and Paris, 1868), p. 45.

12. See Cabrol, "Elevation," DACL IV/2, col. 2661.

13. See Ronald C.D. Jasper and Geoffrey J. Cuming, eds., *Prayers of the Eucharist, Early and Reformed* (London: Collins, 1975), p. 113.

14. PG 4, col. 137. "Pseudo-Dionysius" was a mystical theologian who flourished about the year 500, probably in Syria. In his work on "The Ecclesiastical Hierarchy," he mentions the custom of showing the consecrated gifts to the people: "Then, after the prayers, he [the presider] takes the holy gifts, uncovers them and lifts them; otherwise, the gifts remain covered until time for communion." Text in PG 4, col. 443.

15. See F.E. Brightman, *Liturgies Eastern and Western* (Oxford: Clarendon Press, 1896; reprinted, 1965), p. 395. The following rubric is also found: "The deacon comes to the doors, and lifting the holy cup, he shows it to the people, and says, 'Approach with fear of God and with love.'" Further examples of the "Holy things to the holy" formula may be found in Cabrol, "Elevation," DACL IV/2, cols. 2663-2664.

16. See Edward Yarnold, ed., *The Awe-Inspiring Rites of Initiation* (London: St. Paul Publications, 1973), pp. 173, 227-230.

17. Yarnold, *Awe-Inspiring Rites*, p. 228.

18. Ibid., pp. 245-246.

19. See E.C. Ratcliff, ed., *Expositio Antiquae Liturgiae Gallicanae* (Henry Bradshaw Society, Vol. 98; London: HBS, 1971), p. 10. Ratcliff died before he had the opportunity to complete his critical notes on the text; it seems, however, that he denied Germanus's authorship of the *Exposition*; see: Alexis van der Mensbrugghe, "L'Expositio Missae Gallicanae: est-elle de Saint Germain de Paris (+ 575)?" *Messager de l'Exarchate de Patriarche russe en Europe occidentale* 8 (1959), 217-249.

20. Ratcliff, *Expositio*, p. 10.

21. On the eucharistic "tower" (*turris*) as a vessel of reservation for the eucharist, see W.H. Freestone, *The Sacrament Re-*

served (Alcuin Club Collections, XXI; London: A.R. Mowbray and Co., 1917), p. 217.

22. See Paul Ricoeur, *The Symbolism of Evil*, translated by Emerson Buchanan (Boston: Beacon Press, 1967; paperback edition, 1969), pp. 10-18.

23. See John Dominic Crossan, *The Dark Interval* (Niles, Ill.: Argus Communications, 1975), pp, 54-62.

24. See Crossan, *Dark Interval*, pp. 57-72.

25. On the notion of "root metaphors," see Victor Turner, *Dramas, Fields, and Metaphors. Symbolic Action in Human Society*. (Ithaca, New York: Cornell University Press, 1974), pp. 24-32.

26. See Leander Keck, *Paul and His Letters* (Proclamation Commentaries; Philadelphia: Fortress Press, 1979), pp. 32-48 (interpretation of Jesus' death as "sacrifice").

27. Ambrose, *On the Sacraments*, IV.14; text in Yarnold, *Awe-Inspiring Rites*, p. 133.

28. Text from E.G. Cuthbert and F. Atchley, trans., *Ordo Romanus Primus* (London: The De La More Press, 1905), p. 129.

29. See the discussion in Michel Andrieu, *Les Ordines Romani du haut moyen age* (5 vols.; Spicilegium Sacrum Lovaniense 11, 23, 24, 28, 29; Louvain: 1931–1961), Vol. II, pp. 52-64.

30. Andrieu, *Les Ordines*, II, p. 98.

31. Ibid., II, p. 101.

32. Ibid., II, p. 62.

33. See Ignatius, *Letter to the Philadelphians*, 4: "Make certain, therefore, that you all observe one common Eucharist; for there is but one Body of our Lord Jesus Christ, and but one cup of union with His Blood, and one single altar of sacrifice— even as also there is but one bishop, with his clergy and my own fellows-servitors the deacons." In Maxwell Staniforth, trans., *Early Christian Writings* (New York: Penguin Books, 1968), p. 112.

34. Amalarius of Metz, *Epistola ad Hilduinum Abbatem*, in J.M. Hanssens, ed., *Amalarii Episcopi Opera Liturgica Omnia* (Studi e

Testi 138-140, 3 vols., Città del Vaticano: Biblioteca Apostolica Vaticana, 1948), III, p. 358.

35. Amalarius of Metz, *Ordinis Missae Expositio*, II.15, in Hanssens, ed., *Amalarii . . . Opera*, III, p. 320.

36. Amalarius's allegorical interpretations—the *fermentum* as a sign of the "return of Christ's soul to his body"—is obviously meant to be an allusion to the resurrection. But it should be noted that what Amalarius describes is not resurrection in the New Testament's sense of that term, but resuscitation, the return of a dead man to his former life through a reunion of body and soul.

37. As we have noted earlier in this chapter, elements of "dramatic" and "allegorical" interpretation of liturgical rites appears already in earlier commentators like Theodore of Mopsuestia (– 428).

Chapter Three

Controversy and Estrangement

INTRODUCTION

The trend toward allegorizing the liturgy, toward transforming pastoral rites into ritual dramas, achieved special prominence during the Carolingian epoch. Commentators like Amalarius of Metz, whose work was referred
to in the previous chapter, were fond of investing each
gesture of the liturgy with a hidden "mystical" meaning. Even the most practical actions of the liturgical
ministers were interpreted as scenes from the life of
Jesus. For example, when the subdeacon moved to the
ambo in order to read the epistle at a Solemn Mass,
Amalarius interpreted the movement in light of the gospel account of the ministry of John the Baptist. The subdeacon, Amalarius speculated, represents John: for that
reason, he reads the epistle from a *lower* step at the
ambo—since John's preaching was inferior to that of
Christ.[1]

It is important to note, however, that allegorizing of the
sort engaged in by Amalarius was directed toward the
liturgy itself. However fanciful his interpretations may
appear to be, Amalarius focused his comments on the
liturgical rites, rather than upon paraliturgical or extra-
liturgical ceremonies involving the eucharist. Amalarius
thus had nothing to say about those cultic and devotional practices that emerged later in the medieval
period, practices such as solemn exposition of the
eucharist, processions with the Blessed Sacrament, or
Benediction. In the case of Amalarius we have a dramatic interpretation of the liturgy rather than an extra-
liturgical dramatization of the eucharist.

Nevertheless it was during the Carolingian epoch that
the first signs of an extra-liturgical cult of the eucharist

appeared. Just as at an earlier period sacred food had achieved ritual independence from community meal, so in the early medieval period the eucharistic food began to gain cultic independence from the eucharistic liturgy. Several factors contributed to the appearance of this cultic dramatization of the eucharistic species. One such factor was theological: in the early ninth century a eucharistic controversy arose in the Latin West, and questions were posed about the exact nature of the change that occurs in the sacramental elements of bread and wine. The principal antagonists in this controversy, Paschasius Radbertus and Ratramnus, were both monks of the Abbey of Corbie, but the dispute soon gained notoriety beyond the borders of their monastery. The notion that a change occurs in the eucharistic bread and wine was of course not new, but earlier writers such as Ambrose and Augustine had been content merely to affirm the change and to suggest its source (the words of Jesus, the action of the Spirit). Similarly, the notion that Christ is present and offers himself to believers in the eucharist was ancient and traditional, but earlier documents such as the *First Apology* of Justin Martyr or the *Apostolic Tradition* of Hippolytus had been content simply to affirm such a presence without attempting a philosophically sophisticated explanation of its precise modality. By the early ninth century, however, philosophical questions about eucharistic change and presence were being debated, and conflicting solutions were being proposed.

A second factor was also at work during the Carolingian epoch. The liturgies of the western churches were subjected to a period of intense cross-fertilization. Charlemagne was anxious to reform the liturgy in his empire on the basis of models imported from the Roman church. The native liturgy that had existed in much of the Frankish empire—the old Gallican Rite—was thus exposed to Roman influence. In point of fact, however, what resulted from this meeting of two different ritual families was neither Gallican nor Roman, but a ritual hybrid. This Gallican-Roman hybrid, the result of a cross-fertilization of liturgical traditions, eventually made its way back to Rome itself. Much of the earlier Roman Rite, still reflected in documents like *Ordo Romanus Primus*, disappeared. At the same time, the Gallican Rite vanished except in a few local churches that maintained strong attachment to native customs.

During this period of liturgical cross-fertilization, a new phenomenon emerged: the inclusion of texts for private or devotional prayers within the eucharistic celebration, particularly at the communion rite. The earliest examples of such prayers come from ninth-century sacramentaries, especially in those produced in a Gallican milieu. Some of these prayers, such as the one which begins, "Lord Jesus Christ, Son of the living God," were destined for a long history in the Latin liturgical books; indeed, the prayer just mentioned is still included in the sacramentary as reformed by the Second Vatican Council.

A third factor that helped reshape Christian worship during the Carolingian epoch was a linguistic one. By the ninth century Latin was no longer widely understood except by clerics who had studied it, usually in monastic schools. Actually, the dissolution of Latin as a *lingua franca* used by virtually all socioeconomic classes was already well underway three centuries earlier. Gregory of Tours, in the sixth century, complained that the written Latin of his era was marred by glaring errors of syntax and grammar:

"You do not know how to distinguish the nouns: you frequently use the feminine in place of the masculine, and the masculine in place of the neuter. Despite the authority of illustrious writers whom one should respect, you often fail to use prepositions the way you ought. You put prepositions that take the accusative case before words that are in the ablative case—and viceversa."[2]

68

From the viewpoint of modern linguistics, Gregory's complaint is unjustified: the dissolution of older syntactical and grammatical rules is simply a sign that language is changing, that it still has sufficient vitality to reshape itself. In any case, the process of change in the Latin language was irreversible. By the ninth century the discrepancy between the formal written language and the ordinary speech of the people was so great in places like northern France that bishops were instructed to translate their Latin sermons into the actual speech of the people. A council at Tours in 813 decreed "that all bishops, in their sermons, provide exhortations that edify the people, and that they translate these sermons into old French (*rustica romana lingua*) or into German, so that everyone can understand them."[3]

This conciliar decree is one of the first bits of ecclesiastical documentation that explicitly refers to the existence of a new language in France. By the middle of the ninth century works actually written in old French had appeared.

The same pattern of linguistic evolution emerged elsewhere in Europe; by the end of the tenth century vernaculars were known in Italy and Spain as well.[4] The importance of this development cannot be overemphasized. Language is, after all, more than a mere instrument or tool of thinking and expression. In an important sense, langauge is thought; words constitute reality. As John Dominic Crossan has said: "Reality is neither in here in the mind nor out there in the world; it is the interplay of both mind and world in language . . . being human means living in language and calling that process reality. . . ."[5]

The appearance of new vernacular languages in Europe during the ninth and tenth centuries thus signaled a profound cultural and intellectual change that was bound to influence forms of Christian worship. The language of the people and the specialized hieratic language used by the clergy in liturgy had become, by the tenth century, two forms of speech deeply estranged from one another.[6]

A fourth factor that contributed to liturgical change in the Carolingian era was the composition and compilation of prayers (and sometimes of liturgical poetry) that emphasized internal, psychological sentiments of an intensely personal and private character. Several collections of *libelli precum* (little books of prayers) from this period are known. Among the works attributed to Alcuin, Charlemagne's court liturgist, is a *Libellus sacrarum precum* that contains prayers, liturgical hymns, litanies and poetry.[7] The work may not have been Alcuin's; it is based on a manuscript that seems to date from about the year 900. Nevertheless the booklet is typical of a genre that became popular in the Carolingian era. This *libellus* contains several curious pieces, including the following prayer attributed to St. John the Evangelist:

"Lord Jesus Christ,
I beg you, through your mercy and constancy,
to grant me forgiveness of my sins.
Open to me the door of life, for I am knocking;
and do not let the prince of darkness hinder me.
Let not the footsteps of pride come near me,
nor a foreign hand touch me.
Sustain me according to your word,
and guide me to the fellowship of your feast,
where all your friends celebrate with you."[8]

Many of the prayers collected in this *libellus* contain personal confessions of sinfulness and petitions for pardon. It is possible, indeed, that some of them were used as forms of self-examination and preparation for the sacrament of penance in its Irish tariff form.[9] In any case, some of the prayers include detailed descriptions of sins, real or imagined, for which the devout individual is encouraged to seek forgiveness. An example:

"I have fallen into sins,

I have collapsed into faults. . . .
My feet rushed, as though they were birds,
toward evil that was spurred on by lust;
heedless of obedience to your commands,
my sturdy legs carried me off to wickedness.
My knees gladly bent to fornication, rather than adoration;
I did not hesitate to sully myself
with every uncleanness, through the use of my thighs
and genitals. . . .
My stomach and bowels were constantly bloated
with drunkenness and over-eating. . . ."[10]

Prayers like this one may sound like scripts for a questionable film, but they reveal the genuine needs and concerns of the people who compiled and used them. Indeed, they are possibly a more accurate reflection of the spiritual climate of the era than are the official liturgical texts contained in sacramentaries, antiphonaries and other approved books.

A fifth and final factor at work during the Carolingian era was the emergence of cultic attention to the eucharist outside the celebration of Mass. Some of the earliest hints of an extra-liturgical cult of the eucharist appear in works written for solitaries. The *Regula Solitariorum*, written toward the end of the ninth or beginning of the tenth century by a presbyter named Grimlac, speaks of the recluse as a person who lives constantly in the presence of Christ.[11] This unyielding attention to Christ's presence is fostered by the solitary contemplative's style of life: withdrawal from the world, unceasing prayer, *lectio divina*, and frequent, even daily, reception of the eucharist. Grimlac's discussion of the place of the eucharist in the recluse's piety is interesting for several reasons. First, it suggests that solitaries who are priests may celebrate the liturgy *alone* each day.[12] Although this is not our earliest reference to private Mass, it indicates that by the late ninth century such solitary celebrations were considered praiseworthy. Secondly, Grimlac's

71

view of the eucharist is colored by interests that could almost be described as clericalist. In his discussion of the solitary's personal hygiene, Grimlac raised questions about beards and baths—always a touchy subject in monastic literature. Beards, Grimlac suggested, are a concession to vanity: "If holiness depends on beards," he noted, citing Gregory the Great, "then nobody is holier than a goat!"[13] That quip aside, Grimlac goes on to reveal his real concern:

"I think it is appropriate for solitaries—especially those who celebrate the holy mysteries—to shave and cut their hair every forty days. . . . Moreover, let them have a large vessel in the hermitage, so that the priests may enjoy the use of baths in order to cleanse their bodies. Perhaps someone will object: 'St. Anthony never bathed himself.' To him, I would briefly reply: 'True, St. Anthony never bathed—but he never sang Mass, either.' Therefore, let the priests bathe according to their own discretion, so that they may be clean and worthy when they celebrate the holy mysteries."[14]

Grimlac's prescriptions concerning baths and beards indicate a shift in understanding the relation between priesthood and eucharist. The priest, according to the *Regula Solitariorum*, is a sacral person rather than a pastoral leader who serves a community's liturgical prayer and action. There is a definite trend toward hallowing the status of a priest because of his intimate relation to the holy mysteries. In view of the priest's inherent sacrality, even the time-honored ascetic disciplines (no shaving, no bathing) are condemned out of deference to the sacrament he celebrates.

While the *Regula Solitariorum* offers no explicit evidence about extra-liturgical customs surrounding the eucharist, it unquestionably outlines a view of the eucharist different from what we have encountered in the first and second chapters of this book. The priest is becoming a hieratic specialist, with knowledge of a language (and thus a reality) different from that of ordinary believers. Moreover the priest is able to celebrate the sacrament quite independently of a congregation; his own contemplative piety and motivation are sufficient grounds for celebrating. By the time we reach the Carolingian era, the eucharist has not only achieved ritual independence from its originating context in a meal, it has also achieved cultic independence from the community. Since the priest (and very few others) can control the specialized hieratic language of the celebration, he can also claim a certain possession of the sacrament. For to possess language is to possess the reality; and conversely, to lose control of the words is to forfeit one's claim to the reality.

All five of these factors contributed to the emergence, later in the medieval period, of a eucharistic cult outside Mass. In the pages that follow, these factors will be explored in greater detail. For the moment, however, it is important to reiterate the overwhelming significance of the third factor identified in this introduction: the evolution of vernacular languages in Europe and the consequent transformation of Latin into a specialized speech possessed primarily by sacerdotal experts. If one accepts John Dominic Crossan's contention that reality itself is constituted by the "interplay of mind and world in language," then the linguistic evolution described above assumes major liturgical and theological significance. It could be said, perhaps, that the development of an extra-liturgical eucharistic cult represents an attempt to reassert the people's claim on the sacrament through an alternative language of devotion that relies on strong visual images (seeing the Lord exposed in the sacred host) and popular gestures (processions, blessings and the like).

THE EUCHARISTIC CONTROVERSIES
OF THE NINTH CENTURY
In the year 831, Paschasius Radbertus, a monk and later

abbot of the Benedictine monastery of Corbie, published a treatise entitled *De Corpore et Sanguine Domini* ("On the Body and Blood of the Lord").[15] The publication of this work, originally written for members of the monastic community, marked a dramatic turning point in the history of eucharistic theology in the Latin West, for Paschasius's book represented the first attempt to deal with the eucharist in a systematically doctrinal way. Earlier works, such as the mystagogic catecheses of prominent bishops like Ambrose and Cyril of Jerusalem, treated the eucharist in its liturgical context as the consummating act of Christian initiation. As we have noted in the introduction to this chapter, these earlier patristic commentaries were generally content to affirm the church's eucharistic faith without probing very deeply into questions about change and presence.

With the appearance of *De Corpore et Sanguine Domini*, however, a different theological interest in the eucharist revealed itself. For one thing, Paschasius wrote about the eucharist *not* as one of the initiatory sacraments, but as an independent theological reality isolated from its immediate liturgical context. Moreover the questions that Paschasius raised differed, as one might expect, from those that concerned earlier church fathers like Ambrose, Augustine, Cyril, or John Chrysostom. For the earlier fathers, doctrine was derived from doxology, from the liturgical actions of prayer and thanksgiving in the eucharist: *lex orandi*, *lex credendi*. For Paschasius, however, it was possible to raise questions about eucharistic doctrine that did not flow immediately from the experience and ritual action of a community at prayer.

The questions that preoccupied a Carolingian theologian like Paschasius were ones that dealt with issues like these:

1) What is the relation between the eucharistic body of Christ and the historical body of Jesus who lived, died,

rose, and ascended to the Father?

2) How can one explain the "real presence" of Christ in the eucharist—especially since the sacrament is often celebrated in many different places at the same time?

3) What is the difference in the bread and wine before and after the consecration?

4) What is the relation between the sacramental signs (bread, wine) and the realities which those signs signify (Christ's true body and blood)?

Paschasius approached these similar questions about the eucharist by insisting on the utter *realism* of Christ's presence. For him, there was virtually no difference between the sacramental or "eucharistic" body of Christ and the historical body born of the Virgin: "just as the true flesh [of Christ] was created, without intercourse, from the Virgin through the Spirit, so through the same [Spirit], the same body and blood of Christ is mystically consecrated from the substance of bread and wine. . . . Hence he says, indeed, that this is nothing else than true flesh and true blood—although mystically [present]."[16]

Paschasius's rather crude equation of the sacramental body with the historical body of Christ seemed, of course, to suggest a carnal or materialistic interpretation of the eucharist that earlier church fathers like Augustine might have found repulsive. And indeed there are passages in *De Corpore et Sanguine Domini* where a type of mystical "cannibalism" seems to have infected Paschasius's thinking on the subject. He cites approvingly, for example, hagiographical legends that speak of miraculous "bleeding hosts":

"No one who reads the lives and deeds of saints can remain unaware that often these mystical sacraments of the body and blood have been revealed under the visible form of a lamb or the actual color of flesh and blood. This has been done either on behalf of the doubtful or on behalf of those who love Christ more fervently. In this way Christ graciously offers faith to the unbelieving: when the gifts are broken or the host is offered, a lamb appears in the hands [of the priest] and blood flows in the chalice as at a sacrifice. What is thus hidden in mystery becomes manifest to doubters through a miracle."[17]

Passages like this one reveal Paschasius's emphatically realistic perception of the Lord's presence in the eucharist. In a sense, the sacramental elements of bread and wine are merely veils that hide the natural flesh and blood of Christ: "the body that was born of the Virgin Mary . . . that hung on the cross, that was buried in the tomb, that rose from the dead, that entered the heavens, that now, as high priest forever, daily intercedes for us."[18] It could be said, perhaps, that Paschasius's position represents a failure to take the sacramental signs with full seriousness: the elements of bread and wine are, after the consecration, a kind of mirage, an envelope that merely conceals the natural qualities of Christ's body.

The intensity of Paschasius's eucharistic realism is also evident in his discussion of image (*figura*) and truth (*veritas*) in the sacrament. While he was prepared to admit a distinction between these terms, he seems to have been uncomfortable with it. Perhaps he feared that the language of signs and images (*figurae*) threatened his conviction about the realism of Christ's eucharistic presence. In the passage that follows, Paschasius attempts to clarify the relation between image and truth as these terms are applied to the sacrament:

"Because this sacrament is mystical, we cannot deny that it is an image (*figuram*). But if it is an image, we need to ask how it can also be truth. For every image is the image of something else, and always refers to that something. . . . No one who reads the Bible denies that the images of the Old Testament were shadows. This mystery [the eucharist] is either truth—or an image, and thus a shadow. We must certainly ask, therefore, whether this whole thing should be called truth, without any shadow of falsehood—or whether such a thing ought to be called a mystery.

"It [the eucharist] seems to be an *image* when it is broken, when something is understood about the visible species that differs from our fleshly powers of seeing and tasting, when blood is mixed with water in the chalice. But at the same time, this sacrament of faith is rightly called *truth*. It is truth when the body and blood of Christ are produced from the substance of bread and wine by the power and word of the Spirit; but it is an image when the priest makes some external gesture which serves to recall the sacred Passion at the altar. . . .

"But if we look at the matter correctly, we can see that [the eucharist] is simultaneously image and truth. What is experienced externally [in this sacrament] is an image or figure of truth; but what is rightly believed or understood internally about this [sacrament] is truth. For not every image is merely shadow or falsehood. . . .

"Thus, for example, as children we learned the signs or letters of the alphabet before we achieved gradually, the ability to read; then we learned the spiritual sense and understanding of written texts. So also we are led from the humanity of Christ to the divinity of the Father— and thus Christ is rightly called the image or sign of the Father. . . .

"He [Christ] left us this sacrament—a visible figure and image of his flesh and blood—so that our mind and our flesh could be more richly nourished through them, and so that we could grasp things invisible and spiritual through faith. What is externally perceived in this sacrament is an image or sign; but what is received internally is truth, and no mere shadow. . . ."[19]

I have cited this passage from Paschasius's work at some length because it represents one of the earliest efforts in

Latin theology to work out the exact relation between *sign (figura:* bread and wine) and *things signified (veritas:* the body and blood of Christ) in the sacramental theology of the eucharist. Paschasius's solution to this problem is rather ingenious, and it partially anticipates conclusions drawn several centuries later by scholastic theologians. He is careful to note, for example, that the relation between image and truth is a real one—but one that can be perceived only through faith. Paschasius also suggests that the external signs (figures, images) of the eucharist produce a triggering effect that ushers the believer into the invisible and spiritual truth of the sacrament.[20]

Paschasius's discussion of image and truth in the eucharist also reveals that he rejected the "butcher-shop theology" which Augustine had found so repulsive. Eating and drinking the eucharist is an act of spiritual nourishment; nowhere does Paschasius assert that Christians literally "tear the flesh" or "crush the bones" of Christ when they participate in this sacrament.[21] Unfortunately, some of Paschasius's illustrations—his stories of bleeding hosts, for example—exhibited a crude realism that conflicted with his more refined theological formulations. In a revised edition of his *De Corpore et Sanguine Domini*, published in 844, Paschasius included a story about an old ascetic who, though his life was virtuous, remained ignorant about many points of Catholic doctrine.[22] One day this old man was approached by two younger monks who attempted to explain that what is present in the eucharist is the natural body of Christ *(naturale corpus Christi).*[23] The old man was skeptical of this explanation, but he prayed to God for enlightenment on the subject. Next Sunday at Mass a strange phenomenon occurred while the three men looked on. As the offerings of bread were brought in, the two younger ascetics saw "with their mind's eye"

"[a form] like a young child lying on the altar. When the presbyter extended his hand and broke the bread, an angel of the Lord, with knife in hand, descended from heaven and sacrificed the child, pouring its blood into the chalice. And when the presbyter broke the bread into small pieces, the angel cut up the child's members into little parts.

"When the old man came forward to receive holy communion, a piece of flesh soaked in blood was given to him. When he saw it, he trembled and cried out: 'Lord, I believe that the bread which is placed on the altar is your body, and the cup is your blood.' And immediately, the flesh in his hand became bread, according to the mystery. . . .

"The other ascetics said to [the old man]: God knows that human nature cannot bear to eat raw flesh; therefore he transformed his body into bread and his blood into wine for those who receive it in faith."[24]

It is difficult to reconcile this rather crude story with Paschasius's more sophisticated remarks about image and truth in the sacrament. We must remember, however, that Paschasius regarded the eucharist as a miracle of God's omnipotent power: at each consecration, he believed, God creates or multiplies the natural body of Christ, making it physically present on the altar under the guise of bread and wine.[25] To use the language of a later era, the bread and wine are "annihilated"; their appearances remain, however, because "God knows that human nature cannot bear to eat raw flesh."

We can summarize Paschasius's thinking on the eucharist by relating it to the questions posed earlier in this section of the chapter.

1) The eucharistic body and the historical body of Christ are identical for the sacrament contains the natural body born of a virgin, crucified, and risen.

2) Paschasius held for an emphatic, almost literal, realism regarding the presence of Christ in the eucharist. Indeed, his illustrations—with their refer-

ences to bleeding hosts and miraculous apparitions of the Lord in the bread—suggested a crudely materialistic view of the sacrament. God creates, multiplies the natural body of Christ at each eucharist; the consecration is thus a miraculous demonstration of divine power.

3) After the consecration, the elements of bread and wine become mere masks, envelopes that hide what is literally (physically) present on the altar: the flesh and blood of Christ. For this reason Paschasius could cite approvingly the story of the old ascetic who discovers a "piece of flesh soaked in blood" in his hand at communion time. It seems that after the consecration the bread and wine serve merely to conceal what would otherwise cause revulsion in the communicant (raw flesh and blood).

4) Finally, Paschasius was willing to admit a distinction between image and truth in the sacrament, between the visible signs (bread, wine) and the invisible realities (presence of the Lord's body and blood and participation in them). He implied that the images trigger a movement that permits the believer to grasp in faith the spiritual realities signified by them.

Oppostition to Paschasius: Ratramnus
Paschasius Radbertus's effort to combine Ambrosian realism and Augustinian sacramentalism was, in many respects, an admirable one.[26] Despite its problems of theological formulation and precision, it was a serious attempt to offer an intelligible account of the church's faith concerning the eucharistic presence of Christ to a largely uneducated audience of monks. For many of Paschasius's more sophisticated contemporaries, however, the theory smacked too strongly of crass materialism, of "butcher-shop theology." Even though Paschasius had insisted that the ultimate purposes of the eucharist were to nourish the soul, forgive sins, and unite Christians to the body of Christ (the church), his illustrations promoted a static and carnal assessment of

the Lord's eucharistic presence.[27] Worse still, his theology appeared to confirm popular scruples about crushing and tearing Christ's flesh through the actions of eating and drinking.

At the urging of Emperor Charles the Bald, who found Paschasius's theology excessively realistic, another monk of Corbie, Ratramnus, composed a treatise on the same subject.[28] Like his teacher Paschasius, Ratramnus affirmed the real presence of Christ in the sacrament. The disagreement between the two men was not over whether Christ is present (both agreed that he is), but over how his presence should be understood by believers. Ratramnus refused to identify the eucharistic body with the historical body of Christ. What is offered to Christians in the sacrament is *not* the body of Christ that appeared on earth and will be revealed to us in heaven:

". . . we are taught that the body in which Christ suffered and the blood which flowed from His side as He hung from the cross differ greatly from this body which the faithful celebrate daily in the mystery of Christ's passion, and from this blood which the faithful drink, in order that it may be the mystery of that blood by which the world was redeemed."[29]

This passage shows that Ratramnus had little sympathy for Paschasius's stories about bleeding hosts and miraculous appearances of Christ in the bread and cup. What is at stake, Ratramnus insisted, is the nature of a sacrament (a mystery). The presence of Christ is real and sacramental—not real and literal (physical, carnal, material). To hold that Christ is present according the natural mode of flesh and blood would, according to Ratramnus, destroy the very notion of a sacrament:

"For if that mystery is celebrated under no figure at all, it is no longer properly called a mystery. Since that cannot be called a mystery in which there is nothing hidden, nothing covered with some sort of veil. But that bread which is made the body of Christ through the ministry of the priest manifests itself externally to the senses as one thing, and yet internally it demands recognition from the minds of the faithful as something different."[30]

Ratramnus did not deny that something real and objective happens to bread and wine in the celebration of the eucharist. But he argued that the manner in which this happens is properly called *sacramental*.[31] The sacramental elements do not capture or entrap the natural flesh and blood of Christ, nor do they become mirages or envelopes that act as a crust to conceal raw flesh and dripping blood (as Paschasius's examples suggested). As sacrament, Ratramnus argued, the eucharist appeals to faith, not to any natural mode of recognition whether sensate or intellectual.

"Externally, it [the eucharist] retains the form of bread which before it was; the colour of bread is seen; the aroma of bread is caught. Internally, however, something else far more precious, far more excellent, is intimated, since there is shown what is heavenly, what is divine, that is, the body of Christ, which is seen not by the senses of flesh, but, perceived by the minds of the faithful, received and eaten."[32]

This text shows that Ratramnus perceived the central question about the eucharist as one of sacrament and faith, rather than one of material realism. Unlike Paschasius, whose primary concern seems to have been the actual presence of Christ's natural body, Ratramnus directed his attention to the nature of sacrament and the necessity of faith for the proper perception of sacramental signs. "It is one thing for material food to feed the body," Ratramnus wrote, "another to nourish souls with the substance of eternal life."[33] As sacrament addressed to faith, the eucharist is spiritual food; eating it, Christians feed upon the real body and blood of Christ—but not in a carnal or material way. Ratramnus noted, moreover, that the mystery ("sacrament") of

82

eucharistic bread and wine signifies not only the personal body of the Risen Christ but also the ecclesial body, the church. In a passage of his work strongly influenced by Augustine, Ratramnus wrote:

"St. Augustine teaches us that just as the bread placed on the altar signifies the body of Christ, so also it [signifies] the body of the people who receive it. . . . For what is placed on the Lord's table contains not only the sacramental (*mysterium*) of Christ, but also the sacrament of the body of the faithful people."[34]

Ratramnus was aware that his spiritual and ecclesiological interpretation of the Lord's presence in the eucharist might lead some to think he was denying traditional doctrine. He defended himself in *De Corpore et Sanguine Domini* by appealing to the relation between sacrament and faith:

"It should not be thought that because we say these things the Lord's body and blood is not consumed by the faithful in the mystery of a sacrament; for faith receives not what the eye sees but what it believes. This is spiritual food and spiritual drink that spiritually nourishes the soul and gives life of everlasting fulness. Thus did the Saviour himself speak, commending this mystery: 'It is the spirit that gives life; the flesh profits nothing.'"[35]

Ratramnus thus sought to understand the real presence in a way that would not compromise the integrity of sacramental signs or the necessity of faith for perceiving them. Some of his formulations, indeed, anticipated the vocabulary of later medieval scholasticism. He spoke, for instance, of the mode of Christ's presence as "substantial": "the body and blood of Christ which the faithful receive in church are images [signs], according to their visible appearance; but according to their invisible substance—that is, according to the power of the divine Word—the body and blood of Christ truly exist. As visible creatures [of bread and wine] they nourish the body;

as the greater power of substance, they feed and sanctify the minds of the faithful."[36] Although such formulations lack the precision of later theologians like Thomas Aquinas, they affirm that the Lord's presence in the eucharist is real and substantial.

Like Paschasius before him, Ratramnus distinguished between image (*figura*) or sacrament (*mysterium, sacramentum*) and truth (*veritas*). But whereas Paschasius seemed to feel such a distinction might lead to a denial of Christ's presence, Ratramnus regarded it as essential to a proper understanding of eucharistic doctrine. In a section of his work dealing with the theology of St. Ambrose, Ratramnus quoted the following passage and then offered his own commentary upon it:

"'It was true flesh that was crucified and buried; and this [the eucharist] is truly the sacrament of that flesh. For the Lord Jesus himself cried, 'This is my body.' (St. Ambrose)."

"How carefully, how prudently this distinction is made! Concerning the flesh that was crucified and buried— that is, insofar as Christ himself was crucified and buried—[Ambrose]said: This is the true flesh of Christ. But concerning that which is consumed in the sacrament, he said: This is truly the sacrament of that flesh. [Ambrose] thus distinguished between the sacrament of flesh and the truth of flesh. In the truth of flesh taken from the Virgin, [Ambrose] says Christ was crucified and buried. But the mystery now celebrated by the church he would call the sacrament of that true flesh which was crucified."[37]

Although the language of the passage is a bit awkward, Ratramnus's theological intentions are clear. Phrases like "the true flesh" or "the truth of flesh" refer to the actual historical body of Christ that was born, crucified, buried. This historical body, Ratramnus argued, is not literally or physically "re-created" in the sacrament. What the church celebrates, however, is a true *sacramen-*

tum of that body. In short, the eucharist is a true "mystery" of the flesh of Christ, but it is not a physical re-creation of the natural body of Christ.

In summary, Ratramnus would have answered the questions outlined at the beginning of this section of the chapter differently from the way Paschasius responded to them:

1) According to Ratramnus, the eucharist is a sacrament of Christ's natural historical body, but it is not to be literally or physically identified with that body.

2) Christ is truly present in the eucharist, but this presence does not demand that God "re-create" or "multiply" Christ's flesh at every consecration. Nor is the presence materialistic; there is no room for bleeding hosts in Ratramnus's theory.

3) At the church's eucharist, therefore, the bread and wine act as true signs: they offer to believers the substance of Christ's body and blood, but the distinction between sign and thing signified, between image and truth, remains. The sacramental signs are not mere envelopes that contain raw flesh and blood.

4) The relation between signs (bread, wine) and truth (Christ's body and blood) is real: through the sacramental elements Christians are fed spiritually with the substance of Christ's true flesh and blood. But the sacrament is perceived through faith, not through any natural operation of the human senses or the human intellect.

Against Paschasius's perhaps exaggerated realism, Ratramnus thus proposed a more emphatically sacramental understanding of eucharistic and presence. Like Augustine before him, Ratramnus stressed the spiritual nature of eucharistic eating and drinking, actions that appeal to faith and not to any sensate or materialistic perceptions of flesh and blood. He recognized that the sacrament celebrates both the *corpus Christi mysticum* (eucharist) and the *corpus Christi quod est ecclesia* (church).[38]

EUCHARISTIC PIETY
The eucharistic controversies of the ninth century did not lead immediately to extra-liturgical veneration of the eucharistic species. Christians of the Carolingian period were not yet familiar with customs like eucharistic exposition, Benediction, processions or visits to the Blessed Sacrament. Still, just as new theological questions about the eucharist emerged during this period, so a new eucharistic piety also developed. Elements of this piety are revealed in both liturgical sources and extra-liturgical documents (e.g., prayerbooks, *libri penitentiales*, hagiographical legends, popular stories). In the following pages we will sketch some of the fundamental features of this new eucharistic piety.

Changes in the Practice of Giving Communion
In our discussion of Paschasius Radbertus's eucharistic theology, we came across a story about an old ascetic who had doubts about the nature of Christ's presence in the sacrament. One small liturgical detail from that story concerns us here: the old man received communion *in his hand*. In light of recent liturgical reforms this detail causes us no surprise. Nor, apparently, did Paschasius think the practice was unusual; he offers neither explanation nor apology for it. And indeed, there is no reason why he should have: communion in the hand was the ordinary custom, frequently mentioned by ecclesiastical writers.[39]

During the ninth century, however, the practice of giving communion in the hand began to change. There is evidence, for example, that is some ninth-century churches, the eucharist was placed in the *mouth* of the lay person.[40] *Ordo Romanus X*, which describes Mass celebrated by a bishop in a cathedral served by canons regular, gives the following description of the communion rite:

"The presbyters and deacons, after kissing the bishop, receive the body of Christ from him in their hands; they will communicate at the left side of the altar.

"But the subdeacons, after kissing the bishop's hand, receive the body of Christ from him in their mouths."[41]

This *Ordo*, probably compiled in Mainz sometime between 900 and 950, implies that all persons who are not at least in deacons' orders must be communicated in the mouth, not in the hand. Although the *Ordo* describes only the communion of the liturgical ministers (itself an interesting point), one may legitimately infer that lay communicants, like subdeacons and lesser ministers, are to receive orally.

The custom described in *Ordo Romanus X* reflects a development that had actually begun earlier. A ninth-century council of bishops at Rouen, for instance, had decreed: "Let not the eucharist be put in the hand of any lay man or woman, but only in the mouth."[42] This conciliar prohibition is open to a variety of interpretations. It could be argued, for example, that the council was reacting against superstitious abuses connected with the eucharist. There are collections of medieval stories which abound with examples of the sacrament used for bizarre purposes. Caesarius of Heisterbach (ca. 1180–1240) reports the case of a woman who used the eucharist as an aphrodisiac; he also tells of another lady who laid the consecrated bread in a beehive in order to cure sick bees.[43] But these stories come from a later era, long after the custom of communicating lay persons orally had already evolved. Besides, the stories indicate that when the practice of communion in the hand was replaced by communion placed in the mouth, it did not prevent abuse.

A more plausible interpretation of the prohibition against placing the eucharist in the hands of lay persons has been hinted at in the introduction to this chapter. Increasingly, the eucharist was becoming a rite performd by the clergy, as opposed to an action celebrated by the entire community. The rise of vernacular languages contributed to the distancing of lay persons from altar and sanctuary. The hieratic language used by clerical specialists gave the latter enormous control over sacred actions. Only those who "knew the language" were qualified to handle objects as sacred as the eucharistic species. It was during this period, too, that the custom of anointing a priest's hands at ordination developed. The *Missale Francorum*, a Gallican sacramentary of the eighth century, includes two formulas for this purpose.[44] The first of them reads: "May these hands be consecrated and sanctified through this anointing and our blessing, so that whatever they bless may be blessed and whatever they sanctify may be sanctified."[45]

The second formula is longer and suggests a theology of the priesthood that is heavily influenced by Old Testament images of prophecy and kingship:

"May these hands be anointed with holy oil and with the chrism of holiness. As Samuel anointed David king and prophet, so may [these hands] be anointed and perfected in the name of God the Father and of the Son and of the Holy Spirit—as we trace upon them the image of the holy cross of our Lord and Savior Jesus Christ, who freed us from death and leads us to the kingdom of heaven."[46]

These two formulas for anointing the hands of a priest are the earliest examples we possess.[47] It is significant that the examples come from Gallican territory, the same region in which the prohibition against giving communion to the laity in their hands first appeared. Bruno Kleinheyer has shown that the custom of hand-anointing probably derives from ordination practices in the British Isles; from there the custom made its way onto the continent.[48] Significantly, too, the sources (both insular and continental) associate the anointing not only with images of prophecy and kingship, but also with the specifically sacerdotal action of consecrating the eucharist. In a sacramentary of the abbey of St. Denis that dates from the middle of the ninth century, the following text appears: "O Lord, bless and sanctify these hands of your priest so that they may consecrate victims (*hostias*) which are offered for the sins and negligences of your people. . . ."[49]

This text states, quite unambigiously, that the ordination liturgy gives the ordained person the unique power to consecrate the eucharistic gifts.[50] And this was precisely the interpretation given to the rite by liturgical commentators of the ninth century. Amalarius of Metz (+ 850) commented in his *Liber officialis*: "Our bishops maintain this custom: they anoint the hands of presbyters with oil. Their reason for doing this is quite evident: [hands] that offer victims (*hostias*) to God should be pure. . . ."[51]

Amalarius's interpretation marks an important stage in the evolution of this anointing ritual. In the earliest formulas, such as the one cited above from the eighth-century *Missale Francorum*, the anointing signified little more than a blessing. Rather quickly, however, this simple blessing was invested with deeper significance: the priest is anointed like David, who was king and prophet. Finally, the anointing assumed an explicitly sacramental meaning: these hands are blessed with power to consecrate the eucharistic species. By the middle of the ninth century, this latter interpretation was common.

The Gallican custom of anointing a priest's hands at ordination, imported in the eighth century from the British Isles, did not influence the Roman liturgy until at least the tenth century.[52] Nor did the Gallican liturgical books adopt the insular practice completely: the anointing of the deacon's hands, mentioned in British sources like the Pontificals of Egbert and Robert, was omitted in Frankish documents.[53] Still, the custom of anointing the presbyters had become so powerfully entrenched by Charlemagne's time that even the emperor's desire for a return to Roman liturgical customs could not eradicate it. The sacramentaries produced during the Carolingian reform continued to include the hand-anointing alongside the prayers borrowed from Roman sacramentaries like the *Hadrianum*.

In my opinion, the custom of anointing the priest's hands—together with its interpretation as "power to consecrate the eucharist"—contributed significantly to the change from communion in the hand to communion in the mouth for laity. Not only was the priest a person who knew the "secret sacred language" of the liturgy, he was also one who had been anointed, as kings and prophets are, with powers unavailable to ordinary lay persons. Both factors—knowledge of a hieratic ritual language and access to the holy power of consecration through anointing—contributed to the priest's stature as a sacred person whose relation to the eucharist differed essentially from that of lay believers. The priest alone had knowledge of the sacred texts; he alone had power to transform the elements of bread and wine. And since that transformation, according to the theology of thinkers like Paschasius Radbertus, produced nothing less that the "natural historical body of Jesus" on the altar, the priest could claim a relation to God that was quite extraordinary. Given these developments, it is small wonder that lay persons were gradually prohibited from touching the sacramental species, and that the privilege of handling the body and blood of the Lord was reserved to those whose hands had been anointed for the purpose.

But the gradual change from communion in the hand to communion in the mouth was only one example of a shift in eucharistic practice during the Carolingian epoch. Other factors also affected the relationship between lay persons and the eucharist. Among them were the practice of distributing communion after Mass for practical reasons, and the gradual removal of the eucharistic cup from the laity.

The earliest reference to the custom of delaying communion until after Mass comes from the beginning of the ninth century. In an *Ordo* written by Abbot Angilbert of St. Riquier (+ 814), the following instructions are found:[54]

"I have determined that on the most holy day of Easter, as well as on Christmas Day, the brethren [monks] and all the rest who appear in the Church of the Holy Savior for Mass should receive communion in that same church. While the brethren and the rest of the clergy are receiving communion from the priest who sang the Mass that day, let two other priests—assisted by two deacons and [two] subdeacons—distribute communion. One [of these priests] communicates the men, while the other communicates the women, so that the clergy and people may communicate at the same time and thus be able to hear the blessing and conclusion of the Mass. When everything is over, let them depart, praising and blessing the Lord. After all this is done, the two priests mentioned earlier should take their places—one at the door, the other at the other door—so that they may distribute communion to the servants as they come down from the ambulatory. After all this has been done, the priests, together with their ministers, go to the bottom step [of the chancel] in order to communicate those who were not able to receive at the other places mentioned above. . . ."[55]

This text indicates that distributing communion to some people after Mass was not considered an ordinary practice. The days spoken of—Easter and Christmas—were obviously times when an unusually large number of communicants might be expected. We cannot, therefore, appeal to Angilbert's *Ordo* as evidence for a regular custom of delaying communion for the people until after Mass. Indeed, even on the busier days of Easter and

Christmas, Angilbert clearly states that some of the people communicate at the same time as the monks and the clergy do. Nevertheless, Angilbert's solution to the problem of communicating large numbers on great festivals exerted a powerful attraction. In subsequent centuries this solution became ordinary in churches where numerous communicants could be expected, especially at Easter.[56]

It was during the ninth century, too, that lay persons began to be denied direct access to the eucharistic cup. This was also a gradual development. Already in the early eighth century there is evidence for the use of a reed or straw (*pugillaris, calamus, fistula*) in the administration of the chalice. *Ordo Romanus Primus*, a document compiled about 700 A.D. by someone with detailed knowledge about liturgical rites at the papal court in Rome, gives these instructions for communicating the people at a solemn eucharist:

"The chief bishop receives the chalice from the archdeacon, and stands at the corner of the altar; he communicates the remaining ranks down to the chief counsellor. Then the archdeacon receives the chalice from him, and pours it into . . . the bowl, and hands the chalice to a district subdeacon, who gives him the reed (*pugillarem*) with which he communicates the people."[57]

Although use of the reed did not prevent the laity from receiving from the cup, it did introduce another distinction between clerical and lay communicants: clergy receive directly from the cup; lay persons must use a straw. *Ordo Romanus Primus* gives no reason for the practice, though perhaps the large size of the chalice was felt to increase the danger of spilling its contents.

Another method of giving communion that prevented the laity from directly handling the cup was intinction.[58] In the West, our earliest references to this custom appear in seventh-century conciliar legislation. These early references to intinction are generally unfavorable.

The Fourth Council of Braga (Spain), which met in 675, seems to have forbidden sacramental intinction (dipping consecrated bread into consecrated wine):

"Although every crime and sin is blotted out by the sacrifices offered to God, what expiation can be made to the Lord for sins committed in the very act of offering sacrifice? For we have heard that some [priests], led astray by schismatic ambition, offer milk instead of wine at the divine sacrifice—contrary to the divine commands and apostolic custom; others offer the people eucharist that has been intincted at communion; and still others communicate the people with grapes, rather than with wine made from them, in the sacrament of the Lord's chalice. . . . But the gospel says 'Jesus took bread and cup, blessed them, and gave them to his disciples.'. . . The practice of giving the people eucharistic communion by means of intinction has no authority in the gospel, where [we read that] he gave his disciples his body and blood: the bread was given separately and the cup was given separately. We read that Christ gave intincted bread to no one except to that disciple whom he revealed as a traitor by offering him a morsel that had been dipped (*intincta*)."[59]

The Council's argument against intinction—that it was contrary to the clear intention of scripture and that it evoked the scene of Judas's exposure as a traitor—was repeated by theologians in later centuries.[60] Despite such unfavorable assessments, however, the practice gained popularity. How general intinction was in the ninth century is difficult to determine, though it does seem to have been commonly used in two situations: communion of the sick and the liturgy of the presanctified on Good Friday. Regino of Prüm (ca. 840–915), whose collection of canonical and synodical legislation became a foundation for canon law in the West, mentions use of intincted bread in the ministry to the ill:

"Every priest should have a pyx or some other container

worthy of so great a sacrament, in which the Lord's body may be carefully kept for use in viaticum. . . . The holy oblation should be intincted in the blood of Christ so that the presbyter may truly say to the sick person: 'May the body and blood of the Lord preserve you. . . .' Because of [danger from] mice and wicked people, [the sacrament] should always be kept on the altar. Every third day it should be changed, i.e., it should be consumed by the presbyter, and another, consecrated the same day, be put in its place; otherwise if it is reserved too long, it may (God forbid!) become moldy."[61]

It is significant that the reason Regino gives for intinction is not practical convenience (e.g., the greater ease of swallowing moistened bread) but the integrity of the sacramental signs: the formula of distribution refers to the body *and blood* of the Lord. Even though the ill person was not literally drinking from the cup, Regino seems to have been concerned that both species be administered. The theological theory of concomitance, which emphasized that Christ is present, whole and entire, under either species alone, had not yet developed.[62]

Despite the unfavorable reaction of councils like IV Braga, and despite the theological concern of canonists like Regino of Prüm, intinction gained ground, especially in rites of communion for the ill and dying. Another rite that involved intinction was the liturgy of the presanctified on Good Friday. Prior to the seventh century, there is no evidence for a communion service at Rome on that day; according to ancient custom, the two days before Easter were times of fasting.[63] But *Ordo Romanus* XXIII, compiled sometime between 700 and 750, indicates that in the Roman parish liturgies, communion was given to the people on Good Friday. The papal liturgy celebrated at St. John Lateran, however, maintained the older custom: neither the pope nor his deacons communicated. That these two different customs existed simultaneously, at least for awhile, is clear from the text of OR XXIII:

"There [at St. John Lateran], the pope does not communicate, nor do the deacons. Whoever wishes to communicate, however, may do so from the cylindrical boxes (*capsis*) in which the sacrifice from Holy Thursday has been reserved. Whoever does not want to communicate there [at St. John Lateran] may go to other churches in Rome or to the parishes for communion."[64]

Adrian Nocent remarks that the Good Friday communion at Rome was given under forms of bread and wine, both having been reserved from the liturgy of Holy Thursday.[65] The text of OR XXIII is somewhat unclear on this point, though its use of the word *capsa* (a cylindrical vessel used to store the reserved bread) may indicate that only one form was used. In any case, by the early ninth century, another custom had developed: the bread, reserved from Holy Thursday, was dropped into a cup of unconsecrated wine—and through this contact the wine was considered consecrated.[66] Although later theologians were appalled by the theory of consecration by contact, the custom spread in the ninth and tenth centuries. In the tenth-century Romano-Germanic Pontifical, edited at Mainz about 950, the theory is clearly reflected:

"After they say 'Amen' [to the embolism that follows the Lord's Prayer], he [the bishop] receives from the sacred gifts and puts [a particle of bread] into the chalice; he says nothing at this point unless, perhaps, he wishes to say something privately. The 'Peace of the Lord' is not said because the sign of peace is not exchanged among those present. [The bishop] sanctifies the unconsecrated wine with the consecrated bread. They all communicate in silence."[67]

What the Romano-Germanic Pontifical describes was, in effect, a modified form of intinction which maintained use of the cup through the theory of consecration by contact. It is possible that the practical difficulties of reserving large quantities of consecrated wine from the Holy Thursday liturgy prompted the solution described here. Effectively, however, it meant that the actual eucharistic cup had disappeared from the Good Friday liturgy—if, indeed, it was ever used. And because the theory of consecration by contact was so unacceptable to many theologians in subsequent centuries, a trend began toward restricting communion to the celebrant alone in the liturgy of the presanctified. By the time we reach the Roman Pontifical of the thirteenth century, only the celebrant communicates at the Good Firday service.[68]

Little by little, therefore, the use of the eucharistic cup was removed from lay persons. In part this removal was prompted by practical circumstances: e.g., the special difficulties connected with communion of the ill and with communion from the reserved species on days like Good Friday. But theological theories also contributed to the cup's gradual disappearance. Concomitance and "consecration by contact" helped to defend the legitimacy of separating the people from the cup at communion.

In sum, the ninth century was a watershed in the history of the relation between the people and eucharistic communion. During that period, communion in the mouth began to replace communion in the hand; communion after Mass began to appear as a pastoral solution for large numbers of communicants on major feasts; the cup began to disappear as an integral part of the people's communion. It was a case, perhaps, of the extraordinary exception becoming the pastoral (though not the theological) norm. Clinical forms of communion, such as the intincted bread given to persons in extremis, gradually gained acceptability for all situations. And theological speculation about issues like the concomitant presence of the whole Christ in each sacramental element, helped seal what had begun as an extraordinary pastoral procedure.

Such was the emerging liturgical situation as it affected the ritual of eucharistic communion during the Carolingian epoch. But looking at rituals is one thing; discovering what ordinary people thought about them is another. From the Carolingian era we do, however, possess examples of the kind of religious instruction that was given by clergy to lay persons and even by parents to their children. During the ninth century the earliest Christian catechism in question-and-answer form appeared[69]; it was designed to instruct children in the rudiments of the Creed, the Bible, the sacraments, and prayer. We also possess valuable catechisms that cover similar topics for adult lay men and women.[70] Most of these documents offer some instruction on the eucharistic liturgy, and that is the point that will concern us in the following paragraphs.

In his catechism, *The Lay Way of Life*, Bishop Jonas of Orleans (818–843) discussed eucharistic communion within the larger context of his remarks about Christian marriage. Of particular concern to Jonas were questions about worthy reception and frequency of eucharistic communion. The bishop was critical of Christians who, without good reason, receive communion infrequently.

"There are some, burdened by sin, who are rightly deprived of participation in so great a sacrament by the judgment of a priest. What is even more perilous and worthy of correction, there are a good many who withdraw from this sacrament partly out of carelessness, partly out of sloth. Such people hardly ever [receive] in the course of the year, except on the three great feasts, and then, more out of custom than out of devotion. These latter either do not know, or do not want to know, that the soul deprived of spiritual food dies just as the body does if deprived of food and drink."[71]

Jonas then went on to cite references in the New Testament and in the church Fathers that speak of the conditions required for fruitful reception of communion. He quotes Jerome's opinion that married persons ought to abstain from sexual intercourse for a time before approaching Christ's body in the eucharist.[72] Similarly, he cites Gregory the Great and Isidore of Seville to support both his views about abstention from sex for married people who intend to receive communion and his views about penitents who presume to receive before they have truly repented of their sins.[73] Despite the somewhat negative language of his advice, Jonas clearly intended to *encourage* frequent communion and, at the same time, to discourage reception without prior reflection and preparation:

"Every one of the faithful should recognize the dangers that surround this matter; for unless he eats and drinks he will have no life in himself—and if he eats and drinks unworthily, he eats and drinks judgment for himself. Let each one prepare himself so that often and with due discretion, he may receive the gift of redemption pure in soul and body."[74]

Jonas's *The Lay Way of Life* thus provided moral advice and pastoral counsel for the vast majority of Christians who were neither members of the clergy nor members of religious communities.

Another example of pastoral instruction for lay persons appears in an anonymous ninth-century question-and-answer catechism. This catechism, entitled *Disputatio Puerorum*, includes, among other items, a discussion of eucharistic doctrine and liturgy.[75] Most of the discussion is derived from Isidore of Seville's *Etymologiae*, a seventh-century encyclopedia of information about both secular and theological matters. The author of the catechism offered these explanations about the Mass:
Q. Where does the term "Mass" come from ?
A. From *emittendo* (sending out, dismissing).
Q. For what reason?
A. Because at the time of the sacrifice there is a dismissal

when the catechumens are ordered to depart by the deacon who says: "If any catechumen remains, let him depart." Those who are not yet reborn [through baptism] cannot be present at the sacrament of the altar.
Q. You mentioned sacrifice; why is it called that?
A. It is called sacrifice because it is a "holy thing done" (*sacrum factum*): by a mystical prayer it is consecrated for us in memory of the Lord's passion. Hence, at his command, we call this the body and blood of Christ, for it is sanctified from the fruits of the earth and becomes a sacrament by the invisible working of God's Spirit. The Greeks call this sacrament of bread and cup "eucharist," which in Latin is translated "thanksgiving". . . .
Q. What is a sacrifice?
A. A victim and whatever is burned or placed on an altar is a sacrifice. Because whatever is given to God is either dedicated or consecrated. . . .[76]

After this discussion of the vocabulary used by Christians to describe the eucharist, the author of the catechism explained the "seven prayers of the Mass." Once again, he relied on Isidore of Seville for his interpretation:

Q. I humbly ask that you not refuse to show me what is contained in this Mass.
A. Insofar as I understand it, I will tell you. In the order of the whole Mass, there are seven prayers.
Q. What are they?
A. The first is the one that goes "The Lord be with you" or "Let us pray." It is an admonition to the people, to stir them up for worshiping God. The second is the collect . . . an invocation to God that he may graciously receive the people's prayers and offerings. The third prayer is uttered for those who make offerings, or for the faithful departed, in the collect which is said at the "offertory". . . . The fourth prayer follows the kiss of peace . . . and goes from "Lift up your hearts" to "through Christ our Lord." The fifth is called the *inlatio*, the prayer to sanctify the oblation; it goes from

"Through him the angels praise" to "Hosanna in the highest!" In this prayer all of earth's creatures and heaven's powers are invited to praise. Then the sixth prayer follows: "You, therefore, most loving Father"; it is a confirmation of the sacrament, so that the offering sanctified by the Holy Spirit may conform to [the Lord's] body and blood. Finally, the seventh prayer is the one which our Lord taught his disciples to pray: "Our Father, who art in heaven. . . ."[77]
Several features make this description of the eucharistic liturgy interesting. First of all, the author describes the eucharist as it would have been celebrated in the Gallican (or Old Spanish) Rite, not in the Roman Rite. Such things as the kiss of peace before the eucharistic prayer and the use of technical terms like *inlatio* indicate that the author was thinking of the Gallican liturgy.[78] In the Roman eucharist described in *Ordo Romanus Primus* (ca. 700), the kiss of peace precedes communion, and the use of *inlatio* to refer to the first part of the eucharistic prayer is absent. The dismissal of the catechumens, mentioned in the catechism's explanation of the term "Mass" also reflects Gallican practice, where the formula continued in use long after it had disappeared from the Roman Rite.[79]

Of interest, too, is the catechism's implied theology of the eucharist. The author never alludes to the words of the Lord as a "consecration formula." Indeed, the institution account is never singled out for special commentary, though the author included a phrase-by-phrase explanation of the Lord's Prayer.[80] Nor are questions about eucharistic presence and change, debated by ninth-century theologians like Paschasius Radbertus and Ratramnus, discussed in this catechism. The author of the *Disputatio Puerorum* was content simply to affirm that the eucharist is an "offering sanctified by the Holy Spirit," that it "conforms to Christ's body and blood."[81] If this catechism is representative of religious instruction

given Christians during the ninth century, one may
conclude that the eucharistic debates among theologians
were largely disregarded by or unknown to pastors and
catechists.

A final example of religious instruction in the Carolingian era comes from a short manual written by a mother
for her son. Dhouda was a French noblewoman who
married Duke Bernard of Aquitaine in 824. Her *Liber
manualis*, written between 841 and 843, was addressed
to her eldest son William, who was probably a page at
the court of Charles the Bald.[82] Only a few chapters of
Dhouda's work are extant, but those that remain include
instruction on both personal prayer and public worship.
In a chapter on reverence in prayer, Dhouda recommended these bedtime devotions:

"Pray with your mouth, cry out with your heart, make
petitions while you work, so that every day and night,
every hour and moment, God may always assist you.
When you lie down to rest on your bed, say this: 'God,
come to my assistance; Lord, make haste to help me,'
and the 'Glory be . . .' Then say the Lord's Prayer, and
after you have finished it, say: 'You have guarded me,
God, throughout the day; guard me now through this
night, if it is your will. May I deserve to be protected
under the shadow of your wings, filled with the Holy
Spirit, armed with your royal defense, surrounded by a
guard of angels. . . .' When you have completed this
[prayer], make a cross on your forehead and trace upon
your bed an image of that cross by which you were
redeemed, saying this: 'I adore your cross, Lord, and I
believe in your holy resurrection. Your holy cross is with
me. . . . The cross is my salvation; the cross is my defense; the cross is forever my protection and refuge. . . .'
And similarly [say this]: 'I adore your cross, Lord; I recall your glorious passion. . . .' May this cross and blessing always be with those whom I, weak Dhouda, frequently mention [in prayer]. And like the dew of Her-
mon which falls on the heights of Zion, or like oil on the

head, running down upon the beard of Aaron, so may the anointing of Jesus of Nazareth, the Son of God, descend and remain upon you wherever you travel and upon your brother, who, after you, was the second to come forth from my womb."[83]

Dhouda's devotional recommendations reflect the popular piety of the period. Similar styles of prayer, including the "salutations of the holy cross," are found in the late ninth-century *Libellus precum* mentioned in the introduction to this chapter.[84] Dhouda's *Manual* indicates that at this period devotional prayers were still strongly influenced by biblical and liturgical language. The cross—and the altar (though Dhouda does not mention it)—were the central objects of Christian devotion; the eucharistic species were not yet regarded as appropriate objects of private veneration and prayer.[85] When Dhouda spoke of the eucharist, therefore, she was thinking of the actual celebration of the liturgy. She encouraged William to pray at Mass for all the departed, especially his father:

"You should see to it that the solemnities of Masses and sacrifices are frequently offered for him, and indeed, for all the faithful departed. There is no better prayer. . . . It is said of the incomparable Judas [Maccabeus]: 'It is a holy and pious thought to pray for the dead, and to offer sacrifices for them so that they may be freed from their sins.'"[86]

Although praying for the dead and offering eucharist on their behalf was already an ancient Christian practice by Dhouda's time,[87] the Carolingian period marked a significant stage of growth in the cult of the dead, in the multiplication of prayers and Masses on their behalf.[88] What could be called a cultic industry of praying for the dead, at both Divine Office and Mass, emerged in the ninth and tenth centuries. Monasteries, especially, were often endowed by wealthy patrons for the precise purpose of offering a perpetual round of prayers and Masses for the dead. Dhouda's recommendation to William thus reflects an expanding cultic industry that was destined to continue and grow throughout the later medieval period.[89]

These three examples—Jonas's *The Lay Way of Life*, the anonymous ninth century catechism, and Dhouda's *Manual*—indicate that during the Carolingian epoch pastors and parents took the responsibility of religious instruction for the people seriously. A similar seriousness can be detected in offical decrees from Carolingian councils and synods. The *Capitulary* of Bishop Theodulph of Orleans (ca. 750–821), for example, insists "that the priests establish schools in every town and village, and if any of the faithful wish to entrust their children to them to learn letters, that they refuse not to accept them but with all charity teach them . . . and let them exact no price from the children for their teaching nor receive anything from them save what parents may offer voluntarily and with affection."[90]

In effect, Theodulph was establishing a system of free parochial education at a diocesan-wide level. Monasteries, too, were instructed to establish schools "in which boys may be taught the Psalms, the system of musical notation, singing, arithmetic and grammer."[91]

The eucharistic piety and theology reflected in these catechetical materials also reveal the seriousness with which pastors and catechists encouraged participation in the liturgy. Frequent communion preceded by adequate personal preparation was the theme in Jonas of Orlean's *The Lay Way of Life*. The eucharist as "sacrament by the invisible working of God's Spirit" was the theological keynote of the anonymous *Disputatio Puerorum*. And participation in the liturgy as the premiere way of praying for the dead was Dhouda's counsel to her son at court. Despite the rise and increasing popularity of liturgical practices like the private Mass, Carolingian bishops continued to insist that eucharistic

worship is a communal act, not a private devotion.[92]
Bishop Theodulph's *Capitulary*, for example, decreed:

"A priest should never celebrate Mass alone; for just as
it cannot be celebrated without the priest's greeting, so
it cannot be celebrated without the people's response.
Most certainly, therefore, Mass ought never to be celebrated by one individual alone. For there must be others
who stand about with the priest; others whom he may
greet; others who may respond to him."[93]

Clearly, a bishop like Theodulph considered solitary
celebration of the eucharist abusive, contrary to the very
nature of liturgical action and liturgical roles. His conviction was representative: the norm of eucharistic celebration during the Carolingian epoch remained public and
communal, not private and devotional.

PRIVATE PRAYERS IN THE LITURGY
Though public celebration of the eucharist remained
normative, it was during the Carolingian era that
prayers of a private or devotional nature first began to
enter upon the liturgical action. The earliest evidence for
private prayers at the communion rite appears in the
ninth century. The Sacramentary of Amiens, which appears to date from the second half of the ninth century,
contains a full set of private formulas that are intended
to accompany the priest's actions at Mass.[94] Among the
formulas are prayers for vesting, for approaching the
altar at the beginning of Mass, for personal use while
the *Sanctus* is being sung, and for communion. The
communion prayers are familiar ones. Before receiving
the priest says:

"Lord, Jesus Christ, Son of the living God,
by the will of the Father and the work of the Holy Spirit,
your death brought life to the world.
By your holy body and blood free me from all my sins,
and from every evil.
Keep me faithful to your teaching,

and never let me be parted from you."[95]

After communion, the priest is directed to say:
"What we have received with our mouth, Lord,
may we also bear in our mind:
so that this temporal gift
may become an everlasting remedy."[96]

Both these prayers were incorporated into the Missal of
Pius V (1570) and are still found, in slightly altered
form, in the Missal of Paul VI (1970).

Similar prayers for the priest's communion were included in other ninth-century sources. The
"Prayerbook" of Charles the Bald (+ 877), for instance,
contains this text:

"Lord, holy Father, almighty and eternal God,
may I so receive the body and blood of your Son,
our Lord Jesus Christ,
that I may find forgiveness of my sins
and be filled with your Holy Spirit.
For you are God, and in you is God,
and beside you there is no other;
your kingdom lasts forever and ever."[97]

Like the formulas in the Sacramentary of Amiens, this
one has had a long history. Incorporated into the tenth-
century sacramentaries of Tours, Fulda, and Chartres, it
kept reappearing throughout the middle ages and, more
recently, in the Missal for the dioceses of Lyons (1904)
and Braga (1924).[98]

In British sources, too, private prayers for the priest's
communion began appearing at about this time. Among
a collection of texts printed by Martene in his *De Antiquis
Ecclesiae Ritibus* is the following, taken from an old
Sarum manuscript:

"God, Father,
Font and Origin of all goodness,
your mercy caused your only-begotten Son

to descend for us to the depths of the world.
You willed that he take the flesh
which I now hold here in my hands
(*here the priest bows and speaks to the host:*)
I adore you; I glorify you;
with all the intensity of my heart I praise you.
And I pray that your will not leave your servants,
but that you will forgive our sins. . . ."[99]

A bit further on, the text of this prayer continues:
"Before he receives, let him humbly say to the body:
Hail forever, most holy flesh of Christ,
before all else and above all else
the highest sweetness! . . .
Then, with great devotion, let him say to the blood:
Hail forever, heavenly drink,
before all else and above all else
the highest sweetness!"[100]

The intense eucharistic realism of these texts from the
Sarum usage calls to mind the sacramental theology
supported by Paschasius Radbertus and opposed by
Ratramnus. These formulas provide, moreover, some of
the earliest examples of speaking to the sacramental
species. The rubrics explicitly direct the celebrant to
address the "body" and "blood" with words of personal
devotion. The intimate encounter between a solitary individual and the "flesh and blood" of Christ occupy
center stage in these formulas. The Augustinian view,
reiterated by Ratramnus, that "what is placed on the
Lord's table contains not only the sacrament of Christ,
but also the sacrament of the body of the faithful
people" has receded far into the background.

The appearance of private prayers in the communion
rite thus marks another important stage in the evolution
of eucharistic piety. It is to be noted that most of these
prayers were composed for the use of *priests*—another
indication, along with the ritual custom of anointing
discussed above, that a new perception of the priest's

special relation to the eucharist was emerging during this period. Just as, earlier, the eucharist achieved ritual independence from a meal, so now, increasingly, the priest was achieving sacramental and liturgical independence from the rest of the people. The power to consecrate the elements is uniquely his power. The priest alone can touch the flesh of Christ with his own hands. Nor is the priest bound by what others are doing in the liturgy; while the people are singing *Sanctus*, for example, he is free to busy himself with prayers of personal devotion, as the following text and rubric from the Sacramentary of Amiens illustrate: *"While the 'Holy' is slowly being sung, the priest quickly leaves off his singing, and says [this] prayer:* God, you desire not the death of sinners but their repentance; in your great pity, do not reject me, a weak and miserable sinner. . . ."[101]

That such practices were becoming common in the ninth century is attested by conciliar and episcopal admonitions against them. Archbishop Herardus of Tours (ca. 858) had to remind priests of their obligation to sing with the people: "Presbyters should not begin the secret prayer [canon, eucharistic prayer] until the 'Holy' is finished; rather, they should sing the 'Holy' with the people."[102] The appearance of private prayers in the liturgy thus reflected not only a shift of emphasis in eucharistic piety, but also a shift of understanding about the relation of priest and people to the sacramental action.

CONSECRATION OF EUCHARISTIC VESSELS
Another example of the increasingly clericalized view of the eucharist that was developing in the Carolingian epoch comes from texts for blessing sacred vessels and other church furnishings. These texts first appear in sacramentaries of Gallican provenance such as the *Missale Francorum*, and they may originally have been part of the liturgy for consecrating churches.[103] In the *Missale Francorum* the formulas for blessing chalice, paten, and

altar linens follow immediately after the texts and rubrics for consecrating an altar:

"For consecrating a paten: We consecrate and sanctify this paten for confecting (*ad conficiendum*) in it the body of our Lord Jesus Christ, who endured the cross for the salvation of us all, and who reigns forever."[104]

"For consecrating a chalice: Let us pray, beloved brothers, that with the breath of divine grace, the Lord our God will sanctify this chalice consecrated for service, and that he will direct the fulness of his divine grace toward the blessing of humankind."[105]

The *Missale Francorum* also contains a formula for consecrating a "chrismal," i.e., a vessel used for reserving the Blessed Sacrament[106]:

"Almighty God, Trinity, pour forth the richness of your grace into our hands, so that through our blessing this vessel may be sanctified and may, through the grace of the Holy Spirit, become a new sepulchre for the body of Christ."[107]

These same prayers of blessing for paten, chalice and chrismal reappeared in the Romano-Germanic Pontifical of the tenth century (ca. 950), and from here they made their way into the Roman pontificals of the twelfth and thirteenth centuries.[108] The texts manifest the eucharistic preoccupations of the time: the power of consecrating the body and blood of Christ, and the strongly localized sense of presence suggested by referring to the vessel of reservation as "a new sepulchre for the body of Christ."

One is reminded, too, that during this period the liturgy for consecrating churches sometimes included provision for sealing a consecrated host within the crypt or saint's tomb (*confessio*) over which the high altar was built. Reference to such a practice is found as early as the mid-eighth century in *Ordo Romanus* XLII. This Ordo describes the ancient Roman practice of consecrating an altar by means of two ritual acts: 1) depositing the relics of a saint in the *confessio*, and 2) celebrating the eucharist. Included with the relics in OR XLII are three particles of consecrated eucharistic bread: "He [the bishop] deposits three particles of the Lord's body within the crypt tomb (*confessio*); three portions of incense, as well as the relics, are also deposited there."[109] This custom of burying the eucharist along with the relics in the ritual of consecrating an altar was strongly opposed by canonists, but it survived in some places until at least the fourteenth century.[110]

The customs just described are interesting because they reflect the transference of an ancient Christian piety— reverence for the relics of saints, especially martyrs— onto the eucharistic species themselves.[111] Just as it was customary to deposit the relics of martyrs in or under the altar, so it became common to deposit the Lord's body (the consecrated elements) in the same spot. The altar was no longer a table from which the Christian people were fed, but a sepulchre in which the relics of Christ and his saints were carefully enshrined. The altar itself was in process of transformation from table to reliquary. Such ideas were reenforced by a decline in the reception of communion, as well as by the notion that the priest alone controlled what was happening at the altar.

EUCHARIST AND PENANCE
Still another change in eucharistic theology and piety during this period is reflected in the practices surrounding the discipline of penance. In the early seventh century, probably, the Irish system of tariff penance made its way onto the European continent.[112] Unlike the public canonical penance of an earlier era, tariff penance allowed the Christian to confess sins frequently to a priest or monk in private and to receive absolution from him. Confessors were guided in the assignment of penances by a chart of tariffs contained in the *Libri Penitentiales* (penitential books). These documents, which

began appearing as early as the late sixth century, not only listed sins and their corresponding penances but also outlined ways in which a penance, usually fasting, could be commuted. Among such commutations were prayers and Masses.

If, for example, one committed a sin which, according to the tariffs, required one year of fasting as a penance, according to the *Irish Canons* of the sixth century, such a penance could be commuted in the following manner:

"Commutation for a year of fasting: to spend three days in the tomb [cave] of a dead [saint?], without eating, drinking, or sleeping and without taking off one's clothes. During this time the sinner will chant the psalms or recite the hours of the Office, according to the judgment of the priest."[113]

Other commutations besides the macabre one described above were available to penitents:

"Another commutation for a year of fasting: to spend three days in church without eating, drinking or sleeping—completely naked, and without sitting down. During this time the sinner will chant the psalms with the canticles and will recite the Divine Office. During the course of these prayers he will make twelve genuflections, all this after having confessed his sins before the priest and before the people."[114]

Such penances were obviously harsh and humiliating. There gradually developed another system of commutations which, though somewhat costly, lessened the humiliating burden of fasting and public exposure. This alternative system involved having Masses said for the forgiveness of sins and paying a specified sum to the parish priest (or monk priest) who said them. A list of such "Mass stipends," with their penitential equivalences, can be found in the eighth-century Penitential of Bede. There we read: "One hundred and twenty Masses, plus three psalters and three hundred strokes [in a beating], are equivalent to one hundred gold coins."[115] This meant, effectively, that the payment of a hundred gold pieces (in the currency of the day) could satisfy accumulated penances which, according to the system of commutations, amounted to 120 Masses, 3 recitations of the psalter, and 300 strokes in a beating. That such Masses were said for penitents is attested by the liturgical books of the period, which begin to include entire Mass formulas "for the forgiveness of sins." The old Gelasian Sacramentary (eighth century) provides such a formula, as does the Romano-Germanic Pontifical (tenth century). Here, for example, is the opening collect from a Mass *ad reconciliandum paenitentem* in the Gelasian Sacramentary: "Almighty and eternal God, in your mercy forgive the sins of this sinner who has confessed to you. Let not the guilt of his conscience harm him with punishment, but may the liberality of your kindness bring him pardon."[116] The corresponding collect of a Mass in the Romano-Germanic Pontifical reads:

"Lord, you were pleased with the prayers and confessions of the publican; may you also be pleased with your servant N. In your kindness, hear the prayers of your servant so that he may continue to live in repentance. May his constancy in prayer gain him your speedy pardon, so that united once more to your holy altar and sacraments, he may receive anew your heavenly grace."[117]

These prayers seem to presuppose that the penitent is present at the Mass and that readmission to eucharistic communion still constitutes the ultimate sign of reconciliation. The texts likewise indicate that at this stage in the development of tariff penance, a penitential period still separated the initial confession of sins to a confessor from the final acts of absolution and reconciliation. Later, however, the situation changed: absolution followed immediately upon the penitent's confession of sins, and the penance assigned by the priest was done afterwards.[118] Later still, in the thirteenth century, confession came to be regarded as the ordinary prerequisite for receiving holy communion.[119]

COMMUNION OF THE SICK

Prior to the Carolingian reform of the ninth century, the rite of clinical communion for the ill seems to have had little liturgical or canonical regulation, though the practice itself was an ancient one in the church, already alluded to by Justin Martyr about 150 A.D. Nor was the pastoral responsibility of taking communion to the sick limited to the clergy: lay persons sometimes served as ministers and, occasionally, the ill gave themselves communion from the sacrament reserved in their homes or on their persons.[120] Moreover, the liturgical books compiled prior to the eighth century, such as the Verona (Leonine) Sacramentary, provide no formulas for clinical communion. In the eighth century, however, texts related to the pastoral care of the ill began to appear. The old Gelasian Sacramentary, for example, includes two sets of texts: one, a series of prayers for ill persons at home; the other, a collection of Mass prayers *pro infirmum (sic)*.[121] Since the Gelasian gives no rubrics with these prayers, it is not clear whether they were intended for use in a rite of clinical communion. It is, however, a fair inference that the Gelasian Mass *pro infirmum* was celebrated (in a private home, possibly) to provide the ill with communion. Another eighth century text, *Ordo Romanus* XLIX (ca. 700–750), provides a brief ritual for an ill Christian *in extremis*:

"As soon as you see him approach the end, he is to be communicated with the holy sacrifice, even if he has eaten that day; because communion will be for him a deference and an aid unto the resurrection of the just. . .

"After he has received communion, the Lord's passion is to be read in the presence of the ill person, be he presbyter or deacon."[122]

Neither the Gelasian Sacramentary nor *Ordo Romanus* XLIX offers any direct information about the ritual for communicating the ill or dying, nor do they indicate who the ordinary minister of such a rite might have been. Nor, finally, do they tell us whether the sick person was communicated in both species or only in the form of bread.[123] By the ninth century, however, our evidence becomes much more detailed and explicit. Reform-minded liturgists and theologians of the Carolingian period began to insist that the laity be prohibited from giving communion to the sick, and that the ritual be reserved to priests alone. In his diocesan *Capitula* Hincmar of Rheims (ca. 806–882) decreed: "Is it not the priest himself who visits the sick, anoints with holy oil and gives communion himself and not through another? Moreover, does not the priest give communion to the people, not entrusting the communion to some layman to take to his house because someone is sick?"[124]

Besides prohibiting lay persons from administering the eucharist to the sick, ninth-century sources also reveal that a definite rite for clinical communion was emerging. Roger Béraudy remarks that three basic types of communion ritual for the ill developed.

The first involved bringing the ill person directly to church for communion. In the *Capitulary* of Bishop Theodulph of Orleans, discussed earlier in this chapter, this was the custom: "First of all, penance is administered to the ill person. Then, if his condition permits, he is bathed, dressed in white clothing, and brought to the church, where he lies on sackcloth sprinkled with ashes."[125]

There follows, in Theodulph's description, an elaborate ritual. Ashes are imposed on the head and chest of the ill person, and the seven penitential psalms are recited.[126] Following the imposition of ashes and a litany, the sick one is anointed with fifteen signs of the cross.

These anointings are described in great detail; in effect, they cover the entire body of the ailing Christian.[127] After the aniontings have been completed, the Lord's Prayer and the Creed are recited. Communion follows:

"Then the priest gives him [the ill person] the sign of peace, and communicates him saying: 'May the body and blood of the Lord bring you forgiveness of all your sins and preserve you unto everlasting life.' After another prayer, the priest concludes by saying: 'Let us bless the Lord'; and all respond 'Thanks be to God. . . .' For the next seven days the priest visits the sick one and pours forth prayers over him. . . ."[128]

Theodulph's rite thus combines penance, anointing of the sick, and communion—which appears to be administered from the reserved sacrament, since nothing is said about an actual celebration of the eucharist.[129]

The second type of ritual that developed during this era involved celebrating the eucharist in the home of the sick man or woman. The *Vita* of St. Dunstan of Canterbury (ca. 909–988) includes a story in which the holy bishop receives a vision of a woman who lies dying in her home. The woman tells Dunstan: "There is one final thing that (if I may so speak) I command you to do: tomorrow morning at the crack of dawn, make me a sharer in the sacred anointing and in the body of the Lord. For if I am fortified by these mysteries, I shall not be confounded when I speak with my enemies in the gateway."[130]

Dunstan complied with the woman's wish and, early the next day, set out for her house, where he celebrated Mass and gave her "the body and blood of the Lord." So strengthened, the woman died and was buried in the church of St. Mary at Glastonbury. It is probable, as Béraudy suggests, that special Mass formularies were composed for occasions like these.[131]

The third type of ritual (and the one that became most

common in the church's actual practice) involved bringing the eucharist to the home of the sick or dying person. As we have seen, the remote roots of this custom
stretch back at least to the second century (Justin Martyr). Probably because it was more convenient than
bringing the sick person to church or celebrating Mass in
the home, this third form of clinical communion eventually displaced the others. Even in religious communities, this became the preferred method of communicating the ill. The *Regularis Concordia*, a tenth-
century monastic document from England, provides the
following description:

". . . after the Morrow Mass the celebrant, having taken
off the chasuble, and the other ministers of that Mass,
bearing with them the Eucharist, preceded by acolytes
and thurifer, with the whole community shall go to visit
the sick brother, singing the Penitential psalms, followed by the litanies and prayers and, on the first day
only, the anointing with oil: the sick brother shall then
receive Communion. If the sickness improves, the visiting shall be discontinued, but if not, it shall be kept up
until the death of that brother."[132]

One is struck immediately by the similarity between this
description and that provided in the previous century
by the *Capitulary* of Theodulph of Orleans. The major
discrepancies between the two are 1) the omission of
penance in the *Regularis Concordia* (though penitential
psalms and litanies are said), and 2) the place where the
rituals are celebrated (Theodulph: church; *Regularis Concordia*: sickroom). But there is another difference, and it
is an important one. In Theodulph's *Capitulary*, there is
no mention of external signs of reverence that accompany the administration of communion. Indeed, in contrast to the elaborate ritual that surrounds the action of
anointing the sick, the communion rite itself seems quite
brief and unadorned. The *Regularis Concordia*, however,
speaks of a rather solemn procession with the eucharist,
complete with incense and extra ministers. That these

115

cultic signs of reverence are attached to the *eucharist* rather than to the holy oils seems clear because the rite is repeated each day, as long as necessary, even though the anointing is done but once.[133]

Here, it seems to me, we are at the threshold of cultic attention paid to the eucharistic species outside the immediate celebration of Mass.[134] Within a hundred years after the appearance of the *Regularis Concordia*, the signs of such cultic attention will increase dramatically. The *Monastic Constitutions* of Lanfranc, an eleventh-century monastic customary also from England, indicate that on certain occasions the eucharist is solemnly carried in procession, incensed, signaled by a perpetually burning lamp, and "adored" with genuflections.[135] In the following chapter, we shall see that Lafranc himself, who became the archbishop of Canterbury in 1070, was a leading figure in promoting cultic reverence for the eucharist even outside Mass.

SUMMARY
It is sometimes argued that the cult of the eucharist outside Mass was a direct outgrowth of theological debate and conflict over questions of real presence and substantial change. That such controversy played some role in the evolution of an extra-liturgical cult is unquestionably true. The triumph of Paschasius Radbertus's eucharistic realism, for example, may well have contributed to the popular view that the "natural historical body of Christ" is somehow physically localized in the sacramental species of bread and wine. Historically, however, the debate between Paschasius Radbertus and Ratramnus did not reach full maturity until long after the two antagonists were dead. Not until the middle of the eleventh century, with the controversy surrounding the theology of Berengarius of Tours, did the church's highest leadership officially intervene to declare in favor of Radbertus's brand of eucharistic realism.[136]

Despite the importance of such theological controversy,

116

however, it seems that the sources of the cult of the eucharist outside Mass are more readily discovered in the evolution of the liturgy itself. The first two chapters of this book examined that evolution as it unfolded in the earlier centuries of the Christian era. There, we noticed the emergence of two patterns: 1) the movement from holy meal to sacred food (Chapter One), and 2) the movement from communal symbol to ritual drama (Chapter Two). The first of these movements resulted in the ritual disengagement of the eucharist from its originating source in a community meal that seals a new covenant in the blood of Christ. The second movement resulted in an increasingly allegorized interpretation of ritual acts and communal symbols in the eucharist.

In this chapter we have seen a third pattern unfold: the priest's relation to the eucharist becoming estranged from that of the people. This estrangement is evident in several important shifts affecting liturgical piety and practice during the Carolingian epoch. A quick review of them will bring this chapter to a close.

1) During this period several changes in the manner of giving communion to the people emerge: the cup begins to be withdrawn from the laity, communion is sometimes delayed until after Mass, the eucharist is placed in the mouth rather than in the hand of the lay communicant. At the same time, the hieratic character of sacerdotal specialists is enhanced through the rite of anointing hands at ordination.

2) Catechesis of the people remains a high priority, but the language of the liturgy itself has become foreign to all but the most cultivated persons (clerics, monks, the merchant classes and the nobility). The rise of vernacular languages and literature, already evident by the ninth century, produced emphatic dissonance between the popular speech of ordinary social life and the hieratic speech of worship.

3) Private prayers of devotion, formulas for consecrating

liturgical vessels, and Masses connected with commutations of tariff penance also appear during this period. Solitary celebrations of the eucharist by individual priests, though often opposed by bishops and councils, become increasingly common.

4) Finally, the first signs of cultic attention to the eucharistic species outside Mass appear. These signs first emerge in specific circumstances such as communion of the sick.

In my opinion, the most important of all these factors is the linguistic one. Language, Martin Heidegger argued, is the "house" of being, the place where being dwells.[137] In an essay on "Hölderlin and the Essence of Poetry," Heidegger wrote: "Language is not a tool at his [man's] disposal, rather it is that event which disposes of the supreme possibility of human existence."[138] The primordial purpose of language, long recognized by poets, is thus to give being a home or, as Robert Funk has put it, "Being calls to man, and in responding he, in turn, calls being out of chaos, so to speak, by giving it a place to dwell in language."[139]

A revolution in language is thus a revolution in metaphysics, in the way human beings perceive, experience, and construct "what is."[140] This kind of metaphysical upheaval was already well underway during the Carolingian epoch. The appearance of vernacular language and literature was a decisively revolutionary phenomenon. Linguistically, the Latin liturgy was becoming identified with those social classes who could afford to cultivate an archaic language: landowners and merchants, nobles and royalty, monks and clerics.

The vernacular revolution in language was thus also a sociological fact of profound importance. Access to language provides access not only to being (Heidegger) but to power as well.[141] And the reverse is likewise true: loss of language implies loss of being, loss of power. The growing inaccessibility of Latin to ordinary lay worshipers during this period corresponded, in effect, to a loss of political and religious power.[142] Increasingly, liturgy—as well as the larger arena of political life—fell under the control of those who possessed the language (Latin) in which official affairs were conducted. In short, the linguistic revolution helped promote the political and liturgical disenfranchisement of lay persons in the church. As Amos Wilder has remarked, "The language of a people is its fate."[143]

Given this situation, it is not surprising that people began seeking an alternative language in which to express religious and political convictions. As we shall see in the next chapter, this alternative language frequently took the form of devotional speech and gesture: eating and drinking the eucharist gave way to ocular communion with the sacred host; direct participation in the prayer and song of worship was replaced by gazing at the consecrated elements.

NOTES

1. See Amalarius of Metz, *Codex Expositionis II, XIV*, in J.M. Hanssens, ed., *Amalarii Episcopi Opera Liturgica Omnia* (Studi e Testi 138-140, 3 vols., Città del Vaticano: Biblioteca Apostolica Vaticana, 1948), I, pp. 274-275.

2. Text cited in Blandine-Dominique Berger, *Le Drame liturgique de Paques* (Théologie historique, no. 37; Paris: Beauchesne, 1976), p. 90.

3. Text cited in Berger, *Le Drame*, p. 91.

4. See ibid., p. 91.

5. See John Dominic Crossan, *The Dark Interval* (Niles, Ill.: Argus Communications, 1975), p. 37.

6. See Berger, *Le Drame*, p. 91.

7. Text in PL 101, cols. 1383-1416.

8. PL 101, col. 1383.

9. The system of Irish tariff penance, with its emphasis on

private confessions to a minister, seems to have been imported onto the European continent by the early seventh century. For further discussion see Nathan Mitchell, "The Many Ways to Reconciliation: An Historical Synopsis of Christian Penance," in *The Rite of Penance: Commentaries*, Vol. III: Background and Directions (Washington, D.C.: The Liturgical Conference, 1978), pp. 20-37.

10. PL 101, col. 1404.

11. Text of the *Regula Solitariorum* may be found in PL 103, cols. 575-664.

12. PL 103, col. 625.

13. PL 103, col. 642.

14. PL 103, cols. 642-643.

15. The critical edition of the text of Paschasius Radbertus's treatise may be found in: Beda Paulus, ed., Paschasius Radbertus: *De Corpore et Sanguine Domini* (Corpus Christianorum, continuatio mediaevalis 16; Turnholt: Brepols, 1969).

16. Paschasius Radbertus, *De Corpore*, IV; ed. Paulus, p. 28.

17. Paschasius Radbertus, *De Corpore*, XIV, ed. Paulus, p. 86.

18. Ibid., VII, ed. Paulus, p. 38.

19. Ibid., IV, ed. Paulus, pp. 28-30.

20. For a modern discussion of the "heuristic" or "triggering" effect of symbols see Paul Ricoeur, *The Symbolism of Evil*, translated by Emerson Buchanan (Boston: Beacon Press, 1967; paperback edition, 1969), pp. 14-18.

21. In the eleventh century, Berengarius of Tours was required to confess that when the faithful chew the eucharist bread they truly "crush" the bones and "tear" the flesh of the Lord. See DS 690.

22. See Paschasius Radbertus, *De Corpore*, ed. Paulus, pp. 88-89.

23. Ibid., XIV, ed. Paulus, p. 88.

24. Ibid., XIV, ed. Paulus, pp. 88-89.

25. See ibid., IV; XII, ed. Paulus, pp. 27-31; 76-83.

26. On the difference in emphasis between Augustine's sacramentalism and Ambrose's realism, see Paul Palmer, *Sacraments and Worship* (London: Darton, Longman & Todd, 1954, paperback edition) pp. 201-213.

27. See Paschasius Radbertus, *De Corpore*, ed. Paulus, I-IV, pp. 13-31.

28. Ratramnus's work was also entitled *De Corpore et Sanguine Domini*; it may be found in PL 121, cols. 125-170.

29. Ratramnus, *De Corpore*, 69; PL 121, col. 154-155; translation in Palmer, *Sacraments and Worship*, p. 225.

30. Ibid., 9; PL 121, cols. 130-131; translation in Palmer, *Sacraments and Worship*, p. 224.

31. Ratramnus defined sacraments as follows: "We call them sacraments because under the cover of material things, the divine power grants salvation (in a hidden manner) to those who receive them faithfully." PL 121, col. 147.

32. Ratramnus, *De Corpore*, 9; PL 121, col. 131; translation in Palmer, *Sacraments and Worship*, pp. 224-225.

33. Ibid., 69; PL 121, cols. 155-156; translation in Palmer, *Sacraments and Worship*, p. 226.

34. Ibid., 96; PL 121, cols. 168-169.

35. Ibid., 101; PL 121, col. 170.

36. Ibid., 49; PL 121, col. 147.

37. Ibid., 57; PL 121, col. 150-151.

38. On the important shift in terminology, from *corpus Christi* (as *church*) to *corpus Christi mysticum* (as church), see Henri de Lubac, *Corpus Mysticum; l'Eucharistic et l'Eglise au Moyen age; Etude historique* (2nd ed. rev. and aug.; Paris: Aubier, 1949), pp. 89-135.

39. See Bishops' Committee on the Liturgy, *The Body of Christ* (Washington, D.C.: NCCB, 1977), pp. 10-13, for examples.

40. See W.H. Freestone, *The Sacrament Reserved* (Alcuin Club Collections, XXI; London: A.R. Mowbray and Co., 1917), p. 137, n. 1.

41. Text in Michel Andrieu, ed., *Les Ordines Romani du haut*

moyen age (5 vols.; Spicilegium Sacrum Lovaniense 11, 23, 24, 28, 29; Louvain: 1931–1961), Vol. II, p. 361.

42. Cited in Bishops' Committee, *The Body of Christ*, p. 14.

43. Cited in Adolf Franz, *Die Messe im deutschen Mittelalter* (Freiburg im Breisgau/St. Louis: Herder, 1902), pp. 96-97.

44. Leo Cunibert Mohlberg, ed., *Missale Francorum* (Rerum Ecclesiasticarum Documenta; Series Major; Fontes II; Rome: Herder, 1957), nn. 33, 34; p. 10.

45. *Missale Francorum*, n. 33; ed. Mohlberg, p. 10.

46. *Missale Francorum*, n. 34; ed. Mohlberg, p. 10.

47. The first formula ("May these hands be consecrated") is also found in the manuscript Vat. Reg. 316, the "ancient" Gelasian Sacramentary. See Leo Cunibert Mohlberg, ed., *Liber Sacramentorum Romanae Aeclesiae Ordinis Circuli* (Rerum Ecclesiasticarum Documenta; Series Major; Fontes IV; Rome: Herder, 1960), n. 756; p. 119.

48. See Bruno Kleinheyer, *Die Priesterweihe im Römischen Ritus* (Trierer Theologische Studien, Bd. 12; Trier: Paulinus-Verlag, 1962), pp. 114-122.

49. Text in J.S. Assemani, *Codex Liturgicus* (Rome: 1719–1728), T. 8, p. 128.

50. See the discussion in Kleinheyer, *Die Preisterweihe*, pp. 119-120.

51. Amalarius of Metz, *Liber officialis*, in J.M. Hanssens, *Amalarii Episcopi Opera Liturgica Omnia* (3 vols.; Studi e Testi 138-140; Città del Vaticano: Biblioteca Apostolica Vaticana, 1948), II, p. 227.

52. The earliest evidence for the custom of hand-anointing at Rome appears to come from *Ordo Romanus XXXV* (ca. 925).

53. See Kleinheyer, *Die Priesterweihe*, p. 122.

54. For details about Angilbert and his work, see Angelus Häussling, *Mönchskonvent und Eucharistiefeier* (LFQ 58; Münster: Aschendorffsche, 1973), pp. 52-58.

55. Angilbert, *Institutio de diuersitate officiorum*, VIII; in Kassius Hallinger, ed., *Corpus Consuetudinum Monasticarum*, I: *Initia*

Consuetudinis Benedictinae (Siegburg: F. Schmitt, 1963), pp. 295-296.

56. See A.-G. Martimort *et al.*, *The Church at Prayer: The Eucharist*, trans. by Austin Flannery *et al.* (New York: Herder and Herder, 1973), pp. 206-207.

57. Text translated in Ronald C.D. Jasper and Geoffrey J. Cuming, eds., *Prayers of the Eucharist, Early and Reformed* (London: Collins, 1975), pp. 114-115.

58. By "intinction" here is meant the dipping of the consecrated bread into consecrated wine. Another form of intinction—sometimes called "nonsacramental"—involved steeping the eucharistic bread in an unconsecrated liquid in order to make its consumption easier. See Freestone, *The Sacrament Reserved*, pp. 144-145.

59. Text in Mansi XI: col. 155.

60. For examples of the arguments for and against intinction in the tenth to the twelfth centuries, see Freestone, *The Sacrament Reserved*, pp. 154-165.

61. Text in PL 132: col. 205.

62. On concomitance, see Freestone, *The Sacrament Reserved*, pp. 152-165. A more detailed discussion of this theory will be found in Chapter Four of this book.

63. See Adrian Nocent, *The Liturgical Year*, translated by Matthew J. O'Connell (4 vols.; Collegeville, Minn.: The Liturgical Press, 1977), Vol. 3, p. 72.

64. *Ordo Romanus* XXIII.22; ed. Andrieu, III, p. 272.

65. Nocent, *The Liturgical Year*, Vol. 3, p. 73.

66. Ibid.

67. Cyrille Vogel, ed., *Le Pontificale romano-germanique du dixième siècle* (Studi e Testi 226-227; 2 vols.; Città del Vaticano: Biblioteca Apostolica Vaticana, 1963), II, pp. 92-93.

68. See Michel Andrieu, *Le pontificale romain au Moyen-Age*, (4 vols.; Studi e Testi 86-88, 99; Città del Vaticano: Biblioteca. Apostolica Vaticana, 1938-1941), II, pp. 469, 541-578.

69. This catechism is printed among the spurious works some-

times attributed to Alcuin of York in PL 101: cols. 1099-1144.

70. An example may be found in Jonas of Orleans, *De Institutione Laicali*, PL 106: cols. 121-278.

71. Jonas of Orleans, *De Institutione Laicali*, II.18; PL 106: col. 202.

72. Ibid.

73. Ibid., PL 106: col. 203.

74. Ibid., PL 106: col. 204.

75. Text in PL 101: cols. 1099-1144.

76. *Disputatio Puerorum*; PL 101: col. 1134.

77. Ibid.; PL 101: cols. 1135-1136.

78. See E.C. Ratcliff, ed., *Expositio Antiquae Liturgiae Gallicanae* (Henry Bradshaw Society, Vol. 98; London: HBS, 1971), pp. 13-15.

79. J.A. Jungmann, *The Mass of the Roman Rite: Its Origin and Development (Missarum Solemnia)*, tr. by F.A. Brunner (2 vols; New York: Benziger, 1955) I, pp. 477-478 (in the 5th German ed. of 1962, I, pp. 606-614).

80. *Disputatio Puerorum*, PL 101: col. 1136.

81. The pastoral instructions of Bishop Jonas of Orleans, discussed above, also avoid questions about presence and change in the eucharist.

82. See Edouard Boudurand, *L'Education carolingienne; le Manuel de Dhouda* (Paris: Picard, 1887).

83. PL 106: cols. 112-113.

84. PL 101: col. 1412. See also André Wilmart, ed., *Libelli Precum Quattuor Aevi Karolini* (Rome: Ephemerides Liturgicae, 1940), pp. 14, 37, 55, for further examples of devotions in honor of the holy cross.

85. On devotion to the altar during this period of history, see Louis Gougaud, *Devotional and Ascetic Practices in the Middle Ages*, translated by C.C. Bateman (London: Burns, Oates and Washbourne, 1927), pp. 51-65.

86. PL 106: col. 116.

87. See the discussion of the ancient Christian rites for the dead in Richard Rutherford, *The Death of a Christian: The Rite of Funerals* (New York: Pueblo Publishing Company, 1980), pp. 3-36.

88. See Renata Wolff, "Patterns of Medieval Monastic Reforms," *The American Benedictine Review* 18 (1967), 375-384.

89. See Geoffrey Rowell, *The Liturgy of Christian Burial* (Alcuin Club Collections, 59; London: SPCK, 1977), pp. 68-73.

90. Mansi, XIII: col. 998-999.

91. MGH, *Leges*, I, pp. 53f.

92. On the rise of private Masses, see Theodore Klauser, *A Short History of the Western Liturgy*, translated by John Halliburton (2nd ed.: New York: Oxford University Press, 1979), pp. 96-97, 101-108.

93. Mansi, XIII: col. 996.

94. See texts and commentary in Victor Leroquais, "L'Ordo Missae du sacramentaire d'Amiens," *Ephemerides Liturgicae* 41 (1927), 435-445.

95. Text in Leroquais, "L'Ordo Missae," p. 444.

96. Ibid.

97. Jungmann, *The Mass of the Roman Rite*, II, p. 346 (5th German ed., II, p. 429).

98. See ibid. See also André Wilmart, "Prières pour la Communion," *Ephemerides Liturgicae* 43 (1929), 320-328.

99. Edmond Martène, *De antiquis ecclesiae ritibus libri tres* (4 vols.; Antwerp: John Baptist Novelli, 1763–1764), Book I, Chapter 4, n. XXIV, p. 241.

100. Ibid.

101. Leroquais, "L'Ordo Missae," p. 442.

102. See text in Thomas F. Simmons, ed., *The Lay Folks Mass Book* (Early English Text Society, 71; London: N. Truebner and Co., 1899), p. xxiv.

103. See Adolf Franz, *Die kirchlichen Benediktionen im Mittelalter* (2 vols.; Freiburg im Breisgau: Herdersche, 1909), I, p. 57.

125

104. *Missale Francorum*, 62; ed. Mohlberg, p. 18.

105. *Missale Francorum*, 64; ed. Mohlberg, p. 19.

106. *Missale Francorum*, 68; ed. Mohlberg, p. 19. For the "chrismal" as a vessel for eucharistic reservation, especially in the Celtic churches, see Freestone, *The Sacrament Reserved*, pp. 205-207.

107. *Missale Francorum*, 68; ed. Mohlberg, p. 19.

108. See Vogel, *Le Pontificale romano-germanique*, I, nn. 87, 88, 92; pp. 155-156.

109. *Ordo Romanus* XLII, 11; ed. Andrieu, IV, p. 400.

110. See E. Bertaud, "Devotion eucharistique," *Dictionnaire de Spiritualité*, IV/2, col. 1624.

111. On the cult of relics in early Christianity, see H. Leclercq, "Reliques et Reliquaires," DACL XIV/2, cols. 2294-2359.

112. See N. Mitchell, "The Many Ways to Reconciliation: An Historical Synopsis of Christian Penance," in *The Rite of Penance: Commentaries,* Volume III: Background and Directions (Washington, D.C.: The Liturgical Conference, 1978), pp. 32-35.

113. Text in Cyrille Vogel, *Le Pécheur et la pénitence au Moyen âge* (Chretiens de tous les temps, 30; Paris: Cerf, 1969), p. 124.

114. Ibid., p. 124.

115. Ibid., p. 127.

116. *Gelasian Sacramentary* (Vat. Reg. 316), 360; ed. Mohlberg (see note 47), p. 57.

117. *Romano-Germanic Pontifical*, ed. Vogel, II, p. 278.

118. Vogel, *Le Pécheur*, p. 31.

119. See J. Leclercq, F. Vandenbroucke, and L. Bouyer, *A History of Christian Spirituality*, Vol. II; translated by the Benedictines of Holme Eden Abbey (London: Burns and Oates, 1968), pp. 246-247.

120. See Roger Béraudy, "Eucharistic Worship Outside the Mass," in A.-G. Martimort, *The Church at Prayer: The Eucharist,* translated by Austin Flannery *et al.* (New York: Herder and

Herder, 1973), pp. 198-199.

121. *Gelasian Sacramentary* (Vat. Reg. 316), 1535-1542; ed. Mohlberg, pp. 221-222.

122. *Ordo Romanus* XLIX; ed. Andrieu, IV, p. 529.

123. In some places communion for the sick in both kinds continued until at least the twelfth century. See Béraudy, "Eucharistic Worship," pp. 200-201.

124. Text cited from Béraudy, "Eucharistic Worship," p. 200.

125. Theodulph, *Capitulare*; PL 105: col. 220.

126. *Gelasian Sacramentary* (Vat. Reg. 316), 78-83; ed. Mohlberg, pp. 17-18.

127. Theodulph, *Capitulare*; PL 105: col. 221.

128. Ibid.; PL 105: col. 222.

129. The *Romano-Germanic Pontifical* has a rite for the ill that resembles that of Theodulph; see ed. Vogel, II, pp. 258-269.

130. PL 137: col. 427.

131. Béraudy, "Eucharistic Worship," p. 201.

132. Thomas Symons, ed., trans., *Regularis Concordia* (New York: Oxford University Press, 1953), p. 64.

133. See *Regularis Concordia*, ed. Symons, p. 64, note.

134. It is true, of course, that the connection between community eucharist and clinical communion was still strong in the *Regularis Concordia*: the rite of communicating the ill follows immediately after the early morning Mass and is presided over by the celebrant of that Mass.

135. David Knowles, ed., *The Monastic Constitutions of Lanfranc* (New York: Oxford University Press, 1951), pp. 31, 41.

136. It was in the eleventh century that Ratramnus's work was condemned as heterodox; see Palmer, *Sacraments and Worship*, pp. 221-231.

137. See Martin Heidegger, *Poetry, Language, Thought*, translated by Albert Hofstadter (New York: Harper Colophon Books, 1971), pp. 213-229. See also Robert W. Funk, *Language, Hermeneutic, and Word of God* (New York: Harper and

Row, 1966), pp. 37-46.

138. See Martin Heidegger, *Existence and Being*, translated by Douglas Scott (Chicago: Henry Regnery Co., 1949), p. 276.

139. See Funk, *Language*, p. 39.

140. See Donald Hall, *Remembering Poets* (New York: Harper Colophon Books, 1978), pp. 195-199.

141. It is well known that in archaic cultures, knowledge of a person's name gives one power over that person. Similarly, the ability to name things gives one control over them. Cf. the power of "naming the animals" given to "Adam" in Genesis 2.20.

142. See Jeffrey Burton Russell, *A History of Medieval Christianity; Prophecy and Order* (New York: Crowell, 1968), pp. 82-98.

143. Cited in Funk, *Language*, p. 19.

Debate and Desire

INTRODUCTION

Throughout the Carolingian epoch, as we have seen in the previous chapter, the norm of eucharistic practice remained active participation in the liturgy consummated by eating and drinking the sacramental species. Although the frequency of communion seems to have declined, and although the people's access to the eucharist was gradually restricted (through withdrawal of the cup, for instance), the catechetical materials of that period indicate that Christians were encouraged to communicate devoutly and frequently. "There is no better prayer" than the eucharist, the pious Dhouda wrote to her son William. "The soul deprived of spiritual food dies just as the body does if deprived of food and drink," Bishop Jonas of Orleans warned Christians who communicated infrequently.

In the tenth and eleventh centuries, however, attitudes toward the eucharist underwent an emphatic change, and this change resulted, as we shall see, in the rise of eucharistic cult and devotions that were unknown in earlier centuries. The nature of this change can perhaps best be gauged through an inspection of two monastic documents mentioned at the end of Chapter Three: the *Regularis Concordia* (tenth century) and the *Monastic Constitutions* of Lanfranc (eleventh century). On Palm Sunday, according to the *Regularis Concordia*, a procession with palms is held with the entire community—monks and schoolchildren—taking part. The document's description of this procession would not surprise contemporary Christians: familiar hymns, such as "All Glory, Laud and Honor," are sung and the palms are blessed, carried into church, and held during the singing of the Passion:

". . . the procession shall go forth. As soon as the
Mother church is reached the procession shall wait
while the children, who have gone on before, sing *Gloria
laus* with its verses, to which all shall answer *Gloria laus*,
as the custom is. . . . When all have entered and the
response is finished they shall do as has been said before, holding their palms in their hands until the Offertory has been sung. . . ."[1]

These Palm Sunday ceremonies are well known, as are
their origins in the church at Jerusalem, where popular
"shrine liturgies" had developed at the holy places of
Jesus' life by at least the late fourth century.[2] But by the
time we reach Lanfranc's *Monastic Constitutions* in the
late eleventh century, some significant alterations in the
Palm Sunday liturgy have appeared. For one thing, Lanfranc's liturgy is far more elaborate. In addition to the
priest and deacon, the ministers of the procession include candle-bearers, servants with banners, a lay
brother carrying a bucket of holy water, two thurifers,
and subdeacons carrying two gospel books. Just when
the procession is ready to begin,

". . . two priests shall come forward, vested in albs, to
carry the shrine, which shall have been brought thither
by these same priests a little before daybreak; in it the
Body of Christ shall have been laid. Those who carry the
banners and cross and the rest . . . shall go straight to
this shrine. . . those who bear the shrine shall pass
down between the ranks of the *statio*, preceded by those
who carry the banners and by the other servers . . . all
keeping the same order in returning that they had in
going. As they pass all shall genuflect. . . . When they
come to the gates of the city they shall halt, forming two
ranks with such space between as the place may
provide; the shrine shall be set upon a table covered
with a cloth before the gates in such manner that the
bearers standing on either side shall face the shrine in
their midst. There shall be fair hangings and curtains
prepared above the gateway."[3]

130

Once the crowd has reached the doors of the church, the shrine containing the Blessed Sacrament is "set down upon a table covered with a cloth."[4]

Quite obviously, Lanfranc has transformed the Palm Sunday procession into a solemn procession of the Blessed Sacrament, complete with candles, incense, and genuflections. The procession is even punctuated by stations along the way, at the gates of the city and again at the doors of the church, where the shrine is finally deposited. Nothing of this sort appears in tenth-century sources that describe the Palm Sunday liturgy. The Romano-Germanic Pontifical (RGP) (ca. 950), for example, describes a blessing and procession with palms that is similar to the one found in *Regularis Concordia*.[5] In the RGP, the processional cross (with its relics) is the center of attention; the rubrics direct that it be venerated by clergy and people during the course of the procession through the city.[6] There is no mention of using the Blessed Sacrament in the procession, although RGP does include a second order of service for Palm Sunday that involves a portable shrine in which the gospels are solemnly carried.[7] This shrine (*portatorium*) is placed in front of the altar before the liturgy begins. As the procession gets underway, deacons, accompanied by candle-bearers, thurifers, and banner-bearers, lift the shrine containing the gospels and carry it through the streets.[8] The people sing the familiar hymns, including "All Glory, Laud and Honor," while flowers and branches are strewn in the path of those carrying the gospels.[9]

It appears, then, that in Lanfranc's ceremonial for Palm Sunday, the earlier objects of popular veneration— cross, relics or gospels—have been replaced by the eucharistic species. The liturgical gestures of reverence (lights, incense) accorded to the earlier cult objects in the procession have been transferred to the reserved sacrament. When did this ritual transference take place? It is difficult to assign a precise date, but there is evidence for such transference before the end of the tenth century. Once again, a contrast between two documents will illustrate the point.

In *Regularis Concordia*, there appears some of our earliest evidence for the liturgical dramas that became so popular in the middle ages. Somewhat predictably, the drama appears during the liturgy for Holy Week. On Good Friday, after the main parts of the liturgy have been completed, *Regularis Concordia* describes a ritual for entombing the cross in a special sepulchre that has been constructed on the altar:

"On that part of the altar where there is space for it there shall be a representation as it were of a sepulchre, hung about with a curtain, in which the holy Cross, when it has been venerated, shall be placed in the following manner: the deacons who carried the Cross before shall come forward and, having wrapped the Cross in a napkin . . . they shall bear it thence . . . to the place of the sepulchre. When they have laid the cross therein, in imitation as it were of the burial of the Body of our Lord Jesus Christ, they shall sing the antiphon *Sepulto Domino*. . . . In that same place the holy Cross shall be guarded with all reverence until the night of the Lord's Resurrection."[10]

The alert reader will easily guess what happens in *Regularis Concordia* early on Easter Sunday morning. The Mass of the Paschal Vigil is celebrated on Saturday afternoon (after the office of None); then, at Matins, before sunrise on Easter Sunday, the following ritual occurs:

"While the third lesson [of Matins] is being read, four of the brethren shall vest, one of whom, wearing an alb as though for some different purpose, shall enter and go stealthily to the place of the sepulchre, and sit there quietly, holding a palm in his hand. Then, while the third response is being sung, the other three brethren, vested in copes and holding thuribles in their hands,

shall enter in their turn and go to the place of the sepulchre, step by step, as though searching for something."[11]

The author then explains that all this is done in imitation
of the women who brought spices and perfumes to
anoint Jesus' body. The ritual continues with the famous
dialogue between "the angel" and "the women":
"Whom do you seek?" "Jesus of Nazareth." "He is not
here; he is risen!"[12] The women are then invited to inspect the sepulchre more closely; they discover

"the place void of the Cross and with only the linen in
which the Cross had been wrapped. Seeing this the
three shall lay down their thuribles in that same sepulchre and, taking the linen, shall hold it up before the
clergy; and, as though showing that the Lord was risen
and was no longer wrapped in it, they shall sing this
antiphon: *Surrexit Dominus de sepulchro*."[13]

The short drama ended, the prior of the monastery intones *Te Deum*, while all the church bells peal; the hour
of Lauds follows immediately.

Unlike the allegorical and dramatic interpretations of
ritual discussed in Chapter Two, *Regularis Concordia* actually incorporates dramatic action and dialogue into the
liturgy of Good Friday and Easter Sunday morning.
During the tenth and eleventh centuries such liturgical
"mystery plays" became widespread in Europe.[14] In
their earliest form, the plays seem to have revolved
around the *cross* as the cultic object venerated on Palm
Sunday, hidden in the tomb on Good Friday and vanished from it on Easter morning. But before the end of
the tenth century, there is evidence that the Good Friday *depositio* and the Easter Sunday *visitatio* (or *elevatio*)
are beginning to center on the Blessed Sacrament as the
cultic object "buried" and then "resurrected."

In the *Life of Saint Ulrich*, a hagiographical work roughly
contemporaneous with *Regularis Concordia*, the eucharist

that remains after the liturgy of the presanctified on Good Friday is symbolically "buried." Ulrich's biographer alludes to this custom in the following passage:

"On Good Friday, having carefully completed the canonical hours . . . as on Holy Thursday . . . [Ulrich] hastened to recite the psalter early in the morning. After celebrating the holy mysteries of God [the Good Friday liturgy of the presanctified] and nourishing his people with the sacred body of Christ, he placed what remained [of the eucharist] in a sepulchre, according to custom. . . . "[15]

The biography continues with a description of the Paschal Vigil and its baptisms. Then Ulrich's activities on Easter Sunday are depicted:

"After Prime on the holy and long-awaited day of Easter, he [Ulrich] entered the church of St. Ambrose where, on Good Friday, Christ's body had been placed in the 'tomb.' There, assisted by a few clerics, he celebrated a Mass of the Holy Trinity. After having finished this Mass, he put on solemn vestments; meanwhile, the clergy had gathered at the portico of this same church [St. Ambrose]. Taking with him the body of Christ and the gospels, and accompanied by candles, incense, and the voices of children singing appropriate acclamations, he made his way to the church of John the Baptist, where he sang Terce. . . ."[16]

Although Ulrich's biography does not explicitly describe a ritual for "burying" (*depositio*) and "raising" (*elevatio*) the host, the custom itself is clearly implied. The cross of *Regularis Concordia's* Good Friday/Easter drama has become a consecrated host in Ulrich's biography. But in contrast to the *Regularis*, the *Life of Ulrich* makes no mention of dramatic role-playing, action or dialogue. Unlike the monks who assume the roles of the angel and the three spice-bearing women, Ulrich is not pictured as assuming any role beyond that of his liturgical ministry as bishop. To sum up the comparison:

Regularis Concordia:
"burying" of the *cross*; "visit to the tomb."
Dramatic roles, action, dialogue.

Life of Ulrich:
"burying" of the host; "visit to the tomb."
No reference to dramatic roles, action, dialogue.

A century later, in the *Monastic Constitutions* of Lafranc, the customs of *depositio* and *visitatio/elevatio* for Good Friday and Easter are missing altogether.[17] But there is plenty of evidence that other monasteries and cathedral churches kept the custom alive and even expanded its dramatic elements.[18] A thirteenth-century liturgical directory for the church at Soissons, provides an elaborate ceremony for the visit to the tomb at the end of Matins on Easter morning. The liturgical ministers are assigned dramatic roles—two angels, three women—and attention is paid to such things as costuming and sound effects (precise regulations are given for ringing the church's bells at various points in the drama).[19] In the Soissons directory the host is the central object of attention at the visit to the tomb drama, although on Good Friday it is the *gospel book* which is entombed in the sepulchre.[20] After the dialogue between the angels and the women, the host is solemnly borne in procession to the main altar of the church. Candles, crosses, thuribles, banners, and the pealing of bells accompany the procession, while two priests (one on either side of the minister carrying the sacrament) constantly incense the host.[21]

Ceremonies like this one at Soissons continued to be popular all over Europe throughout the middle ages. Even on the eve of the Reformation in the sixteenth century, early printed missals and breviaries continued to include the "visit to the tomb."[22] The cultic objects used in these rites (cross, gospel book, host) varied from place to place; sometimes a combination of them appeared, as in the Soissons ritual described above.

135

My purpose in providing these examples from the tenth to the thirteenth centuries is twofold. First, they bear witness to an increasingly popular attitude toward the eucharistic elements: in these rites of "burial" and "visitation," the sacrament is viewed not as something to be eaten and drunk in the context of Mass or communion of the sick, but as a cultic object to be reverenced for its own sake in situations *outside* Mass. Secondly, this movement toward adoration of the elements as cultic objects first appears within the historical evolution of the liturgy itself. It was not cultic devotion that gave rise to liturgical development, but liturgical development that gave rise to cultic devotion. The gestures of eucharistic adoration and reverence first appear in direct connection with liturgical rites: the "burial" of the host at the end of the Good Friday liturgy; the "visit to the tomb" at the end of Matins on Easter Sunday; the procession with the Blessed Sacrament in the Palm Sunday ceremonies described in Lanfranc's *Constitutions*. To put the matter baldly, eucharistic devotions such as processions, adoration, and exposition first emerge *within the liturgy itself*.

Having said that, however, it must be added that other factors also played a role in the development of the cult of the eucharist outside Mass. One of these factors was certainly theological. During the eleventh and twelfth centuries a number of important debates about the nature of sacramental signs, the moment of consecration, and the theory of concomitance influenced liturgical and extra-liturgical attitudes toward the eucharist. These debates will be discussed in the pages that follow. And in the second half of the chapter, the development of popular eucharistic customs such as reservation, processions, exposition, and Benediction will be traced.

I. THE EUCHARISTIC CONTROVERSIES OF THE ELEVENTH AND TWELFTH CENTURIES

Can Symbols be "Real"?

Berengarius of Tours
At a synod held at Rome in 1059, during the pontificate of Nicholas II, the theologian and teacher Berengarius of Tours was forced to make the following confession of faith:

"I, Berengarius, . . . acknowledging the true and apostolic faith, anathematize every heresy, especially that one for which heretofore I have been infamous: which [heresy] attempted to prove that the bread and wine which are placed on the altar remain merely a sacrament after consecration—and not the true body and blood of our Lord Jesus Christ; and further, that [the body and blood] are touched and broken by the hands of the priests and crushed by the teeth of the faithful in a sacramental manner only—and not physically (*sensualiter*). I assent to the Holy Roman Church and the Apostolic See, and I confess with mouth and heart that . . . the bread and wine which are placed on the altar are not merely a sacrament after consecration, but are rather the true body and blood of our Lord Jesus Christ—and that these are truly, physically and not merely sacramentally, touched and broken by the hands of the priests and crushed by the teeth of the faithful."[23]

The text of this confession is reasonably clear: it suggests that Berengarius had been teaching that the Lord's presence in the eucharist is sacramental, not physical in a manner perceptible by the human senses (*sensualiter*). This position is described by the confession as heresy, and Berengarius is depicted as assenting to the view of "the Holy Roman Church and the Apostolic See," viz., that Christ's eucharistic presence is not merely sacramental but actual and physical in such a way that the body and blood are broken by the hands of the priest and crushed by the teeth of the faithful.

The intense eucharistic realism of Berengarius's confession is shocking. It sounds very much like the butcher-shop theology that Augustine opposed so vehemently in the late fourth and early fifth centuries. Even if one allows for a bit of polemic hyperbole, the insistence on crushing and breaking the Lord's body seems altogether too violent even for a staunch eucharistic realist. What was Berengarius teaching that prompted so intense a reaction?

To answer this question, we need to recall the ninth-century debate between Paschasius Radbertus and Ratramnus, discussed in Chapter Three. Paschasius championed the realist position in eucharistic theology and, though he tried to soften their impact, his stories of bleeding hosts and miraculous appearances of Christ's body in the bread indicate a preference for physical interpretations. On the other hand, Ratramnus, following the lead of Augustine, proposed a more specifically *sacramental* interpretation of Christ's eucharistic presence. Both men affirmed that the Lord is truly present when the sacrament is celebrated, but Paschasius tended to locate Christ's historical body *physically* in the bread and wine, while Ratramnus preferred to speak of the presence as spiritual and sacramental, i.e., as not bound to any natural law of physical location or sensate perception.

In their own lifetimes, neither Paschasius nor Ratramnus was condemned as heretical. It was felt, apparently, that as long as Christ's eucharistic presence was affirmed, theological interpretation of its meaning could vary. As time went on, however, theologians sought greater clarity about issues like eucharistic presence, the "change" that occurs in bread and wine, the nature and structure of a sacrament. Underlying such theological issues were prickly philosophical questions: how can a physical thing like bread *be* or *become* something else? what is the nature of a body's presence to other realities? does a sign (symbol) *do* anything real, or does it merely represent something else? These and other philosophical questions obviously had a bearing on a theologian's attempt to interpret the eucharist. In the eleventh and twelfth centuries, particularly, an effort was made to hammer out a language in which the philosophical implications of eucharistic doctrine could be intelligently discussed.

But philosophical and theological language was only one source of debate during Berengarius's career; another source was political. We sometimes forget that medieval bishops and popes were rarely accorded automatic allegiance from the people—still less from the nobility and royalty. A medieval prelate often had to struggle to establish a constituency that would support him against other claimants to power. Medieval politics was thus a guerrilla theatre that mixed theological controversy with political opportunity, schemes for convenient marriages with plans for the annexation of duchies and kingdoms, threats of excommunication with power plays of complex magnitude. Political realities played an emphatic role in the careers of eleventh-century scholars like Berengarius and Lanfranc, his eventual opponent on matters of eucharistic orthodoxy.[24] Berengarius's teaching career, for example, was profoundly affected both for good and for ill by the increasing political tension in the 1040s and 1050s between William the Conqueror, duke of Normandy, and Geoffrey Martel, count of Anjou.[25] Pope Leo IX (1049–1054) was also involved, for he had made a successful tour through several French dioceses in 1049, ostensibly to hold councils and dedicate churches but factually to monitor the political situation as well. At a council in Rheims in 1049, Leo had temporarily excommunicated Geoffrey for imprisoning Gervase, the bishop of Le Mans—an action that pleased Duke William and the Norman bishops, who were (rightly) suspicious of Geoffrey's political designs on Normandy. Effectively, the papal intervention succeeded in consolidating William's power to the north

139

and undermining Geoffrey's position in the south of France. As a result, Geoffrey's patronage and protection of court scholars like Berengarius became far less effective.[26] It will be remembered, too, that Lanfranc, who eventually became Berengarius's most dedicated detractor, belonged to the monastery of Bec in Normandy, and thus fell under the influence of William's patronage.

In short, one must speak of the politics of eucharistic controversy in eleventh-century France. Thinkers like Berengarius and Lanfranc were inevitably drawn into the larger political struggle between north (William) and south (Geoffrey). Indeed, one reason for Berengarius's eventual condemnation may well have been the declining power of his chief political patron.

It is clear, however, that political patronage, with its unpredictable fortunes, would have had little impact on the question of eucharistic doctrine had not Berengarius himself achieved notoriety as a clever and controversial theologian. For the works of this teacher from Tours were widely read, discussed and criticized during the mid-eleventh century.[27] Jean de Montclos has suggested that Berengarius's eucharistic theology was constructed on three levels.[28] Each of these levels implies a question central to a theological interpretation of eucharistic doctrine.

1) What is meant by the "real presence" of Christ? Do the bread and wine change—and if so, how? Can one say that the bread and wine somehow "become" the Lord's body and blood?

2) What does it mean to speak of the eucharist as a "sacrament"? If something is a sacrament, is it also "real" or is it merely a sign of something else, an "image"?

3) What does a well-disposed Christian actually "receive" in eucharistic "communion"? How is this communion related to the issues raised in levels 1 (real presence) and 2 (sacrament)?

140

Let us see how Berengarius dealt with these questions—and why his solutions to them aroused such debate and hostility.[29]

Real Presence: There can be little doubt that Berengarius intended to affirm the real presence of Christ's body and blood in the sacrament of the eucharist, even though his formulations were considered inadequate by his opponents. Berengarius insisted, however, that presence and change in the bread and wine were two separate issues: the real presence of Christ in the eucharist does not depend in any way on changing the nature of the bread and wine.[30] Indeed, in *De Sacra Coena*, written after his condemnation at Rome in 1059, Berengarius concluded that "whoever affirms that the body of Christ, in whole or in part, is touched by the hands of the priest at the altar, or broken, or crushed, by the teeth—except insofar as this pertains to the *sacrament* [the sacramental signs themselves]—speaks against the truth and against the dignity of the teaching of Christ."[31] The nature of bread and wine remain unchanged in the eucharist; they do not "become" something else (viz., Christ's body and blood). One can thus speak of a change or conversion only in the sense that in the eucharistic celebration bread and wine become *sacraments* (sacramental signs). To insist upon any natural (i.e., physical) change in the bread and wine would be contrary, Berengarius felt, to the principles of nature.[32] He staunchly opposed those "sensualists" who held that in the eucharist one material reality (bread) is physically changed into another material reality (Christ's body and blood).

On christological grounds, too, Berengarius resisted the notion of any physical change in the eucharist. The body of Christ, having conquered death, is no longer subject to suffering and morality; the risen and glorified Lord cannot therefore be injured by a priest's hands or a Christian's teeth.[33] In the thirteenth century, Thomas Aquinas would also appeal to this notion of Christ's impassibility in order to prove that while the sacramen-

141

tal species are broken in the liturgy, Christ's own glorified body is *not* broken.[34] To think otherwise, Berengarius protested, would be tantamount to calling the truth of Christ's resurrection into doubt.

On both philosophical and theological grounds, therefore, Berengarius opposed contemporary views of change in the eucharist: first, because according to his philosophy of nature, one material thing cannot physically replace another; secondly, because the theology of Christ's resurrection prohibits any notion of change in the glorified body. As far as Berengarius was concerned, the language of change could be used only to speak of the way in which bread and wine become sacraments.

Sacrament: How, then, did Berengarius understand "sacrament"? Like many other theologians of his time, he appealed to Augustine's formula: a sacrament is the "sign of a sacred thing" (*signum rei sacrae*).[35] In the same breath, Berengarius added Augustine's definition of "sign" (*signum*): "You find a definition of 'sign' by the same author in his book *On Christian Doctrine*: 'A sign is something beyond the outward appearance which the senses perceive; by doing one thing it brings something else to mind.' He did not say 'to hand, to the mouth, to the teeth, to the stomach,' but: 'to mind.'"[36] It was the Augustinian connection between "sign" and human intelligence (mind, thought, reasoning) that particularly attracted Berengarius. Every visible sign points to something else invisible, and the relation between these two is perceived through the operation of human intelligence. This fundamental structure of a sign remains even in the case of sacraments: something visible and earthly (the sign) signals something else invisible and divine (the signified). The sacramental relation between visible earthly sign and invisible divine signified is grasped only through the operation of intelligence and faith.[37]

As sacrament and sign, therefore, the eucharist has

142

nothing to do with physical change in material realities. What lies on the altar after the consecration is not the flesh and blood of Christ, but the sacraments of that flesh and blood. In his "Letter to Adelman of Liege," Berengarius struggled to clarify what he meant by appealing once more to Augustine:

"Blessed Augustine offered a distinction between sacraments and the things that sacraments signify in the twenty-first book of *The City of God*, where he remarks: 'He [Christ] shows what it means to eat the body of Christ in reality, and not sacramentally.' Similarly, in one of his sermons: 'The sacrament of this reality is consumed at the Lord's table daily in some places, at specified intervals in others. For some [the sacrament] is life; for others, ruin. But the reality itself [leads] every man to life, and no one to ruin.' And in [his commentary on John's] gospel: 'Because of this, whoever does not remain in Christ and Christ in him undoubtedly does not eat his flesh or drink his blood—even if he receives the sacrament of this reality daily. . . .'"[38]

In Augustine's distinction between *sacrament* (*sacramentum*: visible earthly sign) and *reality* (*res*: invisible divine thing signified), Berengarius felt he had grasped an essential key to eucharistic doctrine. The bread and wine are sacraments that signal the spiritual, invisible reality of Christ's body and blood (the *res*, to use Augustine's term). These two, sacrament and reality, are essentially related, but the relation can be grasped only through the power of faith and intellect. One who receives the eucharist worthily thus receives both sacrament and reality; but this reception is a spiritual eating, not a physical "breaking of bones" or "tearing of flesh."

We can now begin to see why Berengarius was so violently opposed to all theories of a natural or physical change in the elements of bread and wine. If such a change really occurred, then the elements would no longer be a sacrament. If that were the case, then the bread and wine would no longer be capable of signaling spiritual reality (Christ's true body and blood). At stake in eucharistic theology, as Berengarius understood it, were two crucial principles: 1) the human need for signs that are accessible both to intellect and to faith, and 2) the absolute integrity of Christ's glorified humanity. Through his (and Augustine's) distinction between sacrament and reality, Berengarius felt he had defended both these principles.

Unfortunately for Berengarius, many theologians of the eleventh century were unwilling to accept his distinction. For them, sacrament and reality (or truth, *veritas*) were utterly opposite notions.[39] Despite Berengarius's efforts to show that the two were intrinsically related through intellect and faith, his opponents interpreted his sacramentalism as a denial of the reality or "truth" of Christ's presence in the eucharist. Against such sacramentalism, therefore, other theologians asserted a crude realism, insisting that the bread and wine are not only changed, but physically converted into the flesh of Christ, "broken by the hands of the priest and crushed by the teeth of the faithful." Realism of this sort was what Berengarius was forced to confess at the Council of Rome in 1059.

Communion: As we have seen, Berengarius was convinced that Christians truly partake of Christ's body and blood (the reality signaled by the sacrament) in the eucharist. Nor did he think the Lord's body was merely a spiritual phantasm. As Jean de Montclos has written:

"The expression 'body of Christ' should not be taken as an illusion; it signifies, for Berengarius, that the historical body of Christ, which is now in heaven, was and is a true body—and not, as the Manichaeans believed, simply an 'apparition.' The reality of the incarnation is the pledge of efficacity in the eucharist, which, through the signification of sacraments, puts us spiritually in touch with Christ in his authentic humanity."[40]

Berengarius believed, then, that the eucharist establishes a *real* (though spiritual) communion between the believer, worthily disposed, and the *real* body and blood of Christ. In that sense he was willing to admit that Christ's body becomes present on the altar. But in Berengarius's thinking this spiritual communion, though real, seemed to remain at the level of an interior psychological event, and the prevailing thought of his day was not content with that. After all, a real communion between Christ and believer is also effected through faith and grace. In what way, then, would the eucharist differ from them? To this question Berengarius does not seem to have found a fully satisfying answer.

Lanfranc's Reaction to Berengarius

Although the tempest over Berengarius's controversial theology brewed throughout the 1050s, it was not until about 1063 that Lanfranc became fully involved in the dispute. By then, Lanfranc was abbot of the monastery of St. Stephen's in Caen, and had become a prominent figure in Norman political circles.[41] The *Liber de Corpore et Sanguine Domini* (1063) was Lanfranc's response to "Berengarius, the adversary of the Catholic Church."[42] The identification of Berengarius as "adversary of the Catholic Church" is significant: it underscores the deeper political resonances of the debate and indicates Lanfranc's political and papal patronage.

Just as Berengarius had rediscovered the sacramentalism of Augustine, so Lanfranc claimed to have resurrected an insight from Ambrose's *De Sacramentis*.[43] In Chapter IX of the *Liber de Corpore et Sanguine Domini*, Lanfranc indignantly accused Berengarius of misquoting and misconstruing Ambrose's work. In the following passage, Lanfranc claims to cite what Berengarius had said:

"*Berengarius:* Through consecration at the altar, bread and wine become a sacrament of religion—but they do not cease to be what they were; rather, they are what they were and are changed into something else, as blessed Ambrose says in his book *De Sacramentis*.

"Lanfranc: O demented mind! O impudently lying man! . . . You dare to bring Ambrose in as witness. . . . Even if you were to bring in all the books Ambrose ever wrote about the sacraments or other matters . . . you would never be able to find anything like that said or explained by him. . . ."[44]

As a matter of fact, Lanfranc was correct; Berengarius's quotation was faulty. The disputed passage from Ambrose actually reads as follows: "To answer your question, then, before the consecration it was not the body of Christ, but after the consecration I tell you that it is now the body of Christ. He spoke and it was made, he commanded and it was created."[45]

Lanfranc had what he needed: an unambiguous patristic testimony which affirmed 1) that God's power (word) can change what already exists into something else, and 2) that such a change occurs precisely at the consecration of the eucharistic bread and wine. Moreover, Lanfranc could accuse his opponent of being an unreliable scholar who twisted authoritative evidence to suit his own malignant purposes.

The text from Ambrose is pivotal for understanding Lanfranc's brand of eucharistic realism. Against Berengarius's philosophy of nature, which insisted that one material reality cannot be changed into another, Lanfranc argued that God's infinite power can and does in the eucharist cause such a change to happen. God is the One who can "change what already exists into something else." Lanfranc was thus led to draw radically different conclusions about real presence, sacrament, and communion:

Real Presence: In the eucharist, Lanfranc affirmed, the earthly elements of bread and wine are changed into Christ's true body and blood: "We believe that through

146

the ministry of the priest, the earthly substances on the Lord's table are sanctified by divine power in a manner that is unspeakable, incomprehensible, marvelous; and that [these substances] are changed into the essence of the Lord's body, even though the appearances of earthly elements remain. . . ."[46] Here Lanfranc orchestrated a theme that would become familiar in later scholastic theology: there is a distinction between outward appearances (bread and wine) and hidden truth (body and blood). Against Berengarius's christological objection (Christ's glorified body is impassible), Lanfranc offered two responses: first, that in the eucharist the flesh and blood of Christ are not received according to their actual appearances, but according to the appearances of ordinary food; second, that through his divine power the Word can offer his flesh to be broken and eaten on earth, while it remains intact in heaven.[47]

Sacrament: Lanfranc's distinction between "outward appearances" and "hidden truth" also shaped his understanding of sacrament. The appearances mean nothing without the hidden truth (Christ's body and blood) which they signify. If the bread and wine are only sacramental (as Berengarius seemed to imply), if there is no hidden *change* in them, then the entire meaning of the eucharist is destroyed. Lanfranc thus accused his opponent of having a superficial understanding of the structure of sacraments, of reducing signs to mere shells empty of their hidden (but real) content. Once more, Ambrose is the patristic source of Lanfranc's insistence that the interior reality of the sacramental elements is changed by God's power: Ambrose "attests, indeed, that what existed according to its visible appearances [bread and wine] is now changed in its interior essence into those things [body and blood] which, before, were not."[48]

Here we are at the heart of the opposition between these two theologians. For Berengarius, the sacrament is destroyed if bread and wine are changed into something else; for Lanfranc, the sacrament is destroyed if bread and wine are not changed into something else. For Berengarius, the reality (body and blood) signaled by the sacramental signs must remain independent of those signs; for Lanfranc, the signs must be changed into that reality. Berengarius insisted on keeping sacrament distinct from reality, while admitting that the two are genuinely related; Lanfranc insisted on reconciling sacrament and reality, while distinguishing between outward appearances and hidden truth.

Communion: In holy communion, therefore, Christians feed upon the true flesh and blood of Christ, though they eat the flesh under the visible appearances of bread and drink the blood under the visible appearances of wine. Lanfranc distinguished, however, between the *flesh* of Christ and the *body* of Christ. Though these two realities are essentially the same, their qualities are different.[49] As it now exists in heaven, the *body* of Christ remains intact, impervious to further suffering and death; as it exists in the eucharist, the *flesh* of Christ is truly eaten: "with a bodily mouth, we bodily eat and drink."[50] We can see here how Lanfranc coordinated two sets of distinctions:

Sacrament: outward appearances (bread and wine)
hidden truth (flesh and blood of Christ)

Christ: Body (now in heaven, glorified and impassible)
Flesh (eaten by Christians, broken by the priest's hands)

Receiving the outward appearances *means* receiving the hidden truth, though their qualities are different (bread and wine are not bloody; Christ's flesh and blood are). Likewise, eating Christ's flesh means partaking of his body, though the two possess different qualities (the body is impassible; the flesh is not).

Lanfranc defended his somewhat unusual distinction

148

between flesh and body by appealing to a scriptural example. No one doubts, he said, that the widow of Sarepta ate oil from the jar which the prophet Elijah miraculously filled; yet scripture testifies that the jar never ran dry, even after the widow and her son had eaten from it for a year (1 Kings 17.7- 16). This is the case with the eucharist as well: we eat Christ's flesh and blood daily, yet the body of Christ remains whole and intact in heaven.[51] The example strikes modern readers as a bit bizarre, but it reveals something important about Lanfranc's sacramental and christological distinctions outlined above. In both Christ and the sacraments, a partial reality is to be distinguished from a total reality.[52] Thus we have:

Sacrament: partial reality (outward appearances of bread and wine)
total reality (hidden truth of Christ's flesh and blood)

Christ: partial reality (flesh and blood of the eucharist)
total reality (body of Christ now glorified in heaven)

Distinctions of this sort allowed Lanfranc to overcome the apparent opposition between sacramentalism and realism, between appearances and truth, between a body that is glorified in heaven and flesh that is eaten on earth. All these oppositions could be reconciled, Lanfranc felt, if one were willing to make the proper distinctions. Later medieval theology was willing—and Lanfranc's thinking played a major role in the subsequent development of eucharistic theology.[53]

Summary
The importance of the conflict between Berengarius and Lanfranc should not be underestimated. In a sense, the scope of the conflict was truly international, and its political repercussions were as far-reaching as its theologi-

cal ones. One should not forget that within a few years of publishing the *Liber de Corpore et Sanguine Domini*, Lanfranc had become an archbishop in the primatial see of Canterbury, and that Duke William of Normandy had become the conquerer of England. Nor should one overlook the impact which this debate had on the subsequent shape of eucharistic theology and piety in the West. To summarize:

1) Despite unresolved problems in his language and his theory of sacramental signs, Berengarius forced Latin theologians to confront the inadequacies of a crudely realistic approach to the eucharist. By challenging the notion of change in the eucharistic elements, Berengarius helped move theology away from naturalistic interpretations of the transformation of bread and wine into Christ's body and blood. And by insisting of the fundamental importance of Christ's resurrection, he opened the way to a better understanding of the relation between the historical person of Jesus and the eucharistic body of the Lord.

2) Lanfranc's originality as a theologian must also be noted. Although his distinctions were not altogether satisfactory, they paved the way for later thinkers like Aquinas. Moreover, Lanfranc was able to reconcile the unresolved differences between eucharistic "realism" and "sacramentalism" that had emerged in the ninth-century controversy between Paschasius Radbertus and Ratramnus.[54] The two Carolingians had disagreed over whether or not the eucharistic body and the historical body of Christ were identical: Paschasius said they were; Ratramnus denied it. Spurred on by the challenge from Berengarius, Lanfranc proposed a mediating distinction: the two bodies are essentially the same, but their appearances are different. In the eucharist, Christ's flesh appears hidden by forms of bread and wine (partial reality); in heaven, Christ's historical body, crucified and now exalted, is whole and intact.[55]

3) Neither theologian was able to resolve all the problems they encountered in eucharistic doctrine. Only later, after a more sophisticated understanding of Aristotle's philosophical distinction between substance and accidents had emerged, was medieval theology able to liberate itself from the ultra-realism associated with "bleeding hosts."[56] But a beginning had been made: Christian theology could begin to see that the eucharist is real without being crudely realistic, and symbolic (sacramental) without being unreal.

When Does the Consecration Happen?
Berengarius died about 1088, and Lanfranc about 1089; but for better or worse, eucharistic controversy did not die when they did. By the mid-twelfth century, most western theologians could agree that bread and wine are really changed into Christ's body and blood, and that the change happens in virtue of the words of Christ spoken by the priest in the eucharistic prayer. But a new question then arose: what is the exact moment of consecration? Do all the words, for both bread and cup, need to be said before any change happens? Or is the bread already consecrated as soon as the priest has said "This is my body"?

To scholars of our own day, such questions seem poorly posed—and to Christians living outside academia they may sound absurd. But in the twelfth century such issues were taken very seriously. There appears to be, moreover, a direct connection between the debates about the moment of consecration and the liturgical custom of elevating the host at Mass.[57] What were the theological issues involved in this controversy, and how did they contribute to the further development of eucharistic cult and devotion?

Three Schools of Thought
As V.L. Kennedy has assessed the evidence, three schools of thought about the moment of consecration emerged between the years 1160 and 1208.[58]

The "safe" school: As Berengarius had discovered in the
1050s, theology can be hazardous to one's health and
reputation. In every age there seem to be theologians
who prefer to hedge their bets, pursuing a safe course
through theological thickets that are potentially dangerous. Such a theologian was Peter of Troyes, a scholar
who taught at Paris during the 1160s and received the
astonishing surname *Comester* (Peter the Eater). Peter
developed a formula that circulated widely in Europe,
possibly because it was sufficiently ambiguous to be
considered safe, and sufficiently exact to be considered
acceptable. The formula ran: *Quando totum dictum est,
totum factum est*—When everything has been said,
everything has been done.[59] This clever theologial jingle
left the door open just enough: it clearly affirmed that
the consecration is accomplished by the words of Christ,
but it left each person free to decide whether it happens
all at once or separately (for the bread, then for the cup).

The "separate consecration" school: Peter's formula left
many theologians unsatisfied. Stephen Langton, who
taught at Paris as early as 1180 and was later nominated
as Archbishop of Canterbury (1206), preferred the view
that each species is consecrated separately.[60] In one of
his *Quaestiones*, Stephen wondered why the church had
not literally imitated the actions of Jesus: first consecrating and distributing the bread, then the wine.[61] But as a
devout ecclesiastic, Stephen accepted the church's actual practice (consecration of the species first; distribution later) and even tried defending it by suggesting that
Jesus himself may actually have done the same thing.
Other theologians, like Simon of Tournai, argued that
each consecration (for bread, then for cup) is *de facto*
independently effective, but that in actual practice (*de
debito*) one cannot take place without the other.[62]

The "single consecration" school: The champion of the
third school was another Peter, surnamed *Cantor* (the
Singer). Peter the Singer was as clear as Peter the Eater
had been ambiguous. If a priest were to stop after the

words "This is my body," Peter Cantor argued, no consecration would have taken place.[63] His logic was straightforward:

A true body cannot exist without blood;
But there is no blood in this sacrament until the wine is consecrated;
Therefore, the bread is not truly consecrated until the entire formula for both species has been said by the priest.

In short, Peter was arguing that the two clauses of the consecratory formula are so interdependent that one is not effective without the other.[64]

The Underlying Issues

Although much of this debate seems like theological hair-splitting, there were in fact some basic points about doctrine and liturgical practice at stake. For example:

a) If Christians are denied the eucharist cup, are they therefore denied access to Christ's blood? Or are the Lord's body and blood present simultaneously in each of the two species (the theory of concomitance)?

b) If Christians kneel and adore the host before the wine has been consecrated, are they guilty of idolatry? Peter the Singer said yes, because at that point in the Mass, given his theory, bread is still only bread.

c) Does mere contact with the consecrated bread effect a consecration of the wine? This practice was fairly common in earlier centuries of the church's life, as we have seen in Chapter Three. But it was vigorously opposed by theologians like Peter the Singer in the late twelfth century.

d) Is a practice like intinction legitimate? Is there any theological justification for it?

e) Should the consecrated bread and wine be shown to the people that they might offer them adoration? If so, at what point in the liturgy should this be done?[65]

These and similar questions were part of the results from the twelfth century debates about the moment of consecration. The very fact that such questions could be discussed seriously is significant: it reveals that attention has shifted away from the liturgy as an action of the whole community, and from communion as the ratification of that action, toward the climactic moment of the liturgical drama, the consecration. The liturgy itself is perceived not as the "work of the people" (its etymological definition), but as a theophany that inspires wonder and adoration. Peter of Roissy (+ ca. 1213), a priest who worked for a number of years in the diocese of Paris, bore witness to this increasingly theophanic perception of the eucharistic liturgy in a manual written for other priests:

"What should we say when the priest elevates the host? At these well-known words the priest lifts the host, saying: 'He took bread in his holy and venerable hands.' It is a praise-worthy custom in the church that people prostrate on the earth with their hands joined and raised to heaven, because at that point the Lord comes upon the altar. With reverence and honor they ought to receive him, saying with the prophet: 'Lord, have mercy on us, for we have long awaited you. . . .'"[66]

Official Reactions
The text just cited from Peter of Roissy is especially interesting because it reveals three things: 1) the custom of elevating the host had already begun in the late twelfth century; 2) this elevation was not directly connected with the words of consecration, but rather with the words describing Jesus' actions at the Last Supper; and 3) it was customary for people to prostrate at this point in the liturgy. Were these gestures of popular adoration and supplication a spontaneous reaction to the liturgical theophany, or did they result from official decisions on the part of the church's leadership?

The answer to this question is "both." It seems reasonably certain that before the end of the twelfth century, the custom of the priest holding the host aloft at the words "On the night before he suffered, he took bread . . ." was well established. This custom is what Edouard Dumoutet called "the ancient form of elevation" at Mass, and it was more an imitative gesture recalling Jesus' actions than a testimony to the moment of consecration.[67] But at the same time, theological quarrels about the consecration, outlined above, did provoke official reaction, and this reaction led to a change in the manner and meaning of elevating the host.

Sometime between 1205 and 1208, a synod was convoked at Paris to deal with questions of eucharistic doctrine and liturgical practice.[68] There were several problems facing the synod, among them[69]:

1) Controversy about the moment of consecration, especially in light of Peter the Singer's position (one clause of the consecration formula is not effective without the other). Peter had died in 1197, but the controversy had continued.

2) The already-established popularity of elevation in its earlier form, and the danger of encouraging material idolatry if the people adored the host before it was actually consecrated.

3) Questions involving unintentional mishaps in the celebration of Mass: e.g., what should a priest do if he reaches the end of the eucharistic prayer and discovers he had failed to put wine in the chalice?

The Parisian synod seems to have acted on all these questions, some of its decisions (regarding the elevation, for example) were to affect liturgical practice for centuries.[70] First of all, the synod rejected Peter the Singer's position about a single consecration, and sided with the theological majority which held for separate consecration (the second of the "schools" described earlier). This becomes evident when we read the synodical canon that deals with elevating the host:

155

"In the canon of the Mass, when they begin the words 'On the day before . . .,' presbyters are ordered not to elevate the host immediately so that it may be seen by all the people; rather, they are to hold it just in front of their chest until they have said the words 'This is my body.' At that point, they elevate the host so that all may see it."[71]

In effect, the synodical decree prohibited the earlier manner of elevation connected with the imitation of Jesus' actions, and insisted upon a consecratory elevation that follows the formula "This is my body."[72] This indicates, rather decisively, that the synod had resolved the theological controversy in favor of the "separate consecration" school. It also shows that the synod felt the host should not be exposed to public view until after it was consecrated. Obviously, the synod accepted the theological consensus, reached earlier in the eleventh and twelfth centuries; that consecration is effected through the words of the Lord said by the priest.

The Parisian synod also addressed itself to the problem of unintentional mishaps in the celebration of Mass:

"If through negligence it should happen that no wine or water are found in the chalice after the canon and consecration have been completed, the priest should immediately pour both into the chalice and repeat the consecration from that point in the canon [which reads]: 'In the same way, after supper . . .' all the way to the end . . ."[73]

Here again, the synod's intention of supporting the "separate consecration" school and rejecting Peter the Singer's position is evident. The canon just cited clearly assumes that, given the circumstances, the bread is already consecrated and there is no need to repeat the words "This is my body." In order to prevent such mistakes in the future, however, the synod directed that "red wine should be offered in the chalice because white wine looks too much like water."[74]

156

Summary
These historical facts show that while the custom of
elevating the host at Mass did not originate as a consecratory action, it developed in that direction after the
early years of the thirteenth century, partly because of
popular desire to see the host (Dumoutet), and partly
because of official intervention by synods like the one
held at Paris (ca. 1205–1208). Underlying the liturgical
custom was a theological issue: precisely how are
Christ's body and blood present in the two species offered at the eucharist? It was this issue that prompted
the rise of different schools of thought about the moment of consecration. In the section of this chapter that
follows, we shall see how the issue was resolved.

Debates Over Concomitance and Intinction

Concomitance and Conversion
The Berengarian controversy had forced theologians to
seek ways of expressing the church's traditional faith
that Christ is truly present in the eucharist in more
abstract and precise theological language. This search
for an acceptable theological language touched especially upon questions of change and presence in the sacrament. Earlier, we saw how Lanfranc tried to hammer
out a language for eucharistic doctrine based on distinctions between appearances and truth, flesh and body,
partial and total reality. We saw, too, the difficulties
Berengarius had in dealing with the language of change
in the sacramental elements.

During the period between 1160 and 1210, theologians
began working with a technical distinction between
concomitance and conversion. These words were aimed
at clarifying how Christ is "whole and entire, body and
blood, soul and divinity" present in each of the sacramental species. The question was closely related to the
discussion about the exact moment of consecration, for
it will be remembered that Peter the Singer's objection
to the "separate consecration" theory was that "a body

cannot exist without blood," and that no blood exists in the eucharist until the chalice has also been consecrated. As a way of overcoming Peter's objection, theologians came up with the following distinction.

Concomitance: When the bread is consecrated into Christ's body, it follows as a necessary consequence that the blood is also present, since it is true that a body cannot exist without blood. Christ's blood is thus concomitantly or consequentially present as soon as the bread is consecrated.

Conversion: When the cup is consecrated, however, there is a direct and immediate transformation or conversion of the wine into Christ's blood.

This somewhat awkward distinction amounted to a partial concession to Peter's objection: a body without blood is nothing more than a cadavar. At the same time, however, it allows adherents of the "separate consecration" school to maintain their viewpoint. For the distinction permitted a theologian to say that:

Christ's blood is present under the species of bread through the mode of concomitance; hence it is perfectly acceptable for Christians to reverence and adore the host after the words "This is my body," for the host contains the whole Christ, body and blood, soul and divinity.

Christ's blood is present under the species of wine through the mode of immediate, direct conversion; hence the mode by which Christ's blood is present in the consecrated wine differs from the mode by which it is present in the bread.

These distinctions seem very remote from the actual experience of most Christians in the eucharistic liturgy. But for better or worse, the theory of concomitance and conversion had a decisive impact on the shape of worship.

158

The eucharistic cup: In Chapter Three we saw the beginning of a gradual denial of the eucharistic cup to the laity during the Carolingian epoch. Now, in the late twelfth century, this custom was provided with a theological rationale. Since Christ's blood is concomitantly present in the consecrated bread, the cup is unnecessary: lay persons receive the whole Christ, body and blood, when they receive in the species of bread alone. It is not surprising, therefore, that in the thirteenth century giving the cup to the laity declined even further.

Gestures at Mass: In a similar way, the theory of concomitance provided justification for the consecratory interpretation of the elevation at Mass. The host is lifted not in imitation of Jesus' actions ("he took bread, blessed, broke, gave"), but as a signal that the consecration has taken place, and that gestures of adoration are thus appropriate.

In these examples, theological theory, popular custom, and pastoral decision combined to alter the shape of liturgical celebration. Even today, the cup has not been fully restored to lay Christians, and the custom of showing the consecrated species to the people is still part of the eucharistic rite. True, of course, some of these liturgical consequences were unintentional. For example, the synod of Paris discussed above did not intend that its implicit approval of the "separate consecration" theory should result in a total denial of the cup to lay persons. The synod spoke, for instance, of keeping the cups used for communicating the sick "clean and appropriately decorated."[75] But the same synod also insisted on genuflection as the appropriate sign of reverence for the laity when in the presence of the sacrament: "The laity are to be frequently admonished that whenever they see the body of Christ being carried, they should immediately genuflect, as to their Lord and Creator; and they should pray with hands joined until it has passed by."[76] As the thirteenth century began, eucharistic liturgy and piety were entering a new era,

159

one in which, as we shall see in Part II of this chapter, the cult of the sacrament outside Mass blossomed fully.

Intinction

The theory of concomitance, despite its perhaps unforeseen consequences for liturgical practice, was actually an attempt to resolve certain problems in the relationship between christology and eucharistic theology. These problems had already arisen in the ninth century, and they emerged again in the eleventh:

Ninth Century:
Relation between the "historical person of Christ" and the eucharistic body of the Lord (Paschasius, Ratramnus)

Eleventh Century:
Relation between Christ's glorified body in heaven and Christ's flesh in the eucharist (Berengarius, Lanfranc)

Now, in the twelfth century, a new aspect was added to these complex christological and eucharistic questions:

Twelfth Century:
Relation between Christ's body and blood in each one of the sacramental species (the bread, the wine)

Concomitance was, then, something more than a frivolous academic debate; it was an effort, however imperfect, to affirm that in the eucharist Christ's real humanity is made wholly present and available to Christians through sacramental signs. By speaking of Christ's body and blood as wholly present in each species (though in different modes), theologians were saying 1) that Christ's presence in the sacrament is a genuinely human one—a living body, not a cadaver; and 2) that Christians encounter the whole Christ, not merely a part of him, when they receive communion.

But the development of the theory of concomitance raised further questions. If Christ is wholly present in both the bread and wine, are customs like intinction

160

legitimate or desirable? Obviously, intinction originated as an attempt to preserve the ideal of eating and drinking the eucharist in extraordinary situations where actual use of the cup was impractical, e.g., for the ill and dying.[77] It had continued in use even in ordinary situations after the cup began to be withdrawn from the laity in the ninth century. Now that the theory of concomitance had developed to legitimate this withdrawal, was intinction called into question as well?

Many theologians of the eleventh and twelfth centuries thought it was. Some argued, for instance, that dipping the bread into the chalice recalled the unwholesome example of Judas, the Lord's betrayer. But by the middle of the eleventh century a new reason, political in nature, had been found for opposing intinction. In 1054, the religious quarrel between East and West, which had simmered for centuries, finally exploded in bitter and mutual excommunication. Theological polemicists like Cardinal Humbert were busy finding pretexts, however flimsy, to extend and deepen the rift. Humbert argued, for instance, that while the East practiced intinction, the West administered bread and cup separately. In fact, this was not accurate: the West had known the custom of intinction for centuries.[78] But in an era of acrimonious polemic, such distortions were readily seized upon as hallowed fact. Denunciation of intinction thus became a badge of political and religious allegiance in the West's battle against the East.

Not everyone accepted Humbert's mendacious interpretation of western liturgy. Some theologians, such as William of Champeaux, bishop of Chalons-sur-Marne (+ 1121), supported intinction, denouncing the objection based on Judas's example as frivolous.[79] William was acquainted with the theory of concomitance and even accepted it, but he argued that use of both species even in the form of intinction was more faithful to Jesus' example. William's argument holds interest because it shows that even after concomitance had become a fashionable theory, some theologian still insisted that it was more desirable to communicate Christians in both species.

But the political winds were blowing the other way. Prominent church leaders like Anselm of Canterbury (+ 1109) led the fight against intinction, and by the end of the twelfth century, Cardinal Lotario de' Conti di Segni (later Pope Innocent III) was insisting that intinction must cease altogether.[80] Innocent went so far as to say that anyone who denied concomitance was a heretic.[81]

Around the beginning of the thirteenth century, therefore, the majority opinion among theologians was running strongly against intinction, and the practice was well on its way to extinction. Even so, the notion that Christians ought to eat and drink at the eucharist survived in curious ways. During this period there are numerous accounts that indicate popular attachment to the ablution water (and wine) used by priests to purify their fingers after communion.[82] The ablutions were popularly believed to possess miraculous powers of healing.[83] Despite the abuse and superstition often associated with these popular customs, it is possible that the offering of the priest's ablutions to the laity was a kind of surrogate for the eucharistic cup. The same could be said for the popular medieval custom of offering communicants a draught of ordinary wine after they had received the bread.

Each of the theological controversies described in Part I of this chapter contributed both to alterations in the eucharistic liturgy itself and to the eventual appearance of an elaborate eucharistic cult outside Mass.

1) The theology of Berengarius not only precipitated a crisis in eucharistic doctrine, it also focused greater attention on the real presence. Not insignificantly, our earliest evidence for a full-fledged procession with the Blessed Sacrament appears in the monastic customary of Lanfranc, Berengarius's most prominent theological

162

nemesis. Although this procession was still connected with a liturgical event, Palm Sunday, it is easy to see how the custom could achieve independence from the liturgy.

2) The twelfth-century quarrels over the exact moment of consecration further focused attention on change and presence in the sacramental elements. As we have seen, the resolution of this debate in synods like the one at Paris (ca. 1208), helped popularize a change in the manner and meaning of elevating the host at Mass. And the elevation, as we will discover in Part II of this chapter, probably provides the earliest example of eucharistic exposition.

3) Finally, the development of the theory of eucharistic concomitance supplied theological legitimation for a growing liturgical custom, the withdrawal of the cup from the laity, and the eventual abandonment of intinction as well. This step perhaps more than any other contributed to a eucharistic piety centered almost exclusively on the host. Eucharistic devotion and cult outside Mass became, in fact, devotion to the host.

II. THE RISE OF A EUCHARISTIC CULT OUTSIDE MASS
Although the theological debates described in Part I of this chapter contributed to the development of a cult of the eucharist outside Mass, it was the evolution of the liturgy itself that prompted the rise of many devotional customs. In the early stages of their development, these customs seem to have fallen into four principal categories:

1) Devotional visits to the reserved sacrament;
2) Processions in which the sacrament, concealed in a container or exposed to public view, was carried about;
3) Exposition of the sacrament to the gaze of the faithful;
4) Benediction, in which a solemn blessing with the eucharistic bread was imparted to the people, often at the conclusion of a procession or a period of exposition.

Each of these customs has survived in one form or another until the present. Their historical origins will be explored in the pages that follow.

Visiting the Reserved Sacrament
The custom of reserving the consecrated eucharistic species for communicating the ill, the dying, or those absent from the Sunday assembly, is an ancient one. As we saw in Chapter One, Justin Martyr (ca. 150) already knew the custom of taking communion to those prevented from attending the liturgy. And less than a century later, the *Apostolic Tradition* of Hippolytus speaks of Christians who carry the eucharist to their homes for the sake of communicating on weekdays. These sources indicate that the earliest forms of eucharistic reservation involved either Christian persons (the deacons, in Justin's account) or Christian homes (Hippolytus). Much later, the eucharist was reserved in or near the church building—in a box kept in the sacristy, in containers built or suspended in the main body of the church near the altar (eucharistic towers, pyxes in the shape of doves), in niches constructed in the church wall (aumbries), or, increasingly after the sixteenth and seventeenth centuries, in tabernacles placed directly on the principal altar.

These and other modes of eucharistic reservation have been examined in great detail by scholars like W.H. Freestone and Archdale King. As their studies show, the original and primary purpose of reserving the eucharist was pastoral, to provide communion for the ill or dying (*viaticum*) as well as for those absent from the community's Mass. It is not necessary to repeat the long history of eucharistic reservation here; our attention will be focused instead upon devotional customs such as visits to the reserved sacrament. It can be shown, I think, that the custom of visiting the eucharistic species has its roots in the eleventh century, when the devotional practice of saluting the consecrated host just before communion appeared.

164

In a manuscript missal from Troyes, copied sometime in the second half of the eleventh century, the priest is directed to salute the body of the Lord immediately before receiving communion. The rubric reads "Salvation of the Lord's Body," and a short prayer follows: "Hail forever, most holy flesh! My highest and everlasting sweetness!"[84]

Such salutations, wherein the priest spoke directly to the consecrated host, became popular in the middle ages and were introduced in numerous manuscript missals of the period.[85]

When the custom of elevating the host after the consecration appeared at the end of the twelfth century, the "salutation of the Lord's body," originally attached to private devotions by the priest before communion, was often transferred to the moment of elevation. An early example of this appears in the *Ancrene Riwle*, an English rule of life for women living as solitaries near a church. Although the exact author of the *Riwle* is uncertain, the document seems to have been written about the year 1200 by a well-educated cleric.[86] The first part of the *Riwle* contains a generous number of directions for the recluse's daily private devotion and liturgical prayer. Among the practices recommended by the author are a set of salutations addressed to the Blessed Sacrament on the high altar of the church:

"When you are quite ready, sprinkle yourself with holy water . . . and turn your thoughts to the Body and precious Blood of God on the high altar and fall on your knees toward Him with these greetings: Hail, author of our creation! Hail, price of our redemption! Hail, viaticum of our journey! Hail, reward of our hope! Hail, consolation of our time of waiting! Be Thou our joy, who art to be our reward; let our glory be in Thee throughout all ages for ever. O Lord, be always with us, take away the dark night, wash away all our sin, give us Thy holy relief. . . ."[87]

165

The solitary is also directed to say these salutations when "the priest holds up the Host during Mass, and before the *Confiteor* if [she is] going to communicate."[88] During the fourteenth and fifteenth centuries, such devotions, sometimes called *orationes ad elevationem*, appeared frequently in Books of Hours.[89]

Of special interest for our purposes is the *Ancrene Riwle's* reference to a devotional salutation of the reserved eucharist *outside* the immediate context of Mass. In effect, the solitaries for whom this document was written were encouraged to include a kind of visit to the reserved sacrament among their daily devotions. Although their enclosure in a hermitage probably prevented their actually going into the church building to salute the sacrament, these recluses were instructed to visit "the Body and precious Blood of God" in thought, and to kneel "toward Him with [their] greetings."

The *Ancrene Riwle* thus supplies us with one of our earliest examples of regular daily prayer before the sacrament reserved. It suggests, too, that the origins of this devotion are located in the liturgy: the priest's private salutation of the sacrament before communion, already known in the eleventh century, became a popular form of greeting the Lord after the elevation appeared in the late twelfth century. In the *Ancrene Riwle*, this greeting has been extended beyond the liturgical situation to include daily devotion to the sacrament reserved outside Mass.

By the beginning of the thirteenth century, therefore, the notion of visiting the place of eucharistic reservation and praying there had made its debut. This type of piety seems originally to have been more popular among clergy and religious than among the laity. It should be noted, too, that prior to the beginning of the thirteenth century, there is virtually no evidence for devotional visits to the sacrament or for prayer addressed to the Lord in the eucharistic species outside the context of the liturgy. Earlier in the middle ages, Christians expressed personal devotion by visiting the altars in a church rather than by visiting the place of eucharistic reservation. This altar piety may well have been carried over from the ancient Christian cult of the martyrs, whose relics and tombs were revered and visited, particularly on the martyr's "birthday" (*dies natalis*, day of martyrdom). During the Carolingian epoch, for example, visiting the altars of a church was considered a hallmark of authentic piety. Bishop Jonas of Orleans (+ 844), whose work was alluded to in Chapter Three, criticized lay persons who neglected to visit and pray in the churches where relics were kept.[90]

Jonas's pastoral criticism reflects an era that regarded the altar as holy both because of what was done there (celebration of the Lord's sacrifice) and because of what was kept there (relics of saints, especially martyrs). By the beginning of the thirteenth century, however, it had become increasingly common to reserve the eucharistic species on or very near the principal altar of the church.[91] It should not be thought, however, that reservation on the altar was an innovation of thirteenth-century piety and ecclesiastical discipline. As early as the late ninth and early tenth centuries, the canonist Regino of Prüm (+ 915) had referred to reservation of the eucharist *super altare*. In his collection of canonical regulations, Regino recorded the following: "Every presbyter should have a pyx or vessel worthy of such a sacrament wherein the Lord's body may be carefully reserved for viaticum. . . . The holy oblation should be intincted in the blood of Christ . . . and should always be kept on the altar (*super altare*). . . ."[92] Not until the thirteenth century, however, did an ecumenical council explicitly legislate that the sacrament was to be kept under lock and key in church. Canon 20 of the Fourth Lateran Council (1215) reads: "We decree that in all churches the chrism and the eucharist be kept in safe custody under lock and key: so that no bold hand may get ahold of them for horrible and shameless purposes."[93]

Although the Lateran Council did not specify the exact method for safekeeping the eucharist, local diocesan synods of the same century were more explicit. In England, for example, Archbishop Peckham of Canterbury (ca. 1225–1292), commenting on canon 20 of the Lateran Council insisted that every parish church have a *tabernaculum* in which the pyx containing the eucharist might be kept: "In every parish church there should be a tabernacle with a lock (*tabernaculum cum clausura*) . . . in which a beautiful pyx containing the Lord's Body and covered with linens should be kept. . . ."[94] Whether Peckham's tabernacle was a structure placed directly on the altar is doubtful. It is more likely that the tabernacle (or *sacramentarium*) was an immovable stone structure built into the wall of the church near the altar.[95]

From the thirteenth century onward, then, reserving the eucharist in a prominent place on or near the altar becomes normal. Earlier places of reservation, such as the church sacristy, were considered inappropriate or unsafe. There remained, however, a substantial amount of variety in the actual manner of safekeeping the eucharist. The Fourth Lateran Council spoke of lock and key; Archbishop Peckham insisted on construction of a "tabernacle"; some French churches continued to have aumbries built into the walls or pillars of the sanctuary; still other churches, especially in England, suspended a pyx containing the eucharist above the high altar.[96] Eucharistic "towers" or "sacrament houses" were also popular, particularly in France and Germany.[97] The modern tabernacle, placed in the center of the main altar of the church, is a relatively recent invention, and did not become common until the sixteenth century and later.

Two factors, then, seem to have contributed to the rise of devotional prayer before the Blessed Sacrament in the early thirteenth century. One of these was liturgical; the other, architectural. Liturgically, the introduction of the elevation helped to popularize the custom of saluting the Lord present in the eucharistic species. We have seen how the priest's private salutation of the Lord's body before communion (already evident in missals of the eleventh century) was transferred to the moment of consecration and elevation and extended to the people, who were then encouraged to hail the Lord when they saw the host elevated by the celebrant. In the *Ancrene Riwle*, this popular custom of saluting the sacrament has been extended even further: the anchoresses are invited to reverence the "body and precious blood of God" on the altar in their morning devotions. Architecturally, the shift toward reserving the sacrament on or near the principal altar of the church reflected a change of attitude toward the altar itself. The earlier connection between altar and relics, with its probable roots in the ancient Christian cult of the martyrs, seems to have been modified. The altar is perceived increasingly as the privileged place where the supreme relic of Christian faith, the Lord's body, is kept under lock and key.

It is probable, too, that the devotional custom of visiting and praying before the reserved sacrament first arose among religious communities. Already in the late eleventh century, the *Monastic Constitutions* of Lanfranc speak of incensing the sacrament and kneeling in adoration before it: "They go to the place where, on Holy Thursday, the body of the Lord had been laid; after putting incense in the thurible, he [the priest] incenses [the sacrament] and gives it to the deacon to carry. . . . When they draw near to the altar, all the brethren should genuflect, adoring the body of the Lord. . . ."[98] The ritual described here is, of course, a very specific and limited one: the liturgy of Good Friday, with its Mass of the Presanctified. Still, it offers another instance of cultic attention to the sacramental species within the context of a religious community's life and liturgy. In the century following the appearance of Lanfranc's *Constitutions*, another element was added to the growing cult of the reserved eucharist: a burning candle marking the spot where the Lord's body was kept.[99]

In summary, it can be said that the devotional customs of visiting, saluting, and praying before the Blessed Sacrament reserved in church first seem to emerge in the late twelfth or early thirteenth centuries. Early evidence indicates that such customs were initially promoted in religious communities or among solitary persons especially devoted to contemplative prayer, e.g., the recluses of the *Ancrene Riwle*. The devotional visit appears to have developed from elements that had previously made their way into the eucharistic liturgy:

1) The priest's private salutation of the sacrament before communion (eleventh century);
2) The popular salutation of the sacrament at the elevation (end of the twelfth and beginning of the thirteenth centuries);
3) Recommendations to adore the reserved sacrament *outside* the times of liturgical celebration (thirteenth century).

The altar piety of the earlier middle ages, with its attention to the relics of saints, especially martyrs, was giving way to a eucharistic piety centered on the consecrated host.

Eucharistic Processions

Palm Sunday Processions
As early as the late eleventh century there is evidence for liturgical processions in which the sacrament of the Lord's body was carried about. The *Monastic Constitutions* of Lanfranc witness to the practice of carrying the sacrament in solemn procession on Palm Sunday. As we have seen, Lanfranc's use of the sacrament appears to have been a departure from earlier European customs, which reveal that the cross, the gospels, or relics were

more usually carried in the Palm Sunday procession.

It is difficult to determine exactly how widely and how quickly Lanfranc's Palm Sunday procession with the eucharist caught on in other churches. There is evidence from fifteenth and sixteenth century English sources that the sacrament was carried in the procession with palms, and one may assume that the custom had developed from liturgical practices of the sort described by Lanfranc. In the editions of the Sarum Missal published during the late fifteenth and early sixteenth centuries, for example, the rubrics direct that during the procession with palms "a bier be prepared containing the relics, together with the Body of Christ suspended in a pyx."[100] A similar rubric is found in the early sixteenth century Sarum Processional (first printed edition, 1508).[101] The Processional adds that lights, incense, and banners accompany the procession.[102] The Hereford Missal (first printed edition, 1502) repeats the same sort of information for Palm Sunday.[103]

Outside these English sources, however, there is scant evidence for the use of the sacrament in the procession on Palm Sunday. The Roman Pontifical of the twelfth century, for example, does not mention it.[104] In the thirteenth-century Pontifical of the Roman Curia, the sacrament does not seem to have been carried in procession on Palm Sunday, though it was borne into the church at the beginning of the Good Friday liturgy, and the pope is directed to reverence the species before they are carried to the sacristy, where they remain until needed for the communion rite.[105] The Pontifical of William Durandus (1293–1295), which became the prototype for later editions of the Roman Pontifical, gives no indication of a procession with the sacrament on either Palm Sunday or Good Friday. On Good Friday, only the gospel book is carried in the procession from the sacristy to the altar at the beginning of the liturgy. Similarly, in the first printed edition of the Roman Missal, published at Milan in 1474, there is no evidence that the Palm Sunday procession included use of the Blessed Sacrament. [106]

One is tempted to think, therefore, that the custom described by Lanfranc became popular in England but not on the European continent. What did become popular, from the late thirteenth century onward, was the procession with the Blessed Sacrament on the feast of Corpus Christi. The origins of this feast have been well investigated. Here, it will suffice to summarize that research.

Corpus Christi: Feast and Procession

The appearance of the feast of Corpus Christi in the thirteenth century needs to be understood against a background that is both socioeconomic and religious. The person usually cited as responsible for promoting the feast is Juliana of Liège (1193–1258), abbess of the Augustinian cannonesses of Mt. Cornillon. But Juliana's desire to spread devotion to the eucharist in this way makes more sense if we situate it within the larger framework of Belgian social and religious life of the period.

During this period there occurred in Europe an important economic shift from a predominantly agrarian culture centered on the highly structured life of the feudal manor to an increasingly urban and "industrial" one centered in towns. With the end of Moslem domination of commerce in the Mediterranean, Europe's geographic and economic horizons expanded considerably. New routes for commerce opened up, exports of natural resources and agricultural commodities became more profitable, and the rivers of central Europe became important internal arteries for the expansion of trade. In Flanders and the Low Countries the cloth industry arose, providing new jobs and promoting the exodus from feudal manor to medieval town. The population of these towns was often unstable; newcomers had to face an intense period of social readjustment and change. As

Norman Cohn has observed, the town quickly became a gathering place for the dissenter and the discontented:

"Journeymen and unskilled workers, peasants without land or with too little land to support them, beggars and vagabonds, the unemployed and those threatened with unemployment, the many who for one reason or another could find no assured and recognized place— such people, living in a state of chronic frustration and anxiety, formed the most impulsive and unstable elements in medieval society."[107]

In addition to these profound social, economic, and political changes, Europe experienced increasing pressure from religious dissenters in the twelfth and thirteenth centuries. Many of these dissenters seem to have been associated with what came to be known as "apostolic life" movements, which were attempts to imitate the behavior and ideals of early Christians in the time of the apostles. Some of these movements were strongly sacramental in orientation, while others were just as vigorously antisacramental.[108] Among the latter were a group known as *Cathari*, who seemed to believe that the material world belonged to a god of evil.[109] Although the origins of the *Cathari* are still disputed, their dualistic doctrine led them to deny both the truth of Jesus' humanity (it was an appearance, they said, not an actuality) as well as the efficacy of sacraments.[110] By the middle of the twelfth century, *Cathari* had begun to appear in Europe, especially in the region around Liège.

This was not the first time that Christians in Liège had been confronted by antisacramental enthusiasts. In the first quarter of the eleventh century (ca. 1025), a certain Gondolfo of Italy had aroused controversy there with his apparent rejection of baptism, eucharist, penance, and marriage. His ideas were attacked by Bishop Gerard of Liège, but dissenters were not easily routed by episcopal admonitions. Throughout the eleventh century, and even into the twelfth, Liège was regularly invaded by dissidents whose particular object of scorn seems to have been the eucharist.[111]

But the Cathari, and their dissident predecessors at Liège in the eleventh century, were not the only religious movement to affect this city. Another group were the women who came to be known as Beguines. Some writers have argued that this apostolic life movement originated with Lambert le Begue, a preacher of the late twelfth century who urged clerical reform and a return to simplicity of life in his church at Liège, but Lambert's role as founder of the movement is doubtful.[112] It can be said, however, that Lambert initiated a way of life for "holy women" (*mulieres sanctae*) at his church, and that this group possibly served as a model for the later Beguines.

As a specific group, the Benguines seem to have developed in four stages. Before the beginning of the thirteenth century, they were simply women devoted to ecstatic contemplation and simplicity of life, who lived alone or in small groups. By about 1200, they had formed into a religious association separate from the ordinary Christians of the city. Next, they appear to have established infirmaries; finally they created autonomous parishes.[113] The Beguines were not a religious order in the later sense of that term; they were not bound by vows, were not subject to papal enclosure, and did not totally renounce the possiblity of marriage.[114] Their piety seems to have centered on the eucharist and the humanity of Jesus, particularly the passion.[115]

All these factors need to be taken into account if we are to understand the milieu in which the festival of Corpus Christi originated: the changing pattern of Europe's economic and social life in the twelfth and thirteenth centuries, the migration from manor to town, the presence of religious dissidents at Liège, some of whom were staunchly antisacramental, and the rise of apos-

174

tolic life movements like the Beguines, whose piety was oriented toward the eucharist. It seems certain that Juliana of Liège was associated with the Beguines, though she was probably not an actual member of the movement. Of even greater significance was the association between the Beguines and Jacques Pantaleon, canon of St. Lambert and archdeacon of Liège. Pantaleon drew up a rule for the *beguinae clausae*, gave approbation to the feast of Corpus Christi at Liège, and later (as Pope Urban IV) published the bull *Transiturus*, which officially approved the festival for the universal church.[116]

Although *Transiturus* was published on 11 August 1264, Urban IV died in October of that year, and the bull remained a dead letter for almost fifty years. Despite that, the feast of Corpus Christi had taken root and began to spread thoughout Europe. Although she died before papal approval of the feast had been given, Juliana had worked tirelessly to popularize it. For almost forty years (ca. 1208–1246) she sought advice and approval for the feast from theologians and church officials. In 1246, Bishop Robert of Liège gave permission to celebrate Corpus Christi in his diocese, though he encountered opposition from his cathedral canons, who wondered why the daily eucharist was not sufficient honor shown toward the sacrament.[117] The bishop died before he could officially promulgate the feast, but soon a liturgical office for Corpus Christi appeared, possibly written by Juliana and her confessor, John of Lausanne.[118]

Despite the deaths of its early promoters, Juliana and Urban IV, the feast spread rather rapidly to other churches and dioceses. By the end of the thirteenth century it had been adopted in Venice (1295) and Wurzburg (1298), and soon the religious orders followed suite: Cluny (1315), Citeaux (1318), the Franciscans (1319), the Augustinians (before 1326), the Dominicans (by 1324 the entire order had adopted it).[119] In Rome, the feast was adopted on 1 November 1317.[120]

Originally, it seems, the feast of Corpus Christi did not include a procession with the Blessed Sacrament. But the idea caught on rather quickly, and there is evidence for a Corpus Christi procession at Cologne as early as 1279.[121] By the fourteenth century the procession had become popular in many dioceses: Ipswich (1325); Genoa (1325); Milan (1326); Rome (1350).[122] Why did these processions gain such popularity? Was it because the people were eager to see the host exposed? To answer these questions accurately we must turn to a third form of eucharistic cult: exposition of the Blessed Sacrament.

Eucharistic Exposition
The earliest form of exposing the eucharistic species to the people was the rite that took place immediately before communion, when the gifts were lifted with the words "Holy things for the holy" or a similar formula. Until the beginning of the thirteenth century, this was the only point in the western eucharistic liturgies at which the people were invited to gaze upon the species and reverence them. With the introduction of elevation at the consecration about the year 1200, however, the people were also invited to adore the Lord immediately after the words of consecration had been spoken by the priest. The great popularity of elevation is attested by numerous stories, not all of them edifying. Early sermons preached to the people about the meaning of the elevation reveal a rather straightforward, uncomplicated piety. Bishop Berthold of Regensburg, for example, wrote these words: "Behold, this is the Son of God, who shows his wounds to the Father. . . . This is the Son of God who died on the cross for you: you must therefore bear whatever cross is laid upon you patiently. Behold, this is the Son of God who will come for judgment, and to whom you must give an account."[123]

As time went on, however, preaching about the elevation became more extravagant and its claims more reckless. As had happened earlier with the ritual of the eucharist, allegorical interpretations became popular. The elevation was compared, for example, to the vision of Jacob recorded in Genesis 32.24f. Just as Jacob's experience had led to profound changes in his life—lameness, renewal of his soul, and a change of his name—so the elevated species offered miraculous powers to the beholder: a weakening of sinful lusts, strength of soul to endure dangers, and the writing of one's name by God in the book of life (Rev 3.12).[124] The story of Moses and the burning bush (Ex 3.5) was also cited as an exemplar, and the faithful were encouraged to remove their shoes at the elevation.[125] Various spiritual and physical benefits were attached to the moment of elevation: restoration of sight to the blind; freedom from a sudden death; the grace of final perseverance in faith.[126]

As we saw in our discussion of the origins of Corpus Christi, the intense social, economic, and political changes sweeping Europe in the twelfth and thirteenth centuries may account for the almost apocalyptic tone of some of this eucharistic piety. In an uncertain age of transition from a feudal-agrarian economy to an urban-industrial one, people are often inclined to react with violence of either a religious or political sort.[127] In some cases this violent impulse seems to have taken the form of religious dissent (e.g., the *Cathari*, the Beguines); in other cases it took the form of concentration on those elements of Jesus' life closest to the experience of medieval Christians: suffering and death (the passion), human emotions, flesh and blood (eucharistic realism).

In the fourteenth century, increasingly, the elevation was seen as the supreme moment of the eucharistic celebration. For that reason, medieval Christians sometimes felt free to leave church once the elevation was ended. Henry of Hesse (+ 1397), who had once been chancellor of the University of Paris, wryly commented that it might have been better if the host were concealed from the people, since many of them run off to taverns as soon as the elevation ends.[128] Quoting John 20.29, Henry quipped: "Blessed are those who have not seen, yet have believed!"[129] Other church leaders complained that people dashed from church to church in an effort to witness the "miracle" of the elevation several times in a single day.[130] Occasionally priests were asked—and paid—by the people to repeat the elevation two or three times during the Mass, or to hold the host aloft for protracted periods. Bishops and synods regarded this as an abuse. Matthias of Cracow, for example, hinted that priests who repeated the elevation were merely greedy for money.[131]

Unlike the earlier practice of showing the species to the people at communion time, which had as its primary purpose an invitation to receive the sacrament, the elevation was directed toward contemplative adoration— "ocular communion" with the Lord. It would seem logical that elevation led to exposition of the sacrament for prolonged periods of time. But the evidence suggests that there were as many as three different sources at work in the development of exposition:

1) The first of these was associated with eucharist for the dying. In some places in the thirteenth century showing the sacrament to the dying Christian seems to have replaced viaticum. Though the practice was condemned by some diocesan synods, it was authorized by others and the custom was reflected later in the rituals of several German dioceses.[132] The practice is mentioned, too, in the lives of some thirteenth century saints like Juliana of Liège (+ 1258) and Ida of Nivelles (+ 1231).[133] This substitution of exposition for viaticum seems to have been encouraged in cases where the dying person was either too ill or too feeble to partake of the sacramental species.

2) A second source for the development of exposition was the Corpus Christi festival. Originally, the feast

178

seems not to have involved either processions or exposition. In his bull *Transiturus*, Urban IV insisted on the intimate connection between the feast and the eucharistic liturgy.[134] He proposed an indulgence of 100 days to all who would attend matins, Mass, and vespers on the feast, as well as an additional indulgence of 40 days to all who assisted at the lesser hours of prime, terce, sext, none, and compline.[135] Each day during the octave of the feast, moreover, Urban offered indulgences to those who participated in matins, Mass, and vespers. The pope's idea seems to have been to encourage Christians toward more active participation in the liturgy, both the liturgy of the hours and the eucharist. Not until the fourteenth century (1316) did Pope John XXII command as obligatory the Corpus Christi procession.[136]

As we have seen, however, the liturgical interests of Urban IV were quickly superseded by the popularity of processions with the Blessed Sacrament. And that leads us back to the questions raised at the end of the preceding section: how was the eucharist exposed to the people? There is evidence that monstrances existed in the latter half of the thirteenth century.[137] The inventories of churches and the wills of prominent ecclesiastical personages supply evidence for this, as do miniatures painted during the fourteenth century, in which the host is depicted in a monstrance or other transparent container.[138] The will of Archbishop Robert of Rheims (+ 1324), for example, speaks of "a gold cross with precious stones and a crystal in the middle, in which the Body of Christ is placed and carried on the feast of the Blessed Sacrament."[139] This is an interesting reference because in the year of Robert's death (1324) the Corpus Christi procession was still a very recent institution at Rheims.[140] Apart from this feast, moreover, there is scant evidence in the early fourteenth century for prolonged exposition of the sacrament or use of a monstrance.[141]

3) Popular piety contributed a third source for the development of eucharistic exposition. The widespread

popularity of momentary forms of exposition, like the elevation at Mass, has already been discussed. In a sense, elevation as momentary exposition was extended and further solemnized through the Corpus Christi procession. A still further extension of exposition occurred when processions with the sacrament were held on the days within the octave of Corpus Christi.[142] This rapid expansion seems to have been a response to popular piety and also, perhaps, to commercial interest on the part of merchants and guildsmen in medieval towns. In England, particularly, Corpus Christi became an occasion for popular pageantry, drama, and carnival. At Coventry, for instance, pageants and plays were part of the Corpus Christi celebration as early as 1324.[143] As earlier the liturgy of Good Friday and Easter had given rise to dramas surrounding the sepulchre and its visitation by the spice-bearing women, so the fourteenth century produced cycles of Corpus Christi plays at cities like Coventry, York, and Wakefield.[144]

Thus far our examples of eucharistic exposition have emerged from within the liturgy itself—the custom of showing the sacrament to the people at communion, the elevation after the words of consecration, the liturgy of the ill and dying, and the festival of Corpus Christi, with its eventual processions. When and how did the custom of eucharistic exposition *independent of the liturgy* arise?

There is no reliable evidence for independent exposition, either continuously or for a specified period of time, prior to the close of the fourteenth century.[145] The evidence first appears in the life of Dorothea of Danzig (+ 1394) written by her confessor, John Marienwerder. Dorothea was a married woman and mother who lived as a recluse in her later years. Her piety was centered on the eucharist in all its aspects: Mass, reserved sacrament, exposed sacrament. Her biographer wrote: "Attracted by the fragrance of this life-giving Sacrament, the Spouse from her childhood until death had an intense longing to see the Sacred Host, and if in one day she saw it a hundred times, as on some occasions actually happened, she lost nothing of her craving to see It yet another."[146] One may wonder how Dorothea was able to see the host so frequently. It seems that about the year 1380 a popular custom of exposing the sacrament in a monstrance had arisen in some parts of Germany.[147] This form of continuous exposition was not immediately connected with public worship; it seems to derive, indeed, from a modification in the manner of reserving the sacrament. In short, a monstrance or *ostentorium* was being used to reserve the sacrament in church, possibly in response to popular desire to see the host.

The practice of continuous exposition became sufficiently widespread to cause concern among theologians and church leaders, especially in the fifteenth century. In 1452, a council of Cologne, under the presidency of Nicholas of Cusa, legate of Pope Nicholas V, insisted that exposition and processions with the Blessed Sacrament be limited to Corpus Christi and its octave.[148] Other occasions required explicit episcopal permission and were to be undertaken only in extraordinary cases. Prominent theologians of the period, like Jean Gerson (+ 1429), expressed serious reservations about these forms of extra-liturgical exposition. Gerson felt that people would do better to raise their minds toward invisible realities, and he cautioned against the superstitious beliefs that sometimes surrounded the piety of gazing at the host.[149]

Benediction of the Blessed Sacrament
All three of the customs discussed thus far—visits and prayer before the Blessed Sacrament, processions, and exposition—have their roots in the evolution of the eucharistic rite itself. Benediction, the fourth and final custom to be analyzed here, is also derived from liturgical sources. The first of these sources is connected with the liturgy of the hours; the second, with the liturgy of Corpus Christi.

The Liturgy of the Hours: During the first half of the thirteenth century in Italy, a popular evening devotion known as the *laude* arose. The devotion consisted of Latin or vernacular songs addressed to the Virgin Mary, sung by the people, probably at the conclusion of canonical offices like vespers or compline.[150] These popular Marian hymns were disseminated throughout Europe under different names: *Salut* in France; *Lof* in Flanders. Elsewhere they were simply referred to as *Salve*, the first word of the well-known hymn *Salve, Regina* (Hail, holy Queen). The custom of concluding an hour of the Divine Office with a Marian hymn or antiphon was an old one probably known by at least the tenth century, especially in monastic communities. Even to this day, the liturgy of the hours as reformed by the Second Vatican Council provides for the singing of a Marian antiphon at the close of night prayer (compline). In the thirteenth and fourteenth centuries local synods and councils required or recommended this custom. A council at Toulouse in 1231, for example, recommended a Saturday evening devotion in church that consisted, substantially, of vespers in honor of the Virgin.[151] Less than a century later (1302) a council at Penafiel, Spain, required that the *Salve, Regina* be sung each day after compline in every church.[152]

In the fourteenth century it became increasingly popular to perform these evening devotions (*laude*) in the presence of the Blessed Sacrament exposed to the view of the faithful. The original purpose of this exposition was to lend solemnity to the devotion, rather than to increase the honor paid to the sacrament.[153] As Herbert Thurston has remarked, "The *Salut* itself was the substantial element, the exposition and final blessing were only accessories."[154] Thurston's reference to a "final blessing" is important, for it seems that at the conclusion of the devotional *laude* (*Salut, Salve*) it had become customary to bless the people with the sacramental bread. This kind of blessing was not, in itself, an innova-

182

tion. It is possible, for example, that earlier in the middle ages communion of the ill or dying concluded with a blessing of the people with a pyx or other covered vessel containing the sacrament.[155] Earlier still, people were commonly blessed at the conclusion of services with sacred objects such as the cross or the relics of saints.

What *was* innovative in the fourteenth century was benediction of the people with the sacrament visibly exposed in a monstrance or other similar vessel. To understand how and why this happened, we must look at the second source for the custom of Benediction, the procession and exposition on the feast of Corpus Christi.

The Liturgy of Corpus Christi: As early as 1301 at the Benedictine monastery of Hildesheim, Germany, the Corpus Christi procession, itself still a recent innovation, included a "station" or pause in the procession during which the people sang an antiphon while the priest blessed them with the sacrament.[156] This appears to be the first literary evidence for Benediction of the Blessed Sacrament, though it is not absolutely clear whether the host was exposed to public view in a monstrance. By the late fourteenth century the practice of concluding the procession with Benediction seems to have become commonplace, and given the widespread popularity of exposition in late fourteenth century Germany, particularly, it is likely that this Benediction was performed with a monstrance or similar vessel.

After the middle of the fourteenth century, moreover, eucharistic processions, possibly with a concluding Benediction, were extended to major feasts other than Corpus Christi and its octave. Christmas, Easter, Pentecost, All Saints, and the dedication of a church were often solemnized by a procession with the Blessed Sacrament, as were days commemorating civic occasions (e.g., the coronation of a monarch, victory in a battle or war, deliverance from calamity or disease).[157] The desire for more frequent and prolonged exposition of the eucharist sometimes led to customs of dubious liturgical or theological merit. At Minden in eastern Germany, for instance, it became customary after about 1336 to expose the eucharist during both Mass and the hours of the Divine Office.[158] At about the same period (1345) in Augsburg, the archpriest Rudolph complained that the people blessed their crops with the sacrament daily from the feast of Corpus Christi until the end of the harvest season.[159] This method of seeking divine insurance for fruitful harvests prevailed elsewhere, too; Charles Borromeo refers to its lingering presence in Italy in the sixteenth century.[160]

The two liturgical sources of Benediction—the devotional *laude* at the end of vespers or compline and the Corpus Christi procession—reveal that the custom originated as a dismissal rite attached to some other liturgical service. We may conclude that originally Benediction of the Blessed Sacrament was not perceived as an independent ritual; instead, it served as a solemn conclusion to another liturgy. It was not Benediction *per se* that supplied the central motive for a gathering of Christians.

SUMMARY
In Part II of this chapter we have explored the origins of four popular customs that hint at a cult of the eucharist outside the immediate context of Mass: visits, processions, exposition, and Benediction. Several patterns emerge from this exploration, and it may be useful to summarize them here:

1) All four customs originate within the evolution of the eucharistic liturgy itself. Visits appear to derive from the ancient custom of reserving the sacrament primarily for use in communion of the sick or viaticum. Processions first appear in connection with the rites of Holy Week (Lanfranc's provisions for Palm Sunday). Exposition emerges from several sources: the ancient practice of showing the sacrament to the people at communion

time; the medieval custom of elevation; the liturgy of the ill and dying; the festival of Corpus Christi. And finally, Benediction begins as the solemn conclusion to other liturgical events such as the Divine Office and the Corpus Christi procession.

2) Until the fifteenth century at least, there is no question of the devotional cult of the eucharist replacing the liturgy.[161] On the contrary, documents like the *Transiturus* of Urban IV reveal a bold insistence on participation in the liturgy as the ordinary norm of eucharistic piety and devotion. Events such as processions, exposition and Benediction were regarded as extraordinary solemn actions. There is evidence, as we have seen, for offical resistance against prolonged and frequent exposition of the sacrament.

3) These customs obviously reveal a popular change of perception in the meaning and purpose of the eucharistic elements. Their original significance as food and drink for the people of God, while not lost, was modified and reinterpreted. The cultic and devotional attitudes which in an earlier era were directed toward objects such as relics, altars, and the gospels were ritually transferred to the eucharistic species, especially the host. This ritual transference is evident in the customs studied here: visits and prayer at the altars of a church (a form of pilgrimage to the shrine of saints) have become visits to the eucharist enshrined in a place of reservation; objects traditionally carried in procession, such as crosses, relics, and the book of gospels, now include the sacrament of the Lord's body; the custom of displaying precious objects to the view of the faithful for veneration has been transferred to the eucharist as well in the custom of exposition; and the solemn conclusion to a liturgical event, in which the people were often blessed with cross and/or relics has given rise to Benediction of the Blessed Sacrament.

4) Finally, it should be noted that many of the customs

identified here seem to have appeared first in religious communities. Popular cultic gestures toward the eucharist, such as genuflection, incensation of the sacrament, and the use of processional lights first appear in monastic literature like the *Constitutions* of Lanfranc.

We may conclude, then, that the appearance of a devotional cult of the eucharist outside Mass is best explained from within the evolution of the liturgy itself. Unquestionably, theological debate, as well as sociopolitical and economic factors, played a role too. The custom of elevation, for example, seems to have been a response to a specific theological controversy about the exact moment of consecration in the late twelfth century. Similarly, the feast of Corpus Christi with its accompanying practice of eucharistic processions arose in an era of profound social readjustment and religious dissent. But it must be emphasized that at their origins eucharistic devotions were not designed to eliminate or replace the normative expression of faith in the celebration of the liturgy. Throughout the period studied in this chapter eucharistic devotions are seen as ways to encourage, not inhibit, popular participation in both Mass and the liturgy of the hours.

NOTES

1. Thomas Symons, ed., *Regularis Concordia* (New York: Oxford University Press, 1953), pp. 35-36.

2. See John Wilkinson, trans., *Egeria's Travels* (London: SPCK, 1971) for a detailed description of these shrine liturgies.

3. David Knowles, ed., trans., *The Monastic Constitutions of Lanfranc* (New York: Oxford University Press, 1951), pp. 23-25.

4. Ibid., p. 25.

5. See Cyrille Vogel, ed., *Le Pontificale romano-germanique du dixième siècle* (Studi e Testi 226-227; 2 vols.; Città del Vaticano: Biblioteca Apostolica Vaticana, 1963), II, pp. 40-51.

6. Ibid., II, pp. 47-48.

7. Ibid., II, pp. 51-52.

8. Ibid., II, p. 52.

9. See ibid., II, p. 52. The Romano-Germanic Pontifical gives a third order of service as well; it resembles the first and includes veneration of the cross.

10. *Regularis Concordia*, ed. Symons, pp. 44-45.

11. Ibid., pp. 49-50.

12. Ibid., p. 50.

13. Ibid., p. 50.

14. See Blandine-Dominique Berger, *Le Drame liturgique de Paques* (Théologie historique, 37; Paris: Beauchesne, 1976), pp. 247-256, for a listing of the sources that contain dramas connected with the *visitatio sepulchri*.

15. PL 135: col. 1020.

16. PL 135: col. 1021.

17. *The Monastic Constitutions of Lanfranc*, ed. Knowles, pp. 38-48.

18. See Berger, *Le Drame liturgique*, pp. 247-256, for sources.

19. See Karl Young, *The Drama of the Medieval Church* (2 vols.; Oxford: Clarendon Press, 1933), I, pp. 305, 624-625.

20. Young, *Drama*, I, pp. 624-625.

21. Ibid., I, p. 305.

22. See Walter Howard Frere and Langton E.G. Brown, eds., *The Hereford Breviary* (3 vols.; Henry Bradshaw Society, 26, 40, 46; London: Harrison and Sons, 1904–1915), I, pp. 324-325.

23. DS 690.

24. See Margaret Gibson, *Lanfranc of Bec* (Oxford: Clarendon Press, 1978), pp. 63-97.

25. Ibid., pp. 64-65.

26. Ibid., p. 65.

27. Ibid., pp. 65-66.

28. Jean de Montclos, *Lanfranc et Bérengar. La Controverse eucharistique du XI siècle* (Spicilegium Sacrum Lovaniense, Etudes et Documents, 37; Louvain, 1971), p. 433.

29. A word should be said about Berengarius's works, many of which have not been published in modern critical editions. *De Sacra Coena* is perhaps Berengarius's most comprehensive treatment of eucharistic doctrine. For a description of this work's contents, see de Montclos, pp. 503-515. Berengarius's letters to friends and to opponents are also important. See especially de Montclos, pp. 125-148, 531-539.

30. See de Montclos, *Lanfranc et Bérengar*, p. 142.

31. Berengarius, *De Sacra Coena*, 166; text in de Montclos, p. 514.

32. See de Montclos, *Lanfranc et Bérengar*, p. 143.

33. Ibid.

34. Thomas Aquinas, *Summa Theologiae*, III, 77, 7.

35. See Berengarius, "Letter to Adelman of Liège," lines 22-27; text in de Montclos, p. 532.

36. Ibid.

37. Ibid., p. 147.

38. Ibid., pp. 535-536.

39. Ibid., p. 597, s.v. *sacramentum*.

40. See de Montclos, *Lanfranc et Bérengar*, p. 147.

41. See Gibson, *Lanfranc of Bec*, p. 70.

42. Text of Lanfranc's *Liber de Corpore et Sanguine Domini* may be found in PL 150: cols. 407-442.

43. Lanfranc had been at work on an edition of Ambrose while he was still a monk at the abbey of Bec. See Gibson, *Lanfranc of Bec*, p. 83.

44. PL 150: col. 419.

45. Ambrose, *De Sacramentis*, IV.15; translated in Edward Yarnold, ed., *The Awe-Inspiring Rites of Initiation* (London: St. Paul Publications, 1971), p. 134.

46. PL 150: col. 430.

47. PL 150: cols. 429-430; see de Montclos, *Lanfranc et Bérengar*, pp. 358-359.

48. PL 150: col. 420.

49. See PL 150: col. 427.

50. PL 150: col. 429.

51. PL 150: col. 427.

52. See de Montclos, *Lanfranc et Bérengar*, p. 384.

53. On the influence of Lanfranc among later scholastic theologians, see de Montclos, *Lanfranc et Bérengar*, pp. 448-478.

54. See the discussion of Paschasius Radbertus and Ratramnus in Chapter Three, in the section entitled "The Eucharistic Controversies of the Ninth Century."

55. See PL 150: col. 424; see also de Montclos, *Lanfranc et Bérengar*, p. 450.

56. See de Montclos, *Lanfranc et Bérengar*, s.v. "Accidents— Substance," p. 580.

57. This is the position of V.L. Kennedy, "The Moment of Consecration and the Elevation of the Host," *Medieval Studies* 6 (1944), 121-150. Edouard Dumoutet, on the other hand, argued that the custom of elevating the host emerged as a response to popular desire to gaze at the consecrated species. See E. Dumoutet, *Le Desir de Voir l'Hostie* (Paris: Gabriel Beauchesne, 1926). Dumoutet argues (p. 50) that the practice of elevating the host already existed before the controversies over the moment of consecration became widespread. He contends, further, that by the time Bishop Odo of Paris directed that elevation be adopted in all churches in his diocese, the moment of consecration had become a dead issue. Kennedy, however, claims that Dumoutet's evidence for popular devotion (seeing the host, ocular communion) is actually derived from the period after Odo's decree at the Parisian synod (between 1205–1208).

58. Kennedy, "The Moment of Consecration," pp. 147-148.

59. Ibid., pp. 124-125.

60. Langton was the first writer who explicitly referred to the custom of genuflecting after the words over the bread have been said. See Kennedy, "The Moment of Consecration," p. 137.

61. See Kennedy, "The Moment of Consecration," pp. 136-137 for texts and discussion.

62. Ibid., pp. 128-129.

63. Ibid., p. 139.

64. Ibid., p. 140.

65. As we have seen in Chapter Two, the eucharist was shown to the people at communion time at a fairly early period of the church's history.

66. Text in Kennedy, "The Moment of Consecration," p. 149, n. 124.

67. See Dumoutet, *Le Désir de Voir l'Hostie*, p. 50; also Kennedy, "The Moment of Consecration," p. 149.

68. On the date of this synod, see V.L. Kennedy, "The Date of the Parisian Decree on the Elevation of the Host," *Medieval Studies* 8 (1946), 87-96.

69. See Kennedy, "The Moment of Consecration," pp. 149-150.

70. The decrees of the Parisian synod are printed in Mansi, XXII, cols. 675-686. Kennedy, however, has suggested that this collection of synodical decrees may actually represent the work of several different synods. He also feels that the synodical decree requiring elevation of the host after the formula of consecration, rather than at the words "On the day before he suffered," appeared later than 1208, the year in which Bishop Odo of Paris (1196–1208) died. See Kennedy, "The Date of the Parisian Decree," p. 96, for his conclusions.

71. Mansi XXII: col. 682.

72. The Parisian synod spoke only of elevating the *bread*. Elevation of the chalice does not seem to have become common until the fourteenth or fifteenth centuries. See Dumoutet, *Le Désir de Voir l'Hostie*, pp. 57-58.

73. Mansi XXII: cols. 681-682.

74. Mansi XXII: col. 682.

75. Mansi XXII: col. 677.

76. Mansi XXII: col. 678. This synod also specified that the eucharist be kept under lock and key "on a more beautiful part of the altar in the principal church" (Mansi XXII: col. 678).

77. See W.H. Freestone, *The Sacrament Reserved* (Alcuin Club Collections, XXI; London: A.R. Mowbray and Co., 1917), pp. 144-145.

78. See Freestone, *The Sacrament Reserved*, pp. 155-156.

79. Ibid., pp. 160.

80. Ibid., pp. 164-165.

81. PL 217: col. 866.

82. See Adolf Franz, *Die Messe im deutschen Mittelalter* (Freiburg im Breisgau: Herdersche, 1902), pp. 105-114.

83. Ibid., p. 109; Franz gives the story of a woman supposedly cured of blindness after smearing her eyes with wine from the ablutions of Archbishop Herbert of Cologne.

84. Text in André Wilmart, *Auteurs spirituels et Textes dévots du Moyen âge* (Etudes d'Histoire Littéraire, Paris: Etudes Augustiniennes, 1971; reprint of 1932 edition), p. 20.

85. See above, Chapter Three, p. 00, for similar texts from the Sarum rite.

86. See M.B. Salu, ed., *The Ancrene Riwle* (London: Burns and Oates, 1955), pp. xxiii-xxvi.

87. Ibid., p. 7.

88. Ibid.

89. See Gerard Sitwell, "Private Devotions in the *Ancrene Riwle*," in Salu, p. 193.

90. See PL 106: col. 150.

91. See Peter Browe, *Die Verehrung der Eucharistie im Mittelalter* (Rome: Herder, 1967; reprint of the 1933 edition), pp. 18-19.

92. Regino, *Notitiae*, I.70; in PL 132: col. 205.

93. Text in Freestone, *The Sacrament Reserved*, p. 190, n. 4.

94. Ibid., p. 191, n. 1.

95. Ibid., p. 191, nn. 1 and 2.

96. Ibid., pp. 190-195.

97. Ibid., pp. 192, 216-218.

98. *The Monastic Constitutions of Lanfranc*, ed. Knowles, p. 41.

99. See Browe, *Die Verehrung*, p. 17.

100. See F.H. Dickinson, ed., *Missale ad usum insignis et praeclarae ecclesiae Sarum* (London: J. Parker and Co., 1861–1883; reprint: Gregg International Publishers, 1969) col. 258.

101. See W.G. Henderson, ed., *Processionale ad usum insignis ac praeclarae ecclesiae Sarum* (Leeds: M'Corquodale and Co., 1882; reprint: Gregg International Publishers, 1969), p. 49.

102. Ibid., p. 51.

103. See W.G. Henderson, ed., *Missale ad usum percelebris ecclesiae Herfordensis* (London: 1874; reprint: Gregg International Publishers, 1969), p. 80.

104. See Michel Andrieu, ed., *Le pontificale romain au Moyen-Age* (4 vols.; Studi e Testi 86-88, 99; Città del Vaticano: Biblioteca Apostolica Vaticana, 1938–1941), I, pp. 210-214.

105. Ibid., II, p. 465.

106. See Robert Lippe, ed., *Missale Romanum* (Henry Bradshaw Society, 17; London, 1899).

107. Norman Cohn, *The Pursuit of the Millenium* (2nd ed.; New York: Harper and Row, 1961), pp. 29-30.

108. See Walter Wakefield and Austin Evans, *Heresies of the High Middle Ages* (Records of Civilization: Sources and Studies; New York: Columbia University Press, 1969), pp. 6-7.

109. Wakefield and Evans, *Heresies*, p. 8.

110. Ibid.

111. See Jeffrey Burton Russell, *Dissent and Reform in the Early Middle Ages* (Los Angeles: University of California Press, 1965), pp. 21-23, 41-43.

112. See Ernest W. McDonnell, *The Beguines and Beghards in*

Medieval Culture (New Jersey: Rutgers University Press, 1954), p. 72.

113. Ibid., pp. 5-6.

114. Ibid., pp. 310, 321.

115.

116. Ibid., pp. 306-307.

117. See Emile Bertaud, "Devotion eucharistique," *Dictionnaire de Spiritualite*, IV/2, col. 1625.

118. See McDonnell, *The Beguines*, p. 307.

119. See Bertaud, "Devotion eucharistique," col. 1626.

120. Ibid.

121. See Roger Béraudy, "Eucharistic Worship Outside the Mass," in A.-G. Martimort, *The Church at Prayer: The Eucharist*, translated by Austin Flannery *et al.* (New York: Herder and Herder, 1973), p. 224, n. 1.

122. Ibid.

123. Cited in Franz, *Die Messe*, p. 101.

124. Ibid., pp. 101-102.

125. Ibid., p. 102.

126. Ibid., p. 103.

127. See Cohn, *The Pursuit of the Millenium*, pp. 29-30.

128. See Dumoutet, *Le Desir de Voir l'Hostie*, pp. 30-31.

129. Ibid.

130. Franz, *Die Messe*, p. 104.

131. Ibid., p. 105, n. 1.

132. Dumoutet, *Le Desir de Voir l'Hostie*, pp. 76-77.

133. Ibid., p. 76.

134. See Lambert Beauduin, *Mélanges liturgiques* (Louvain: Abbaye du Mont César, Centre liturgique, 1954), p. 209.

135. Ibid., p. 210.

136. Ibid.

137. Dumoutet, *Le Desir de Voir l'Hostie*, p. 81.

138. Ibid., p. 82.

139. For text see ibid., p. 82, n. 3.

140. Ibid., pp. 82-83.

141. Ibid., p. 83.

142. Beauduin, *Mélanges liturgiques*, p. 210.

143. See Herbert Thurston, "Benediction of the Blessed Sacrament," *The Month* 98 (1901), 68.

144. Ibid.

145. Ibid.

146. Text cited ibid., p. 58.

147. Ibid., p. 59. Dumoutet suggests that the practice of continuous exposition may have arisen as early as 1330: *Le Desir de Voir l'Hostie*, p. 83.

148. See Beauduin, *Mélanges liturgiques*, p. 210.

149. See Dumoutet, *Le Desir de Voir l'Hostie*, pp. 31-33.

150. See Herbert Thurston, "Our English Benediction Service," *The Month* 106 (1905), 394-404.

151. See Beauduin, *Mélanges liturgiques*, p. 211.

152. Ibid.

153. Thurston, "Our English Benediction Service," p. 395.

154. Ibid.

155. See Thurston, "Benediction of the Blessed Sacrament," pp. 192-193.

156. See Béraudy, "Eucharistic Worship Outside the Mass," p. 230.

157. Ibid., p. 224.

158. See Mario Righetti, *Manuale di Storia liturgica* (4 vols.; Milan: Editrice Ancora, 1946–1953), III, p. 497, n. 40.

159. See Thurston, "Benediction of the Blessed Sacrament," p. 191.

160. Ibid.

161. See Beauduin, *Mélanges liturgiques*, p. 211.

Conclusion to Part I

The four chapters that comprise Part I of this book
represent an attempt to trace the theological and liturgical evolution that led to a devotional cult of the eucharist
outside Mass. That evolution is best described, in my
opinion, through four distinct stages of development:
from holy meal to sacred food (Chapter One); from
communal symbol to ritual drama (Chapter Two); from
controversy among theologians to the people's linguistic
estrangement from the Mass (Chapter Three); and finally, from academic debates about eucharistic change
and presence to the popular desire to see the host
(Chapter Four). Before commenting on the Second Vatican Council's reforms of "Holy Communion and Worship of the Eucharist Outside Mass," it may be profitable to summarize the results of our theological and liturgical investigation.

1) The first stage of development reveals that at an early
period of history, perhaps well within New Testament
times, the celebration of the Lord's Supper achieved
ritual independence from its original context in a community meal. The meal became superfluous, with the
result that attention shifted toward the sacred food. Two
other forms of disengagement also appear within the
first centuries of Christian history: the gradual loosening
of the connection between Lord's Day and Lord's Supper through the celebration of the eucharist on days
other than Sunday; and the separation of holy communion from the public liturgy through customs like communion at home on weekdays and communion for the
ill and dying.

2) During the second stage of development, the com-

munal symbols of eating and drinking the eucharist begin to be given an allegorical interpretation. Perceived as a sacred drama, the eucharist is interpreted as the unfolding "in mystery" of Jesus' life, passion, and resurrection. Interpretations of this sort already appear during the fourth century in the writings of bishops like Theodore of Mopsuestia. An important shift in liturgical sensibility is the result: the holy table becomes an allegorical figure of Jesus' tomb; the bringing of gifts to the altar becomes a funeral procession in which deacons solemnly bear the Lord's body for mystical burial; the action of sacrifice (praise and thanksgiving, eating and drinking) becomes a dramatic rehearsal of historical events from the past (Jesus' death, resurrection). In this process, symbols are perceived as historical allegories (commemorations); actions are regarded as objects; and liturgical verbs become nouns (things to be contemplated).

3) During the Carolingian epoch the allegorization of liturgical rites achieves special prominence in the work of commentators like Amalarius of Metz. At the same time serious theological controversy about the nature and meaning of Christ's presence in the eucharist emerges in the debate between Paschasius Radbertus and Ratramnus. More important, however, is the deepening estrangement between the people and the eucharistic liturgy. The signals of this estrangement are several: the gradual withdrawal of the cup from the laity begins to appear in the ninth century; the rise of vernacular languages and literatures separates the people linguistically from the sacred speech (Latin) controlled by hieratic specialists (priests); private sacerdotal prayers of devotion arise within the liturgical rites; the first signs of *cultic* attention to the eucharistic species outside Mass emerge.

4) By the late eleventh century, finally, the signs of a cult of the eucharist outside Mass have definitely appeared: in Lanfranc's description of a Palm Sunday procession

197

with the Blessed Sacrament, for example. Theological debate, such as the controversy between Lanfranc and Berengarius over the question of Christ's real presence in the eucharist, doubtless played some role in the evolution of this cult. So did sociopolitical and economic factors in medieval Europe, as we have seen in our discussion of the origins of Corpus Christi. But it is clear that the evolution of the liturgy itself provides the originating source for the popular eucharistic customs that emerge in the eleventh through the fourteenth centuries. Visits to the Blessed Sacrament, processions, exposition, and Benediction can all be traced back to liturgical roots.

The cult of the eucharist outside Mass developed, therefore, not as an attempt to replace or devalue participation in the liturgy, but as a way to encourage it. Urban IV's bull *Transiturus*, which officially approved the festival of Corpus Christi in 1264, was a summons to increased participation in both Mass and the liturgy of the hours. Despite abuses and superstitions that sometimes accompanied the development of eucharistic devotions, their original intention seems clear: to invite people to fuller participation in the liturgical life of the Christian assembly.

The Reforms
of Eucharistic Worship Outside Mass

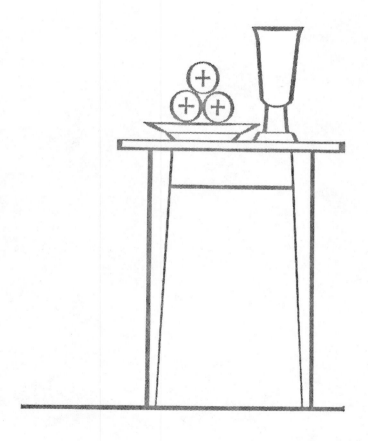

Introduction

When the Decree, "Holy Communion and Worship of the Eucharist Outside Mass," appeared on 21 June 1973, it marked the appearance of something rather innovative in the area of liturgical legislation. Never before had there been an attempt to gather, in a single systematic piece of legislation, all the relevant texts, rites, and rubrics pertaining to holy communion outside Mass, communion of the sick and viaticum administered by an extraordinary minister, and forms of eucharistic worship such as exposition, Benediction, processions, and congresses. Until recently, too, there was considerable debate about whether customs like Benediction of the Blessed Sacrament were to be considered "liturgy." At its origins, as we have seen in Chapter Four, Benediction was not an independent rite, but a solemn conclusion or dismissal attached to another liturgical service: an hour of the Divine Office or the procession on the feast of Corpus Christi. This original situation was still reflected in the Roman Ritual of 1614 (the so-called Tridentine ritual), where Benediction is never referred to as an independent liturgy, but is described only in connection with the procession on Corpus Christi and with the rite of communion for the sick.[1] This suggests that the notion of Benediction as an independent service, a liturgy in its own right, was rather late in developing. And indeed, not until 1958 did a decree of the Sacred Congregation of Rites explicitly affirm that Benediction is a "true liturgical function."[2]

During the period between the Council of Trent and our own day, therefore, there was discussion and sometimes disagreement about which aspects of eucharistic devotion were genuinely liturgical. The discussion was complicated by two further factors.

1) The *Roman Ritual* of 1614, referred to in the preceding paragraph, was strongly "recommended" to all dioceses, but was not absolutely mandatory. This meant that even after the Council of Trent local diocesan usage continued to vary (sometimes considerably) from place to place, as it had, indeed, throughout the middle ages.

2) Secondly, the period after Trent witnessed the rise of numerous devotions, eucharistic confraternities, religious communities devoted to perpetual adoration, and popular customs like the Forty Hours Devotion. Some of these practices, such as the ceremonies for Forty Hours, eventually made their way into the later editions of the Roman Ritual; but again, there remained a great deal of local variation—and it was not always clear what belonged to public worship and what belonged to the area of popular but nonliturgical devotion. A few words about both these factors will set the stage for examining the recently reformed rites of holy communion and worship of the eucharist outside Mass.

The Roman Ritual of 1614: The remote ancestor of the liturgical book we ordinarily call a "ritual" is the *libellus ordinis* (*libellus officialis*), a small manual of directions and rubrics for carrying out services that may have existed as early as the seventh century. These took various forms, sometimes in conjunction with other volumes like the sacramentary, which ordinarily provided only the presidential prayers of the liturgy and gave few, if any, rubrics. These *libelli* were intended primarily for priests serving in parishes. By the eleventh and twelfth centuries, the *Manuale* or *liber manualis* (handbook) appeared. Like the *libellus ordinis*, the *Manuale* was designed to assist parish priests in the performance of liturgical rites; it was thus also known as the *sacerdotale* (priest's book), the *pastorale* (pastoral book), or the *alphabeta sacerdotis* (priest's basic book). Sometimes these handbooks contained not only information about the proper administration of sacraments, but a handy compendium of canon law as well.[3]

Some of the priests' manuals that developed during the medieval period included material in the vernacular. An example is the Englishman John Myrc's "Instructions for Parish Priests," a vernacular translation of a Latin work (*Pars Oculi*) that appeared about 1450. Myrc's "Instructions" provide, in English verse, a treatise on pastoral theology; they also contain information about hearing confessions, classifying sins, baptizing Christians, and catechizing people in fundamental elements of faith. Myrc's book was, in effect, a species of vernacular *rituale*. The existence of such books indicates that prior to the Council of Trent the vernacular was used not only in preaching and catechizing but in certain parts of the liturgy itself: e.g., in the exchange of vows at a wedding, in the liturgy of penance (the penitent's confession, the confessor's advice), and in the questions and answers of godparents at baptism.[4]

Like the late medieval missals, breviaries and antiphonals, the priest's "ritual" thus existed in a variety of forms. The reformation of the major liturgical books mandated by the Council of Trent bore fruit in 1568 (the breviary) and 1570 (the missal), but it was not until 1614 that Pope Paul V ordered the publication of the *Rituale Romanum*.[5] In the apostolic constitution that accompanied the ritual, the pope alluded to the "great multitude of rituals" that were already in existence, but urged all "patriarchs, archbishops, bishops, vicars, abbots and parish priests" to use the new ritual in the administration of the sacraments.[6] Despite the papal exhortation, however, local diocesan rituals continued to be published and used. At the same time, the *Rituale Romanum* was regularly revised and updated. In 1752 an enlarged edition of it appeared; in 1884 Pope Leo XIII ordered an *editio typica*; and in 1925 a revised edition was published. Further changes were made in the

203

Rituale during the pontificates of Pius XII (1952) and John XXIII (1960).

Frequent changes and additions are, of course, predictable in a book intended primarily for use in the pastoral celebration of the liturgy. And in a sense, the *rituale* was never a completely comprehensive book that included all the material a parish priest might need for presiding at sacraments or at nonsacramental liturgies. A case in point is Benediction of the Blessed Sacrament. By the sixteenth and seventeenth centuries Benediction has certainly achieved a quasi-independent existence, though it was still frequently used as a solemn conclusion to other services. But the *Rituale Romanum* of 1614 provided no independent form for it; as we have noted, Benediction was mentioned only in connection with the procession on Corpus Christi and with the rite of communion for the sick. Factually, it was the form associated with the Corpus Christi procession that shaped the development of Benediction. Its characteristic features, as outlined in the 1614 Ritual, included:

exposition of the sacrament on the altar;
incensation of the sacrament;
the verses *Tantum ergo* and *Genitori* from the hymn *Pange Lingua*;
the verse *Panem de caelo*, with the response *Omne delectamentum*;
the collect *Deus, qui nobis sub sacramento mirabili*;
the blessing of the people in the form of a cross, in silence;
reposition of the sacrament.[7]

During the seventeenth and eighteenth centuries, this basic format for Benediction (with the addition of further prayers, litanies, and hymns such as *O Salutaris*) began appearing not in official books like the *Rituale*, but in prayerbooks and manuals of popular Christian devotion.[8] These developments will be examined in greater detail in Chapter Seven; for the moment I merely want to emphasize that much of what became the "liturgy" of Benediction reflected popular but unofficial custom. Official documents, in contrast, remained quite conservative on matters like eucharistic exposition, Benediction and processions. The authoritative regulation of such practices generally took the form of restriction and limitation, rather than positive encouragement. Thus, for instance, the Sacred Congregation of Rites (established in 1588) insisted that exposition of the sacrament be severely limited. Through a decree of 31 May 1642, the Congregation distinguished sharply between public and private exposition, insisting that the former required a grave reason and episcopal approval:

"The ancient decrees on this matter are to be observed, namely: Religious orders are not permitted to expose the sacrament of the most holy eucharist for public adoration in their own churches, unless there is a public reason approved by the ordinary. For a private cause, however, [exposition] is permitted as long as the sacrament is not taken from the tabernacle, and as long as it remains covered so that the sacred host may not be seen."[9]

That the reason for exposition had to be both serious and public was reiterated by the Congregation in a decree of 13 February 1666; replying to a question from the archbishop of Ragusa it commented:

"Exposition of the Blessed Sacrament in churches of religious orders . . . should be done and regulated by the judgment of the archbishop, in order to avoid the absurdities and scandals which may arise through frequent exposition. The archbishop should determine the reasons that justify exposition, the appropriate place and hours, as well as the security and decency of the sacrament."[10]

Further decrees of the Congregation of Rites forbade things like exposition in the ciborium and the placing of relics and statues on the altar of exposition. Restrictions were also made about the celebration of Mass at an altar on which the Blessed Sacrament was exposed. Indeed, the *Caeremoniale Episcoporum* (1600) expressed some regret that this situation should arise at all: "It would be far more desirable if, on the altar where the blessed sacrament is, Masses were not celebrated—a custom we see having been observed in antiquity."[11]

These examples indicate that at the level of official pronouncement, in documents like the *Rituale Romanum* of 1614 and the decrees of the Congregation of Rites, the attitude toward eucharistic devotions and cult of the sacrament outside Mass has generally been cautious, not to say prohibitive. This may help explain why the church's leadership was reluctant to provide official rites for customs like exposition or (until recent times) to speak of Benediction as a Christian "liturgy." Officially, the church has always insisted that the norm of eucharistic devotion in the life of Christians is participation in Mass. This insistence became even firmer after the Council of Trent, and is vigorously reflected in the quotations cited above.

The Spread of Devotions
Despite official caution about the cult of the eucharist outside Mass, the period after Trent was marked by a multiplication of devotional customs. This was prompted, in part, by the rise of eucharistic confraternities and by communities of religious dedicated to adoration of the Blessed Sacrament. The eucharistic confraternities, which were confederated into a kind of "archconfraternity" by Pope Paul III in 1539, actually traced their roots back to the thirteenth century. Groups like the Gray Penitents of Avignon began appearing in the first half of the thirteenth century; their purpose was to do reparation for the alleged outrages committed against the eucharist by religious dissidents such as the *Cathari* and the Albigensians. By the end of that century, similar groups had sprung up in Belgium, Holland, and

Italy. These were not religious orders or communities in the technical sense; they were rather like pious associations of lay people who accompanied the Blessed Sacrament whenever it was carried to the sick or borne in a procession.[12]

By the early fourteenth century, however, congregations of religious dedicated to the Blessed Sacrament did appear. In 1328, for instance, the Cistercian Andre di Paolo established the "white monks" or brothers of the Blessed Sacrament in order to honor all aspects of Christ's eucharistic presence. (These monks eventually merged with the Olivetan Benedictines in 1582).[13] By the seventeenth century, numerous attempts were being made to found religious congregations that would engage in perpetual adoration of the eucharist. Bishop Sebastian Zamet (+ 1655) and the more famous Angelique Arnauld (+ 1661) organized such a congregation, and though it flourished for about five years (1633–1638), it seems not to have lasted. In 1639, two other French Christians attempted similar foundations: Jeanne Chezard de Matel (+ 1670) opened the first house of a group known as the Order of the Incarnate Word and of the Blessed Sacrament; at Marseilles a former Dominican, Antoine le Quien (1601–1676) established a house of religious women vowed to perpetual adoration. A short time later (1652), Catherine de Bar (+ 1698) started a community of Benedictines of the Blessed Sacrament at Paris.

Significantly, perhaps, many of these seventeenth-century efforts to found religious communities devoted to the eucharist began in France at about the time the Jansenist controversy was brewing. Angelique Arnauld, abbess of the Benedictine community of Port-Royal, was an older sister of Antoine Arnauld, whose book *On Frequent Communion* set off a great controversy when it appeared in 1643. Antoine had emphasized the necessity of thorough preparation before receiving the eucharist and the dispositions required if one were to communicate frequently. Although he had not intended to discourage frequent communion, the rigor of his proposals for preparation was seen by his Jesuit opponents as unduly harsh and unmanageable for ordinary Christians. In 1653, Pope Innocent X formally condemned certain propositions associated with Jansenist theology; three years later (1656) Arnauld himself was censured by the Sorbonne and solemnly degraded.[14]

It is well known that Angelique Arnauld was strongly attracted to the Jansenist ideas propagated by her brother; in fact, Antoine had lived at Port-Royal after his ordination to the priesthood in 1641. There can be little doubt that the two shared common attitudes toward the eucharist: intense reverence, combined with insistence on a thorough, morally rigorous preparation for holy communion. Angelique Arnauld's interest in forming a community of religious dedicated to perpetual adoration fits this attitudinal pattern, for a prime purpose of the "perpetual adoration movement" was to do reparation for the laxity, sacrilege, and abuses committed against the sacrament.

In light of the Jansenist crisis in seventeenth-century theology—and in view of Jansenist interest in issues like reverence for the eucharist and frequency of communion—the cautious attitude of church officials toward adoration, exposition and Benediction makes more sense. It will be remembered that most of the examples of official reaction to eucharistic devotions cited earlier in this introduction appeared in the seventeenth century and were often directed toward churches run by religious communities. Quite plausibly, there is a connection between official caution and unofficial fear that some forms of eucharistic piety and devotion might be tainted by Jansenist principles. For the Jansenist controversy did not die when the Arnaulds did. The movement spread to many different parts of Europe, including Italy and the Austro-Hungarian empire; and as it spread Jansenism developed into several distinct branches that parted significantly from the opinions of the early Jansenist Fathers like Arnauld and Saint Cyran. The Jansenism at work in the thinking of Scipio de Ricci and the Synod of Pistoia in 1786, for example, took positions on liturgical matters that were not of immediate concern to Arnauld in his book *On Frequent Communion*. Pistoia insisted on simplicity and a return to "ancient Christian custom" in public worship, and thus legislated against more than one altar in church, against the custom of communicating the people with hosts consecrated at another Mass, and against what the synod considered superstitious abuses connected with popular eucharistic piety. Pistoian Jansenism attempted to reassert the centrality of the eucharistic liturgy, and was therefore hostile to forms of popular cult that seemed to distract people from full participation in Mass.

Like the seventeenth-century French Jansenism of Antoine and Angelique Arnauld, the eighteenth-century Jansenism of Scipio de Ricci received papal condemnation. Pope PiusVI's bull *Auctorem Fidei* (28 August 1794) repudiated the decisions reached at Pistoia, as well as the theological assumptions on which they were based. One can see that Jansenism, in its various historical forms, worked both for and against the cult of the eucharist outside Mass. One can see, too, that like the origins of elevation in the twelfth century and of the feast of Corpus Christi in the thirteenth, eucharistic devotion continued to be touched by political and ecclesiastical controversy. The reluctance of church leaders to approve customs like exposition, except under extraordinary circumstances, may have been motivated as much by political considerations (Jansenism) as by theological ones (emphasis on the Mass as central). For when it was combined with religio-political ideas like Josephinism or Gallicanism, which emphasized the power of prince and bishops against encroachment by the pope, Jansenism became a powerful threat against the very notion of papal leadership.

209

The historical period after Trent can thus be characterized as simultaneously a time of popular development and official caution in the matter of eucharistic worship outside Mass. Popular movements toward public exposition and perpetual adoration were countered by official admonitions against "absurdities and scandals"; the growing popularity of devotions like Benediction were met with extreme reticence in official books like the *Rituale Romanum*. Not until the twentieth century did the church's highest leadership attempt to systematize the ensemble of eucharistic devotions and customs into a pattern of explicitly *liturgical* forms for worship of the eucharist outside Mass.

THE SECOND VATICAN COUNCIL

The *Constitution on the Sacred Liturgy* (1963) had already raised the issue of popular devotions and their relation to liturgical worship. In section 13 of the Constitution, the following comments were made: "Popular devotions of the Christian people are to be highly commended. . . . But these devotions should be so drawn up that they harmonize with the liturgical seasons, accord with the sacred liturgy, are in some fashion derived from it, and lead the people to it. . . ."[15] Although the popular devotions referred to by the Constitution obviously include other customs besides eucharistic ones, the Consilium charged with the implementation of liturgical reforms moved rather quickly after the close of the Council to issue an instruction on eucharistic worship (25 May 1967). This instruction not only outlined basic principles of eucharistic theology, viewed from a liturgical perspective; it also included a section entitled "The Worship of the Eucharist as a Permanent Sacrament."[16] Devotions, processions, exposition and Benediction are described, and norms for their celebration given. Since these norms provided the framework for the rites published in 1973, it will be useful here to summarize them according to topical headings.

Eucharistic devotions: The *Instruction on Eucharistic Worship* repeats the Council's statement from the *Constitution on the Liturgy*: popular devotions must 1) be derived from the liturgy in some way, 2) harmonize with the liturgy, 3) lead people back to the liturgy "which of its nature is far superior to these devotions."[17] By repeating the Council's position on devotions, the Instruction implicitly recognizes two important points: first, that not all eucharistic customs are liturgical ones; and secondly, that active participation in "the eucharistic sacrifice" remains the ultimate norm and criterion against which all other customs, devotional or liturgical, are to be assessed. Significantly, the General Instruction that accompanies the 1973 rites for holy communion and worship of the eucharist outside of Mass, begins with a brief theological and liturgical discussion of the relation between Mass and the eucharist as a permanent sacrament.[18]

Processions: The Instruction of 1967 appeals to the Corpus Christi procession as the implicit model for this form of public eucharistic devotion. But the document recognizes that today such expressions of piety may not be opportune always and everywhere; hence the local bishop is given discretionary authority to decide if, when, and how such processions are to be held in his diocese.

Exposition: We have already seen that, in the seventeenth century particularly, the Congregation of Rites was very cautious about granting permission for frequent or prolonged exposition. The Instruction carefully notes that exposition "should be seen, by signs, in its relation to the Mass" and insists that the sacrament was instituted "above all with the purpose of nourishing, healing and sustaining us."[19] To that end, basic norms for exposing the eucharist, briefly or for longer periods, are outlined:

1) Celebration of Mass in the area of the church where

211

exposition is being held is forbidden. If Mass is to be celebrated in the same area of the church, the exposition should be interrupted.

2) Either a monstrance or a ciborium may be used for exposition.

3) If the exposition is for a brief period of time only, the eucharist is placed on the altar table; if exposition is prolonged a "throne" may be used.

4) The period of exposition may be accompanied by scripture readings, homily, song, moments for silent reflection, and brief exhortations. Exposition concludes with Benediction.

5) A solemn annual exposition for a more protracted period may be held "if it is seen that there will be a reasonable number of the faithful," and if the local ordinary gives his consent.[20] The period of exposition need not be continuous (as it was, e.g., in the well-known Forty Hours Devotion).

6) For a grave general need, local ordinaries may order a prolonged exposition of the Blessed Sacrament "in those churches where there are large numbers of the faithful."[21]

7) The practice of exposing the sacrament merely for the sake of Benediction after Mass is forbidden.

The liturgical principles underlying these several norms are quite clear: first, the eucharist was instituted primarily for nourishment, healing, and sustenance; exposition is always subordinate to eating and drinking at the liturgy; and secondly, the presence of the people at prayer is a fundamental criterion for determining the appropriateness and the duration of exposition. It is clear, too, that the Instruction understands eucharistic devotions as a prolongation of the liturgical action, and not as cult objects to be paraded indiscriminately before the public's gaze.

Many modes of presence: Perhaps the most evocative section of the Instruction of 1967 is devoted to the many modes of Christ's presence in the celebrating assembly. Following the lead of the *Constitution on the Liturgy* (section 7), the 1967 Instruction significantly enlarges our understanding of the term "real presence." The Lord is present, first, in the assembly that gathers in his name; He is present too in the Word proclaimed and preached, in the person who presides at eucharist, in the sacramental elements. All these presences are *real*, and thus the "presence of Christ under the species 'is called real not in an exclusive sense, as if the other kinds of presence were not real, but par excellence.'"[22]

The importance of this theological point about the many modes of Christ's real presence should not be neglected, because it establishes the fundamental framework for understanding the worship of the eucharist outside Mass. Liturgical devotion to the Lord present in the reserved sacrament makes sense only if one recognizes that this presence is situated within a much larger context: assembly, Word, minister(s), liturgy. This is unquestionably the reason why the Instruction insists that such things as eucharistic exposition "should be seen, by signs, in its relation to the Mass," and should involve the presence of the people at prayer.

As we shall see in the chapters that follow, the principles laid down in the 1967 Instruction provided the pastoral and theological framework for the 1973 document "Holy Communion and Worship of the Eucharist Outside Mass." We turn now to commentary on the principal parts of this latter document: holy communion outside of Mass (Chapter Five); administration of communion and viaticum by an extraordinary minister (Chapter Six); and forms of eucharistic worship (Chapter Seven). Part II will conclude with a discussion of the relation between popular devotions and official worship (Chapter Eight).

NOTES

1. See *Rituale Romanum Pauli V Pontificis Maximi iussu editum* (Rome, 1615), pp. 66 (communion of the sick), 219-220 (Corpus Christi). The "benediction" that concludes the rite of communion of the sick is a nonsolemn form: after returning to church from the house of the sick person, the minister is directed to bless the people with the sacrament contained in the pyx and covered with a veil.

2. See the decree of the Sacred Congregation of Rites "De Musica Sacra et Sacra Liturgia ad Mentem Litterarum Encyclicarum Pii Papae XII" (3 September, 1958), AAS 50 (1958), 630-663. In no. 47 of this decree, the phrase "vera actio liturgica" is used in reference to Benediction (p. 646).

3. For further details about the historical evolution of the *Rituale*, see Lancelot Sheppard, *The Liturgical Books* (Twentieth Century Encyclopedia of Catholicism, 109; New York: Hawthorn Books, 1962), pp. 81-84.

4. See Edward Peacock, ed., *John Myrc's Instructions for Parish Priests* (Early English Text Society, 31; London: Truebner and Co., 1868), pp. iii-vi.

5. The Roman Pontifical was revised and published after the Council of Trent by order of Pope Clement VIII in 1596.

6. For the text of the apostolic constitution of Paul V, see *Rituale Romanum* (1614), unnumbered pages at the beginning of the book. The constitution was regularly reprinted in subsequent editions of the *Rituale*.

7. See *Rituale Romanum* (1614), pp. 219-220.

8. See Herbert Thurston, "Our English Benediction Service," *The Month* 106 (1905), 396-402.

9. Cited in Lambert Beauduin, *Mélanges liturgiques* (Louvain: Abbaye du Mont César, Centre liturgique, 1954), p. 216.

10. Ibid., p. 217.

11. Ibid., p. 218.

12. See Emile Bertaud, "Dévotion eucharistique," *Dictionnaire de Spiritualité*, IV/2, col. 1632.

13. Ibid.

214

14. See F. Ellen Weaver, *The Evolution of the Reform of Port-Royal* (Paris: Beauchesne, 1978), pp. 72-76.

15. *Constitution on the Liturgy*, 13; text translated in James J. Megivern, ed., *Worship and Liturgy* (Official Catholic Teachings; Wilmington, N.C.: McGrath Publishing Company, 1978), p. 202.

16. See "Instruction on Eucharistic Worship" (IEW), in Megivern, *Worship and Liturgy*, pp. 335-342.

17. IEW, 51; Megivern, *Worship and Liturgy*, p. 336.

18. See "Holy Communion and Worship of the Eucharist Outside Mass," in *The Rites* (2 vols.; New York: Pueblo Publishing Company, 1976-1980), I, pp. 455-456. Hereafter references to this document will be cited: HCWE, I (the volume of the Pueblo edition), followed by the appropriate page reference.

19. IEW, 60; Megivern, *Worship and Liturgy*, p. 339.

20. IEW, 63; Megivern, *Worship and Liturgy*, pp. 340-341.

21. IEW, 64; Megivern, *Worship and Liturgy*, p. 341.

22. IEW, 9; Megivern, *Worship and Liturgy*, pp. 315-316.

Chapter Five

Holy Communion Outside Mass

INTRODUCTION

The evidence for Christians receiving the eucharist *outside* the celebration of Mass is ancient. As we have seen in Chapter One, the occasional disengagement of the eucharistic species from their liturgical context happened at a rather early period of the church's history. Sometimes this disengagement took the form of carrying the sacrament to those who were absent from the Sunday liturgy (Justin Martyr, ca. 150); sometimes the eucharistic bread was taken home for a domestic communion on weekdays (*Apostolic Tradition*, ca. 215). There is early evidence, too, for taking the eucharist to those explicitly identified as ill or dying. Eusebius of Caesarea (ca. 260–340), often called the Father of Church History, records the story of Serapion, a third-century Christian from Alexandria who had lapsed from the faith under pressure of persecution.[1] When he lay dying, Serapion called for his grandson, asking him to summon a priest. Since the priest was ill and unable to come, he gave the young boy a portion of the eucharist, instructing him to soak it and let the drops fall into the old man's mouth. The boy did as instructed, and Serapion, having received viaticum, yielded his spirit to the Lord.[2] The story suggests that by the third century the custom of giving communion to the dying (in this case, as a sign of reconciliation for a lapsed Christian) was familiar.

The origins of communion outside Mass thus reflect two different types of pastoral situation. The first type might be described as *domestic*: it involves a regular pattern of communion, often in the private setting of a home, by Christians who do not face any special emergency (such as grave illness or danger of death). The second type has sometimes been called *clinical*: it reflects an extraordinary situation of illness or danger where the eucharist is regarded as viaticum (food for the final journey of the Christian in death).[3] It should be noted, too, that in the church's early history communion outside Mass did not necessarily require the ministry of ordained persons. Although Justin Martyr mentions deacons and the old man Serapion (in Eusebius's story) requests a priest, it is clear that the eucharist was often administered, in both domestic and clinical situations, by lay persons.[4]

In this chapter we will focus our attention on those rites for communion outside Mass which do not involve ministry to the ill or dying. The 1973 Roman document on holy communion and worship of the eucharist outside Mass provides two liturgical rites for this purpose:

1) A rite of communion joined with a fuller celebration of God's Word (*Ritus cum ampliore Verbi Dei celebratione*), which includes provision for one or two biblical readings taken from the lectionary for the day, from texts assigned to votive Masses of the eucharist or the Precious Blood, or from readings proposed in the appendix to the ritual[5];

2) A shorter ritual created for use when there is not a sufficiently large community present for a full celebration of the liturgy of the word (e.g., when only one or two people are to be communicated). In this second format the minister is directed simply to read a brief passage about "the bread of life" after the introductory rites and before the distribution of communion.[6]

In providing these two liturgies for communion outside Mass, the Congregation for Divine Worship was venturing into somewhat innovative territory. For although the custom of Christians receiving the eucharist outside Mass is ancient, antiquity provides little evidence of official rites designed for this purpose. Not even the *Rituale Romanum* of 1614 devoted much attention to the procedures for communicating people outside Mass; its rites, as we shall see, was extremely terse and independent of any liturgy of the word.

This chapter will explore some of the historical, theological, and pastoral influences that appear to have shaped the new rites of communion outside Mass. Beginning with four historical models derived from the earlier centuries of Christian life, we will turn to the Ritual of 1614, then on to a more detailed examination of the rites published in 1973. A discussion of the theological and pastoral significance of the rites for communion outside Mass will conclude the chapter.

FOUR HISTORICAL MODELS

A Domestic Communion Ritual (Apostolic Tradition, 215)
In the introduction to Chapter One the text of Hippolytus's *Apostolic Tradition* was quoted as an example of a "domestic communion ritual." It was noted, too, that the Christian custom of carrying the eucharist home from the Sunday liturgy appears to have been widespread, at least until the fourth century when influential leaders like St. Jerome began complaining of abuses. Despite these patristic complaints, however, the custom of taking communion home and receiving it there on weekdays seems to have continued in some places until as late as the seventh or eighth centuries.[7]

How was this domestic communion ritual performed? According to the *Apostolic Tradition*, the rite was extremely simple: The sacrament in the form of bread is carried home without, apparently, any special ceremonial signs of reverence or adoration. It is reserved in a safe place where mice cannot reach it and where it will not be lost. It is to be received by Christians only, before the ordinary food of a meal is consumed. When the eucharistic bread is eaten, the communicant also blesses a cup of wine, which is received as "the antitype of the blood of Christ."[8]

Significantly, the *Apostolic Tradition* refers to this

eucharist received in a domestic ritual as "the body of Christ . . . not to be despised."[9] The one who eats it in faith is promised protection from harm: "even if some deadly thing is given him, after that it shall not overpower him."[10] And the communicant is similarly warned to be reverent with the cup "blessed in the name of God," because if it is treated carelessly "you will be guilty of the blood, as one who despises the price with which he has been bought."[11]

Several points about this simple rite are noteworthy. First, it takes place in the home, apart from the liturgical assembly. It is, secondly, unattached to any other religious ritual. Thirdly, there is no ordained minister involved—not even, apparently, for the blessing of the cup. Finally, the specialized vocabulary of Christian eucharist is applied to both bread and cup (body of Christ, blood of Christ), and the effects of the sacrament are specified (communion with the Lord, protection from harm). The author of this text was clearly convinced that what Christians received in their homes on weekdays was the same thing they received in the liturgical assembly on Sunday. Clearly, too, the author was not embarrassed by what liturgists of a later era might consider a conflict between "private devotion" and "public worship."

A Monastic Communion Ritual (The Rule of the Master, ca. 500-525)
One place where the custom of receiving communion outside Mass on weekdays appears to have survived, even after Jerome's assaults on it in the late fourth century, was in monasteries. The *Rule of the Master*, a monastic document written sometime during the first quarter of the sixth century in the vicinity of Rome, testifies to a daily communion ritual independent of Mass.[12] Chapters 21 and 22 of this rule provide a detailed picture of the practice. The communion liturgy is celebrated in the oratory immediately after the monks

219

have sung the hour of none (ca. 3 P.M.) and before they retire to the refectory for their daily meal.[13] After all the monks have exchanged the sign of peace, the abbot (a layman, according to RM) receives communion under both species.[14] Those who have been busy preparing the community's meal are then summoned; after entering the oratory, they pray briefly, exchange the sign of peace with the abbot, and receive the eucharist (both species).[15] Then the rest of the community communicates from the bread and cup, deanery by deanery.[16] Following communion, all the monks go directly to the refectory, where the meal begins with a rather elaborate ceremony of breaking bread and distributing individual cups of wine.[17]

Several significant features of this monastic communion ritual deserve comment. It will be noticed, first, that the rite is preceded by a liturgy of the word (the hour of none), which would have included psalmody, prayer and two readings from the Bible: a passage from the apostle, and another from the gospel.[18] Secondly, the rite takes place in the oratory, the ordinary "space" for the liturgical assembly of monks. Communion is distributed under both species (the cup probably having been consecrated "by contact"), with the abbot (a layman) presiding at the liturgical action. Thirdly, the communion rite flows directly into a ceremonial meal in the monastic refectory. The meal is worth describing because it resembles, in structure and theme, that form of religious supper popularly known as an "agape." A basket of bread is lowered with a pulley to the abbot's table "to give the impression that the provisions of God's workmen are coming down from heaven."[19] The abbot makes the sign of the cross over the bread, breaks it, takes a portion for himself, and raises it so that it "will be blessed by the Lord."[20] Bread is then distributed to the deans of the monastery, who take it around to the tables.[21] Then wine is given out in individual cups to the abbot and all members of the community. The meal it-

220

self follows, with a blessing said over each dish served; when all have eaten, water for washing the hands is brought around to each table, and the supper concludes with the serving of a warm beverage (probably mulled wine).[22]

The ritual pattern of this meal and the language used to describe it have obviously been influenced by the eucharistic liturgy. The abbot, for example, is directed to bless, break, lift, and distribute the bread, while each "course" of the meal is accompanied by formulas of thanksgiving and blessing.[23] Taken together, the ensemble of rites outlined in RM 21–23 constitutes a rather impressive liturgy: celebration of the word (the hour of none); eucharistic communion under both species; a ceremonial meal resembling an agape. Nowhere is the presence of an ordained minister required for daily communion; and on Sundays the Master's monks appear to have celebrated with the local parish community.[24]

The Liturgy of the Presanctified Gifts
In the two communion rituals just described it is obvious that the bread was taken to a private home or a monastic house from the parish's celebration on Sunday. The cup, in all probability, was consecrated "by contact" with the bread.[25] Both these rituals—domestic and monastic—were, in effect, liturgies of the presanctified gifts, i.e., rites which made use of eucharist consecrated on some earlier occasion. In the West, however, the term "liturgy of the presanctified" is used in a technical sense to mean a shortened form of Mass in which there is no eucharistic prayer and thus no consecration of bread and wine. More specifically, the Mass of the presanctified referred to the liturgy on one day of the church year: Good Firday.

Ordinarily it is assumed that the liturgy of the presanctified originated in the East and subsequently influenced the West. This may have been the case, but in fact

221

our first clear testimonies to the custom, in both East and West, come from the same period: the seventh century. In the *Chronicon Paschale* written at Constantinople during the reign of Patriarch Sergius (610–638), there is unambiguous evidence for a liturgy of the presanctified on days both within and outside the season of Lent.[26] Toward the end of the seventh century the council in Trullo (692) indicates that this form of liturgy was celebrated on virtually all days in Lent except for Saturdays, Sundays, and the feast of the Annunciation.[27] And by the ninth century, a horologion of the monastery of St. Sabas provides formularies for a daily communion ritual with presanctified gifts.[28]

In the West, the first evidence for a liturgy of the presanctified gifts also appears in the seventh century. In the ancient Gelasian Sacramentary (*Sacramentarium Gelasianum Vetus*), the brief rubrics for Holy Thursday and Good Friday indicate that such a liturgy is known.[29] The ministers are instructed to reserve a portion of "the sacrifice" after the Chrism Mass of Thursday "so that they may communicate" the next day.[30] On Good Friday, after the solemn prayers of the faithful have been completed, the deacons are instructed to enter the sacristy, in order to take "the body and blood of the Lord which remains from the previous day and place it upon the altar."[31] After the Lord's Prayer has been said and the cross adored, they communicate from the presanctified gifts.

In *Ordo Romanus* XXIII, a Latin document roughly contemporaneous with the ancient Gelasian Sacramentary, there is a rather curious but significant rubric: at the Good Friday liturgy celebrated by the pope there is no communion at all.[32] Those Roman Christians who wish to communicate on this day may, however, receive at one of the parish churches in the city.[33] Two different practices are clearly reflected in this document: one is associated with the papal liturgy (no communion), while the other is connected with liturgy in the parish churches of Rome (communion from the presanctified gifts). These two divergent customs seem to have existed side by side during the seventh and eighth centuries, and of the two, the papal custom certainly represents the more ancient and conservative one. Pope Innocent I (401–417), for example, wrote to Bishop Decentius of Gubbio that according to ancient apostolic custom the Roman Church fasts on the two days before Easter (Friday and Saturday), and for that reason does not celebrate the mysteries.[34]

The notion that celebrating the eucharist on Good Friday is inappropriate persisted stubbornly in the West for centuries. In the Romano-Germanic Pontifical (ca. 950), the Good Friday liturgy includes communion, but also alludes to the custom mentioned by Innocent I: "On Good Friday . . . Mass is not sung; nor is it celebrated on Holy Saturday until the vigil at night."[35] Nevertheless, the earlier medieval pontificals show that communion on this day was popular. The Pontifical of the Roman Curia (twelfth century) mentions that "all who wish" receive the sacrament in silence.[36] In the following century, however, the communion of the people on Good Friday seems to have faded. The Pontifical of the Roman Curia (thirteenth century) indicates that only the presiding prelate receives the eucharist.[37] A similar situation is revealed in the Pontifical of William Durandus, which became the model for later medieval pontificals in the West.[38] By the end of the thirteenth century, therefore, the Good Friday communion from the presanctified gifts appears to have been restricted to the presiding celebrant alone.

What was the ritual shape of this liturgy of the presanctified in the medieval West? According to the Romano-Germanic Pontifical, the rite for Good Friday was divided into two parts: a liturgy of the word, celebrated in the late morning and concluding with the solemn prayers; and a liturgy of adoration of the cross with communion, celebrated toward evening (ad ves-

223

peram). This latter liturgy included[39]: preparation of the cross in front of the altar (the cross is held by two acolytes); singing of the *Hagios ho Theos* (Holy God), the Reproaches, and the *Ecce lignum crucis* ("Behold the wood of the cross"); adoration of the cross by the bishop, clergy and people. After the cross has been returned to its proper place, two subdeacons and two presbyters proceed to the sacristy, where they gather up the eucharistic bread reserved from the liturgy of Holy Thursday. The bread, together with a cup of unconsecrated wine, is brought to the altar. The bishop then intones the introduction to the Lord's Prayer, which is sung (together with its embolism, "Deliver us, Lord"). After receiving from the bread, the bishop drops a small particle into the cup: "he sanctifies the unconsecrated wine through the consecrated bread."[40] All present then communicate from bread and cup in silence.

One will notice that in this liturgy, the communion ritual has been clearly separated from the liturgy of the word (celebrated earlier in the day), and has become attached to the liturgy of adoration of the cross. This is significant because the medieval rites for Good Friday manifest the same tendency we have observed earlier in the liturgical evolution of Palm Sunday: a ritual transference of cultic gestures from the cross to the Blessed Sacrament. Just as in Lanfranc's *Monastic Constitutions* (eleventh century) the Palm Sunday procession became, effectively, a procession with the Blessed Sacrament, so a similar phenomenon appears in connection with Good Friday. For example, *Ordo Romanus* XXIII (ca. 700–750) indicates that a relic of the true cross is solemnly carried in the procession from the Lateran basilica to the stational church (Holy Cross in Jerusalem) where the liturgy is to be celebrated. By the time of the Pontifical of the Roman Curia (twelfth century), however, it is a small box (*capsa*) containing the eucharistic species that is processionally transported from the Lateran to the

224

stational church. This same document also reveals that at the Good Friday communion rite (the liturgy of the presanctified) the elements reserved from Holy Thursday are solemnly incensed.[41] Similar provisions are found in the Pontifical of the Roman Curia (thirteenth century), where the *capsa* in which the sacrament is borne in the procession is described as *adornata* (decorated). In this latter document, too, the Good Friday liturgy of the presanctified has been expanded to include: 1) the "offertory" rite with its accompanying prayers (*Suscipe, sancta Trinitas, In spiritu humilitatis,* etc.); 2) an incensation of the presanctified gifts and the altar; and 3) the invitation *Orate, fratres* . . . (the rite then continues with "Let us pray," "Taught by our Savior's command . . .," "Our Father," mixing of the bread in a chalice of unconsecrated wine, and communion of the celebrant alone).[42]

In the West, therefore, the liturgy of the presanctified in the technical sense of the term gradually evolved from a parish custom of communion on Good Friday (*Ordo Romanus* XXIII) to a rather elaborate devotional rite connected with the solemn adoration of the cross. During the evolution of this liturgy, moreover, we see in the Pontifical of the Roman Curia (thirteenth century) a ritual transference of gestures of homage and adoration from cross alone (OR XXIII) to both cross and eucharistic elements. Further, the popular custom of receiving communion, connected with parish liturgy in OR XXIII, disappears; by the end of the thirteenth century the celebrant alone receives at the Good Friday Mass of the presanctified. Finally, this liturgy takes on the characteristics of a "simulated Mass" in which offertory prayers, incensations, *Orate, fratres,* Lord's prayer and embolism are included. What began as a form of communion for the people outside Mass on Good Friday became a solemn liturgy of adoration (cross, eucharistic species) in which the people were prohibited from receiving the sacrament.

225

Communion After Mass

In the West during the ninth century, under the pretext of practical necessity, the communion of the people was sometimes delayed until after the celebration of Mass.[43] As we have noted in Chapter Three, this practice seems first to have appeared in the *Ordo* of Abbot Angilbert of St. Riquier, which directs that on some great festivals like Christmas and Easter, some of the people may have to be communicated after the liturgy has ended. Quite clearly, Angilbert's *Ordo* did not intend to recommend this as a regular custom appropriate for all situations. Indeed, even on days when large crowds might make the communion of all at Mass difficult, the *Ordo* spells out directions for facilitating the rite "so that clergy and people may communicate at the same time and thus be able to hear the blessing and conclusion of the Mass."

But once the solution of delaying communion until after Mass was proposed, it proved attractive. Medieval *ordines* indicate that the custom became rather widespread, especially at popular communion seasons like Easter. The *Ordo ecclesiae Lateranensis* (twelfth century), for example, places the communion of the newly baptized at the end of Mass during the octaves of Easter and Pentecost.[44] In England during the thirteenth century, churches belonging to the Gilbertine order had the custom of distributing communion to the laity after Mass on Easter Day. Explicit instructions are provided for this in the *Ordinale Gilbertinum*:

"On Easter Day, if lay people are to receive communion, as many hosts as seem necessary to communicate the number who will gather are set aside for consecration . . . When Mass is over . . . the priest takes off his chasuble; he then pronounces absolution over the people, who prostrate and beat their breasts while saying the Lord's Prayer. He admonishes them not to over-eat or over-drink on that day after they have received the eucharist. Then, with great care, he communicates those who approach. Two [servers] hold a cloth between the priest and the communicants; one of them offers it to those who come up for communion, while the other [server] offers them a cup of wine mixed with water from which they drink."[45]

This text reveals not only that the laity are communicated after Mass, but that the ritual is prefaced by instruction about the dispositions required for receiving.[46] The ritual itself is simple: the priest says a formula of absolution (use of the *Confiteor* as a preparation prayer for communion was common in medieval Latin rites); the people say the Lord's Prayer; after receiving, the communicants receive an ablution of wine and water—a functional way to purify the mouth after reception, but possibly a ritual remnant of communion under both species as well. One will also notice the text's concern for proper reverence toward the sacrament: the cloth handed to the communicants serves to catch any particles that might fall when the eucharist is distributed.

The Gilbertine ordinal provides a brief rite for those occasions when communion is given immediately or very soon after Mass. Nothing is said about distributing communion at other periods unrelated to the time of the eucharistic celebration. And, indeed, not until after the Council of Trent does there appear an independent rite for communion outside Mass unrelated to the time of the liturgical action.

It should be noted that this "practical" solution of delaying communion of the laity until after Mass actually represents the final stage of an evolutionary process. Some brief attention to that process may be useful here.

a) As early as the sixth century there is clear evidence that growing numbers of western Christians attended Mass without receiving communion. Caesarius of Arles (470–542), for example, complained that many people leave church after the readings or after the preparation of the gifts because they do not intend to communicate.[47] For this reason, probably, councils began legislat-

227

ing that Christians must remain at the liturgy until they have received the priest's blessing.[48]

b) The priest's blessing referred to in such legislation was not, however, the final act of the dismissal rite, but rather a blessing of those who were not going to communicate given immediately after the Lord's Prayer or the sign of peace.[49] By the sixth century, then, it had become customary in some quarters to dismiss the noncommunicants prior to the people's communion. Gregory the Great (ca. 540–604) seems to have been familiar with this custom. In Book Two of his *Dialogues*, he quotes the deacon's cry before communion, "Whoever is not a communicant should depart!"[50] It may be that Gregory was thinking of persons who were under some ban of official excommunication, but it is not likely that these would have remained at Mass until the communion. More probably he was referring to noncommunicants.[51]

c) By the sixth and seventh centuries, therefore, the communion of the faithful at Mass had begun to appear as a kind of appendix still closely related to the eucharistic action but not absolutely essential. During the Carolingian era, reform-minded leaders resisted this impression by decreeing that all Christians should remain at Mass until the final dismissal (the *Ite, missa est*).[52] By this time, however, declining numbers of communicants at Mass had transformed the communion rite into an affair primarily for the celebrant. On those rare days when large numbers of people did communicate—at Christmas or Easter, for example—it seemed expedient not to "delay" the Mass, and so the custom of distributing the eucharist immediately afterwards developed. That is the situation reflected in ninth century sources like the *Ordo* of Abbot Angilbert and the twelfth-century Gilbertine Rite. Even so, no independent liturgical rite for communion outside Mass appeared until after the Council of Trent.

These four historical models thus reveal that while the practice of receiving communion apart from the liturgy developed early on in the church's history, it took much longer for a definite liturgical rite for communion *extra missam* to appear. The clearest example of such a rite emerges from a monastic document, the early sixth-century *Rule of the Master*; there, as we have seen, a ritual for daily communion after the hour of none and before the principal meal is spelled out in rather elaborate detail. We can sum up the evidence from these historical models with the following observations.

1) The oldest documented form of communion *extra missam* is the reception of eucharist in the home (the domestic ritual). This custom seems to have arisen by the second half of the second century and continued in popularity until at least the late fourth century (later, in some places).

2) The earliest evidence for an independent ritual of communion outside Mass appears in monastic sources like the *Rule of the Master*.

3) Apart from domestic rituals such as the one outlined in the *Apostolic Tradition* and monastic customs like the one contained in RM, the time for distributing communion apart from Mass seems to have been immediately after the liturgical celebration. This is the practice reflected, for example, in the *Ordo* of Abbot Angilbert and in the *Ordinale Gilbertinum*.

4) Again, apart from documents like RM, no official independent liturgical rite for distributing the eucharist outside Mass appears in the West until after the Council of Trent. The exception, of course, was for communion of the ill and dying; but that topic will be discussed in the following chapter.

By the sixteenth century the practice of giving people communion immediately after Mass had become sufficiently widespread as to create the need for some kind of ritual. There is evidence that local churches sometimes created their own rites for this purpose. Bernard Dreygerwolt, who was pastor of the Jakobikirche in Muenster from 1508 until 1523, noted in his parish records that communion immediately after Mass was customary on Christmas, Holy Thursday, and Pentecost.[53] The ritual used there resembles the description found in the *Ordinale Gilbertinum*: after Mass, the pastor removes his chasuble; the sequence from the liturgy for Pentecost (*Veni, sancte spiritus*) is then sung for the communicants; communion is distributed (Bernard provides the interesting statistic that about 80 to 100 persons regularly communicated); the Marian antiphon proper to the liturgical season is sung to conclude the rite.[54]

A similar format seems to have been used in other German churches as well during the early part of the sixteenth century.[55] Ordinarily, of course, this communion immediately after Mass involved the distribution of bread alone. But during the period of the Council of Trent, some countries petitioned and received permission for communion in both kinds—even when the eucharist was given *extra missam*. Josef Jungmann notes that after the Council, Germany, Bavaria, Austria, and Bohemia were granted permission to use the cup, under certain specified circumstances. By 1621, however, all such concessions had been withdrawn.[56] Otto Nussbaum cites similar evidence in connection with a synod at Vienna in 1564.[57] The synod had apparently received a rescript from Pope Pius IV, who allowed communion in both kinds to be given after Mass in Austrian territories on Christmas, Easter, and Pentecost, provided that all the ecclesiastical prescriptions for the liturgy had been carefully observed.[58]

By the time the Council of Trent concluded its deliberations in 1563, there were still no universally obligatory liturgical books in the Latin West. Within less than ten years, however, this situation changed: the reformed breviary appeared in 1568, and the Missal of Pius V was published in 1570. For obvious reasons, neither of these books provided a ritual for communion outside Mass; not until the seventeenth century did one appear.[59]

Theology
In the Ritual published by order of Pope Paul V in 1614 a rite for distributing communion outside Mass was included. The texts for this rite, as we shall see, were borrowed from other sources; chiefly, the rite of communion at Mass in the Missal of Pius V (1570), and material from the liturgy of Corpus Christi. There is no reference to a liturgy of the word, nor is there any rubric that restricts the use of the rite to the period immediately after Mass. Nevertheless, the 1614 Ritual seems to have regarded communion outside Mass as anomalous:

"The communion of the people ought to occur within Mass, immediately after the communion of the priest who is celebrating—unless, for a reasonable cause, it is sometimes to be postponed until after Mass. For the prayers said at Mass after communion refer not only to the priest, but also to the other communicants."[60]

This rubric is interesting because it reveals a reluctance to approve the custom of communicating outside Mass. The norm, unquestionably, is communion within the eucharistic celebration itself. The proof of this norm, the Ritual notes, is found in the postcommunion prayers of the liturgy, which consistently use the inclusive language of "we" and "us." The authors of the Ritual seem, therefore, to have resisted the medieval evolution that prompted reduction of the communion at Mass to a rite exclusively concerned with the priest-celebrant.

On this point, the Ritual of 1614 expresses the thinking contained in Trent's decree, "The doctrine of the Sacrifice of the Mass" (17 September 1562).[61] In Chapter 6 of this decree, the bishops had shown a clear preference for sacramental participation by the people at the eucharist: "This holy synod strongly desires that at each Mass, the faithful who are present should communicate not only spiritually but sacramentally through reception of the eucharist. Through this means, the fruits of this most holy sacrifice will reach them more richly. . . ."[62] Although the Council went on to defend the legitimacy of Masses in which the priest alone communicates, it clearly preferred full sacramental participation by all at the liturgy.

The Rite of 1614
The doctrine underlying the ritual for communion outside Mass was thus very precise: the theological norm remains participation by the whole assembly, priest and people, in communion during Mass. Communion *extra missam*, though permissible "for a reasonable cause," is non-normative and exceptional. Ritually, the format provided in the 1614 book is extremely sober; it includes: the confession (*Confiteor*), said by the servers in the name of the people; the absolution (*Misereatur vestri*) said by the priest; the formula of invitation (*Ecce Agnus Dei*) said by the priest as he holds the host up in view of the people; the response (*Domine, non sum dignus*); distribution of communion, with the formula *Corpus Domini nostri Jesu Christi*; the antiphon *O sacrum convivium*, said by the priest as he returns to the altar; the versicle and response (*Panem de caelo . . . /Omne delectamentum*), followed by "Lord hear my prayer"/"And let my cry come unto you"; invitation to prayer and concluding collect (*Deus, qui nobis sub sacramento mirabili . . . ;* in paschaltide, *Spiritum nobis, Domine, tuae caritatis infunde . . .);* final blessing of the people.

There are no surprises in this ritual; its sources are rather easily identified. The use of the "confession and absolution" (*Confiteor/Misereatur*) before communion was common in medieval eucharistic rites.[63] The invitation to communion (*Ecce Agnus Dei*), based on John 1.29,

232

and the response (*Domine, non sum dignus*), the centurion's prayer in Luke 7.6-7, were likewise traditional elements.[64] The formula for distributing communion (*Corpus Domini nostri Jesu Christi*) seems to have appeared by the eleventh or twelfth centuries, and had been incorporated into the Missal of Pius V (1570).[65] From the feast of Corpus Christi came the antiphon, versicle, and response, and the closing prayer said by the priest at the end of the ritual.[66] The alternative closing prayer (for the paschal season) had a long history in the ancient sacramentaries: following its debut in the Verona (Leonine) Sacramentary, it made its way into the Gelasian, and then, in revised form, into the Gregorian. The Ritual of 1614 used the Gregorian form of the prayer: "Lord, pour out the Spirit of your love upon us, so that those who are filled with these paschal sacraments may become one heart through your holiness. Through Christ our Lord. Amen."[67]

As one might expect, the Ritual of 1614 also gives rubrics governing the vesture of the priest who distributes communion, as well as norms for the preparation and behavior of the communicants.

Vesture: The priest (no other "extraordinary" minister is mentioned) is vested in surplice and stole of a color appropriate to the liturgy of the day.[68]

Altar: The rite takes place at the altar; the corporal is laid out on the *mensa* as at Mass, and candles are lighted. The Ritual assumes that the sacrament has been reserved in a tabernacle "appropriately covered with a canopy" and located either on the principal altar of the church or on another altar "where the veneration and cult of so great a sacrament may be fittingly carried out."[69]

Preparation of people: The Ritual indicates that the people should receive "frequently . . . especially on major solemnities." Their preparation includes "sacramental confession" and fasting from the previous midnight.[70]

Who may receive: "All the faithful," the Ritual comments, "are to be admitted to holy communion except those who, for a just reason, are prohibited."[71] Not surprisingly, the list of prohibited persons includes those involved in some kind of public scandal. People who have not yet reached an "understanding" or "taste" for the sacrament (e.g., the very young) are likewise excluded, as are the mentally ill—unless they should have a "lucid interval" and manifest "devotion."[72]

Easter Communion: The Ritual of 1614 includes a section dealing with the Fourth Lateran Council's decree (1215) that all Christians should receive the eucharist "at least once a year" during paschaltide. The parish priest is instructed to keep a list of his parishioners; those who, after being warned, fail to meet this obligation are to be denounced to the Ordinary.[73]

Summary

Two major points emerge from our discussion of the Ritual of 1614. First, the theological and pastoral norm for holy communion remains full participation in the eucharistic liturgy. All forms of communion outside Mass are "exceptional" and thus non-normative. Subsequent editions of the Roman Ritual, including those revised and published in the twentieth century, continued to repeat the admonition contained in the 1614 rite: the communion of the faithful ought to occur at the liturgy "unless, for a reasonable cause, it is sometimes to be postponed until after Mass" for "the prayers said at Mass after communion refer not only to the priest, but also to the other communicants."[74] Secondly, the Ritual of 1614 emphasizes the desirability of frequent communion, the pastor's responsibility to provide regular catechesis about the sacrament, and the individual Christian's obligation to prepare properly for participation in the eucharist. In this the Ritual implicitly recognizes that many of the sixteenth-century reformers' criticisms of medieval Catholic piety and practice were

234

legitimate. It would not be inaccurate to describe the 1614 book as a "reform ritual," one that reasserts the ancient eucharistic norm—communion at Mass—and calls both pastors and people to greater responsibility for instruction and participation.

THE RITUAL OF 1973
Background
Despite the 1614 ritual's insistence that participation in the liturgy is normative, the custom of distributing communion outside Mass, often quite independent of the time at which Mass was celebrated, expanded during the post-Tridentine period. In many cases, it became usual if not "normative" for Catholics to receive communion regularly apart from Mass. There are several reasons for this development, some of which may be usefully outlined here.

Devotions: During the seventeenth and eighteenth centuries, a new wave of eucharistic devotional piety spread in Europe. It was often connected with devotion to the Sacred Heart, which Margaret Mary Alacoque (1647–1690) had worked to promote. Although the origins of devotion to Jesus' human heart go back much further (to medieval writers like Bernard of Clairvaux, Bonaventure, Gertrude of Helfta, and Mechtilde of Magdeburg), it had remained primarily concentrated in religious houses until seventeenth-century proponents like Margaret Mary and John Eudes (1601–1680) revived it as a popular devotion appropriate for all. The seventeenth-century revival included several prominent eucharistic features: reception of holy communion on the first Friday of each month; the holy hour of adoration on each Thursday; prayer and penance in reparation for outrages committed against the sacrament. "First Friday devotions" became enormously popular as did the notion of dedicating every Thursday to "eucharistic reparation."[75]

Not all Catholics were convinced that the cult of the

235

Sacred Heart, with its accompanying eucharistic piety, was desirable or even legitimate. The Synod of Pistoia (1786) repudiated the devotion as abusive and superstitious. Nevertheless, papal approbation of this form of piety was rather frequent, particularly from the end of the eighteenth century onward. In condemning the Synod of Pistoia, for example, Pope Pius VI (1794) implicitly approved devotion to the Sacred Heart.[76] At the end of the nineteenth century, Pope Leo XIII, in his encyclical letter *Annum sacrum* proclaiming 1900 a "holy year," spoke explicitly of the Sacred Heart as "the symbol and the express image of the boundless love of Jesus Christ," and noted that this devotion "is truly and properly addressed to Christ himself."[77] And only twenty-five years ago, Pope Pius XII outlined the theological basis for devotion to the Sacred Heart in his encyclical letter *Haurietis aquas* (15 May 1956). Pope Pius carefully pointed out that attention to the physical heart of Jesus is rooted in the more fundamental Christian doctrine of the hypostatic union between human and divine natures in the person of the Word.[78] He also noted that such devotion to Jesus' heart must always be referred back to this fundamental point of theology.[79]

Despite refined theological discussion pro and con, the immense popularity of Sacred Heart devotions and the nine First Fridays, has continued up to the present. Before the Second Vatican Council, especially, it was the custom in many parishes to distribute communion outside Mass frequently on First Fridays (e.g., every fifteen minutes or half-hour). Often, too the distribution continued even while Mass was being celebrated at the principal altar of the church.

Fasting regulations: The custom of fasting prior to receiving the eucharist is an ancient one in both East and West. Explicit legislation on the subject appears in the Latin churches as early as the late fourth century. North African councils, such as those at Hippo (393) and Carthage (397), expressly refer to the custom of fasting before communion.[80] In a letter written about the year 400, Augustine expresses belief that the custom is universal and that it dates back to apostolic times.[81]

Traditionally, the period of fasting began at midnight on the day when the eucharist was to be received. The Ritual of 1614 reflects this tradition and thus states, in its rubrics for communion outside Mass, that those who receive should be "fasting at least from midnight" (*saltem a media nocte ieiuni*).[82] Ordinarily the fast was strictly interpreted: abstention from *all* food and drink (including water).

In the twentieth century, the eucharistic fast in the Roman church was modified in three stages.

In 1953, Pope Pius XII's Apostolic Constitution *Christus Dominus* decreed that ordinary water does not break the eucharistic fast, although the requirement of abstaining from food from the previous midnight remained in force.[83] Special provisions were made for the ill, for priests required to celebrate several times on a single day, for travelers, and for people whose work is fatiguing.[84]

In 1957, Pius XII modified the eucharistic fast still further through his *motu proprio, Sacram Communionem* (19 March 1957). A three-hour fast from food and alcoholic beverages, and a one-hour fast from nonalcoholic liquids, was established as the ordinary rule for all. Priests were to compute the time of fasting from the beginning of Mass; the people, from the time of receiving communion.[85]

Finally, in 1964, Pope Paul VI reduced the period of fasting from food and drink to one hour before communion. Even this minimum requirement can be dispensed from, especially for the sick, who may, as Pius XII had noted in 1957, take true medicines at any time before communion.[86]

These modifications made it far easier for Catholics to

communicate at whatever Mass they were attending. Before the fasting regulations were relaxed, it was common for people to receive communion outside Mass, particularly if the liturgy was not to be celebrated until a later hour of the morning. This was especially the case in religious communities of men and women, where a "communion Mass" (also called a "meditation Mass," since the time was actually spent in private prayer and devotion) was often celebrated early in the morning—to be followed, later, by the "conventional" or "community" Mass. This meant, incongruously, that the principal eucharistic liturgy of most Sundays and feasts was one in which few, if any, communicated with the priest. The modifications of the eucharistic fast thus helped reassert the ancient norm of communion at the liturgy, rather than before or after the liturgy.

Pastoral practices: During the period after Trent, pastoral practices of questionable propriety also reenforced the idea that eucharistic communion is quite independent from eucharistic action. In many places, for example, it was common for one priest to hear confessions while another celebrated the eucharist. Sometimes people would emerge from the confessional just in time to kneel at the communion rail to receive the sacrament. The notion that active participation in the entire liturgy of the Mass was the best way to prepare for communion had given way to the idea that confession must, or at least should, precede communion. In some places, too, it was customary to begin distributing communion shortly after the priest began the rite of preparing the gifts. The people, after all, had no active voice in the eucharistic prayer (servers or choir took over the dialogue, acclamations, doxologies, etc.), nor was their assistance considered essential to the celebrant's action at the altar. It was thus considered acceptable to accommodate large numbers of communicants by distributing the eucharist while the priest was busy doing "his" prayers.

238

Practices like these had a double effect. First, they intensified the popular impression that "hearing Mass" was one thing, while "going to communion" was quite another—and that two activities need not coincide. Secondly, they appeared to say that even at Mass the people's communion had nothing essential to do with the preparation of the gifts, the sacrificial offering of praise and thanksgiving, and the eucharistic prayer. Since even at Mass the eucharist was frequently given from the reserved sacrament, the act of communion was further estranged from the liturgical action of prayer and praise.

All three of the factors discussed above—devotional, disciplinary, and pastoral—form part of the background that led up to the Second Vatican Council's reform of the rites for communion outside Mass. Preliminary responses to these factors had been made in the 1967 Instruction on Eucharistic Worship. There, it was affirmed that

Devotions must "be derived from" and "lead the people toward" the liturgy;[87]
Mass must be celebrated in such a way that the people are not distracted by "two liturgical celebrations at the same time in the same church";[88]
The people "should normally receive" communion "during Mass," with eucharistic breads consecrated at that liturgy;[89]
The faithful should be "constantly encouraged to accustom themselves to going to confession outside the celebration of Mass";[90]
Although communion may be given outside Mass, "It is necessary to accustom the faithful to receive Communion during the actual celebration of the Eucharist."[91]

These preliminary responses were fleshed out and given definite ritual shape in the 1973 rituals for holy communion and worship of the eucharist outside Mass.

Theological Roots

Like a rondo with a recurrent theme, the liturgical documentation that has emerged since the Council stresses, insistently, the need for adequate catechesis and instruction of the people—not merely about "the changes," but about the theological roots that underlie the changes. As the 1967 *Instruction on Eucharistic Worship* put it: "Suitable catechesis is essential if the mystery of the Eucharist is to take deeper root in the minds and lives of the faithful."[92] Three theological themes consistently recur in the conciliar and postconciliar documentation that deals with eucharist: the normative ecclesiological character of the Sunday Assembly; the many real presences of Christ; and the intimate relation between the two tables, word and sacrament. Some comments about each of these will preface our discussion of the rites for communion outside Mass.

Sunday Assembly: The earliest Christian believers seem to have been conscious of three primary facts surrounding the relation between Jesus and themselves. Two of these facts were historical: 1) Jesus died, and his closest disciples fled, failed their Master at the most critical point of his career; 2) the disciples later reassembled, gathered again in the conviction that Jesus was alive—and that they had somehow been forgiven their failure. The third fact exploded history, turned it inside out, touched off a firestorm at the center of the universe: God had raised Jesus up, vindicating him out of death, thus reversing all human expectations about living and dying. The third fact, in short, was Easter. From that point on, nothing could ever be the same—neither past, nor present, nor future. The very structure of time itself had been altered.

The events that constitute Easter—including not only God's act of raising Jesus but the disciples' experience of forgiveness, conversion, and regathering as well—came to be attached, in celebration and memorial, to the first day of the week. There is evidence that this has already

240

begun to happen in the New Testament era: Paul and the Christians at Troas, for instance, are described by Luke as gathering to break bread "on the first day of the week" (Acts 20.7). By the second century the connection between Sunday and the Lord's resurrection was explicit. Ignatius of Antioch speaks of the Christian custom of keeping Sunday, the "day on which our life arose," in his letter to the Magnesians (written ca. 110).[93] Justin Martyr, writing perhaps four decades after Ignatius, connects Sunday with the first day of creation.[94]

Very early on, then, Sunday came to be understood as a day radically different from all others, an "eighth day" on which an entirely new order of things was breaking into the world. As the memorial of the Easter events, Sunday was seen as the eschatological day—a time out of time that transformed the very notion of temporality. The "time" of Sunday was not to be thought of as limit or measurement, but as potential, the breaking into the world of God's decisive act of liberating humanity through the resurrection of Jesus. In short, Sunday was a sacrament of "that more cheerful order of things" which begins to govern us even before it fully arrives.[95]

It is thus not difficult to understand how early Christians connected Lord's Day (a phrase used in Revelation 1.10) with Lord's Supper (a phrase used by Paul in 1 Corinthians 11.20). The day and the actions (gathering, assembling for prayer, thanksgiving, bread-breaking) were regarded as inseparable, particularly in the theology of writers like Ignatius of Antioch. Repeatedly in his collection of letters, Ignatius insists that in the Sunday eucharist the gathered assembly reveals itself as church: "A valid Eucharist is to be defined as one celebrated by the bishop or by a representative of his. Wherever the bishop appears, the whole congregation is to be present, just as wherever Jesus Christ is, there is the whole Church."[96]

241

Translated into the theological vocabulary of a later era, one can say that for Ignatius the starting-point for all ecclesiology is the Sunday assembly, gathered in communion with the bishop to celebrate the eucharist. Ecclesiology begins with *praxis*, with the actions and experience of those who have come to faith through conversion—and who celebrate that belief by gathering at table, giving thanks, breaking bread and passing the cup. These actions, more than any others, reveal the church for who it is in the world, and it is thus not surprising that the Second Vatican Council referred to the Sunday assembly, gathered for eucharist around its bishop, as the "principal manifestation" (*praecipua manifestatio*) of the church. This is also why contemporary theologians like Karl Rahner can speak of the eucharist as "constituting" the church, as "bringing it into being" in a concrete moment of space and time.

Both the *Instruction on Eucharistic Worship* (1967) and the new rites for holy communion and worship of the eucharist outside Mass (1973) appeal to this kind of ecclesiology rooted in the church's liturgical praxis. In the very first paragraph of the 1967 Instruction, reference is made to the "close and necessary connection between the Eucharist and the mystery of the Church," a theme already adumbrated in the Council's dogmatic constitution on the church, *Lumen Gentium*.[97] And the initial sentence of the General Introduction to the 1973 document reads: "The celebration of the eucharist is the center of the entire Christian life, both for the Church universal and for the local congregations of the Church."[98]

This is unquestionably the reason why the 1973 rites for eucharistic communion and devotions outside Mass are constantly spoken of in relation to the Christian assembly and its liturgical action. The very structure of the document reveals this ecclesiological concern, for each individual section of the document begins with a discus-

242

sion of the primary significance of the community's celebration of eucharist.

The General Introduction to the entire document insists that "the celebration of the eucharist in the sacrifice of the Mass . . . is truly the origin and goal of the worship which is shown to the eucharist outside Mass."[99]

The Introduction to the rite for communion outside Mass reiterates this ecclesiological and liturgical point: "Sacramental communion received during Mass is the more perfect participation in the eucharistic celebration."[100]

The Introduction to the rites for exposition, Benediction, processions, and eucharistic congresses calls attention, likewise, to the ecclesiologically normative character of the Sunday assembly and its liturgical action: "Exposition of the holy eucharist . . . is intended to acknowledge Christ's marvelous presence in the sacrament. . . . This kind of exposition must clearly express the cult of the blessed sacrament in its relationship to the Mass."[101]

The implication of such comments is clear: eucharistic customs that do not reflect the assembly's action as their point of origin are theologically suspect and liturgically unacceptable.

The Many Modes of Christ's Presence: If the Sunday assembly and its action provides the ecclesiological norm for all forms of eucharistic cult, the fact of Christ's many modes of real presence provides the sacramental one. Just as it is impossible to speak of eucharistic devotions without having first spoken of the eucharistic assembly, so it is impossible to make sense of Christ's real presence in this sacrament without having first noted the presence of Christ in the assembly itself, in the Word, and in the liturgical ministers who serve. The overwhelming importance of this theological principle is reflected by its frequent repetition in conciliar and postconciliar documents.

1963, *Constitution on the Liturgy*, section 7: "Christ is always present in His Church, especially in her liturgical celebrations. He is present in the Sacrifice of the Mass, not only in the person of His minister . . . but especially under the eucharistic species. By His power He is present in the sacraments. . . . He is present in His word. . . . He is present . . . when the Church prays and sings. . . ."[102]

1967, *Instruction on Eucharistic Worship*, section 9: "He is always present in a body of the faithful gathered in His name. He is present too in His Word. . . . In the sacrifice of the Eucharist He is present both in the person of the minister . . . and above all under the species of the Eucharist. . . . This presence of Christ under the species is called 'real' not in an exclusive sense, as if the other kinds of presence were not real, but 'par excellence.'"[103]

1973, "Holy Communion and Worship of the Eucharist Outside Mass," section 6: "In the celebration of Mass the chief ways in which Christ is present in his Church gradually become clear. First he is present in the very assembly of the faithful . . . next he is present in his word . . . then in the person of the minister; finally and above all, in the eucharistic sacrament. . . ."[104]

As these texts make clear, it is the structure of the liturgy itself that demonstrates both the fact of Christ's many modes of presence among the Christian people—and the relationship among these modes. Assembly, Word, sacrifice (actions of praise, thanksgiving, offering), species: these four fundamental modes indicate that the full mystery of Christ's real presence originates in the liturgical praxis of the assembly—and always leads back to that assembly gathered to pray, sing, hear the Word, break the bread and share the meal. Even the "prolonged presence" of Christ in the reserved sacrament receives its significance from what the people, led in prayer by their ministers, said and did in the liturgical assembly. The reserved sacramental species, used for

244

communion outside Mass or for the sick and dying, are thus not independent objects, but living icons of a community's action: they are not relics to be admired, but active symbols that continue to invite people to nourishment. [105]

The source of this larger vision of sacrament and modes of real presence are reflected in the work of contemporary theologians like Edward Schillebeeckx and Karl Rahner. Schillebeeckx's formula has become something of a modern classic: Christ is the "sacrament of encounter" between God and humankind. [106] This means, in effect, that the holy humanity of Jesus Christ remains the real and permanently available symbol of the meeting between a God who hungers for humanity and a humanity who hungers for God. In the langauge of transcendental Thomism used by Karl Rahner, Jesus is the irrevocable "real symbol" of God's disclosure and offer of self to the human world and its history. [107] Just as the Word of God is the "real symbol" of the Father who eternally utters himself, and in so uttering simultaneously constitutes both himself as personal Father and the Word as personal Son, so the church is "real symbol" (sacrament) of the incarnate Word in history, and the sacraments are "real symbols" that actualize the church's essence at moments critical or decisive for the community's life. [108]

This larger vision of sacramentality (Christ as *the* sacrament, church as primary sacrament of Christ) has been incorporated into the recent documents that deal with eucharistic worship and devotion. Pastors and teachers are charged with specific responsibility for helping people understand these fundamental points of sacramental theology—including the many modes of Christ's real presence. [109]

The Two Tables—Word and Sacrament: A third theological theme reflected in the 1973 rites for communion outside Mass is the "unity of the two tables"—the table of God's

Word and the table of the Lord's Supper. The theme itself is an ancient one, commented upon, for example, by Cyril of Jerusalem in his catechetical lectures: "Just as bread is suitable for our body, so the Word is well suited to our soul."[110] And we have seen too that the custom of combining liturgy of the Word with liturgy of the Supper is likewise ancient, explicitly referred to as early as Justin Martyr (ca. 150).[111]

As was the case with the ecclesiological theme "Sunday assembly," so this point about the unity of the two tables has been consistently repeated in the conciliar and postconciliar documents.

1963, *Constitution on the Liturgy*, section 56: "The two parts which, in a certain sense, go to make up the Mass, namely, the liturgy of the word and the eucharistic liturgy, are so closely connected with each other that they form but one single act of worship."[112]

1967, *Instruction on Eucharistic Worship*, section 10: "The preaching of the Word is necessary for the very administration of the sacraments, inasmuch as they are sacraments of faith, which is born of the Word and fed by it. This is especially true of the celebration of Mass, in which it is the purpose of the Liturgy of the Word to develop the close connection between the preaching and hearing of the Word of God and the Eucharistic Mystery. . . . Thus the Church is nourished by the bread of life which she finds at the table both of the Word of God and of the Body of Christ."[113]

1973, "Holy Communion and Worship of the Eucharist Outside Mass," section 26: "This rite is to be used chiefly when Mass is not celebrated or when communion is not distributed at scheduled times. The purpose is that the people should be nourished by the word of God. By hearing it they learn that the marvels it proclaims reach their climax in the paschal mystery of which the Mass is a sacramental memorial and in which they share by communion. Nourished by God's Word, they are led on to grateful and fruitful participation in the saving mysteries."[114]

Repetition of this theme is surely no accident. Even when the eucharist is distributed outside Mass, there is a clear preference for situating the act of communion within a celebration of the Word. The two tables are regarded, in these documents, as a single act of nourishment, for the liturgies of Word and bread and cup constitute "but one single act of worship."[115]

Contemporary expression of this ancient doctrine about the unity of the two tables is found, for example, in the writings of Karl Rahner. For some years now, Rahner has been developing the theme of a "continuum" that unites Word and Sacrament within a comprehensive understanding of the way God speaks (discloses, reveals, gives self) to humankind.[116] Working from the biblical notion of *dabar* (speech, utterance, word), Rahner notes that the efficacious Word of God may be addressed to human beings with varying degrees or levels of intensity. God's Word is active, for example, in the Bible, in the historical experience of a community of faith, in tradition, in an assembly of Christians gathered for prayer in Jesus' name, in sacrament. Seen from this point of view, sacraments are efficacious "Word of God" experienced by the community when it gathers precisely as church, as holy sign of God's eschatologically triumphant grace and mercy in the world. Sacraments are thus "performative utterances" (Rahner: *exhibitives Wort*) that not only accomplish what they signify but also "actuate" the church at decisive moments of its local history: e.g., when new members are initiated when mature Christian vocation is discerned and designated (marriage, ordination), when the community's continuing need for spiritual nourishment is met (eucharist). Put another way, sacrament is effective Word of God spoken to and by the church at a moment of maximal intensity in its historical life.[117]

The doctrine of the "unity of the two tables" has importance not only for a modern Roman Catholic understanding of sacrament, but for ecumenical discussion of the issue as well. As Karl Rahner has noted,

"the theologian of both confessions [Catholic and Protestant] can and must seek afresh for a common point of departure in investigating the question of the institution and the existence of sacraments in the Christian Church. I believe that this point of departure is the distinctive theological character of the word uttered in the Church as the eschatological presence of God."[118]

There is increasing evidence that both Protestant and Roman Catholic scholars are seeking out the source of sacramental actions through a renewed appreciation of the Word that "gives what it promises." The 1967 Lutheran-Roman Catholic Statement on the Eucharist, for example, discusses Christ's presence in the liturgy of the table within the more comprehensive framework of "a manifold presence of Christ, the Word of God and Lord of the world":

"We confess a manifold presence of Christ, the Word of God and Lord of the world. The crucified and risen Lord is present in his body, the people of God, for he is present where two or three are gathered in his name (Mt. 18.20). He is present in baptism, for it is Christ himself who baptizes. He is present in the reading of the scriptures and the proclamation of the gospel. He is present in the Lord's supper."[119]

Documents like this one reveal that the ancient dispute between "pulpit" (Protestant) and "altar" (Catholic) is gradually fading in light of a common reappropriation of Augustine's famous definition: sacrament is a "visible word" (*verbum visibile*).

Each of these three theological themes—the Sunday assembly, the many presences of Christ, the unity of the two tables—is reflected in the reformed rites for holy communion and worship of the eucharist outside Mass.

The new rites clearly prefer that when communion is distributed outside Mass, it be done when the people are gathered for a celebration of God's Word.[120] Even the Short Rite for communion includes a brief scriptural reading.[121] "Nourished by God's word," the rite comments, "they are led on to grateful and fruitful participation in the saving mysteries."[122]

The Structure of the Rites
Two basic principles seem to have influenced the structure of the new rites of communion outside Mass.

1) First, these rites are to be perceived and celebrated as continuations of the community's liturgical action in the eucharist. To that end the rites have been consciously modeled on the unitive liturgies of word and table, as the following outline shows.

The Long Rite with the Celebration of the Word

Introductory Rites
    Greeting
    Penitential Rite

Celebration of the Word of God
    One or more readings
    Responsorial psalm
    General intercessions

Holy Communion
    Our Father
    Sign of peace
    Invitation to communion
    Distribution
    Hymn or other appropriate song (optional)
    Prayer after communion

Concluding Rites
    Blessing
    Dismissal

The structure of this rite leaves no doubt that the act of

receiving communion (even outside Mass) is part of a liturgy, celebrated by an assembly of Christians, who are called together by God's word and whose action is rooted in the full eucharistic rite. There seems to be a deliberate attempt to avoid the impression that communion is a purely private affair independent of the liturgy.

2) The second principle calls attention to the dialogal character of all Christian worship. Even the short form for distributing communion outside Mass respects this principle.

The Short Rite with the Celebration of the Word

Introductory Rites
    Greeting (and response of the people)
    Penitential Rite (invitation to reflect; confession)

Reading of the Word (Short Form)

Holy Communion
    Our Father (invitation to pray; minister and people recite the prayer together)
    Invitation to communion (with response)
    Distribution
    Psalm or song (optional)
    Prayer after communion

Concluding Rites
    Blessing
    Dismissal

This short rite, intended for use "when the longer, more elaborate form is unsuitable, especially when there are only one or two for communion and a true community celebration is impossible,"[123] still retains the characteristic liturgical dialogue between minister and people. In the 1614 Ritual, the dialogue had been largely lost: as at Mass, servers took the people's parts (e.g., the *Confiteor*, the responses). In contrast, the 1973 rites make it clear that even when communion is disengaged from the eucharistic liturgy, the people are still active participants, not silent or passive spectators in a devotional drama.

Structurally, then, the reformed rites for communion outside Mass closely adhere to the principles laid down in the Council's Constitution on the Liturgy.

1) The act of receiving communion is always a liturgical act, and thus the presence of an assembly is normative. "It is to be stressed that whenever rites, according to their specific nature, make provision for communal celebration involving the presence and active participation of the faithful, this way of celebrating them is to be preferred, so far as possible, to a celebration that is individual and quasi-private. This principle applies with special force to the celebration of Mass and the administration of the sacraments. . . ."[124]

2) Since communion (even outside Mass) is part of a liturgy, the people have a proper role in the action. "The people should be encouraged to take part by means of verbal expression of praise, responses, the singing of psalms, antiphons, and songs, as well as by actions, gestures, and bodily attitudes. . . ."[125]

3) Since Word and Sacrament are intimately connected in all liturgical actions, eucharistic nourishment should be preceded by nourishment from the scriptures. "Sacred Scripture is of the greatest importance in the celebration of the liturgy. . . . it is from the Scriptures that actions and signs derive their meaning."[126]

Historically, the reformed rites for communion outside Mass are akin to two models studied earlier in this chapter: the monastic ritual found in documents like the *Rule of the Master*, and the liturgy of the presanctified (associated with Good Friday in the West). The following chart will reveal the similarities.

251

Rule of the Master	Liturgy of the Presanctified	New Rites
Liturgy of the Word Monastic office of none, including psalmody, NT reading, gospel	*Liturgy of the Word* Two readings, with intervening chant, followed by gospel of the passion	*Liturgy of the Word* One or two readings (or at least a few verses of scripture)
Intercessions at the end of none (*Rogus Dei*)	Solemn prayers of intercession for all states and conditions of people	General intercessions (longer rite)
Liturgy of Communion	*Liturgy of Communion*	*Liturgy of Communion*
(Our Father probably said at the end of none)	Our Father	Our Father
Exchange of the sign of peace	Communion in both kinds (originally)	Exchange of the sign of peace (longer rite)
Communion in both kinds	Concluding prayer	Communion in form of bread (ordinarily)
Prayer (in the monastic refectory)		Concluding prayer

As this chart shows, the new rites for communion outside Mass are essentially a liturgy of the presanctified gifts, with characteristic elements such as biblical readings, psalmody/song, intercessory prayer, and familiar portions of the eucharistic liturgy (Lord's Prayer, sign of peace, distribution of communion, postcommunion prayer and dismissal). Formerly, the West knew such a liturgy on only one day of the year, Good Friday; many of the eastern churches, by contrast, celebrated the liturgy of the presanctified rather frequently, especially on weekdays in Lent. With the appearance of these new rites, the Roman Church has created a hybrid form of the liturgy of the presanctified that shows indebtedness to both monastic custom (a liturgical rite celebrated in church) and historical precedent (the Good Friday model). Unlike the Eastern custom and the monastic practice revealed in the *Rule of the Master*, however, the reformed Roman rites are not attached to the liturgy of the hours (vespers, none).

THEOLOGICAL SIGNIFICANCE OF THE RITES

Although the customs of receiving communion outside Mass is ancient, as we have seen, its opponents also go back far in the church's history. After the church became a licit religion (*religio licita*) in the Constantinian empire during the fourth century, opposition to the custom grew more vocal and more vehement. In Chapter Two we noted St. Jerome's sardonic description of Christians who would not dare to receive in church, but who think nothing of taking communion in the privacy of their homes. We have noted, too, the church's long-standing official reluctance to create or approve a "liturgy" for communion outside Mass. During the Reformation period, the custom of communicating outside Mass was widely attacked by the reformers—and even the Council of Trent insisted that sacramental communion at Mass was the best mode of participating in the eucharist. Trent's preference was reflected several decades after the council closed by the 1614 Ritual, which reiterated that "the communion of the people ought to occur within Mass." And in the reformed rites that have appeared since the Second Vatican Council, the same message comes across: "Sacramental communion received during Mass is the most perfect participation in the eucharistic celebration."[127]

Does this mean that communion outside Mass is simply a benign abnormality, historically ancient but theologically disreputable? From one point of view the question could be answered affirmatively. In all ages the church has insisted that Mass and communion belong together, liturgically and theologically; only for a serious pastoral reason should the two be separated. Officially, the church has never condoned the indiscriminate distribution of communion outside Mass, though it has defended a Christian's right to request the sacrament "for a reasonable cause" (to quote the 1614 Ritual). The church's official reluctance to approve separation of communion from Mass is still evident in the rituals published in 1973: "The faithful should be encouraged to receive communion during the eucharistic celebration itself. Priests, however, are not to refuse to give communion to the faithful who ask for it even outside Mass."[128]

Clearly, then, the separation of eucharistic communion from eucharistic liturgy is regarded as extraordinary, as a departure from the norm that is legitimate only when serious pastoral circumstances require it. Such circumstances obtain, for example, when no ordained priest is available to celebrate eucharist with the people. In mission territories, especially, this situation is not uncommon; a congregation may be left for months without the sacramental ministry of priest or deacon. Situations of this sort seem to have been envisioned by the 1973 decree *Immensae Caritatis*, which laid down norms for facilitating sacramental communion in particular circumstances.[129] "Provision must be made," the decree noted, "lest reception of communion become impossible or difficult because of insufficient ministers."[130] In order to alleviate this situation, *Immensae Caritatis* provides for the commissioning of special ministers for the eucharist.[131] Such ministers may preside at the long or short rites for distributing communion outside Mass.[132]

The pastoral intention behind the provisions of *Immensae Caritatis* and the rites for distributing holy communion outside Mass is thus obvious: the people are not to be denied access to the eucharist simply because ordained personnel are not available. The special ministers of *Immensae Caritatis* and the liturgy of the presanctified of the new rites seem designed, in the first instance, to meet legitimate pastoral needs in places where a full celebration of the eucharist is impossible.

254

In light of such pastoral situations, the theological significance of the reformed rites for communion outside Mass becomes clearer. These liturgies of the presanctified intend to unite people not only with the Lord present in the eucharistic species, but also with the larger community and its liturgical action. To put it somewhat crudely, these rites are not primarily intended to make the Lord available, but to put people in touch with the action of the full eucharistic assembly. That is unquestionably the reason why the instructions that accompany the new rites make comments like these:

"In fact it is proper that those who are prevented from being present at the community's celebration should be refreshed with the eucharist. In this way they may realize that they are united not only with the Lord's sacrifice but also with the community itself and are supported by the love of their brothers and sisters. . . .

"The faithful should be instructed carefully that, even when they receive communion outside Mass, they are closely united with the sacrifice which perpetuates the sacrifice of the cross. . . ."[133]

As these texts show, to receive communion (even outside Mass) means not only to make contact with the Lord, but to intensify one's relationship with the Christian assembly and its liturgical action. The sacramental symbols of bread and wine are not merely objects or relics that signify Jesus' presence; they are vital signs that signify and effect one's communion with the worshiping people of God. The reformed rites for distributing communion outside Mass thus invite us to a threefold communion: with the Lord, with the assembly, and with the full eucharistic action.

Theologically, the new rites challenge us to expand our understanding of liturgical symbols generally and of the eucharistic elements specifically. Symbols are, after all, actions not objects, verbs not nouns.[134] Nor can symbols

255

be reduced to a single meaning that excludes all others; by nature, they are richly ambiguous, dense with multiple layers of significance. The sacramental symbols of bread and wine are no exception; they too operate simultaneously on several levels of meaning. Early church fathers like Augustine were intensely aware of the multiple meanings that are condensed into the sacramental symbols. In an Easter sermon delivered about the year 410, he wrote:

"No matter how many breads are laid upon the altars of Christ throughout the world today, it is but one bread. What is meant by one bread? St. Paul interpreted it briefly: 'We, being many, are of one body.' This bread is the body of Christ, to which the apostle refers when he addresses the Church: '*Now you are the body of Christ* and his members.' That which you receive, that you yourselves are by the grace of redemption, as you acknowledge when you respond Amen. What you witness here is the sacrament of unity."[135]

Augustine's text means that the eucharistic bread refers not only to the personal body of Jesus dead and risen among his people, but also the corporate body of Christ—the church. In a profound sense, we are what we eat; we receive what we have become—the body of the Lord. Even when they are reserved for communion outside Mass, the sacramental symbols of bread and wine continue to signify and effect what they originally signified and effected in the eucharistic celebration: communion with the Lord, communion with one another, communion with the sacrificial actions of praise and thanksgiving. How is this possible? Because symbols, even when lifted from their original matrix, continue to evoke that matrix and to make its power present among those who interact with the symbols. That is precisely why symbols can survive, even when their original context has been lost or altered.

An example will help to clarify this last point. It is a virtually universal consensus among biblical scholars that the central symbol of Jesus' ministry was the kingdom or reign of God.[136] Originally, of course, the symbol developed as a powerfully condensed sign that evoked two ancient myths fused in Israel's religious experience: the ancient Near Eastern myth of a god who acts as a sovereign, bringing cosmos (order) from chaos each spring; and the specifically Jewish myth of a LORD who intervenes decisively in the history of a chosen people.[137] Even after Israel's origins as an elect people were blurred by the social and political disasters of fallen monarchies and exile, the symbol of kingdom (God acting sovereignly to save people) survived, continued to absorb and reveal new meaning. Shortly before Jesus' time, this symbol acquired the desperate resonances of apocalyptic hope: surely God would intervene, would act again as sovereign, would establish a kingdom by crushing Israel's political oppressors and ushering in a new age of economic prosperity and religious fervor.[138] In his own ministry, however, Jesus appears to have repudiated both the classical and the apocalyptic significance of kingdom symbolism, though he retained the symbol. As preached by Jesus, the reign of God was no longer a time or place, nor even an object of apocalyptic hope; it was a verb, a sudden bursting in of God upon human life and consciousness. God could and would reign anytime, anywhere, Jesus announced, among people who were willing to renounce the ancient human sins of possessiveness (hoarding), ambitiousness (climbing), and control of others (commanding).[139] Among such people—poor, "polluted" by guilt, powerless—God would reign with righteousness, calling forth a new human community based on the voluntary renunciation of hoarding, climbing, and controlling.

Jesus thus appealed to a symbol whose original matrix (in ancient Near Eastern and classical Jewish mythology) had been drastically altered. But the symbol itself survived such alterations of context and achieved power to invite men and women into the new human community

257

envisioned by Jesus. Christians still, in fact, appeal to kingdom as the ultimate symbol of a humanity liberated, reconciled, and brought to peace in the presence of God.

Something similar occurs in the case of the eucharistic symbols. When the eucharist is distributed outside Mass, the original symbol matrix—the liturgical assembly of Christians gathered to give thanks, eat and drink—is eclipsed, but not destroyed. Just as Jesus affirmed God's sovereignty, even though the symbol of kingdom was altered, so the sacramental symbols of eucharist continue to affirm the Lord's presence and the assembly's liturgical action, even though the celebration of Mass is over. In Jesus' preaching, the kingdom retained its symbolic power to offer all people a new experience of God's decisive action in the human world; in the rites for communion outside Mass, the eucharistic elements retain their symbolic power to invite people into communion with the Lord and with one another. In other words, it is precisely because the eucharist is a sacramental symbol that its effectiveness survives even when its original matrix is eclipsed.

The theological justification for communion outside Mass must be rooted, therefore, in an understanding of sacramental symbols: what they are and how they work. Even when holy communion is separated from Mass, the sacramental elements retain their power as symbols, i.e., as invitations to the action of eating and drinking. Precisely because they are sacrament (and thus action, verb), the eucharistic food and drink may legitimately be reserved for the use of those who are prevented from participating in the liturgical assembly. The Christian custom of communicating persons outside Mass thus affirms rather than compromises or denies the sacramental nature of eucharistic liturgy.

258

SUMMARY

This chapter has explored the historical, pastoral, and theological background necessary for understanding the reformed Roman rites for holy communion outside Mass. We have seen that these new rites are truly liturgies, actions of a people gathered and nourished by God's Word. It has been noted, too, that despite the pastoral and theological legitimacy of such rites, the norm of eucharistic worship in the church remains "sacramental communion received during Mass."[140] In the chapter that follows, we shall turn our attention to that special pastoral situation envisaged by the 1973 instruction *Immensae Caritatis*: the administration of communion and viaticum to the sick by an extraordinary minister.

NOTES

1. See Eusebius, *The History of the Church*, Book VI.44, translated by G.A. Williamson (Baltimore: Penguin Books, 1965), pp. 284-285.

2. Ibid.

3. On the term "clinical" as applied to communion for the ill or endangered, see W.H. Freestone, *The Sacrament Reserved* (Alcuin Club Collections, XXI; London: A.R. Mowbray and Co., 1917), pp. 105-106.

4. See Roger Béraudy, "Eucharistic Worship Outside Mass," in A.-G. Martimort, *The Church at Prayer: The Eucharist*, translated by Austin Flannery *et al.* (New York: Herder and Herder, 1973), p. 198.

5. See "Holy Communion and Worship of the Eucharist Outside Mass," in *The Rites* (2 vols. New York: Pueblo Publishing Co., 1976–1980), I, pp. 465-469. Further references to this document will be cited as follows: HCWE, I (volume of the Pueblo edition), followed by appropriate page references.

6. See HCWE, nn. 42-53, I, pp. 470-474.

7. See Freestone, *The Sacrament Reserved*, pp. 40-44.

8. See Geoffrey J. Cuming, *Hippolytus: A Text for Students*

259

(Grove Liturgical Study No. 8; Bramcote, Notts.: Grove Books, 1976), p. 28.

9. Ibid., p. 27.

10. Ibid.

11. Ibid., p. 28.

12. On the date and provenance of the *Rule of the Master*, see Luke Eberle, trans., *The Rule of the Master* (Cistercian Studies Series, 6; Kalamazoo, Mich.: Cistercian Publications, 1977), pp. 73-79.

13. Ibid., p. 171.

14. *Rule of the Master* 21.1, 7; trans. Eberle, p. 171.

15. Ibid., 21.4-12; trans. Eberle, pp. 171-172.

16. Ibid., 22.1-4; trans. Eberle, p. 172.

17. Ibid., 23.1-15; trans. Eberle, pp. 173-174.

18. Ibid., 35; trans. Eberle, p. 199.

19. Ibid., 23.2; trans. Eberle, p. 173.

20. Ibid., 23.3; trans. Eberle, p. 173.

21. Ibid., 23.6-10; trans. Eberle, p. 174.

22. Ibid., 23.15-26; trans. Eberle, pp. 174-175.

23. See ibid., 23.15; 24.18; 27.3-4; trans. Eberle, p. 174 (note). It is possible that the bread and wine distributed at the beginning of the meal were also intended as a *purificatio oris* after communion.

24. See *Rule of the Master*, trans. Eberle, p. 33 (introductory essay).

25. See ibid., pp. 31-32.

26. See Otto Nussbaum, *Die Aufbewahrung der Eucharistie* (Theophaneia, 29; Bonn: Hanstein, 1979), pp. 39-40.

27. Canon 52, Mansi, XI: col. 967; see the comments in Nussbaum, *Die Aufbewahrung*, p. 40.

28. See Nussbaum, *Die Aufbewahrung*, p. 40.

29. Although the manuscript of the *Sacramentarium Gelasianum*

Vetus dates from about 750 A.D. (Vat. Reg. 316), it reflects usages of an earlier period.

30. See Leo Cunibert Mohlberg, ed., *Liber Sacramentorum Romanae Aeclesiae Ordinis Circuli* (Rerum Ecclesiasticarum Documenta; Series Major; Fontes IV; Rome: Herder, 1960), n. 390, p. 63 (this edition is of the *Gelasianum Vetus*).

31. Gelasian Sacramentary, ed. Mohlberg, n. 418, p. 67.

32. See Michel Andrieu, ed., *Les Ordines Romani du haut moyen age* (5 vols.; Spicilegium Sacrum Lovaniense 11, 23, 24, 28, 29; Louvain: 1931–1961), Vol. III, pp. 269-273.

33. *Ordo Romanus* XXIII.22; ed. Andrieu, III, p. 272.

34. Innocent I, *Letter* 25.4; text in PL 20: cols. 555-556.

35. See Cyrille Vogel, ed., *Le Pontificale romano-germanique du dixième siècle* (Studi e Testi 226-227; 2 vols.; Città del Vaticano: Biblioteca Apostolica Vaticana, 1963), n. 304, II, p. 86.

36. See Michel Andrieu, ed., *Le pontificale romain au Moyen-Age* (4 vols. Studi e Testi 86-88, 99; Città del Vaticano: Biblioteca Apostolica Vaticana, 1938–1941), II, pp. 234-237.

37. See Michel Andrieu, *Le pontificale romain au Moyen-Age*, II, pp. 464-469.

38. See ibid., III, pp. 582-587.

39. Ibid., II, pp. 86ff.

40. Ibid., II, p. 93.

41. Ibid., II, pp. 234-237.

42. See ibid., II, pp. 464-469. Innocent III had attempted to simplify the liturgy of the presanctified in the early years of the thirteenth century; see the short recension of the *Roman Pontifical of the XIII Century* in Andrieu's edition, II, pp. 467-469.

43. For the development of similar practices in the East see Nussbaum, *Die Aufbewahrung*, pp. 44-45.

44. See Béraudy, "Eucharistic Worship Outside the Mass," pp. 206-207.

45. R.M. Woolley, ed., *The Gilbertine Rite* (2 vols.; Henry Bradshaw Society, 59-60; London, 1921), I, p. 45.

46. See ibid. The full text instructs the priest or "some other person" to give the people a sermon about: 1) faith in the real presence of Christ in the eucharist; 2) the need for mutual charity in order to make a good communion; 3) the danger of receiving if one has been publicly excommunicated.

47. Caesarius, *Sermon* 73.2; ed. Morin in Corpus Christianorum 103, p. 307. See the comments in Nussbaum, *Die Aufbewahrung*, p. 46.

48. See the Synod of Agde (605), canon 47, in Mansi VIII: col. 332; the Council of Orleans (511), canon 26, in *MGH Conc.*, I, 8 (ed. Maassen).

49. See Nussbaum, *Die Aufbewahrung*, p. 46.

50. See Gregory the Great, *Dialogues, Book II*; translated by Myra L. Uhlfelder (The Library of Liberal Arts; Indianapolis: Bobbs-Merrill, 1967), p. 33.

51. See Nussbaum, *Die Aufbewahrung*. p. 46.

52. See Amalarius of Metz, *Liber Officiorum*, III.36.7, in J.M. Hanssens, ed., *Amalarii Episcopi Opera Liturgica Omnia* (Studi e Testi 138-140; 3 vols.; Città del Vaticano: Biblioteca Apostolica Vaticana, 1948), II, pp. 370-371.

53. See Nussbaum, *Die Aufbewahrung*, p. 50.

54. See ibid., p. 50, n. 105, for the text of Bernard's description.

55. See ibid., p. 50, for further details.

56. See Josef Jungmann, *The Mass of the Roman Rite*, II, p. 386 (5th German edition, II, pp. 478-479).

57. See Nussbaum, *Die Aufbewahrung*, p. 50.

58. See ibid., p. 50, n. 108 for text.

59. At Session 22 of the Council of Trent (1562, reign of Pius IV), a procedure had been established whereby use of the cup for communion of the laity could be petitioned from the Holy See. See the text in DS 1760.

60. See *Rituale Romanum Paule V. Pontificis Maximi iussu editum* (Rome: 1615), p. 60.

61. See DS 1738-1750.

62. See DS 1747.

63. See Jungmann, *The Mass of the Roman Rite*, II, p. 371 (5th German edition, II, pp. 455-463).

64. See N.M. Denis-Boulet, "Analysis of the Rites and Prayers of the Mass," in A.-G. Martimort, ed., *The Church at Prayer: The Eucharist* (see n. 4, above), p. 183.

65. See Béraudy, "Eucharistic Worship Outside the Mass," p. 204.

66. See ibid., p. 208.

67. See *Rituale Romanum* of 1614 (n. 60, above), p. 60.

68. Ibid., p. 58.

69. Ibid., p. 57.

70. Ibid., p. 56.

71. Ibid., p. 57.

72. Ibid., p. 58.

73. Ibid., p. 61.

74. See *Rituale Romanum* (Editio Prima juxta typicam Vaticanam; New York: Benziger Brothers, 1953), p. 102.

75. See, for example, C. McNeiry, *Thursdays with the Blessed Sacrament* (New York: Benziger Brothers, 1917).

76. See DS 2661-2663.

77. See DS 3353.

78. See DS 3922.

79. See DS 3925.

80. See the article "Eucharistic Fast" in *The Oxford Dictionary of the Christian Church*, edited by F.L. Cross and E.A. Livingstone (2nd edition; New York: Oxford University Press, 1974), pp. 477-478. For the conciliar texts, see: Mansi III: col. 923 (Hippo); Mansi III: col. 885 (Carthage).

81. See Augustine, *Letter* 54, in PL 33: col. 203.

82. See *Rituale Romanum* of 1614, p. 56.

83. See James J. Megivern, *Worship and Liturgy* (Official

Catholic Teachings; Wilmington, N.C.: McGrath Publishing Company, 1978), p. 135.

84. Ibid.

85. See ibid., pp. 178-179.

86. See AAS 56 (1964), 212; AAS 57 (1965), 186.

87. See *Instruction on Eucharistic Worship* (IEW), 58; in Megivern, *Worship and Liturgy*, pp. 338-339.

88. IEW, 17; Megivern, *Worship and Liturgy*, p. 320.

89. IEW, 31; Megivern, *Worship and Liturgy*, p. 326.

90. IEW, 35; Megivern, *Worship and Liturgy*, p. 330.

91. IEW, 33; Megivern, *Worship and Liturgy*, p. 328.

92. IEW, 5; Megivern, *Worship and Liturgy*, p. 313.

93. See Ignatius of Antioch, *Letter to the Magnesians*, 9; translated in Robert M. Grant and Jack Sparks, *The Apostolic Fathers* (Nashville: Thomas Nelson, 1978), p. 88.

94. See Justin Martyr, *First Apology*, 67; in: Willy Rordorf *et al.*, *The Eucharist of the Early Christians*, translated by Matthew J. O'Connell (New York: Pueblo Publishing Company, 1978), p. 73.

95. See Robert Capon, *Party Spirit* (New York: William Morrow and Company, 1979), pp. 12-20.

96. See Ignatius Antioch, *Letter to the Smyrnaeans*, 8; translated in Grant and Sparks, *The Apostolic Fathers*, pp. 112-113.

97. See IEW, 1; Megivern, *Worship and Liturgy*, p. 308, with the references in n. 4, p. 438.

98. See HCWE, 1, I, p. 455.

99. Ibid.

100. HCWE, 13, I, p. 459.

101. HCWE, 82, I, p. 486.

102. *Constitution on the Liturgy*, 7; Megivern, *Worship and Liturgy*, p. 200.

103. IEW, 9; Megivern, *Worship and Liturgy*, pp. 315-316.

104. HCWE, 6, I, pp. 456-457.

105. On the notion of symbols as verbs and actions (not nouns or objects), see Nathan Mitchell, "Symbols are Actions, not Objects—New Directions for an Old Problem," *Living Worship* 13 (February, 1977), 1-4.

106. See Edward Schillebeeckx, *Christ, the Sacrament of the Encounter with God*, translated by Paul Barrett *et al.* (New York: Sheed and Ward, 1963), pp. 13-32.

107. On transcendental Thomism, and on Rahner as one of its chief exponents, see Richard P. McBrien, *Catholicism* (2 vols.; Minneapolis: Winston Press, 1980), I, pp. 128-133. On Rahner's notion of the "real symbol" see Karl Rahner, "The Theology of the Symbol" in *Theological Investigations IV*, translated by Kevin Smyth (Baltimore: Helicon Press, 1966), pp. 221-252.

108. On these points see Karl Rahner, *The Church and the Sacraments*, translated by W.J. O'Hara (Quaestiones Disputatae, 9; New York: Herder and Herder, 1963), p. 22.

109. See IEW, 5-15; Megivern, *Worship and Liturgy*, pp. 313-319.

110. Cyril of Jerusalem, *Lecture 4*: "On the Body and Blood of Christ," in Paul Palmer, trans., ed., *Sacraments and Worship* (London: Darton, Longman and Todd, 1957, paperback edition), pp. 24-25.

111. See Justin Martyr, *First Apology*, 67; translated in Willy Rordorf *et al.*, *The Eucharist of the Early Christians*, p. 73.

112. *Constitution on the Liturgy*, 56; Megivern, *Worship and Liturgy*, p. 214.

113. IEW, 10; Megivern, *Worship and Liturgy*, p. 316.

114. HCWE, 26, I, p. 465.

115. *Constitution on the Liturgy*, 56; Megivern, *Worship and Liturgy*, p. 214.

116. See Karl Rahner, "The Word and the Eucharist," *Theological Investigations* IV (see n. 107, above), pp. 253-286.

117. See Karl Rahner, "What is a Sacrament?" *Theological Investigations XIV*, translated by David Bourke (New York: Sea-

bury Press, 1976), pp. 135-148.

118. See Karl Rahner, "What is a Sacrament?" p. 136.

119. Paul C. Empie and T. Austin Murphy, eds., *Lutherans and Catholics in Dialogue, I-III* Minneapolis: Augsburg Publishing House, 1967), III, p. 192.

120. See "Rite for Distributing Holy Communion Outside Mass," *The Rites*, I (see n. 5, above), pp. 465-469.

121. Ibid., I, pp. 470-474.

122. Ibid., I, p. 465.

123. HCWE, 42, I, p. 470.

124. *Constitution on the Liturgy*, 27; Megivern, *Worship and Liturgy*, p. 206.

125. Ibid., 30; Megivern, *Worship and Liturgy*, p. 207.

126. Ibid., 24; Megivern, *Worship and Liturgy*, p. 206.

127. HCWE, 13, I, p. 459.

128. HCWE, 14, I, p. 459.

129. See Bishops' Committee on the Liturgy, *Study Text 1: Holy Communion* (Washington, D.C.: Publications Office, USCC, 1973), pp. 3-10.

130. Ibid., p. 3.

131. Ibid., pp. 4-5.

132. HCWE, 20, I, p. 461.

133. HCWE, 14, 15, I, pp. 459-460.

134. See Mitchell, "Symbols are Actions, not Objects," pp. 1-4.

135. See text cited in Bishops' Committee on the Liturgy, *The Body of Christ* (Washington, D.C.: NCCB, 1977), p. 22.

136. See Norman Perrin, *Jesus and the Language of the Kingdom* (Philadelphia: Fortress Press, 1976), pp. 15-56.

137. Ibid., pp. 19-25.

138. Ibid., pp. 26-29.

139. See Juan Mateos, "El Nuevo Testamento y su Mensaje," in *Nuevo Testamento*, translated and edited by Juan Mateos, Luis Alonso Schökel *et al*. (Huntington, Ind.: Our Sunday Visitor, 1975), pp. 13-44.

140. HCWE, 13, I, p. 459.

Chapter Six

Special Ministers of Communion

INTRODUCTION
On 29 January 1973, the Congregation for the Discipline of the Sacraments issued the decree entitled *Immensae Caritatis*. The document dealt with four items related to holy communion both within and outside of Mass: 1) special ministers for distribution of the eucharist; 2) extension of the faculty to receive communion more than once on the same day; 3) mitigation of the eucharistic fast for the sick and aged; and 4) reception of the eucharist in the hands of the faithful.[1] The pastoral intention of *Immensae Caritatis* is clear: to facilitate reception of communion, especially in situations where there are insufficient numbers of ordained persons or where illness and age prevent people from fulfilling the discipline of eucharistic fasting.

Later in 1973, the published "Rites for Holy Communion and Worship of the Eucharist Outside Mass" included a chapter on administration of communion and viaticum to the sick by an extraordinary minister.[2] The chapter actually provided three rites for use by a special minister of the eucharist: The Ordinary Rite of Communion of the Sick[3]; Short Rite of Communion of the Sick[4]; Viaticum.[5]

It should be noted that these rites were designed precisely for pastoral situations where priests or deacons are either unavailable or prevented (by illness, age, pastoral work) from carrying out this ministry. *Immensae Caritatis* provided norms for the appointment of extraordinary eucharistic ministers; the "Rites for Holy Communion and Worship of the Eucharist Outside Mass" provided liturgical rites for use by these ministers. According to present legislation, therefore, the ministry of communion for the ill and dying may be carried out by both ordained and nonordained persons:

When priests or deacons perform this ministry, they use the forms provided in the "Rite of Anointing and Pastoral Care of the Sick"[6];
When special ministers (including acolytes) take communion to the ill and dying, they use the forms provided in the "Rites for Holy Communion and Worship of the Eucharist Outside Mass."[7]

Structurally, these two sets of rites are similar; the following chart will reveal the major differences between them.

Priests/Deacons	Special Ministers/Acolytes
I. Ordinary Rite of Communion of the Sick	I. Ordinary Rite of Communion of the Sick
Greeting	Greeting
Sprinkling of sick person and room with holy water (optional)	
Penitential Rite	Penitential Rite
Opportunity for sacramental confession	
Other forms	Other forms
Reading from Scripture	Reading from Scripture
Lord's Prayer	Lord's Prayer
Communion	Communion
Concluding Prayer	Concluding Prayer
Blessing	
II. Short Rite of Communion of the Sick	II. Short Rite of Communion of the Sick
Opportunity for sacramental confession	
Introductory antiphon	Introductory antiphon
Communion	Communion
Concluding Prayer	Concluding Prayer
III. Viaticum (outside Mass)	III. Viaticum (outside Mass)
Introductory Rites	Introductory Rites

Sprinkling with holy water (optional)	
Greeting, instruction	Greeting, instruction
Penitential Rite	Penitential Rite
Opportunity for sacramental confession	
Other forms	Other forms
Plenary indulgence for the dying (optional)	
Reading from Scripture	Reading from Scripture
Baptismal Profession of Faith	Baptismal Profession of Faith
Viaticum	Litany
Lord's Prayer	Viaticum
Communion	Lord's Prayer
Concluding Rites	Communion
Prayer	Concluding Rites
Blessing	Prayer
Sign of Peace	

Except for certain elements reserved to priests (e.g., the confession of a sick or dying person), these rites are virtually identical in structure and content. Each of the three rites, moreover, envisions a particular pastoral setting:

Rite I implies a visit to the home of the sick person;
Rite II implies a situation such as a hospital or nursing home, where several people may be receiving communion in separate rooms or buildings;
Rite III restricts its attention to the case of a person who is near death, whether at home or in a medical facility.

The present chapter will focus on these three rites as they are designed for use by special ministers of the eucharist.[8] For that reason, it will not be my purpose to give a complete history and theology of communion of the sick or viaticum; instead, I will concentrate on these rites as they have been associated, historically and pastorally, with special ministers. This chapter will thus be structured along the lines of 1) historical models; 2) the Ritual of 1973 with attention to theological roots,

270

structure of the new rites and theological significance of the rites.

HISTORICAL MODELS

From the earliest centuries of Christian history there is evidence for the participation of lay persons in pastoral ministry for the ill and dying. Until at least the ninth century, for example, Christians were accustomed to anoint themselves and others in time of sickness with oil blessed for this purpose by the bishop.[9] In some cases, the sick were also communicated by lay persons. One such example has already been described in Chapter Five: the third-century Alexandrian Serapion's last communion, administered to him by his grandson. Serapion's situation was perhaps extraordinary, but other hagiographical accounts reveal similar customs. Bede's *History of the English Church and People* includes a charming vignette about the poet Caedmon, monk of Whitby, who appears to have been communicated by lay companions as the time of his death approached.[10] And Gregory the Great's description of Benedict's death suggests that Benedict (a layman) gave himself communion in his last hours.[11]

Bede's and Gregory's allusions to communion in the form of viaticum administered by lay persons emerge, of course, from a specific situation: the life and customs of monastic communities. But it is fairly certain that lay ministers of communion for the sick and dying were not restricted to houses of religious. Negative evidence supplied by conciliar and synodical legislation indicates that for many centuries lay persons were entrusted with this ministry, even though this was sometimes regarded as irregular.

Our purpose here will be to sift the evidence for historical examples of communion taken to the sick and dying by lay men or women. For the sake of convenience in organizing the data, three categories will be discussed:

1) monastic customs; 2) examples of lay ministry; and 3) the ministry of acolytes.

Monks as Ministers

In an eighth-century ecclesiastical handbook of penance known as the *Penitential of Bede*, there is a passage which reads:

"it is permitted to all the faithful when they chance to find unbaptized persons about to die, nay it is commanded, that they snatch souls from the devil by baptism, that is, that they shall with water simply blessed in the name of the Lord baptize these persons in the name of the Father and of the Son and of the Holy Spirit, plunging them in the water or pouring it over them. Hence the faithful who can do it, especially monks, ought both to have a knowledge of baptizing and, if they are going anywhere at a distance, always to have the eucharist with them."[12]

Although Bede's authorship of this handbook has been vigorously disputed by scholars, one thing is clear: the author of this document is familiar with the custom of lay persons, especially monks, carrying the eucharist with them in case it should be needed for the dying. Nor was this custom unusual, it appears, among Christians in the British Isles. Irish hagiographical literature, for example, abounds in stories about monks who carried their chrismals (small vessels containing the eucharist) as they traveled from place to place. The chrismal served a dual purpose: it provided protection as a kind of amulet, and it enabled a monk to give viaticum to those who might need it.[13] Both purposes are reflected in Irish legends about prominent saints. The following story, for instance is taken from the Life of St. Comgall (+ ca. 602).

"One day, when St. Comgall was working alone outside in the fields, he put his chrismal on his cloak. That day, a band of foreign robbers [Picts] fell upon the village

272

with the intent of seizing everything there—both men and beasts. When the foreigners came upon St. Comgall working outside, and when they saw the chrismal on his cloak, they assumed that the chrismal was Comgall's god. And because they feared his god, the robbers dared not touch him."[14]

The second reason for carrying the chrismal—to provide viaticum for the dying—is illustrated by this account of St. Molua: "St. Molua indicated to St. Cronan that his death was near, and received the communion of Christ's body and blood from him. After prayer, a tearful blessing and the kiss of peace, St. Molua returned with his disciples to his own monastery, Cluain Ferta."[15] A variant in the manuscript tradition of Molua's life indicates that Cronan had been carrying the sacrament on his own person, presumably in a chrismal.[16]

These passages testify to the common Irish practice of carrying the sacrament in a chrismal, especially for the sake of providing viaticum. And although the monks in these stories were probably ordained priests,[17] the passage cited above from the *Penitential of Bede* reveals that lay persons were encouraged to adopt the same custom. It can be argued, in any case, that Irish monks, whether ordained or not, were considered appropriate ministers of the eucharist for the sick and dying.

Neither the *Penitential of Bede* nor the Irish hagiographies provide us with a description of any ritual used when viaticum was administered by laity or monks. We know, nevertheless, that from very early times viaticum was considered *the* sacrament of the dying Christian.[18] So great was the concern that a Christian die fortified by the eucharist that extreme measures were sometimes taken to insure the presence of the sacrament at the moment of death.[19] In some cases the eucharist was actually administered to the corpse out of fear, apparently, that Christians might otherwise be endangered by diabolical enemies on their final journey toward God.[20]

This rather curious custom seems to have been widespread in both East and West, especially from the fourth through the seventh centuries.[21]

This perhaps exaggerated concern for providing the dying with viaticum may help explain why carrying the eucharist in a chrismal became so popular in Irish monasticism. Irish monks, whether ordained or not, were more mobile than the ordinary parish clergy for the nonmonastic priests and deacons were required to reside at their churches and to be present there especially on Sundays.[22] Such requirements are reflected, for example, in ancient Irish canonical collections such as the *Collectio canonum Hibernensis*.[23] Other bits of legislation indicate that monastic mobility created problems for resident parish clergy, since monk-priests were popularly regarded as possessing higher status than their parish counterparts.[24]

Ireland was not the only place where monks, even when not ordained, were considered appropriate ministers of the eucharist. As we have seen in the preceding chapter, the Italian community governed by the *Rule of the Master* developed a daily communion service presided over by the abbot, a lay man. Though this service was not designed for communion of the sick or viaticum, it may be safely inferred that a dying monk in that community could receive the sacrament from his lay superior. Leaders of monastic houses, even though they were not ordained, thus seem to have been treated as qualified to distribute the eucharist. Another story from Gregory the Great's *Dialogues* illustrates this point. Benedict, abbot and lay man, is pictured as sending the eucharist to the family of a young monk whose body refused to remain buried: "the man of God gave them a consecrated wafer of the Lord's body and said, 'Go and put this consecrated wafer on his breast and bury him that way.' When this had been done, the earth received his body and kept it, and did not cast it out again."[25] Though the story lacks historical veracity, it does bear witness to popular attitudes toward the eucharist. The young monk in question had left the monastery without permission to visit his parents—and he had died on that very day, apparently without benefit of viaticum. By sending the "consecrated wafer" to the family, Benedict provided a belated viaticum. The story also, incidentally, reflects the abuse of burying the eucharist with the dead.

Monks as ministers of the eucharist, especially in cases involving viaticum, seem to have been fairly common, at least in the period prior to the ninth century. Women religious also performed this ministry sometimes, as appears to be the case in the description of St. Odilia's death (ca. 720).[26] Such monastic customs are probably a survival of the more ancient practice of permitting lay persons to take the eucharist home, where it could be used both for ordinary reception on weekdays and for emergency situations such as grave illness or danger of death. After the fourth century, as we have seen in earlier chapters, the laity's freedom to take the eucharist home was restricted, but these restrictions seem to have been less binding on monks and nuns.

In both East and West, there is thus a consistent if not very detailed pattern of evidence for monastic men and women as special ministers of the eucharist. In addition to the testimony of western documents like the *Rule of the Master* and the Irish *Vitae Sanctorum*, we have corroborative evidence in eastern monastic sources. The letters of Theodore the Studite (+ 826), the renowned Byzantine monastic reformer, contain an interesting reference to the reservation and use of the eucharist by monks and nuns. Theodore had been asked whether or not monks and nuns could act as ministers of communion; his reply follows.

"It is not permitted for anyone who is not a priest to touch the sacred gifts; nor is it permitted to give oneself communion if neither presbyter nor deacon is present—except in case of urgent necessity. In such an event, the following is done: the holy book is placed [on the altar], which is covered with a clean cloth or holy veil. With fearful hand, one then consumes the holy eucharist, which had previously been placed on the altar. . . . Afterwards, whoever has received should cleanse the mouth with wine."[27]

This ninth-century text hints at several important points. Though the administration of the sacrament by nonordained persons is regarded as exceptional, it is not forbidden. The text presupposes, moreover, that the eucharist is reserved regularly in monastic houses of men and women. Finally, there are suggestions of a ritual—even when it is a case of giving oneself communion.

Lay Persons as Ministers
If monastic personnel were viewed as acceptable (though sometimes exceptional) ministers of the eucharist in the earlier centuries of Christian history, what can be said about lay persons who were not members of religious communities? Historical evidence reveals a gradual tendency to prohibit the laity from taking the eucharist to their homes, as well as from taking it to the sick or dying. Such prohibitions begin to appear in the seventh century and are repeated with greater frequency during the ninth century and later. In the paragraphs that follow we shall attempt to see how the laity were gradually excluded from the ministry of communion.

In the first of his funeral orations on his brother Satyrus, Ambrose of Milan tells the story of his sibling's experience of shipwreck. When the disaster occurred Satyrus was still a catechumen, and "though he did not fear death, he was . . . deeply concerned about dying without the Eucharist."[28] A resourceful young man, Satyrus approached some fully initiated Christians aboard the ship, and asked them for the eucharist; he then placed the sacrament in a napkin, tied it around his neck, and jumped into the sea. Ambrose goes on to say that Satyrus's action revealed his deep faith and resulted in his rescue.[29]

The story is important because it reveals that even in the late fourth century lay Christians carried the eucharist with them, especially on journeys that were long and dangerous. And like the stories of peripatetic Irish monks with their chrismals, Ambrose's tale views the eucharist as double protection: an amulet against dangers and viaticum in case of sudden illness or death.

Implicitly, Ambrose's story about Satyrus affirms the propriety of the ancient Christian custom. But Jerome, Ambrose's contemporary, seems to attack the practice of eucharistic reservation in the homes of lay Christians.[30] Ever the suspicious monitor of Christian mores, Jerome, seems to have feared that people might communicate in the privacy of their homes, even when they were ill-prepared to receive at the public celebration in church. How can one account for the apparent discrepancy between these two views, each represented by a prominent church leader of the later fourth century?

In my opinion, the discrepancy is best viewed as a conflict between two values. One value, represented by Ambrose's account of his brother's shipwreck, stresses the critical connection between reception of the eucharist and the death of a Christian. As Alfred Rush has observed, the Roman church placed unusually strong emphasis on having the eucharist in one's mouth at the very point of death.[31] This emphasis would have lent legitimacy to the custom of carrying the eucharist on one's person, especially when embarking on long and difficult journeys, since one could not always depend, in such circumstances, upon the immediate availability of a clergyman. Reservation of the eucharist on one's person or in the home was a kind of insurance that viaticum would be available whenever it was needed. Jerome's opposition to the practice represents, however, a different value. Communion at the eucharist is the sign of communion with the church, its beliefs and its behavior: "what is not allowed in church is not allowed at home."[32] Jerome seems to have felt that the domestic and quasi-private reservation of the eucharist threatened this important ecclesiological principle.

I do not mean to imply that Ambrose and Jerome came into historical conflict over this issue; we have no evidence that either man repudiated the other's view of eucharist. Their different emphases reveal, however, a potential conflict that would later influence church discipline. Ambrose's panegyric on his brother affirms a custom that was destined, in late centuries, for virtual extinction, while Jerome's admonitions are eventually reflected in the church's official opposition against lay involvement in eucharistic reservation and communion of the sick.

By the seventh century, local councils and synods had begun to prohibit lay persons from acting as ministers of communion. The Council in Trullo (692) forbade the laity to distribute communion whenever a bishop, presbyter or deacon was present.[33] Similar legislation appears in the West during the same century. When, for example, a local council meeting at Rouen around the year 650 instructs the clergy to make sure the eucharist is placed "not in the hands but only in the mouth of a lay man or woman," there seems to be an implicit prohibition against eucharistic reservation by laity in their homes.[34]

And yet it is clear that in the seventh century no uniform policy about lay persons as ministers of communion had been developed in either East or West. The canons of the Council in Trullo, for example, were rejected by the pope, and earlier seventh-century writers in the East like John Moschus (+ 619) quite clearly assumed that lay persons could and would reserve the eucharist and administer communion.

Ambiguities of this sort continued through the eighth and ninth centuries, particularly in the West. The "conflict between two values" mentioned earlier seems to have come to a head during this period. On the one hand, sources like the *Penitential of Bede* exhibit concern that viaticum be readily available—and thus monks and lay persons are encouraged always to have the eucharist with them. On the other hand, ecclesiastics like Hincmar of Rheims (ca. 806–882) insisted that their clergy assume responsibility for visiting the ill and taking them communion. Among items to be checked at a parish visitation is this one: "Whether the presbyter himself visits the sick, anoints them with holy oil, and communicates them—and not someone else. The presbyter must give communion, and not hand it over to some layperson to take to the sick."[35] A similar text appears in the canonical collection of Regino of Prum: "Some presbyters hold the divine mysteries in such careless disregard that they hand over the holy body of the Lord to lay men and women to take to the sick. . . . The presbyter himself should communicate the sick."[36]

These objections reveal, of course, that the custom of lay persons taking communion to the ill was still being observed. And despite efforts at liturgical reform during the Carolingian era, the practice was still alive in the tenth century. Among the edicts of Ratherius, who became bishop of Verona in 931, is an admonition that reads: "No [presbyter] should presume to give a lay man or woman communion to be taken to the sick."[37] Examples could be multiplied, but it is reasonably evident that lay ministers of communion for the ill and dying continued to exist, throughout the first millenium of Christian history, despite official denunciations. Even at a later period in the middle ages, councils and synods were willing to recognize that in cases of extreme necessity the laity could legitimately function as eucharistic ministers. This is the tenor of a canon approved at a council of Westminster in 1138: "We decree that the body of Christ be taken to the ill only by a priest or deacon; but in case of pressing necessity it may be taken, with greatest reverence, by anyone."[38]

In principle, therefore, the medieval church seems to have recognized the legitimacy of lay ministers of communion at least in urgent situations. As time went on, however, prohibitions against lay ministry, and even against that of deacons, multiplied. Thirteenth-century English councils frequently forbade priests to let deacons take communion to the sick.[39] It is important to note, however, that these prohibitions were primarily disciplinary and pastoral in nature; they did not call into question the theological legitimacy of communion ministers who were not priests. The intent of synodical statutes forbidding all but the priest to take communion to the sick thus appears to have been corrective; neglect of pastoral responsibility on the part of the presbyters supplied the motive behind these statutes, as the following one from the diocese of York reveals:

"Presbyters should diligently visit the sick on all Sundays and festivals. . . . Nor should they, as some have presumed heretofore, send deacons with the eucharist to the sick, while they [the presbyters] devote themselves to drinking or other delights of the flesh. The presbyters should personally go to the sick and solicitously hear their confessions."[40]

Other thirteenth-century English canons exhibit a similar concern. Canon 35 of the synodical statutes for the diocese of London in the time of Bishop Fulk Basset (ca. 1245–1259) reads, in part: "Presbyters are not permitted to delegate deacons to take the holy body of the Lord to the sick, except out of necessity when the priest himself is absent."[41]

These medieval statutes eventually established the pattern for legislation concerning eucharistic ministers in the Latin church. The 1917 Code of Canon Law reflected this pattern; canon 845 laid down the following provisions:

280

"1. The ordinary minister of holy communion is the priest alone;

2. The extraordinary [minister] is the deacon, if permission has been granted, for a grave reason, by the local ordinary or the pastor; in case of necessity [the permission] may legitimately be presumed."[42]

Until the reforms of the Second Vatican Council appeared, these canons remained in effect. With the publication of *Immensae Caritatis*, however, the situation changed. The category of extraordinary ministers of the eucharist was expanded to include persons who are neither priests, deacons, nor acolytes.[43] These special ministers are recommended particularly in pastoral situations such as the following:

When the number of communicants at Mass is particularly large;
When there is need for a number of eucharistic ministers to care for the sick, e.g., in hospitals;
When there is a grave emergency, e.g., viaticum for a person in proximate danger of death.[44]

Six norms for the selection and work of these special ministers were outlined in *Immensae Caritatis*; a review of them here may be useful.

1) Local ordinaries may permit qualified persons to act as eucharistic ministers, either for a specific occasion or "in case of necessity, in a permanent way." This faculty may be invoked whenever there is no priest, deacon or acolyte present, or when these ministers are prevented from distributing communion because of advanced age, ill health, or other pastoral obligations. The faculty may also be used when the number of communicants at Mass is so great that the celebration would be unduly delayed.

2) With the permission of their local ordinaries, individual priests may appoint qualified persons as extraordinary ministers when there is a genuine need on a specific occasion.

281

3) Auxiliary bishops, episcopal vicars and others may be delegated by the ordinary in a similar fashion.

4) The "qualified persons" so designated for this special ministry include in order of preference: reader (lector); major seminary student; male religious; woman religious; catechist; man; woman. This order of preference, may, however, be changed at the discretion of the local ordinary.

5) The faculty spoken of in norms 1 through 3 may also be extended to the superiors of religious communities (male or female) for use in their own oratories.

6) A recommended ritual for designating special ministers of the eucharist is appended to the text of *Immensae Caritatis*.[45]

These norms were reiterated in a declaration of the Congregation for the Sacraments and Divine Worship on 17 April 1980.[46] This declaration, *Inaestimabile Donum*, did not repeat the earlier provisions for extraordinary ministers of the eucharist, but did label "reprehensible" the attitude of priests who "though present at the celebration, refrain from distributing Communion and leave this task to the laity."[47] Like the thirteenth-century synodical statutes discussed above, this declaration seems motivated not by a desire to exclude special ministers of the eucharist, but by an insistence that priests fulfill their pastoral responsibilities.

In the twenty centuries of Christian history, therefore, the question of special (nonordained) ministers of the eucharist has come full circle. We may summarize this history by noting, first, that the basic pastoral principle which determines who should distribute communion is this: to make the eucharist as widely available as possible to those who reasonably desire it. What is at stake is not the "rights" of ministers, whether ordained or not, but the legitimate need of baptized Christians to participate fully in the eucharist through sacramental communion. It was precisely to facilitate fulfillment of this need, as we have seen, that the church expanded the category of "extraordinary minister" after the Second Vatican Council. It should be noted, secondly, that the existence of lay ministers of communion has ancient roots in Christian tradition. Although the laity have sometimes been barred from this ministry, their exclusion seems to have resulted from a desire to correct the neglect of pastoral responsibility on the part of priests. The restoration of special eucharistic ministers in our own day thus respects the pastoral principle that gave rise to the practice in the first place: easier access to holy communion for all, especially for the ill and dying.[48]

Acolytes as Ministers
In the reformed rite for the institution of acolytes, the presiding bishop is directed to instruct the candidates along these lines:

"As people chosen for the ministry of acolyte, you will have a special role in the Church's ministry. The summit and source of the Church's life is the eucharist, which builds up the Christian community and makes it grow. It is your responsibility to assist priests and deacons in carrying out their ministry, and as extraordinary ministers to give holy communion to the faithful at the liturgy and to the sick."[49]

This text makes explicit allusion to the acolyte as an "extraordinary minister" of the eucharist; at the same time, the ritual of institution and its accompanying instruction makes it clear that this ministry is neither a sacramental order such as diaconate or priesthood nor an office intended exclusively for clerics. As one of two official "ministries" in the Roman Church, the other being that of reader, the acolythate is open to lay men and now embraces the functions formerly reserved to the subdiaconate, an office that has been suppressed.[50]

When, historically, did the acolyte as an extraordinary minister of the eucharist develop? The question is not

283

easy to answer, partly because the origins of the acolythate itself are obscure. Most scholars agree that this ministry was known in the church of Rome by at least the middle of the third century. A letter of Pope Cornelius to Fabius of Antioch, written about 251 and cited by Eusebius in his *Ecclesiastical History*, lists the ministers of the Roman church at that period as including "forty-six presbyters, seven deacons, seven subdeacons, forty-two acolytes."[51] This is an interesting reference, especially when one remembers that in his *Apostolic Tradition* (ca. 215) Hippolytus mentions the ministries of reader and subdeacon, but not that of acolyte. In describing the subdeacon, however, Hippolytus provides a clue that may help clarify the origins of the acolyte's ministry. "Hands shall not be laid on a subdeacon," the author writes, "but he shall be named in order that he may follow the deacons."[52] The last phrase is significant, for the word "acolyte" is derived from the Greek verb *akoloutheo*, meaning "to follow." The job of "following" (assisting, helping) the deacon, identified by Hippolytus as belonging to subdeacons, may in the course of time have been separated into two distinct ministries: that of subdeacon and that of acolyte. Perhaps by the middle of the third century, when Cornelius wrote to Fabius, this separation had been achieved, and thus the pope could speak of the distinct offices.

It must be remembered, however, that at this early period of the church's history great flexibility and diversity existed among the so-called lesser ministries (those below the rank of bishop, presbyter, and deacon). The eastern churches, for example, seem never to have developed a ministry of acolyte in the precise western sense of that term.[53] And even the western churches did not all agree on their lists of lesser ministries; Spain, for instance, had its order of "sacristans" and other churches knew of *fossaria*, gravediggers.[54] One must therefore be cautious in attempting to identify the exact role or functions of ministers like the acolyte in early Christianity.

284

Thus, even if acolytes did exist in Rome by the middle of the third century, we are still left with an unanswered question: when and how did these persons assume responsibility for distributing the eucharist, especially to the sick? Third-century sources such as Cornelius's letter to Fabius are silent about the functions of acolytes, and although Cyprian of Carthage (+ 258) speaks of them as *tabellarii* (couriers entrusted with important confidential messages), this function was also fulfilled by other ministers such as subdeacons or readers.[55]

Perhaps the earliest association between acolytes and eucharistic ministry appears in the legends that surround the famous Roman martyr Tarsicius. Factual information about this young man is meager, but among the epigrams written by Pope Damasus (304–384) is one that reads:

"The Jewish people hurled rocks at Stephen, when he warned them of better things. He it was who seized a trophy from his enemies—and he became the first faithful levite to suffer martyrdom. When holy Tarsicius, bearing the sacraments of Christ, was wickedly pressed to show what he held to the godless, he preferred to be cut down, losing his own life, rather than hand over the heavenly members [of Christ] to the rabid dogs."[56]

It will be noted, of course, that in this epigram Damasus does not explicitly identify Tarsicius as an acolyte; if anything, the context implies that he was a deacon—a "faithful levite" as Stephen was. But in later centuries it became popular to imagine Tarsicius as an acolyte, hardly older than a boy, whose devotion to the eucharist outweighed concern for his own safety. The popularity of this legend was heightened by the sixth-century *Passio sancti Stephani papae*, which perhaps erroneously identified Tarsicius as an acolyte.[57] Toward the conclusion of this *Passio*, the following story is related:

"One day the pagan soldiers found an acolyte whose name was Tarsicius carrying the sacraments of the Body of Christ. The pagans seized him and demanded to know what he carried. But Tarsicius, considering that it was insufferable to cast pearls before swine, refused to show them the holy mysteries. [The soldiers] then beat him with clubs and rocks until he gave up his spirit."[58]

Should one assume, then, that the connection between acolytes and the ministry of taking communion to Christians is simply a piece of hagiographical fiction? Probably not. The letter of Innocent I to Decentius, bishop of Gubbio, indicates that each Sunday acolytes carried the *fermentum* from the bishop's Mass to the titular churches where presbyters were presiding. As we have seen in Chapter One, the size and complexity of the church at Rome in the early fifth century prohibited a gathering of the entire community at the bishop's Mass on Sunday. Innocent explains how this situation was handled: "On Sunday the presbyters at the *tituli* are not able to join us, because of the people entrusted to their care; the *fermentum* consecrated by us is therefore sent to them by acolytes, so that they will not consider themselves separated from communion with us, especially on that day."[59]

Here the connection between acolytes and "bearing the eucharist" is explicit. It should be noted, however, that Innocent says nothing about a special ministry toward the ill and dying, nor does he mention any other task for acolytes beyond that of taking the *fermentum* to the titular churches where presbyters preside on Sundays. Other sources important for the history of the Roman liturgy are surprisingly silent about the existence and role of acolytes. The Verona (Leonine) Sacramentary (ca. 600), for example, provides neither ritual nor prayers for the ordination of acolytes, though it does provide texts for ordaining bishops, deacons, and presbyters.[60] The ancient Gelasian Sacramentary (*Gelasianum Vetus* manuscript ca. 750) which contains a mixture of Roman and Gallican elements, mentions acolytes, but only in a section of the document derived from a Gallican source known as the *Statuta Ecclesiae Antiquae*.[61] In the *Missale Francorum*, a Gallican sacramentary from the late seventh or early eighth century, the text concerning acolytes from the *Statuta Ecclesiae Antiquae* is included, and a prayer for the "blessing of an acolyte" (*benedictio acoliti*) is also provided.[62]

But none of these texts which do include formulas for blessing or ordaining acolytes refer to them as ministers of the eucharist. The *Statuta Ecclesiae Antiquae* speaks of the acolyte in this manner:

"When an acolyte is ordained by the bishop he should be taught how to conduct himself in his office. From the archdeacon he receives the candlestick with a candle, that he may know he is responsible for lighting the lamps of the church. Let him also receive an empty vessel for carrying the wine destined for the eucharist of Christ's blood."[63]

The prayer of blessing for an acolyte found in the *Missale Francorum* is also silent about any ministry of taking communion to others: "Lord, holy Father, almighty and everlasting God, you spoke to Aaron and Moses, [instructing them] to rekindle the lights in the tabernacle of testimony. Be pleased to bless and sanctify this your servant, that he may be an acolyte in your church: through [Jesus Christ . . .]."[64]

Both these texts, it will be noticed, emphasize practical caretaker functions: lighting the candles in church, assuming responsibility for the wine vessels used at Mass. These are, of course, familiar tasks associated, at a later period of history, with altar boys, also called acolytes.

So far, then, our examination of the historical evidence reveals that while acolytes are known to have existed in some churches by the middle of the third century, there is no secure proof that they were considered special ministers of the eucharist. The tradition that connects acolytes with bearing the eucharist, especially to the sick and dying, appears to be based on an erroneous interpretation of Tarsicius popularized by the *Passio sancti Stephani papae* in the sixth century. Pope Innocent I does assign acolytes the task of carrying the *fermentum* to the titular churches in Rome on Sundays, but this function would not in itself make them extraordinary ministers of the eucharist. Nor do the texts and rubrics of the major sacramentaries—Roman, Gallican and mixed varieties—offer us any conclusive proof that acolytes were regularly regarded as qualified ministers of communion.

We must look elsewhere, then, for the roots of the tradition that views acolytes as "extraordinary ministers to give holy communion to the faithful at the liturgy and to the sick."[65] In *Ordo Romanus Primus* (OR I), a detailed outline of papal ceremonies at the eucharist (ca. 700), acolytes play a prominent role. The full text of this *ordo* is too lengthy to reproduce here, but an outline of its contents as they relate to the role of the acolyte may be given.[66]

Preparation of Gifts: The "offertory rite" in OR I is somewhat complex and involves the ministry of bishop (pope), archdeacon, deacons, district subdeacons, presbyter, and acolytes. Two ministerial responsibilities fall to the acolytes: they hold the large bowls into which the wine offered by various categories of people is poured (the wine is brought up in flasks, received by the archdeacon, poured into a large chalice, then poured into a bowl held by the acolyte); and they hold the linen bags into which the offerings of bread are placed. As we shall see, these bowls and linen bags are used later in the Mass when the people receive communion.[67]

Ritual of the Paten: After the preparation of gifts is completed, an acolyte with a linen cloth tied to his neck stands next to the pope, who begins the eucharistic prayer. Inside the cloth, the acolyte holds the paten which is destined for use in the communion ritual.

(Those old enough may remember that the subdeacon performed a similar task at a solemn high Mass.)

Communion Ritual: After the eucharistic prayer is finished and the bread on the altar has been broken in preparation for holy communion, the acolytes who held the linen bags containing the people's offerings bring them to the altar. The bread is broken by deacons, and communion is given to the various ranks of clergy and people by several ministers (pope, bishops, archdeacon, deacons). A similar procedure is followed for the wine: the bowls held by the acolytes are "consecrated by contact," the deacon pouring a small amount from the pope's chalice into them. The chalice used in the communion of the people is filled, as need requires, from these bowls of wine. This method was obviously used in order to accommodate large numbers of communicants, and to avoid the wrong impression that might be created if several chalices were placed on the altar. By using the linen bags of bread and the bowls, held by acolytes at some distance from the altar, OR I was able to maintain the ancient principle that all communicants receive from *one* loaf and *one* cup.

Nowhere in the description of this papal liturgy are acolytes assigned the task of administering communion to the people. Their job is to assist the other ministers (deacons and subdeacons, principally) in preparing the gifts and in seeing that sufficient bread and wine are available at the time of communion. It is interesting that *Ordo Romanus* XXXIV, a description of the rites used for ordinations at Rome and compiled ca. 750, says nothing about the acolyte as a communion minister:

"When Mass has been celebrated, they clothe the cleric (who is to become an acolyte) in planeta (chasuble) and stole.

"When the bishop or the pope comes to give him communion, they beckon him forward and place a little bag over his chasuble; he prostrates, still wearing the little bag, and they offer prayer for him as follows:

"'Through the intercession of the blessed, glorious and ever virgin Mary, and of the blessed apostle Peter, may the Lord save, keep and protect you. Amen.'"[68]

In light of the ceremonies for a papal Mass described in OR I, this ritual for ordaining an acolyte makes sense. The little bag is the appropriate sign of the acolyte's office, for he uses it during the liturgy of the eucharist at the preparation of the gifts and at communion time. Note too that in the earlier Roman rituals for ordination it was customary to clothe even the lesser ministers in chasuble (*planeta*) and stole, for at this period of history the chasuble seems to have been the ordinary liturgical garment for *all* clerics in the Roman church —except for the deacons, whose distinctive garb was the dalmatic.[69] Even in later *ordines* of mixed character (Roman-Gallican), such as OR XXXV (ca. 925), the rubric about vesting the acolyte in chasuble and stole has been kept. In this last *ordo*, however, another feature of the acolyte's ministry is noted: it is his responsibility to carry the chrism so that it may be used by the bishop whenever the need arises.[70]

Our study of the *Ordines romani* reveals that while acolytes were unquestionably regarded as liturgical ministers at the eucharist, there is scarcely any evidence to prove they functioned as special ministers of communion. There is, however, one last source that needs to be examined before concluding our discussion of the eucharistic ministry of acolytes: the famous letter of the Roman deacon John to the nobleman Senarius.[71] Noted for its important information about baptismal practices at Rome, John's letter, written about the year 500, also includes a brief description of acolytes and their ministry.

"Acolytes differ from exorcists in this manner: exorcists are denied the power of carrying the sacraments and of ministering them to the priests. . . . But acolytes receive the vessels for carrying the sacraments, and they exercise their order of ministering to the priests. Thus an exorcist can become an acolyte, but no acolyte can assume the office of exorcist—for that would be no promotion. An acolyte who has acquitted himself well in his ministry may, however, be promoted to the rank of subdeacon. For among us, he is called a subdeacon who carries the sacred chalice in which the bishop offers the mystery of the Lord's blood. And again, if [the subdeacon] has persevered spotless and blameless in his ministry, he may be promoted to the sacred dignity of diaconate or priesthood."[72]

It is reasonably clear from John's letter that the liturgical role of the acolyte, described in detail in OR I (ca. 700), was already established in the Roman church by the year 500. And if we take into account, further, the letter of Innocent I to Decentius of Gubbio, we may conclude that the acolytes's ministry was well known at Rome in the early fifth century (ca. 416).

A common thread runs through all these descriptions of the acolyte and his ministerial role: he is the one responsible for "carrying the sacraments" in the liturgical celebration. Does this mean he was a minister of holy communion? Not exactly. In the sources we have examined here, the acolyte "bears" or "carries" the eucharist (and other elements besides, such as chrism) from one liturgical minister to another. He is, in other words, a kind of liturgical go-between. According to Innocent I, he carries the eucharistic particle (*fermentum*) from the pope's Mass on Sunday to the celebration conducted by presbyters in the titular parishes. According to OR I, he holds the linen bags in which the eucharistic bread is kept, and carries it to those who will break it in preparation for communion. He acts not as one who distributes communion, but as one who assists those who break and distribute the bread.

Our primary historical sources—letters, sacramentaries, *ordines*—do not, therefore, explicitly identify the acolyte as a communion minister. Neither do the major medieval pontificals—from the tenth-century Romano-Germanic Pontifical to the thirteenth-century Pontifical of William Durandus—speak of the acolyte as a minister of communion. Nor, finally, did the pontifical promulgated after the Council of Trent allude to any such task.[73] But one can see how, under the influence of popular legends such as those associated with Tarsicius, the acolyte came to be viewed as an auxiliary minister of the eucharist, especially if a deacon or priest were not available. In this instance, at least, hagiographical fiction seems to have played a more prominent role than historical fact.

THE RITUAL OF 1973

Our historical discussion of special or "extraordinary" ministers of communion reveals that the church's practice in this matter has varied widely over the centuries. Members of religious communities (both men and women), lay persons and acolytes all have been associated at one time or another with the ministry of holy communion, especially for the ill and dying. Restoration of these special ministers through the provisions of *Immensae Caritatis* (1973) is thus very much in accord with the evolving tradition of the church.

Until the recent liturgical reforms, however, there were no official rites for communion of the sick and dying when these are celebrated by special ministers (lay persons, nonordained religious, acolytes). The Tridentine Ritual of 1614, for example, provided rites for the communion of the ill and for viaticum, but these were clearly designed for ordained ministers.[74] Indeed, the 1614 Ritual does not even mention the deacon as a possible extraordinary minister of the eucharist; it confines its

292

comments to the pastor or parish priest (*parochus*). The same situation is reflected in the earlier twentieth-century editions of the Roman Ritual. A revised edition published in 1955 during the pontificate of Pius XII, for instance, speaks only of priests as ministers for communion of the sick or viaticum.[75]

With the restoration of the diaconate as a permanent order in the church, and with the approval of special eucharistic ministers outlined in *Immensae Caritatis*, it was necessary to revise and in some cases create rites for communion of the ill and dying. As we have noted in the introduction to this chapter, deacons who exercise this ministry follow the forms provided in the "Rite of Anointing and Pastoral Care of the Sick." The rites contained in the document "Holy Communion and Worship of the Eucharist Outside Mass" are intended, therefore, only for special ministers (acolytes, nonordained religious, lay persons).

Theological Themes
Many of the themes identified in Chapter Five (rites for communion outside Mass) are present in the rites for communion of the sick by a special minister. Emphasis on the "two tables" of Word and Sacrament is reflected, for instance, in the provision for reading from scripture.[76] And the rites seem to imply that even in the private home of a sick or dying person there should be a gathering of Christians, a liturgical *assembly*.[77] Of perhaps greater significance, however, are the ecclesiological and ministerial implications of these new rites. These implications will be explored in the paragraphs that follow.

Ecclesiology: A frequent complaint heard on the eve of the Second Vatican Council was that the church had become too Romanized, too clericalist. Many Catholic Christians, perhaps the majority, seemed quite unconscious of their own identity as a people on pilgrimage, elected by God's grace to be a sacrament of hope in and for the world. It hardly needs to be said that the changes in ecclesiological understanding before and after the Council are dramatic. If any demonstration of this is needed, one can glance at the enormous difference between the original draft of the Council's dogmatic constitution on the church, prepared by a commission chaired by Cardinal Ottaviani, and the version that was eventually approved under the title *Lumen Gentium*.[78] Here is a topical comparison of the two versions:

First Draft	Final Version
The church militant	The mystery of the church
Membership in the church; necessity of the church for salvation	The People of God
Episcopate and priesthood	Ministry and Hierarchy
Residential bishops	
Religious	
Laity	Laity
Magisterium	The universal call to holiness
Authority and obedience	
Church and State; religious tolerance	Religious
	Pilgrim People
Necessity of evangelization	Mary, Mother of the Church
Ecumenism	

Both the structure and the content of the two versions exhibit profoundly different perceptions of who the church is and how it relates to the world. In the final draft, as Richard McBrien has observed,

"The Church was no longer to be seen initially or primarily . . . as a juridically, hierarchically constituted society which exists to communicate the grace of redemption to all mankind. Rather, it is first and foremost a community of people on march history, a pilgrim people, the very People of God. Within this People of God, there is a fundamental equality of vocation, of commitment, and of dignity."[79]

This vision of a people on the move, united by a "fundamental equality of vocation, of commitment, and of dignity," has unquestionably influenced both doctrine and worship in the postconciliar era. What fundamentally empowers Christians to worship is not the presence of ordained ministers, but the fact of baptismal initiation into the mystery of Jesus dead and rising. This is not a new insight; it was clearly formulated by Thomas Aquinas in the thirteenth century when he wrote that sacramental character (first imparted at baptism) brings the soul "to its fullness in things pertaining to the worship of God in terms of the Christian life as a ritual expression of this."[80] Aquinas was saying, in effect, that living in faith is the fundamental act of worship, that liturgy and life are thus inseparable, and that baptismal character empowers a Christian to "do" cult.

To say this is not, of course, to denigrate the importance of ordained ministry in the church. But it does show that Christians can offer authentic worship even in situations where no ordained person is present. Does a group of baptized lay Christians who gather to pray the liturgy of the hours engage in a genuinely liturgical act? It certainly does. Do the Christians who gather in a sick person's room to hear the scriptures, pray, and receive communion from the hands of a lay minister perform an authentic act of worship? Unquestionably, they do. The point here is not that ordination is unimportant or unnecessary, but simply that liturgy is not limited to events at which ordained personnel preside.

For this reason it is entirely appropriate that communion distributed to the sick or dying by extraordinary ministers be included in the reformed Roman Ritual as genuinely liturgical actions. Worship is, as the *Constitution on the Liturgy* implies, the "supreme manifestation of the church" (*praecipua manifestatio ecclesiae*).[81] And no matter how small or poor the community may be, when it assembles to act as church, it becomes church. A.-M. Roguet has summed up the matter well:

"We can only speak of liturgy when the community acts in so far as it is the Church, and because the Church itself recognizes it under the movement of the Holy Spirit. . . .

"When there is a truly liturgical action, the community which performs it represents the Church, it is the Church. However small and poor a community may be, when it celebrates the liturgy it is a particular Church. This is above all true of local churches, the parishes. But it is also true of personal parishes, of little groups which celebrate the liturgy, and . . . of religious communities."[82]

These new rites for communion of the sick and viaticum thus invite us to embrace a broader vision of both church and worship. They encourage us to see in the liturgical assembly, however small or poor it may be, the church itself caught in the act of becoming. They remind us that liturgical prayer and action are not exhausted by those occasions when a bishop, priest, or deacon presides.

Ministry: Closely related to the ecclesiological theme embedded in these new rites is a ministerial one. There is renewed discussion today about the baptismal priesthood of all Christians, about newly emergent forms of lay ministry in the church.[83] The Council itself spurred this discussion, particularly in the constitution *Lumen Gentium*. In somewhat cautious language the Council declared: "Though they differ essentially and not only in degree, the common priesthood of the faithful and the ministerial or hierarchical priesthood are none the less ordered one to another; each in its own proper way shares in the one priesthood of Christ."[84] The Council then went on to describe the "priestly community" of the baptized as prophetic.[85] In so doing the Council was appealing not only to traditional initiatory images (the baptized Christian as priest, prophet and king), but also to a theme common in Lukan theology: Jesus' Easter gift

296

of the Spirit empowers the entire community as prophets.[86] As George Montague has written:

"Luke, more than any of the evangelists, considers the age of salvation to be the age of the Spirit. This appears first in the emphatic role he gives to the Holy Spirit in the life and ministry of Jesus . . . and then in the church which receives that same Spirit after Jesus' ascension. . . . Christian discipleship involves, in addition to other traditional elements, an entering into the prayer of Jesus through the power of the Holy Spirit. . . .

"The Christian community is therefore primarily a prophetic community, and the Spirit is the spirit of prophecy, taken in its widest sense."[87]

The important point to notice here is that according to Luke's theology, the first and most secure signal of the presence of the prophetic Spirit in the community is prayer. Jesus is thus presented in Luke's gospel as a man dedicated to prayer through the power of the Spirit.[88] And the Christian community, empowered by the same Spirit, is first and foremost a community that gathers for prayer, instruction, fellowship and the breaking of bread (Acts 2.42). Consistently, therefore, Luke narrates his story of ecclesial origins by speaking of a community gathered for prayer and praise. In this, Luke also explains to his readers how the community is related to Jesus, because Jesus too is presented as discovering himself, so to speak, in a context of prayer

Jesus	*Community*
The Spirit descends on Jesus while he is praying (Luke 4.21)	The Spirit descends on the apostles while they are gathered in the place where they devoted themselves to prayer (cf. Acts 1.14; 2.1)
Jesus comes away from his messianic investuture at baptism and immediately goes to the synagogues	After their pentecostal experience the community is

(places of prayer and instruction) (Luke 4.14-15)	empowered for instruction, prayer and praise (See Acts 2.1-47)

Through such parallelisms of structure and content Luke makes a central theological point: the church knows how to pray because it learned it from Jesus and is empowered by the same Spirit that anointed Jesus for his mission and ministry.[89] Time and again Luke reiterates this point by concluding a section of narrative with a stock phrase about the community joyfully gathered for preaching and prayer. These stock phrases are scattered throughout Acts in a manner somewhat similar to Shakespeare's rhyming couplets at the conclusion of dramatic scenes: "And day by day attending the temple together and breaking bread in their homes, they partook of food with glad and generous hearts, praising God" (Acts 2.46-47); "And every day in the temple and at home they did not cease teaching and preaching Jesus as the Christ" (Acts 5.42); "And the word of the Lord spread. . . . And the disciples were filled with joy and with the Holy Spirit" (Acts 13.49, 52).

Luke thus seems to say that the first and most reliable manifestation of the Spirit of prophecy in the church is prayer. If, as the Council suggests, the priestly community of Christians is "prophetic," it is so first because it prays in the name of Jesus and in the power of the Spirit. Prophecy first erupts in prayer, and prayer is the characteristic sign of a prophetic community endowed with the Spirit of the Risen One.

For this reason, perhaps, leadership of the community at prayer has from earliest times been regarded as an essential form of Christian ministry. Prophets who possessed discernible gifts of teaching and prayer were often accorded extremely high status in primitive Christianity, even though these ministers (doubtless including both men and women) were not ordained or ritually designated for an office.[90] In the *Didache*, for example, prophets appear to be among those who proclaim the eucharistic prayer; if they are genuine, they are to be treated with honor and allowed to "give thanks as they please."[91]

At an early stage in the development of Christian ministry, therefore, prayer leadership and ordained leadership were not necessarily coextensive. The ability to lead others in prayer was a gift of the Spirit communicated through faith and baptism—and while ordained persons might well possess this gift, they did not have a monopoly on it. Once again, saying this in no way belittles the fact or functions of ordained officeholders in the community. Just as liturgy includes more than simply those events presided over by ordained officials, so leadership at community prayer is not restricted to those who have been ritually designated to serve or govern the church.

By providing liturgical rites led by nonordained Christians the reformed services for Holy Communion and Worship of the Eucharist Outside Mass affirm this ancient tradition in the church. *Immensae Caritatis* stresses that persons selected for the extraordinary ministry of communion to the sick and dying be qualified.[92] This is a point that ought not be neglected. Persons chosen to be special ministers should have the qualifications demanded of other liturgical leaders: sensitivity to the pastoral situation, ability to lead others in public prayer, skill in proclaiming the Word of God, basic ritual competence. While it is true, as Luke's theology suggests, that the entire Christian community is prophetic and that all possess the Spirit's gift of prayer, not every one is qualified to lead a liturgical assembly.

The new rites for communion of the sick by lay ministers thus provide an opportunity for parishes and other local communities to develop a form of service that has ancient roots in the church: leadership in prayer. As we have seen, this ministry was not and need not be restricted to those Christians chosen for ordained service. It must be remembered that ministry exists in the church not for its own sake, but as pastoral response to human need. While some of these needs continue to require the presence and action of ordained clergy, others may be met by laity qualified to lead others in prayer, praise, and the hearing of the Word. Ultimately, the criterion for all ministry in the church is a common one: "the pastoral benefit of the faithful."[93]

PASTORAL SIGNIFICANCE
The ecclesiological and ministerial implications of the new rites for communion of the sick by special ministers have obvious pastoral repercussions. The parish priest is no longer a solitary sacramental laborer, but the ordained leader of a college of ministers in the local church. Just as the relations among bishops, priests, and deacons are defined by the Council as collegial, so the relation between the priest and other ministers in the parish.[94] The ultimate theological source of collegiality in ministry is, of course, the single baptismal vocation common to all Christians. No matter how high a view one may have about the ontological nature and effects of ordination, what binds Christians together in life and ministry is deeper than what separates or distinguishes them. Plunged into the death and rising of Jesus, all the baptized share corporate responsibility for preaching the gospel, serving those in need, and worshiping the Father in spirit and truth.

It is this collegial understanding of all ministries in the church (whether ordained or not) that qualifies what is meant when we say the church is hierarchical in structure. Hierarchy, in Christians terms, can never mean the domination of some over others, or control of the weak by the strong. The specific nature of Christian hierarchy is collegial, and that means no one in the church may claim lordship over another. For among believers there is one unique lordship: that of Jesus, with whom all

300

have been clothed through conversion, faith, and baptism.

Collegiality and hierarchy are thus mutually modifying terms in the Christian church. Because all ministry is collegial and rooted in the common baptismal vocation, hierarchy refers to degrees of responsibility rather than levels of dominion or control. And because ministry is hierarchical, collegial responsibility can take a variety of forms without any fear of one group encroaching on another's "turf." Collegiality prevents the Christian ministry from becoming a power struggle among virtuosi preening themselves for top billing; hierarchy defines the specific responsibilities of each college of ministers, and thus frees people from the relative chaos created by a lack of structure in social life. In short, collegiality says "we share the responsibility"; hierarchy says "the buck stops here."

The emergence of new lay ministries in the church today, such as those connected with the pastoral care of the sick and dying, is thus a fuller manifestation of the church's structure as simultaneously collegiate and hierarchical. It is important that these new ministers not be regarded as "flunkies" assigned to do the difficult work shunned by the ordained; and it is important, too, that lay ministers not be considered mini-priests or mini-deacons. In this regard it is perhaps unfortunate that the recent Roman documents speak of acolytes and lay persons as "extraordinary" ministers of the eucharist (*ministri extraordinarii*). While it is true that the eucharist is customarily distributed by priests or deacons, ministry itself is not in the first instance an ordained or clerical phenomenon. The ministry of lay persons at the eucharist may be "extraordinary," but lay ministry itself is not. Indeed, the opposite is true: the "ordinary" Christian minister, in virtue of baptism, is the lay man or woman; the "extraordinary" minister is the person chosen to accept the responsibilities of ordination.

Thus the presence of lay men and women distributing communion at the Sunday liturgy or at the bedside of the ill and dying is an entirely ordinary expression of Christian ministry and pastoral care. The ministry of lay persons in the church has value in its own rights, not merely as an extension or surrogate for absent clerics. That is precisely why a special minister of the eucharist does not need to be ordained in order to fulfill this task. Baptism itself empowers Christians to lead others in prayer, to take communion to the sick, to bring viaticum to the dying, to lead a celebration of God's Word. Thus the rites for commissioning ministers of communion, appended to *Immensae Caritatis*, are really celebrations of prayer, Word, and blessing. They are not ordinations involving imposition of hands, transfer of ritual objects (chalice and paten), or special clothing (chasuble and stole).[95]

Pastorally, then, the rites for communion of the sick led by lay ministers provide an opportunity for recovering an ancient Christian insight: ministry is the ordinary mode of life for *all* Christians. It is neither exceptional nor extraordinary; all believers are called by baptism to carry on the service (*diakonia*) of Jesus who was priest not in virtue of any ordination, but in virtue of his self-offering on the cross. To be Christian is to be minister; and to be minister is to be involved in collegial responsibility for the gospel wherever and however it is preached.

SUMMARY
Our attention in this chapter has been focused on a specific issue: the historical, pastoral, and theological significance of eucharistic ministers who are not ordained to the diaconate or priesthood. We have seen that in the history of our tradition several different categories of special eucharistic ministers have emerged: religious men and women, lay men and women, acolytes. Sometimes these persons were officially encour-

aged to engage in pastoral care, especially for the dying. We see an example of this in a document like the *Penitential of Bede*, which urged both monks and laity to carry chrismals containing the eucharist in case there was need to give viaticum. Sometimes, too, there has been aggressive official resistance against nonordained ministers of the eucharist, possibly because the clergy were careless in their own work among the sick and dying. Throughout history, however, there have been special ministers, official or unofficial, who brought the bread of life to those who would otherwise have died without it.

The reemergence of lay eucharistic ministers in our own day thus represents continuity with a long tradition. Their presence and work reminds us that liturgy is not restricted to grand occasions when clergy preside, that church is not limited to solemn assemblies, that ministry is the ordinary vocation of all baptized Christians.

NOTES

1. See Bishops' Committee on the Liturgy, *Study Text 1: Holy Communion* (Washington, D.C.: USCC, 1973), pp. 3-4.

2. For the text of the document "Holy Communion and Worship of the Eucharist Outside Mass," see *The Rites* (2 vols., New York: Pueblo Publishing Company, 1976–1980), I, pp. 475-485 ("Administration of Communion and Viaticum by an Extraordinary Minister"). Further references to this document will be cited as follows: HCWE, I (the volume of the Pueblo edition), followed by the appropriate page references.

3. HCWE, I, pp. 475-478.

4. HCWE, I, pp. 478-479.

5. HCWE, I, pp. 479-483.

6. HCWE, 54; I, p. 475.

7. HCWE, 54; I, p. 475.

8. A forthcoming volume in the Pueblo series of commentaries on the rites as reformed by the Second Vatican Council will

include discussion of the documents on anointing and pastoral care of the sick.

9. See Canadian Conference of Catholic Bishops, *National Bulletin on Liturgy*, 57: Rites for the Sick and Dying (Volume 10; January-February, 1977), pp. 17-18.

10. See Leo Sherley-Price, trans., *Bede: A History of the English Church and People* (Baltimore: Penguin Books, 1960), Book IV.24, pp. 247-248.

11. See Myra Uhlfelder, trans., *Gregory the Great: Dialogues, Book II* (Indianapolis: Bobbs-Merrill, 1967), p. 47.

12. John T. McNeil and Helena M. Gamber, eds., trans., *Medieval Handbooks of Penance* (Records of Civilization, Sources and Studies, XXIX; New York: Columbia University Press, 1938), p. 224.

13. See W.H. Freestone, *The Sacrament Reserved* (Alcuin Club Collections, XXI; London: A.R. Mowbray and Co., 1917), pp. 56-57.

14. Charles Plummer, ed., *Vitae Sanctorum Hiberniae* (2 vols.; Oxford: University Press, 1910; reprinted, 1968), II, p. 11.

15. Plummer, *Vitae Sanctorum Hiberniae*, II, p. 223.

16. See Freestone, *The Sacrament Reserved*, p. 57.

17. For Comgall as priest see Plummer, *Vitae Sanctorum Hiberniae*, I, p. lix.

18. See the evidence assembled by Alfred C. Rush, "The Eucharist, the Sacrament of the Dying in Christian Antiquity," *The Jurist* 34 (1974), 10-35.

19. On the insistence that the eucharist be in the mouth at the moment of death, see Alfred C. Rush, *Death and Burial in Christian Antiquity* (The Catholic University of America Studies in Christian Antiquity, 1; Washington, D.C.: Catholic University of America Press, 1941), pp. 92-93.

20. See Rush, *Death and Burial*, pp. 99-101.

21. See ibid., pp. 99-100.

22. See Patrick J. Corish, "The Christian Mission," in *idem*, general editor, *A History of Irish Catholicism*, Volume 1 (Dublin: Gill and Macmillan, 1971), pp. 36-37.

23. Ibid., p. 37.

24. Ibid.

25. Gregory the Great, *Dialogues*, Book II.24, trans. Uhlfelder, p. 35.

26. See Freestone, *The Sacrament Reserved*, pp. 202, 226.

27. Theodore the Studite, *Letter* 219; PG 99: col. 1661.

28. See Leo P. McCauley *et al.*, trans., *Funeral Orations by Saint Gregory Nazianzen and Saint Ambrose* (Fathers of the Church, 22; New York: Fathers of the Church, 1953), p. 180.

29. Ibid., pp. 180-181.

30. See Chapter One, pp. 16-17.

31. See Rush, *Death and Burial*, pp. 92-93.

32. Jerome, *Letter 49*; text in Isidore Hilberg, ed., *Sancti Eusebii Hieronymi Epistulae* (CSEL, Vol. 54; Vienna: F. Tempsky, 1910), p. 377.

33. Canon 58; text in Mansi XI: col. 969. See the discussion in Freestone, *The Sacrament Reserved*, pp. 226-227.

34. *Caput* I.2; text in Mansi X: cols. 1199-1200. See the discussion in Freestone, *The Sacrament Reserved*, p. 277; questions have been raised about the precise dating of this council.

35. Text in PL 125: col. 779.

36. Text in Freestone, *The Sacrament Reserved*, p. 228.

37. Text in PL 136: col. 560.

38. Text in Freestone, *The Sacrament Reserved*, p. 228.

39. See, for example, the synodal statutes for the diocese of York, ca. 1241–1255, in Frederick Maurice Powicke and C.R. Cheney, eds., *Councils and Synods, with Other Documents Relating to the English Church* (2 vols.; Oxford: Clarendon Press, 1964), I, pp. 488-489; see also the synodal statutes of Bishop Fulk Basset for the diocese of London, ca. 1245–1259 (ibid., I, p. 640); finally, see the synodal statutes of Bishop Gilbert of St. Leofard for the diocese of Chichester, 1289 (ibid., I, p. 1085).

40. See Powicke/Cheney, I, p. 488.

41. Ibid., I, p. 640.

42. *Corpus Iuris Canonici* (Rome: Typis Polyglottis Vaticanis, 1918), p. 334.

43. See BCL *Study Text 1: Holy Communion*, p. 4.

44. Ibid.

45. Ibid., pp. 4-5.

46. See the text of this declaration (*Inaestimabile Donum*) in *Origins* 10 (June 5, 1980).

47. Ibid.

48. See BCL *Study Text 1: Holy Communion*, p. 3.

49. See "Rite of Institution of Readers and Acolytes," in *The Rites* (2 vols.; New York: Pueblo Publishing Company, 1976–1980), I, pp. 743-744.

50. See the *motu proprio* of Pope Paul VI entitled *Ministeria Quaedam*; text in *The Rites*, I, pp. 726-731.

51. See Eusebius, *Ecclesiastical History*, Book VI.43; translated by G.A. Willaimson, *Eusebius: The History of the Church* (Baltimore: Penguin Books, 1965), p. 282.

52. See Geoffrey J. Cuming, *Hippolytus: A Text for Students* (Grove Liturgical Study, No. 8; Bramcote, Notts.: Grove Books, 1976), p. 15.

53. An exception to this may be found in the case of the Armenians. See Henry Denzinger, *Ritus Orientalium* (Würzburg, 1864), II, p. 281.

54. See Bishops' Committee on the Liturgy, *Study Text 3: Ministries in the Church* (Washington, D.C.: USCC, 1974), p. 25. See also: Joseph Crehan, "The Seven Orders of Christ," *Theological Studies* 19 (1958), 81-93.

55. See V. Maurice, "Acolyte", DTC I/1, col. 314.

56. See Antonius Ferrua, ed., *Epigrammata Damasiana* (Sussidi allo Studio delle Antichità Cristiane, II; Città del Vaticano: Pontificio Instituto di Archeologia Cristiana, 1942), p. 117.

57. See E. Day, "Tarsicius, St." in NEC 13, p. 940.

58. Text in *Acta Sanctorum*, August, I, edited by John Carnan-

det (Paris and Rome, 1867), p. 143; full text of the *passio*, pp. 141-143.

59. Text in PL 20: cols. 556-557.

60. See Leo Cunibert Mohlberg, ed., *Sacramentarium Veronense* (Rerum Ecclesiasticarum Documenta, Series Maior, Fontes, I; Rome: Herder, 1956), nn. 942-954, pp. 118-122.

61. See *Sacramentarium Veronense*, ed. Mohlberg, n. 742, p. 116. The *Statuta Ecclesiae Antiquae* is a fifth-century document probably composed by Gennadius of Marseilles (ca. 470); it contains a list of eleven "orders": bishop, presbyter, deacon, subdeacon, acolyte, exorcist, reader, porter, cantor, virgin, and widow. The list was extremely influential in the western churches. See Charles Munier, ed., *Les Statuta Ecclesiae Antiquae* (Bibliothèque de l'Institut de Droit canonique de l'Université de Strasbourg, no. 5; Strasbourg: Presses Universitaires de France, 1960).

62. See Leo Cunibert Mohlberg, ed., *Missale Francorum* (Rerum Ecclesiasticarum Documenta, Series Maior, Fontes, II; Rome: Herder, 1957), nn. 3, 11; pp. 4-5.

63. *Statuta Ecclesiae Antiquae*, n. 94; ed. Munier, pp. 96-97.

64. *Missale Francorum*, ed. Mohlberg, n. 11, p. 4.

65. See "Rite of Institution of Readers and Acolytes," *The Rites*, I, pp. 743-744.

66. Text translated in Ronald Jasper and Geoffrey Cuming, *Prayers of the Eucharist, Early and Reformed* (London: Collins, 1975), pp. 111-114.

67. Ibid., pp. 112-113.

68. See Michel Andrieu, ed., *Les Ordines romani du haut moyen âge* (5 vols.; Spicilegium Sacrum Lovaniense 11, 23, 24, 28, 29; Louvain, 1931–1961), III, p. 603.

69. Ibid., III, p. 603, n. 1. Even deacons sometimes wore the chasuble for liturgical services: see ibid., III, p. 606, n. 10.

70. See *Ordo Romanus*, 35.9; ed. Andrieu, III, pp. 34-35.

71. Text of the letter in PL 59: cols. 400-408.

72. PL 59: cols. 404-405.

73. For the medieval pontificals, see Michel Andrieu, ed., *Le pontificale romain au moyen âge* (4 vols.; Studi e Testi 86-88, 99; Città del Vaticano: Biblioteca Apostolica Vaticana, 1938-1941); see also Cyrille Vogel, ed., *Le Pontificale romano-germanique du dixième siècle* (Studi e Testi 226-227; 2 vols.; Città del Vaticano: Biblioteca Apostolica Vaticana, 1963).

74. See *Rituale Romanum Pauli V Pontificis Maximi Iussu Editum* (Rome, 1615), pp. 62-66.

75. See *Rituale Romanum* (Editio Prima iuxta Typicam Vaticanam; New York: Benziger Brothers, 1955), pp. 103-107.

76. HCWE, I, pp. 276-277; 481.

77. See HCWE, I, pp. 476, 479-480.

78. See Richard McBrien, *Church: The Continuing Quest* (Paramus, N.J.: Newman Press, 1970), pp. 31-33.

79. Ibid., p. 33.

80. Thomas Aquinas, *Summa Theologiae*, IIIa, 63, 1; translation in David Bourke, *St. Thomas Aquinas: Summa Theologiae, Vol. 56: The Sacraments* (New York: McGraw-Hill, 1975), p. 79.

81. See *Constitution on the Liturgy*, nn. 2, 26; in James Megivern, ed., *Worship and Liturgy* (Official Catholic Teachings; Wilmington, N.C.: McGrath Publishing Company, 1978), pp. 197-198; 206.

82. A.-M. Roguet, *The Liturgy of the Hours. The General Instruction with Commentary*, translated by Peter Coughlan and Peter Purdue (Collegeville, Minn.: The Liturgical Press, 1971), p. 84.

83. See, for example, Robert J. Hater, *The Ministry Explosion: A New Awareness of Every Christian's Call to Minister* (Dubuque, Iowa: William C. Brown, 1979).

84. See *Lumen Gentium*, 10; in Austin Flannery, ed., *Vatican Council II: The Conciliar and Post Conciliar Documents* (Collegeville, Minn.: The Liturgical Press, 1975), p. 361.

85. See *Lumen Gentium*, 12; ed. Flannery, p. 363.

86. See George Montague, *The Holy Spirit: Growth of a Biblical Tradition* (New York: Paulist Press, 1976), pp. 300-301.

87. Ibid., p. 300.

88. See ibid., p. 257: "Most significant about Luke's presentation of the Holy Spirit during the ministry is its close relation to the prayer of Jesus."

89. See ibid., pp. 257-258.

90. On the role of prophets and prophecy in the New Testament period, see Edward Earle Ellis, *Prophecy and Hermeneutic in Early Christianity: New Testament Essays* (Wissenschaftliche Untersuchungen zum Neuen Testament, 18; Tübingen: Mohr, 1978).

91. See *Didache*, 10-11; tranlsated in Maxwell Staniforth, *Early Christian Writings* (Baltimore: Penguin Books, 1968), pp. 232-234.

92. See BCL *Study Text 1: Holy Communion*, p. 4.

93. See HCWE, 17; I, p. 461.

94. On collegiality see *Lumen Gentium*, 22; ed. Flannery, pp. 374-376.

95. See the text of these rites in BCL *Study Text 1: Holy Communion*, pp. 37-39.

Chapter Seven

Worship of the Eucharist Outside Mass

INTRODUCTION
In Chapter Four of this book we examined in detail the historical evolution of the cult of the eucharist outside Mass. The primary forms of this cult—processions, exposition, visits to the Blessed Sacrament, and Benediction—were analyzed in light of the theological controversies and the pastoral circumstances that gave them rise. We concluded that the appearance of a eucharistic cult outside Mass is best explained from within the evolution of the liturgy itself. History suggests, therefore, that eucharistic devotions are an outgrowth of liturgical development; they become "problematic" only when their source in the sacramental action of the assembly is ignored or denied.

The 1973 reforms of eucharistic worship outside Mass make every effort to underscore the source of public and private devotion in the liturgical activity of the Christian people: "When the faithful honor Christ present in the sacrament, they should remember that this presence is derived from the sacrifice and is directed toward sacramental and spiritual communon."[1] The postconciliar documents also insist that the prime purpose for reserving the sacrament is communion of the dying; devotion toward (and adoration of) the species remain secondary purposes: "The primary and original reason for reservation of the eucharist outside Mass is the administration of viaticum. The secondary reasons are the giving of communion and the adoration of our Lord Jesus Christ who is present in the sacrament."[2]

In short, the recent reforms of eucharistic devotion outside Mass are based on two fundamental principles: 1) The primary purpose of celebrating the eucharist is to

unite God's People through common participation in eating and drinking a meal;
2) The primary purpose of reserving the eucharist after Mass is to provide viaticum for the dying.

All other expressions of eucharistic piety, whether public or private, liturgical or nonliturgical, are subordinate to these two principles. In this, the Council's reforms are merely a reiteration of ancient Christian thought: the eucharist was instituted as food and drink, not as an object to be gazed upon or carried about. The ultimate test of legitimate eucharistic devotion remains: does it lead the people back to the celebrating assembly; does it encourage a more conscious and active participation in the liturgy?

This chapter focuses attention on three reformed rites of eucharistic cult outside Mass: 1) exposition and Benediction (including prolonged forms of exposition such as those formerly associated with the Forty Hours Devotion); 2) processions; and 3) Eucharistic Congresses. The chapter will be structured along the lines of the two preceding ones. Following some initial historical notes, the structure and contents of the new rites will be discussed. Then the theological significance of the reserved sacrament will be examined, and the chapter will conclude with an assessment of the pastoral value of eucharistic devotions.

HISTORICAL NOTES
Since a detailed account of the origins of eucharistic devotions has already been given in Chapter Four, our attention here will be devoted to three specific items: the Forty Hours Devotion; the celebration of Eucharistic Congresses; and the development of eucharistic devotions in the Roman Catholic Church in the United States.

Forty Hours
The precise historical origins of the Forty Hours Devo-

tion are difficult to establish. There is a consensus, however, that the devotion originated in the sixteenth century, probably in Milan. There, in the year 1527, Gian Antonio Belotti preached a series of Lenten sermons in the Church of the Holy Sepulchre; in them, he urged Christians to spend forty hours before the Blessed Sacrament in order to seek God's help during a time of war. Belotti seems to have recommended that this devotion be observed four times a year: at Easter, Pentecost, Assumption, and Christmas.[3] Within a few years, Belotti's recommendation was taken up and fostered by others—especially by the Capuchin priest Joseph von Ferno. Von Ferno added a new element to the devotion by proposing that a "chain" of Forty Hours expositions be kept in rotation throughout the churches of Milan. By transferring the sacrament from church to church (and keeping watch for forty hours at each place), a year-long round of special prayer and supplication could be established.[4]

The work of two other men in spreading the Forty Hours Devotion must also be mentioned here. Antony Maria Zaccaria, a member of the Clerks Regular of St. Paul (Barnabites), seems to have become an apostle of the devotion as early as 1534. And in 1550, the Oratorian Philip Neri introduced the devotion to the churches of Rome.[5] The popularity of Forty Hours expanded very rapidly. By the latter part of the sixteenth century influential church leaders like Charles Borromeo (+ 1584) spoke of the devotion as though it were ancient custom.[6] Very quickly, too, it seems, Forty Hours came to be associated with carnival time, immediately before the beginning of Lent.[7]

Papal approbation of this new eucharistic devotion was secured rapidly. In 1539, Pope Paul III approved a petition soliciting indulgences for those who participated in it; his confirmation reads, in part:

"Since . . . our beloved son the Vicar General of the Archbishop of Milan at the prayer of the inhabitants of

312

the said city, in order to appease the anger of God provoked by the offences of Christians, and in order to bring to nought the efforts and machinations of the Turks who are pressing forward to the destruction of Christendom, amongst other pious practices, has established a round of prayers and supplications to be offered both by day and night by all the faithful of Christ, before our Lord's Most Sacred Body, in all the churches of the said city, in such a manner that these prayers and supplications are made by the faithful themselves relieving each other in relays for forty hours continuously in each church in succession. . . . We, approving in our Lord so pious an institution, and confirming the same by Our authority. . . ."[8]

This is the earliest magisterial text we possess that explicitly describes and approves the Forty Hours Devotion. Two points, particularly, should be noted in Paul III's response to the petition from Milan. First, the devotion is seen as a kind of reparation in a time of serious social upheavel. The crisis of war, with its concomitant threat of Turkish political supremacy, appears to have supplied immediate motivation for the "round of prayers and supplications," and the crisis is traced to "the anger of God provoked by the offenses of Christians." Secondly, the devotion is a popular one in which "the faithful themselves" relieve one another "in relays for forty hours continuously in each church in succession." Although it may have been fostered initially by clerical enthusiasts (Belotti, von Ferno, Zaccaria, Philip Neri, Charles Borromeo), Forty Hours seems to have caught hold quickly among lay Christians.

In 1560, papal approval of the new devotion was reiterated through a bull of Pope Pius IV. This bull, *Divina disponente clementia* (17 November 1560), gave formal approbation to an archconfraternity of Christians in Rome who were dedicated to prayer and corporal works of mercy, specifically, burying the dead.[9] Citing the custom of the Forty Hours Devotion among members of the archconfraternity, the pope remarked:

"Among other works [of this confraternity] they have determined that each month, certain days and hours be designated [for prayer] in imitation of the forty days Our Lord Jesus Christ spent in fasting in the desert. . . . This prayer also imitates [the example of] the holy apostles and fathers of the early church who prayed to God without ceasing. . . . For forty continuous hours the men and women of this society offer God both vocal and mental prayer. . . . At the beginning of this prayer on the next-to-the-last Sunday of each month, or on another day, [the members of the confraternity] carry the Body of the Lord in procession with appropriate ceremony."[10]

It will be noticed that Pius IV, unlike Paul III, did not stress the connection between Forty Hours and the sociopolitical crisis of war. Instead, he appealed to examples from scripture and tradition: the forty-day fasting of Jesus and the ancient Christian ideal of ceaseless or uninterrupted prayer.[11]

By the end of the sixteenth century, popes had begun to declare generous indulgences for those who participate in the Forty Hours Devotion. In 1592, for example, Pope Clement VIII published the bull *Graves et Diuturnae*, which not only approved the devotion once again but attached a plenary indulgence to it: "To all Christians of either sex who are repentant, have confessed and been refreshed by the most holy sacrament of the eucharist, and have spent at least an hour in prayer in any church where this devotion is celebrated, we grant a plenary indulgence of all their sins."[12] This and other indulgences were reconfirmed by Pope Paul V at the beginning of the seventeenth century in the bull *Romanus Pontifex* (23 May 1606).[13]

In the eighteenth century, too, papal approbation of the Forty Hours Devotion was renewed in the form of the

314

Instructio Clementina.[14] This instruction also outlined all the rites and ceremonies to be observed during the celebration of Forty Hours. Technically speaking, the *Instructio Clementina* represented local usage for the city of Rome; it was not binding on other churches, though many places adopted the Roman customs. Briefly, the *Instructio* provided for the following ceremonies.

1) During Forty Hours the eucharist is to be exposed on the principal altar of the church. All images and statues on or in the vicinity of the altar of exposition are to be covered.[15] Relics of the saints are also prohibited from being kept on the altar during the exposition.[16]

2) The eucharist is to be exposed in a monstrance and placed prominently in view of the faithful (e.g., on a "throne"). Candles are to be kept burning at all times during the period of exposition.[17]

3) No other Mass is to be celebrated at the altar of exposition except those solemn liturgies that open and close the period of the Forty Hours Devotion. The opening Mass (Mass of exposition) is to be a votive Mass of the Blessed Sacrament. On the second day, a votive Mass for Peace is to be celebrated at another altar in the church. The Devotion closes with another votive Mass of the Blessed Sacrament (Mass of reposition). The opening and closing Masses may be accompanied with processions of the Blessed Sacrament, litanies, and prayers.[18]

4) While the Forty Hours Devotion is going on, no Requiem Masses are permitted in the church. If private Masses are celebrated in the church of exposition, no bells may be rung during them.[19]

5) White is the appropriate liturgical color for the ceremonies of Forty Hours both at the Masses and in the processions.[20]

The provisions of the *Instructio Clementina* for the Forty Hours Devotion at Rome were widely imitated and adopted in other dioceses. In the United States, the Second Plenary Council of Baltimore (1866) explicitly mentioned the *Instructio Clementina*, though it noted that pastoral circumstances sometimes made a full observance of the Roman customs unfeasible.[21] Nevertheless, the *Ceremonial for the Use of the Catholic Churches in the United States of America*, published by order of the First Council of Baltimore (1852), contains rites and rubrics for Forty Hours that are virtually indistinguishable from the ceremonies described in the *Instructio Clementina*.[22] Indeed, until the reforms of the Second Vatican Council the celebration of Forty Hours in the United States remained relatively unchanged from the *Instructio Clementina* and the nineteenth-century *Ceremonial*.[23]

This brief historical sketch of the devotion leaves some unanswered questions. Apart from stress caused by social and political circumstances (the crisis of war), what prompted the development of Forty Hours? Did it originate simply as a way to honor the Blessed Sacrament with unusual solemnity, or were other motives at work? In his illuminating essay on the subject, Josef Jungmann suggested that the remote sources of the devotion are to be found in the medieval custom of keeping watch at the "tomb" of Jesus on the last three days of Holy Week (Friday evening until early Sunday morning).[24] As we have seen in Chapter Four, the custom of burying the cross (later, the eucharistic host) in a sepulchre on Good Friday developed as early as the tenth century. Christians were invited to pray at Jesus' "tomb" until, at matins of Easter morning, the "three Marys" visited the sepulchre, discovered it empty, and proclaimed the Lord's resurrection. The period of time covered by this devotion at Jesus' tomb was approximately forty hours (from about 3 P.M. Friday until 3 or 4 A.M. Sunday). We know that this Holy Week devotion was enormously popular throughout medieval Europe, and that it generated numerous liturgical dramas based on the visit of the spice-bearing women to Jesus' grave on Easter morning. [25] We know, too, that the cross buried on Friday and mysteriously resurrected on Sunday was gradually replaced by the consecrated host. In effect, therefore, the Holy Week devotion at Jesus' tomb had become a Forty Hours eucharistic devotion.

It is possible, too, as Jungmann remarked, that the emphasis on Jesus' forty-hour entombment has roots in patristic exegesis and commentary. St. Augustine, for example, who was always fascinated by the mystical significance of numbers, claims that the length of time between Jesus' death and his resurrection was forty hours[26]: "From the hour of death until the dawn of the resurrection there are forty hours." At an early period in liturgical history, moreover, these hours were devoted to fasting—both as preparation for celebrating Pascha and as preparation for initiating candidates at the Easter Vigil.[27] It could be said, then, that the pre-history of the Forty Hours Devotion is rooted in ancient customs commemorating Jesus' passion through roughly forty hours of prayer and fasting.

There are two other themes, however, which were quickly attached to Forty Hours when it emerged in the sixteenth century: Jesus' fasting in the wilderness and the early Christian ideal of incessant prayer (see Luke 18.1; 1 Thess 5.17). Both these are mentioned by Pius IV in his bull of 1560. The theme of incessant prayer is more comprehensible when we remember that, originally, the Forty Hours Devotion passed in relays around the churches of a city so that, in effect, there was a constant round of watching and prayer among the Christians of a particular locale. And the theme of Jesus' fasting clearly points to the penitential character of Forty Hours; for according to Paul III's decree of 1539, the devotion was designed "to appease the anger of God provoked by the offences of Christians."

Originally, then, the focus of Forty Hours was eucharistic only in a secondary way; the primary themes were repentance and reparation; commemoration of Jesus' passion; recollection of Jesus' fasting. By the time the *Instructio Clementina* appeared in the early eighteenth century, however, the focus of the devotion had shifted somewhat. Thanksgiving for the gift and mystery of the eucharist predominated, although the Mass on the second day of the devotion (a votive Mass for peace) recalled the historical origins of Forty Hours in the sixteenth century.

Since the eighteenth century, therefore, Forty Hours has generally been perceived as a solemn festive demonstration of Catholic piety toward the eucharist. Use of an abundance of flowers, candles, incense, and ornate vestments helped reenforce this impression. In a sense the Forty Hours Devotion became a badge of distinctively Catholic identity: a custom, like abstinence from meat on Friday, that differentiated Roman Catholics from other Christians. For many priests, too, it provided an opportunity for fraternizing with clerical friends; in the United States, a social gathering at the sponsoring parish's rectory usually brought the Forty Hours festivities to a conclusion.

Eucharistic Congresses
Eucharistic Congresses, such as the one held at Philadelphia during the American Bicentennial in 1976, are a very recent innovation in the church's history. The idea for such gatherings seems first to have been promoted by Emilie Tamisier (1843–1910). Once a novice with a religious community known as the Servants of the Most Holy Sacrament, Mme. Tamisier felt called to promote the cult of the eucharist throughout the world.[28] She helped organize eucharistic pilgrimages at several French cities (Avignon, Faverney, Douai) between the years 1874 and 1878. The first international Eucharistic Congress did not take place, however, until 1881 in Lille. Organized by Gaston de Segur (+ 1881) and Philibert Vrau (+ 1904), it attracted people from

318

Belgium, England, Spain, France, Holland, and Switzerland. By 1976, forty-one such Eucharistic Congresses had been held.

Almost from the beginning these Eucharistic Congresses included not only liturgies and devotions, but study days and seminars devoted to theological, pastoral, and social topics. At the eleventh Congress in Brussels (1898), for example, public papers were presented on topics such as Christian art, the role of women in Christian family life, Christian responsibility toward the poor, and the church's missionary activity in parts of the world like China and Africa.[29] Perhaps even more astonishing was this Congress's attention to urgent social problems of the day. A paper was presented, for example, on the eucharist and the working class, in which it was argued that the crisis of the late nineteenth century was simultaneously social and religious.[30] The author of this paper, Père L. Lefebvre, insisted that the church must be more attentive to the needs and conditions of the working classes, and that these needs included specifically religious ones.[31] Another paper, given by the Jesuit Père Coubé, addressed the topic of social revolution and the eucharist.[32] Coubé described the contemporary situation in Europe in these terms: "Love and hate, healthy expressions of goodness and sudden explosions of titanic revolt, joyful hope for renewal and pale terror in the face of the unknown: these are the polar opposites between which our society constantly oscillates. Do we not live in an epoch that is chaotic and paradoxical?"[33] Coubé went on to suggest that the eucharist is the ultimate source of unity among all social classes, that it alone has power to destroy "egoism, source of all divisions" and to alleviate or transfigure "suffering, source of all social discontent."[34] In his analysis of solutions offered to the social crisis among working people Coubé was critical of social Darwinism, Nietzschean individualism, and unbridled capitalism.[35] Against these, he proposed a model of social life symbolized by the eucharistic liturgy:

319

"It is only by eating and drinking the eucharist that Christ combats in us that egoism which is the principal obstacle to unity. The form of a meal, which he has chosen for this divine sacrament, in an admirable lesson. . . .

"St. Paul tells us: 'We who share the one bread form one body' . . . Participation in the one meal is one of the most expressive and popular signs and causes of unity among human beings."[36]

It is significant that from their inception Eucharistic Congresses involved themselves in the urgent social problems of their day. Although the analysis and solutions offered by people like Coubé may seem simplistic to late twentieth century readers, one cannot overlook the importance of using an international forum like the Congresses to focus attention on the social, political, economic, and religious needs of humankind. One should also note that Pope Leo XIII, with whose approval the eleventh Congress was held in 1898, was himself deeply interested in the situation of working people in the European community. His encyclical letter *Rerum Novarum* (1891) was, in fact, the first of a series of modern papal documents on peace, social justice, and liberation for workers.

Significantly, therefore, the Eucharistic Congresses were not limited to specifically liturgical and devotional issues. They provided a regular international forum for discussing Christian social responsibility in a rapidly developing world. At the twenty-eighth Congress meeting in Chicago (20-24 June, 1926), for example, a symposium attended by delegates from the United States and ten European and Latin American countries agreed on a plan for an "international Catholic movement for peace."[37] The symposium was sponsored by the Social Action Department of the National Catholic Welfare Conference, and it included roundtable discussions on "nationalism, imperialism, the use of war as a weapon."[38] Included, too, was a discussion on international ethics, as well as proposals for an international conference on the subject of peace in the world. The Chicago Congress also devoted special sectional meetings to the situation of black and Hispanic Catholics in the United States.[39]

Interest in issues of international peace and justice continued to be exhibited at subsequent Eucharistic Congresses. The forty-first Congress at Philadelphia (August 1976) centered attention on the growing problem of world hunger. Mother Teresa of Calcutta, for instance, spoke of her work with the starving people of India; Dom Helder Camara of Brazil passionately denounced injustice in third-world countries.[40] Camara challenged participants at the Congress to face the problems of structural injustice that affect at least two-thirds of the world's population. "The great challenge," he said, "is to change without hate and without violence. . . . It is not sufficient to create certain material goods for people. Men also have hunger for liberty. It is essential. It is impossible for men to accept only material goods; there must also be a freedom to pray. When we have needy persons who are in hunger, though, we don't have the right to discuss, discuss! We must do what our words say!"[41]

As these examples show, the purpose of Eucharistic Congresses has, from the beginning, been inclusive of social and political issues as well as explicitly theological ones. It is worth remembering, perhaps, that at one of the first (national) eucharistic meetings organized by Emilie Tamisier at Paray-le-Moniale in 1873, members of the French government were represented; at Mme. Tamisier's request they knelt at an altar and promised to work against secularism in politics.[42] Undeniably, then, the Eucharistic Congresses have a history of association with the social and political concerns of Catholics. This history is indirectly recognized in the 1973 rites for holy communion and worship of the eucharist outside Mass.

321

In speaking of preparation for a Eucharistic Congress the document notes that primary consideration is to be given to "research and promotion of social undertakings for human development and proper distribution of property, including temporal property, following the example of the primitive Christian community."[43] Such words confirm an insight that seems to have been grasped intuitively by Emilie Tamisier in the nineteenth century: viz., that the eucharistic symbols of bread and wine shared in a meal around a table are an invitation to work for the ultimate unity of the human family.

Eucharistic Devotions in the United States
The final section of these historical notes will be devoted to the development of eucharistic devotions among Roman Catholics in the United States. The work of the First and Second Plenary Councils of Baltimore has already been alluded to. Here, a somewhat more systematic outline of the evidence for eucharistic customs in the American Catholic community will be presented.

One of the earliest official liturgical books for Roman Catholics published in this country was John Aitken's *A Compilation of the Litanies, Vespers Hymns and Anthems as Sung in the Catholic Church* (1787).[44] The book was approved and recommended for use by John Carroll (who had not yet been selected and ordained bishop) and by three other prominent clergymen: Robert Molyneux, Francis Beeston, and Lawrence Graessl.[45] It is a curious collection of Latin and vernacular hymns, psalmody, and music for the Ordinary of the Mass. Settings for Sunday vespers, the Litany of Loretto, and the Requiem Mass are also included in the collection.[46] Much of the musical material is from the eighteenth century, and texts from Protestant hymn writers like Isaac Watts and William Dodd have been liberally borrowed.[47] Aitken also printed some melodies from the repertoire of Gregorian Chant; these are written in modern notation, with somewhat awkward vocal harmonizations added.

322

Of particular interest for our purposes is Aitken's inclusion of the *Tantum Ergo* (two settings), under the heading "The Hymn at Benediction."[48] The presence of this hymn in his collection indicates that Benediction was a popular devotion among the approximately 40,000 Roman Catholics in late eighteenth century America.[49] Interesting, too, is Aitken's printing of a complete setting for Sunday vespers. At the earliest diocesan synod held in the United States under the presidency of Bishop John Carroll in 1791, Sunday vespers and Benediction are mentioned as regular features of worship on the Lord's Day:

"In places [where there are sufficient ministers], the Litany of Loretto of the Blessed Virgin Mary, the principal patron of this diocese, should be sung at the proper hour. After it is completed, let there be a solemn sprinkling with holy water, as it prescribed in the Missal. Then Mass should be celebrated solemnly, with singing; and on more solemn days, if possible, let a deacon and subdeacon assist. After the gospel is over, the prescribed prayers for all ordinary [needs] and for the prosperity of the Republic should be read. The proper gospel for that day should also be read again, in the vernacular. The banns of marriage should be published, as should [announcements about] feast and fast days of observance—and whatever else the people need to be forewarned about. Then there should be a sermon of such nature that it instructs and edifies the hearers, and stirs them up to a more perfect Christian life. In the afternoon, Vespers should be sung; and after that, the Antiphon of the Blessed Virgin proper to the season. Benediction with the Blessed Sacrament should then be given, with solemn singing; afterwards, [there should be] catechetical instruction. It is to be desired that during these services some hymns or prayers be sung in the vernacular."[50]

A comparison between this first synodal description of Sunday worship and the contents of John Aitken's hymnal is revealing. Everything the synod described as normative for the liturgies of Sunday corresponds to the material collected in Aitken's *Compilation*: The Litany of Loretto, the sung Mass, vespers followed by the Antiphon of the Blessed Virgin, Benediction. The use of Benediction as a conclusion to vespers reflects what we have seen in Chapter Four about its origins: blessing the people with the sacrament constituted a solemn dismissal rite for other liturgical services such as vespers and compline.

Subsequent provincial and plenary Councils of Baltimore reaffirmed the decisions of the 1791 synod regarding the cult of the eucharist in parishes of the United States. At the First Provincial Council of Baltimore (October 1829), the bishops decreed that a Book of Ceremonies conforming to the Roman Ritual but written in English be published in this country:

"Since books written in English and dealing with the sacred rites are highly desirable, we decree that a Book of Ceremonies conforming to the Roman Ritual, subject to the judgment of the Holy See, and compiled from approved works [be published], so that all priests and clerics throughout this province may know and observe the rites of the universal Church. Included in this Book should be an explanation of the rites so that the faithful may assist at the sacred functions with greater understanding and edification."[51]

This *Manual of Ceremonies* was published in 1833, sent to the Congregation for the Propagation of the Faith, and approved by Pope Gregory XVI.[52] The *Manual* was, for the most part, a translation of the *Memoriale Rituum* approved in 1724 by Pope Benedict XIII for use in churches where, ordinarily, a single clergyman officiates at the liturgy.[53] Included in this *Manual* are detailed instructions for Benediction with the Blessed Sacrament and for the Forty Hours Exposition.[54] It also includes a rite for Benediction given with the ciborium.[55] It may be useful here, by way of illustration, to outline the 1833 *Manual's* description of Benediction with the Blessed Sacrament.

1) The altar is to be prepared with twelve lighted candles and a "throne or small canopy" placed between the candlesticks. The Blessed Sacrament, exposed in a monstrance, is placed on a corporal beneath the canopy. The officiating priest vests in surplice, white stole and cope; a humeral veil is used at the point in the rite when Benediction is actually given.

2) After the ministers (celebrant, thurifer, and two acolytes) enter the sanctuary, the sacrament is taken from the tabernacle, placed in the monstrance and incensed. "Whilst the Celebrant is incensing the Blessed Sacrament, the choir may sing the *O Salutaris hostia*."

3) Meanwhile, "such hymns, antiphons, and litanies as are approved of by the Church, or any psalm, or mottet extracted from the psalms, may be sung."

4) Then the entire hymn *Pange Lingua*, or at least the last two verses (*Tantum ergo* and *Genitori, Genitoque*), should be sung. The hymn is followed by a versicle (*Panem de caelo*), response (*Omne delectamentum*), and prayer (*Deus, qui nobis*). Other prayers "taken from the Roman Missal" may be added. During the *Tantum ergo* the celebrant incenses the Blessed Sacrament a second time.

5) The actual ceremony of blessing the people with the sacrament then follows. The priest, in humeral veil, turns toward the people with the monstrance in his hands and traces the sign of the cross over them. No hymns are sung at this point, nor does the priest say anything.

6) The priest then places the monstrance back on the altar, removes the humeral veil, and puts the Blessed Sacrament back into the tabernacle. He and the ministers then genuflect and return to the sacristy.

This rite follows very closely the ceremonies described in the Roman Ritual of 1614 for Benediction at the conclusion of the procession on the feast of Corpus Christi.[56] The relatively simple rite contained in the 1833 *Manual of Ceremonies* was implicitly reaffirmed by the Third Provincial Council of Baltimore in October 1837 . That Council insisted that the *Manual* be used "in all the provinces of the United States," so that the liturgical rites "might be uniform everywhere, and so that the customs of the Holy Roman Church might be imitated by all."[57]

At the same time, however, the Third Provincial Council of 1837 exhibited some anxiety about the state of worship in American parishes. Two issues, particularly, appear to have become sensitive: the use of vernacular hymns and prayers in connection with liturgical services and the quality of music sung in churches. It is well known that John Carroll wanted to see at least some use of the vernacular in the American Catholic community. In fact at the first diocesan synod that met in Baltimore in 1791 under Carroll's presidency, there was an explicit desire for "some hymns or prayers . . . in the vernacular." But by the time the Third Provincial Council met, Carroll (+ 1815) had been dead for several years, and there seems to have been growing concern that liturgy in the United States might be out of step with the Roman Rite. Among the decrees of the Third Provincial Council, therefore, we find the following:

"So that everything may be done in order and the solemn rites of the Church may be integrally preserved, we admonish the rectors of churches to keep a careful watch so that abuses that affect church music may be eliminated. . . . Let them take care, therefore, that in the holy sacrifice of the Mass and other divine services, music—and not 'divine services of music'—be used. They should know, too, that according to the rite of the church it is not permitted to sing vernacular songs at Mass or at solemn Vespers."[58]

By the time the First Plenary Council of bishops in the United States met at Baltimore in 1852, it seemed opportune to publish a new edition of the *Manual of Ceremonies* that had been mandated in 1829 and published in 1833.[59] The rites for Benediction contained in the later editions of the *Manual* reflect the Third Provincial Council's concern about use of the vernacular in liturgical services. In the first edition of the *Manual* (1833), for example, there is no explicit prohibition of vernacular hymns at Benediction. Aitken's 1787 *Compilation* had included a generous number of English and German hymns. But later editions of the *Manual of Ceremonies* expressly prohibit vernacular hymns and antiphons at Benediction. The following comparison will indicate the change:

Manual (1833)[60]	*Manual (third edition, 1871)*[61]
Whilst the Celebrant is incensing the Blessed Sacrament, the choir may sing the *O Salutaris hostia*. After it, such hymns, antiphons, and litanies as are approved of by the Church, or any psalm, or mottet extracted from the psalms, may be sung.	Then the priest . . . incenses the Blessed Sacrament . . . bowing before and after. . . . In the meantime, the choir may sing such hymns and antiphons as are approved by the Church, or by ancient usage; nevertheless, they should be in the Latin language. . . .

Considering the popular origins of Benediction in the *laude* (hymns of praise, some of them in the vernacular) that concluded liturgical services like vespers and compline, this later insistence on the use of Latin alone seems odd. One must remember, however, that in the nineteenth century the American Catholic community was under pressure to prove itself on two fronts: to non-Catholics in the United States, it had to prove its patriotism and freedom from undue papal interference;

to Rome, it had to prove its loyalty and strict adherence to customs of the Latin rite. John Carroll's hope for at least "some hymns or prayers . . . in the vernacular" was slow in maturing.

When use of the vernacular did appear in the rite of eucharistic Benediction, it was attached to two items not mentioned in the 1833 or 1871 editions of the *Manual of Ceremonies*: the "Divine Praises" and the familiar recessional hymn "Holy God, We Praise Thy Name." The source of the hymn "Holy God" is rather easy to identify; it appeared under the title "Grosser Gott" in the *Katholisches Gesangbuch*, published in Vienna about 1774.[62] The English translation of the hymn appears to be the work of Clarence Alphonsus Walworth (1820–1900). An American, Walworth had been a member of the Protestant Episcopal Church, was subsequently received into the Roman communion, ordained a priest, and along with Isaac Hecker and others, helped found the Paulists. His translation of "Grosser Gott," a paraphrase of the *Te Deum*, was published in 1853 in the *Catholic Psalmist*.[63] Although it is not clear when "Holy God" began being used as a familiar recessional hymn, its choice was probably related to the custom, referred to in the *Manual of Ceremonies*, of occasionally singing the *Te Deum* at Benediction.[64] Since "Holy God" was in fact a shortened paraphrase of the old Latin hymn, its choice would have seemed entirely appropriate.

The origins of the Divine Praises are a bit more difficult to trace. In his famous handbook of liturgical history, *The Ceremonies of the Roman Rite*, Adrian Fortescue claimed that these ejaculatory invocations ("Blessed be God"/"Blessed be his holy name" . . .) had been composed in Italian by Pope Pius IX.[65] That this was not the case, however, is clear; as early as 1801 Pope Pius VII had granted an indulgence for the recitation of the Divine Praises.[66] It is likely (though not absolutely conclusive) that the invocations were written toward the end of the eighteenth century, possibly by Jesuit Father

Louis Felici. Herbert Thurston, in a short essay on the subject, gives the date 1797 as the time when the Divine Praises first appeared.[67]

Yet it does not seem that the Divine Praises were formulated precisely for the purpose of using them at Benediction. The earliest printed versions are headed by the title "Praises in reparation for blasphemy."[68] Even in late editions of the *Raccolta* this title was repeated.[69] Originally, then, these invocations were a form of reparatory prayer. There is, however, a certain logic in their eventual use at Benediction of the Blessed Sacrament, for in the seventeenth and eighteenth centuries devotions of reparation became connected with the eucharist.[70] Visits, "holy hours," and perpetual adoration were seen not only as expressions of eucharistic faith and piety, but as opportunities to atone for outrages and blasphemies committed against the sacrament.[71]

In the United States, use of the Divine Praises at Benediction seems to have become popular around the end of the nineteenth century. The eighth revised edition of the *Manual of Ceremonies* (under the title *Ceremonial for the Use of the Catholic Churches in the United States of America*), published in 1894, still makes no mention of them.[72] But a popular Catholic *Choir Manual* published in 1914, in accordance with Pius X's *motu proprio* on sacred mustic (1903) provides a musical setting for the Divine Praises in English.[73] It is probable, however, that the custom of using the Divine Praises caught on only gradually in American parishes. A popular Catholic prayerbook, *Key of Heaven*, published in 1909 with the approbation of Cardinal Gibbons, provides official texts and devotional prayers for Benediction and Forty Hours, but the Divine Praises are included only among the vernacular prayers after Mass.[74] Another such prayerbook, *Blessed be God*, published in 1925, however, contains both the Divine Praises and the hymn "Holy God" among the concluding rites of Benediction.[75] Still other prayerbooks of the period, published in both

Great Britain and the United States, contain the Divine Praises but do not explicitly connect them with Benediction of the Blessed Sacrament.[76]

Sources like these reveal the probable development that lies behind use of the Divine Praises at Benediction. Originally, these invocations "in reparation for blasphemy" were prayers of personal and private devotion; as such, as we have seen, they were enriched with indulgences by Pius VII as early as 1801. By the middle of the nineteenth century they had become popular; the number of ejaculations was expanded through additions such as the one made by Pius IX, probably around 1854—"Blessed be her [Mary's] holy and immaculate conception." By the end of the nineteenth century it had become customary in many places to recite the Divine Praises along with the prayers after Mass prescribed in 1884 and 1886 by Leo XIII.[77] In 1897, Leo officially approved, but did not command, use of the Divine Praises among the prayers to be said "kneeling" after the celebration of a private Mass."[78] The threefold invocation of the Sacred Heart among the prayers after Mass ("Most Sacred Heart of Jesus, have mercy on us") was approved in 1904 by Pius X.

In short, the use of the Divine Praises in the liturgy seems to have originated in the nineteenth century among the prayers recited after Mass (the "Leonine" prayers). Their use at the end of Benediction appears to have developed gradually around the end of the century. The list of invocations continued to be expanded: the Sacred Heart was added in 1897 (Leo XIII); St. Joseph, in 1921 (Benedict XV); the Assumption, in 1950 (Pius XII); the Precious Blood, in 1960 (John XXIII); and the Holy Spirit, in 1964 (Paul VI).[79] In the reformed rites of Benediction published in 1973, the Divine Praises are not explicitly mentioned, though a rubric notes that after the blessing and reposition of the sacrament in the tabernacle, "the people may sing or say an acclamation."[80]

330

By the first quarter of the twentieth century, therefore, the customary ritual for eucharistic Benediction in American parishes was fairly well established. It ordinarily included the following elements.

1) An opening hymn (*O Salutaris*) sung by the people (or choir) after the Blessed Sacrament had been exposed on the altar in a monstrance.

2) Incensation of the sacrament; litanies, prayers, and hymns concluding with *Tantum ergo*, versicle and response, and prayer.

3) Blessing of the people with the sacrament in silence.

4) Recitation or singing of the Divine Praises, usually in the vernacular. Sometimes an invocation to the Sacred Heart of Jesus in the eucharist ("May the Heart of Jesus in the most Blessed Sacrament be praised. . . .") was added.

5) Hymn of thanksgiving: Psalm 116 and/or "Holy God."[81]

This ritual pattern for Benediction remained fairly constant in the United States until after the reforms of the Second Vatican Council were put into effect.

For many years Benediction after Sunday Mass or vespers was an extremely popular devotion. It had been mandated, as we have seen, as part of the regular pattern of Sunday worship in American Catholic parishes as early as 1791.[82] Many Catholics living today still remember returning to church on Sunday afternoon for sung vespers and Benediction; sometimes a sermon was included in these services. Prayerbooks and manuals of devotion regularly included the texts and sometimes the music for Sunday vespers.[83] The location of texts for Benediction in these prayerbooks indicates that for centuries there remained in the consciousness of Catholics a lingering memory of the origins of this solemn eucharistic blessing as the conclusion of the dismissal rite at the end of another liturgical service such as vespers or compline.[84]

Forty Hours Devotion in the United States
Benediction was not, however, the only popular eucharistic devotion that developed among Catholics in the United States. The Forty Hours Devotion was another. At the Second Plenary Council of Baltimore (1866), this devotion was discussed, approved and regulated.[85] It is certain, however, that the custom of observing Forty Hours existed in at least some American parishes long before 1866. *The Manual of Ceremonies* (1833) published by order of the First Provincial Council of Baltimore (1829) includes a lengthy appendix in which the ceremonies of Forty Hours are described in detail.[86] Subsequent editions of the *Manual* contained similar information.[87] But the strongest encouragement for the regular observance of Forty Hours on the diocesan level came from St. John Neumann. In 1853, Neumann introduced the devotion into the diocese of Philadelphia; within five years (1858), it had also been introduced into the archdiocese of Baltimore.

The Second Plenary Council thus sought to regulate a eucharistic devotion that had already been in existence for some years. An implicit recognition of this fact is revealed by the language of the Council's decrees:

"The prayers of Forty Hours, which came into use with the approval of Pope Pius IV in the sixteenth century, were more carefully arranged by Pope Clement VIII and were enriched with many indulgences. Far and wide through the Christian world [this devotion has grown], and it has even been solemnly celebrated from time to time in these provinces."[23]

The Council went on to recognize that, given the missionary character of Catholicism in America, it was virtually impossible to observe all the requirements for Forty Hours outlined in the *Instructio Clementina* (1730/1731). It therefore petitioned the Holy See to permit the use of a modified form of the devotion which the pope had already approved for the archdiocese of Baltimore.[89] The modifications granted to churches in the United States included these items:

1) Exposition of the sacrament during the hours of the day only, from morning until evening; at night the eucharist could be reposed in the tabernacle.

2) The procession with the Blessed Sacrament could be omitted if it seemed inappropriate or if there were insufficient space in the vicinity of the church.

3) Indulgences of seven years and seven quarantines were granted to those Christians who visited the church during the times of the solemn exposition.

4) A plenary indulgence was granted to all who, after receiving the sacraments of penance and eucharist, took part in the public ceremonies of Forty Hours.

5) During the period of exposition, all altars in the church were to be regarded as privileged, i.e., a plenary indulgence for a soul in purgatory could be obtained through a Mass celebrated at them.[90]

The Council also decreed that the liturgical ceremonies for each of the three days during the Forty Hours Devotion should be those outlined in the *Ceremonial for the Use of the Catholic Churches in the United States of America*.[91] Not surprisingly, these ceremonies adhered very closely to the provisions of the *Instructio Clementina*.

In popular prayerbooks and manuals of devotion the liturgical aspects of Forty Hours were often ignored in favor of prayers with a strongly sentimental and individualistic orientation. Here, for example, is a portion of a prayer contained in the 1909 edition of the *Key of Heaven* for private use at Forty Hours: "O fairest, O most blooming Flower Jesus! O life that never fadest! O life, by which I live, without which I die! O life by which I rejoice, without which I mourn."[92] Prayers of this sort indicate that with the passage of time some of the original purposes of Forty Hours—prayer for peace, Christ's

333

passion as source of life for all the world, fasting and prayer in memory of Jesus' experience in the desert—had been obscured by attention to more personal and inward matters.

Other Eucharistic Devotions
In addition to customs like Benediction and Forty Hours, Catholic parishes in the United States were encouraged to develop other devotions as well. Visits and private prayer in the presence of the reserved sacrament were explicitly encouraged, for example, by the Second Plenary Council of Baltimore (1866).[93] This Council was careful to point out, however, that the eucharist is intended primarily not as an object of adoration but as spiritual food to be eaten:

"Our beloved redeemer Jesus Christ, in his overwhelming kindness and love for human beings, is always with us in the most venerable mystery of his body and blood. In his supreme love he wills to feed and nourish us, and thus he commanded above all that this wonderful sacrament be eaten as the true food of the soul. By it, life is preserved and strength increased; for he himself has promised: 'Whoever eats me will live because of me.'"[94]

In recommending both private and public devotions toward the eucharist, the Second Plenary Council stated that "through the solemn honor and cult given by all to the Son of God," the souls of the faithful would be "kindled and enflamed with greater love."[95] At the same time the Council brought forward a rather unecumenical argument in favor of the cult of the eucharist outside Mass: "In this region of the world, [such devotions] provide, as it were, a public testimony to our faith against the heretics and unbelievers among whom we live—and who either ignore or ridicule this inscrutable mystery of divine love."[96]

Despite the tone of these words, their underlying sociological significance is patent. As we have seen earlier in this chapter, eucharistic cult and devotion outside Mass provided a "distinctive badge of identity" for a Catholic minority in an overwhelmingly Protestant country. The Council fathers were, in effect, recommending a sociological strategy that is common among minority groups of any culture: defiant display of those things that make the minority different from the majority.[97] The entire ensemble of eucharistic devotions— visits, prayers and adoration before the Blessed Sacrament, Benediction, Forty Hours, Holy Hours—thus served both a religious need and a sociological purpose. On the one hand, these pious exercises helped link American Catholics, many of whom were immigrants, with their European roots. (All the eucharistic devotions we have described in this chapter take their origin in European Catholicism.) This linkage was important because it provided a sort of common devotional language for Catholics in a cultural environment which was often suspicious or actively hostile.[98] On the other hand, these popular devotions provided Catholics with an almost defiant sense of pride in their religious distinctiveness, their uniqueness among the numerous and often conflicting Christian denominations in the United States. In short, the eucharistic devotions offered both linkage with religious roots and tradition, as well as distinctive identity in a religiously pluralistic culture.

One final comment should be made before concluding this section on eucharistic devotions in the United States. In many respects the nineteenth-century church in America was a century ahead of its time. Between 1791, the year of the first diocesan synod in this country, and 1884, the year of the Third Plenary Council of Baltimore, at least ten ecclesiastical councils (seven provincial and three plenary) were held. These meetings involved virtually all the bishops in the United States as well as pastors, theological advisors and consultants. The councils were, in fact, a vigorous demonstration of collegial responsibility in pastoral matters.

As leaders of a church in mission territory, the early American bishops thus seem to have recognized the need for collegial deliberation and action. While they were conscientious about submitting their decisions to Rome for approval, they were also bold in their willingness to experiment with traditional structures.

Roman discomfort with the American church manifested itself rather quickly. In a sharply worded letter sent in 1834 to the American hierarchy, the Congregation for the Propagation of the Faith reminded the Americans that bishops are appointed by Rome, not elected:

"[The Sacred Congregation] wants it to be known by all that in letters written to the Holy See about the appointment of bishops, there should be nothing that suggests 'election,' 'nomination' or 'postulation'—but rather, only 'recommendation.' The form of these letters should in no way imply that the Holy See has an obligation to appoint one of the men recommended [by the American bishops]. The liberty of the Apostolic See in the choice of bishops must remain unhampered. The recommendations merely provide the Congregation with information and knowledge; they do not impose any obligation."[99]

From this letter it is clear that Rome wanted to nip in the bud any thoughts of independence the American bishops might have had in the selection of persons for the episcopal office. At about this same time, it appears, Rome made moves to shut off any possibility of using the vernacular at services like Mass, vespers, and Benediction.

The tension between Roman caution and American boldness remained largely underground until the end of the nineteenth century when the controversy over "Americanism" arose. In a polite but firm letter to Cardinal Gibbons of Baltimore (22 January 1899) Leo XIII condemned certain efforts that were being made in the

336

United States, chiefly by Isaac Hecker and others, to update the formulation of Christian dogma in light of new cultural conditions.[100] These American theologians were also accused of criticizing traditional passive virtues like humility and obedience to authority.[101]

What Leo labeled "Americanism" (*Americanismus*) was probably not a serious threat to Catholic tradition; indeed, people like Isaac Hecker anticipated many of the moves made by the Second Vatican Council, such as the need for updating doctrinal language and the use of communications media in proclaiming the gospel in the modern world. But Leo's letter signaled Roman displeasure with American concerns for human liberty and religious freedom, and, in a sense, served to put the American hierarchy on the defensive. After the "Americanism" controversy blew over, the mood of American Catholicism seemed to change. The collegiate activity of provincial and plenary councils all but disappeared. And the image of the bishop in this country also changed from that of a member of a corporate college who shared pastoral responsibility with others, to that of a representative of Rome who administered papal directives in the local church. For a time, at least, the American experiment in Catholicism had come to an end.

THE NEW RITES (1973)
The reformed rites for worship of the eucharist outside Mass are easily outlined in their structure and contents. The 1973 Roman document provides three rites:
1) A Rite of Eucharistic Exposition and Benediction;[102]
2) A Rite for Eucharistic Processions;[103]
3) An outline for holding Eucharistic Congresses.[104]
These new rites do not speak any longer of the Forty Hours Devotion, but only of "lengthy exposition" on certain occasions approved by the local ordinary.[105]

Exposition and Benediction

The section of the 1973 document entitled "Exposition of the Holy Eucharist" begins by insisting that the "cult of the blessed sacrament" be clearly seen in "its relationship to the Mass."[106] The liturgical celebration of the eucharist, the document notes, "includes in a more perfect way the internal communion to which exposition seeks to lead the faithful."[107] Because Mass remains the supreme expression of eucharistic faith and piety, therefore, the liturgy may never be celebrated in the body of the church during exposition of the blessed sacrament.[108] Should a lengthy period of exposition be held, it is either to be interrupted while Mass is celebrated, or the Mass must be held in some area of the church "distinct from the area of exposition."[109] Gestures of reverence in the presence of the exposed sacrament have been simplified:

"A single genuflection is made in the presence of the blessed sacrament, whether reserved in the tabernacle or exposed for public adoration.

"For exposition of the blessed sacrament in the monstrance, four to six candles are lighted, as at Mass, and incense is used. For exposition of the blessed sacrament in the ciborium, at least two candles should be lighted, and incense may be used."[110]

These simplifications of gesture are obviously intended to avoid the visual impression sometimes given in the past that exposition is a more important event than Mass.[111]

The question of exposition for lengthier period of time is then discussed. It is recommended that in churches where the sacrament is regularly reserved, a "solemn exposition . . . for an extended period of time should take place once a year."[112] This lengthy exposition need not be continuous, particularly if there are only a few worshipers who might be present for it (e.g., during the hours of the night).[113] The reposition of the sacrament

338

(which may not occur more than twice a day) may be done without elaborate ceremony.[114]

Shorter periods of exposition may also be arranged from time to time. These should include a "suitable period for readings of the word of God, songs, prayers, and sufficient time for silent prayer."[115] In no case, however, may exposition be held merely for the sake of giving benediction: "Exposition which is held exclusively for the giving of benediction is prohibited."[116]

The question of perpetual adoration of the eucharist is discussed in relation to those religious communites and "other groups" among whom the practice is required by constitution or regulation.[117] "It is strongly recommended, " the document notes, "that they pattern this holy practice in harmony with the spirit of the liturgy."[118] Thus, if such forms of adoration involve the entire community, "readings, songs, and religious silence" are recommended.

A priest or deacon is the ordinary minister of exposition. In their absence, however, others may fulfill this ministry: Acolytes or special ministers of communion; a member of a religious community or lay association of men or women dedicated to eucharistic adoration 'upon appointment by the local ordinary.' When these latter act as ministers of exposition, they are not permitted to bless the people with the sacrament.[119] When priests or deacons minister, they vest in alb (or surplice over a cassock) and stole; other ministers wear "either liturgical vestments which are usual in the region or the vesture which is suitable for this ministry and which has been approved by the Ordinary."[120] At Benediction, the priest or deacon should wear cope and humeral veil; the cope may be omitted if Benediction takes place with the ciborium.[121]

The Ritual: The reformed rite for eucharistic Benediction embraces four simple stages: exposition of the sacrament, a period of adoration, the blessing of the people, reposition of the sacrament.[122] Structurally, the rites are straightforward:

Exposition: The people assemble and, as the minister approaches the altar carrying the Blessed Sacrament, a song may be sung. The ciborium or monstrance is placed on the altar and incensed.[123]

Adoration: Prayers, songs, and readings from the Bible then follow. A homily or brief exhortation may also be given "to develop a better understanding of the eucharistic mystery."[124] If the exposition is lengthy, parts of the liturgy of the hours may be sung, especially the principal hours of lauds and vespers.

Benediction: As the minister goes to the altar, the people sing "a hymn or other eucharistic song." *O Salutaris* and *Tantum ergo* are not obligatory. The sacrament, if exposed in a monstrance, is incensed and afterward the minister rises and says the prayer "Lord Jesus Christ, you gave us the eucharist. . . ."[125] The deacon or priest then puts on the humeral veil and blesses the people with the monstrance or ciborium. Nothing is said or sung during this blessing.

Reposition: The blessing done, the minister places the sacrament back into the tabernacle; meanwhile, the people may "sing or say an acclamation."[126]

Processions
The historical origins of eucharistic processions, especially those associated with the feast of Corpus Christi, have already been examined in Chapter Four. Only a few comments about the reformed rites of 1973 are necessary here.

The model for all such processions is, as might be expected, the one customarily performed on Corpus Christi. This event receives special mention in the 1973 document:

"The annual procession on the feast of Corpus Christi, or on an appropriate day near this feast, has a special importance and meaning for the pastoral life of the parish or city. It is therefore desirable to continue this procession . . . when today's circumstances permit and when it can truly be a sign of common faith and adoration."[127]

In the Roman Ritual of 1614, the procession on Corpus Christi was the only eucharistic procession, properly speaking, for which a rite was provided.[128] An unusually solemn and festive rite, the procession described in the Ritual of 1614 included these elements:

Decoration of the church and pathway of the procession with carpets, rich tapestries and holy images. After the celebration of Mass, psalms and litanies were sung as the procession began. The sacrament was incensed by the priest, who was vested in white cope. After he received the humeral veil from the deacon, the priest picked up the eucharist in a monstrance and joined the procession, accompanied by ministers, two acolytes, and thurifer.

While the procession was in progress, eucharistic hymns were sung: *Pange Lingua, Sacris solemniis, Verbum supernum, Iesu nostra redemptio, Aeterne Rex altissime.*

After the procession returned to church and the sacrament had been placed on the altar, all knelt while *Tantum ergo* was sung. A versicle and response followed (*Panem de caelo, Omne delectamentum*), and the priest said the prayer *Deus qui nobis.*

Then the people were blessed with the sacrament and the eucharist was replaced in the tabernacle.

Few ritual details for the eucharistic procession are provided in the 1973 document. Much is left to be "arranged in accordance with local customs."[129] Songs and prayers, lights and incense, are mentioned as characteristic elements of the procession; stations at various points along the path of the procession are also recommended. As in the 1614 ritual for Corpus Christi, the procession concludes with Benediction of the Blessed Sacrament.[130]

Eucharistic processions, it should be noted, are not obligatory, not even the one customarily associated with Corpus Christi. It is up to the local ordinary to decide whether this type of public devotion is "opportune in today's circumstances, and to determine the time, place, and order of such processions."[131]

Eucharistic Congresses
Technically speaking, there is no distinctive rite for Eucharistic Congresses. The ordinary regulations for Mass, eucharistic exposition and Benediction, and processions are followed while the congress is in session.[132] The 1973 document devotes most of its attention, therefore, to the planning that should precede such a congress. Two points stand out:

1) ". . . the local church and other churches should undertake studies beforehand concerning the place, theme, and program of the congress."[133] Planning should be interdisciplinary in nature, and should take into account the research of "specialists in theological, bilibcal, liturgical, pastoral, and humane studies."[134]

2) In planning for the Congress, three considerations are primary: catechesis on the eucharist "as the mystery of Christ living and working in the Church"; active participation in the liturgy; and "research and promotion of social undertakings for human development and the proper distribution of property."[135]

These guidelines reflect the historical evolution of the Eucharistic Congresses in the nineteenth century. For as we have seen earlier in this chapter, the meetings were originally organized not only as an expression of eucharistic piety but as an international forum for the discussion of issues central to church and society in the modern world, such as the rights of working people, justice and peace, and the impact of Christian values on the social order. In the 1973 document these concerns are clearly focused. A congress should emphasize not only the church's bond of unity and charity, but the larger world's hunger for human development.

All three reformed rites for the cult of the eucharist outside Mass (exposition and Benediction, processions, congresses) are characterized by the "noble simplicity" called for by the *Constitution on the Liturgy* in its guidelines for liturgical revision.[136] The important role of local custom in the development of these rites is repeatedly recognized and affirmed.[137] At the same time, the 1973 document makes it clear that all forms of eucharistic devotion, however laudable, are subordinate in importance to the community's action at Mass.

THEOLOGICAL ROOTS
The cult of the eucharist outside Mass depends, obviously, on a theology of the sacrament that sees veneration of the consecrated elements as legitimate and even as appropriate or required. Such a theology is not easy to construct or explain, for it always seems to run the danger of compromising the integrity of the eucharist as a liturgical action of the Christian people. If, at its normative origins, the eucharist is "meal," "celebration," "action of the assembly," how can one defend a cult that takes place outside or on the margins of those activities? In a word, how can an action (the liturgy of celebrating eucharist) become an object (cult of the reserved sacrament)? Two issues, then, need to be explored if we are to understand the theological propriety of a eucharistic cult outside Mass: the relation between action and object in the eucharist; and the primacy of eucharistic action.

Action and Object
Among the Christian sacraments the eucharist is unique in that it not only engages people in a common action of

343

praise and thanksgiving and of eating and drinking a meal, but it also produces something that remains —*food* that can still be eaten and drunk. To put it another way, eucharistic activity produces objects that remain even when the immediate actions (taking, blessing, breaking, sharing) have ceased. The relation between action and object is obvious, but the precise meaning of the remaining object is far less apparent.

The early Christian church does not seem to have been very worried about this issue. Justin Martyr (ca. 150) tells us that holy food from the eucharistic table is regularly carried to those who are absent from the assembly's actions. Hippolytus (215) tells us that Christians regularly carried home food from the table, and that they treated this food reverently as the Lord's Body. By at least the later third century there is evidence for the custom of regularly reserving food from the eucharistic meal for use in viaticum.

Until the Carolingian epoch, however, there is no evidence for adoring or venerating the eucharistic bread and wine outside the context of Mass, where action and object are clearly related. We have already seen, in the historical chapters of this book, how such a cult of the eucharist outside Mass developed. Here our attention will focus on the meaning of the eucharist as an object produced by an assembly's action, reverentially reserved and popularly venerated.

It has often been said that the eucharist is an action of love, a celebration of lovers who meet at a meal. It is well known, too, that a meal—if it is genuinely human and Christian—gives rise to things or states which survive: a deepened love, a stronger sense of mutual responsibility, an intensified commitment to one another. If a meal is authentic, we leave the table changed, however slightly; we rise from it different from what we were before. Every meal thus produces something that survives, something that changes us, something that we

344

cannot neglect without becoming less than we were before.

The eucharistic meal shares in this fundamental human intention of all communal dining together. We leave it both refreshed and changed. In every celebration of the Lord's Supper we take one more step toward the final destiny of the whole human family: eating and drinking in the kingdom of God. At the eucharist, bread and wine become the symbols of a destiny and a hope that survive even all our leave-takings from the table. For bread and wine are not only the signs of human activity, "the work of human hands": they are also the symbols of survival. As long as there is eucharistic food we can continue to exist as a community of faith.

The liturgical actions of the Christian assembly thus result in objects that symbolize our survival as a people united in faith and destiny. The eucharistic food that remains after Mass ceases to be a mere object; it becomes an action in its own right, inviting us to return to the table, to commit ourselves more deeply to one another, to work for the ultimate communion of all peoples at the banquet of God's kingdom.

For this reason the eucharistic species are not a mere static thing that represents something or someone the way a photograph might represent a beloved though absent friend or relative. On the contrary, the bread and wine produced by the community's action themselves become real symbols (thus real actions) that continue inviting us to find communion with God by discovering our unity with one another in Christ.[138]

In a nutshell, food can never be divorced from the actions that produced it. It continues to share the quality and meaning of those acts; indeed, it survives them and puts us in touch with the people and the actions that first brought them into being.

If, as we believe, the eucharist is an action of both God and the Christian people simultaneously, then the consequences are clear. As long as they remain food and drink, the eucharistic elements continue acting in the way all symbols act, putting us in touch with what they symbolize: the presence of the Lord, communion with God's people. Even when the eucharist is received outside Mass, we are connected with the action of a people who gathered in faith to express their common faith and destiny in a God who shares self with others in the ordinary deeds of dining at table.

This is what is meant, fundamentally, when the eucharist is spoken of as a permanent sacrament. The eucharistic bread and wine that remain after the celebration of Mass do not suddenly lose their character as real symbols; they are bread and wine that have been permanently altered by the action of Christ's body, head and members, in the liturgy. The relation established in the liturgy between the bread, the people, and the Lord, is a real symbolic, sacramental relation, one that continues to exist as long as the bread and wine remain real food and drink.

A comparison here may be useful. We Christians make a similar claim about the effects of baptismal initiation. Baptism establishes a relation between the Christian person, the Lord, and the community of believers. This relation is regarded as a real one, permanent and unalterable, definitive. Even when the immediate liturgical actions of washing, anointing, and communicating are · over the relation between person, Lord, and community remains real and constant. This is the source of the indescribable dignity that belongs to the Christian person: such a one is an "ikon," an incarnate symbol of God's new covenant with the world in Christ. For like the liturgy of the eucharist, the liturgy of Christian initiation is an action that "produces" an object: Christians are made, not born. As the "object" made in baptism, however, the Christian person is obviously not a "thing," but a living enfleshed symbol of all that God intends for the world.

346

What happens to the Christian person in baptism is analogous to what happens to the actions of the community gathered for eucharist. These eucharistic actions are expressed and objectified in the real symbols of bread and wine. What is encountered in the eucharistic species is thus not only the presence of the Lord, but the actions of his people as well. From this point of view it is clear that devotion to the eucharist outside Mass has nothing to do with "consoling Jesus imprisoned in the tabernacle." For ultimately, even the reserved eucharistic species are destined to be eaten and drunk by God's people.

Here one can see that the relation between action and object in the eucharist comes full circle. Action (liturgy) produces object (the sacramental species); but the object is destined once more for action (eating and drinking by God's people). The eucharist is never destined to remain an object of adoration and piety; it is always returned to the people in the form of spiritual food and drink. We can summarize the point in this sketch:

	produces		returns to
ACTION		*OBJECT*	*ACTION*
(Deed of the community: liturgy; praise and thanksgiving)		(Eucharistic bread and wine)	(Deed of the community; eating and drinking)

All three steps (action–object–action) in the sketch outlined above constitute the full sacramental symbolism of the eucharist. If, on occasion, the "object" (eucharistic bread and wine) is reserved (for communion of the absent, ill or dying, primarily; for veneration secondarily), this does not destroy the symbolic pattern, for ultimately the object is returned to the consummating actions of eating and drinking. The symbolic intentionality of the pattern thus remains constant even when there is a delay between the two phases of community action—between the deed of liturgical praise and thanksgiving and the deed of eating and drinking.

To sum it up, precisely because they are symbols and not merely representational "things," the eucharistic bread and wine may be temporarily reserved before they are returned to the consummate action of eating and drinking. As the 1973 document on worship of the eucharist outside Mass observes, the primary and original purpose of such reservation is always "the administration of viaticum"[139]; any other purpose (distributing communion, adoration) is secondary. Eucharistic reservation and devotion may thus be regarded as a temporary delay in the three-step symbolic pattern of the eucharistic liturgy: action (produces) object (returns to) action.

This explanation will, it is hoped, shed some light on the meaning of popular Catholic customs like visiting and praying before the Blessed Sacrament. The real presence of the Lord in the eucharist carries through the entire three-step symbolic pattern. Even though the mode of that presence may differ as one goes from action to object to action, there can be no doubt that the Lord is really present in all phases of the pattern. For the Lord is present in the liturgical assembly gathered for praise and thanksgiving (action); present in the sacramental species of bread and wine (object); present in the eucharistic food eaten and drunk at communion (action).[140] To visit the Blessed Sacrament is thus to make contact with the Lord and his people, since the eucharistic food is not an object that materializes out of nowhere, but the fruit of a community's liturgical action. Prayer in the presence of the Blessed Sacrament thus unites Christians with the assembly. However intensely personal such prayer may be, however intimate the encounter between believer and Lord, there is always a social dynamic at work in the eucharistic symbols of bread and wine. Action (produces) object (returns to) action. At every phase of this symbolic pattern Christians encounter the real presence of the Lord. If it is authentic, eucharistic devotion always leads the believer

348

back to the Lord's table, back to the celebrating assembly, back to eating and drinking the food that survives even when the meal is ended.

The Primacy of Action

In the preceding paragraphs I have purposely used the phrase "symbolic pattern" in referring to the eucharist. This is important, because the eucharist—as both a sacramental liturgy and a sacramental object of devotion— is not a single symbol but a cluster or intricate pattern of symbols. Our understanding of the eucharist is impoverished to the degree that we neglect any part of the pattern. I have suggested, further, that the pattern involves three basic phases: action–object–action. When we speak about Christ's real presence in the eucharist, we are speaking fundamentally about this entire pattern of symbolic actions and objects. To put it another way, we cannot speak accurately about Christ's real presence in the sacramental species of bread and wine unless we understand that presence as one mode among many. That is why the conciliar and postconciliar documents keep insisting on the "many modes of Christ's presence" in the liturgy.[141] Assembly, Word, ministers, sacramental species: in all these the Lord is truly present, though the modes of that presence differ.

Christ's distinctive presence in the gifts of bread and wine is best understood, therefore, as part of a larger symbolic pattern. The Lord's presence touches this pattern at all points—not merely at the moment of consecration in the eucharist. And there is more. We Christians believe that through God's decisive act in the cross of Christ the entire world has been permeated by grace.[142] The world is not simply a neutral arena without God and without grace; it has already been possessed at its deepest level by God's presence and self-bestowal.[143] Despite its apparent "secularity," despite its vulgar history of death and violence, despite its real injustice and despair, this world, with its history, is the

349

one loved unconditionally by the God of Jesus Christ. Every human being who lives in this world is thus touched by the real presence and love of God even though he or she may be quite unconscious of it. In Karl Rahner's words, the world and its history are already a "sublime liturgy, breathing of death and sacrifice, which God celebrates and causes to be celebrated in and through human history in its freedom."[144]

Our specifically Christian liturgies, our public prayer and sacraments, are thus part of the larger "liturgy of the world." It could be said, in fact, that the Christian sacraments are symbolic expressions of what the world can become if it chooses to be its best self, if and when it chooses to recognize itself as graced and loved unconditionally by God. The eucharist, for example, is a symbol of that communion in love for which the world itself is destined; it expresses the common vocation of all human persons, for all are destined, ultimately, to feast at table in the presence of God. The eucharist celebrates, in short, the common vocation and destiny of all human beings in all times and in all places; it is never merely a "self-proclamation" of the church, still less a private encounter between the individual and the Lord.

If we confess, as we do, that Jesus is really present in the eucharistic bread and wine, then we must recognize that this presence is possible because God has first loved and graced the entire world in Christ. Real presence in the eucharist presupposes the real presence of the Lord in the "liturgy of the world"; in the revealing Word of God; in the assembly of Christians gathered to worship; in the ministry of those who serve church and world. Christ's distinctive presence in the gifts of bread and wine is thus a reality that springs from action (God's decisive act in the cross of Christ; the Christian community's responsive act of praise and thanksgiving) and returns to action (eating and drinking, renewed service by Christians in and for the world). The 1973 document on worship of the eucharist outside Mass makes the point this way: "When the faithful honor Christ present in the sacrament, they should remember that this presence is derived from the sacrifice and is directed toward sacramental and spiritual communion."[145]

An accurate understanding of Christ's presence in the eucharist demands that we affirm the primacy of action over object in this sacrament. For the presence of the Lord in the sacramental elements is not an end in itself, but a reality destined to nourish the church and, ultimately, the world. Any theology which attempts to isolate Christ's presence in bread and wine from the full pattern of symbolic actions by which God embraces the world is misleading at best and pernicious at worst. Similarly, any devotion that refuses to recognize the primacy of the community's worship as the source and consummation of eucharistic action are misguided.

PASTORAL SIGNIFICANCE OF THE NEW RITES

Renewal of the Assembly
A careful reading of the 1973 document on worship of the eucharist outside Mass will make it clear that the Christian assembly itself is the principal focus of renewal in the matter of eucharistic devotions. There can be no liturgical rites for venerating the eucharist, after all, without a community of worshipers. In all the rites provided by the reforms of 1973—exposition and Benediction, processions, eucharistic congresses—the active participation of the Christian assembly is presupposed. Eucharistic devotions are seen not so much as opportunities for expressing piety, but as a means of renewing the assembly itself and of intensifying its participation in the Mass.

Repeatedly, the instructions that accompany "Holy Communion and Worship of the Eucharist Outside Mass" draw attention to the relation between devotions, whether public or personal, and worship.[146] In every case the Christian assembly and its worship are given premiere importance:

"The celebration of the eucharist is the center of the entire Christian life, both for the Church universal and for the local congregations of the Church."[147]

"The faithful should be encouraged to receive communion during the eucharistic celebration itself."[148]

"This kind of exposition must clearly express the cult of the blessed sacrament in its relationship to the Mass."[149]

The structure of the reformed rites for eucharistic cult outside Mass exhibits a similar concern for the primacy of communal worship over private devotion. Every one of the new rites—communion outside Mass, communion of the sick and dying, exposition and Benediction, processions, congresses—is based on common liturgical principles.

The Formative Impact of God's Word: The Christian assembly is called into being by God's Word. That Word— uttered by God in human history, preached by human ministers, heard and heeded in faith—is a decisive *event*, not a catalogue of information.[150] That is why for Paul Christian faith has nothing to do with fidelity to inherited beliefs or customs: it is trustful response to a proclamation, a spoken word. As Leander Keck has observed, the accent on "hearing as the event which awakens faith" is crucial in Paul's theology.[151] But this "hearing of the Word" is not "an inference, deduction, or value judgment on a body of information"; it is not, in other words, an act of or by the self.[152] Why? Because the self can never generate its own salvation. Keck notes: "From Paul's angle, the self that needs salvation can no more generate its own salvation than a psychotic can become his or her own therapist. The self needing salvation must be accosted by a word that offers an alternative and calls for a response. Paul's word for that response is *pistis*, usually translated 'faith.'"[153]

Pauline theology thus sees the Word of God as the "accosting event" that generates faith. The Christian

Church is the assembly of those men and women who have been so accosted, who have responded in trust, and who recognize that salvation can never be a deed done by the self. That is precisely why the church returns, constantly, to the proclamation and hearing of God's Word, especially in the liturgy. That is also why the church recognizes a true presence of Christ in the word of preaching.[154]

Significantly, all the reformed rites for worship of the eucharist outside Mass include the Word as part of the celebration. In this, there is implicit recognition that the Christian assembly, whether it is gathered for Mass or for a eucharistic devotion, is first formed in faith by the Word. In celebrating these rites it is pastorally important not to treat the Word as though it were simply a solemn appendage aimed at making the service lengthier. For unless the Word awakens faith and forms the community of believers, the sacraments themselves are subverted. Without the Word, sacraments become mere ritual manipulation, "acts of the self" seeking its own salvation. Even when it is received and venerated outside Mass, the eucharist presupposes the Word's formative action in the assembly.

Action of the Assembly: Another point clearly emphasized in the document "Holy Communion and Worship of the Eucharist Outside Mass" is that the source of the eucharist lies in the liturgical action of the assembly. The eucharistic species offered to Christians for devotional veneration are not sacral objects secretly produced by sacerdotal magicians. The holy gifts of bread and wine are symbols of creation's fruitfulness ("bread . . . which earth has given," "wine . . . fruit of the vine"), of human labor ("the work of human hands"), and of the assembly's action ("we offer you in thanksgiving . . . this bread, this cup"). In virtue of their baptismal priesthood Christians truly offer the eucharistic sacrifice of praise and thanksgiving.[155] Through their role differs from that of ordained priests, it is not for that reason less

353

important or less valuable. In the worship of the eucharist outside Mass, therefore, Christians recognize that the holy gifts offered for their adoration are their gifts, hallowed by the common prayer of priest and people, offered to all for nourishment. They are truly "holy things for God's holy people," holy things sanctified by the common action of all God's priestly people. The eucharistic elements are not the priest's possession, occasionally exposed like rare jewels to the unwashed masses. They are offered to all and belong to all.

Both these principles—the formative impact of God's Word, the importance of the assembly's action at eucharist—are vital. Eucharistic devotions are not, in the first instance, designed to bolster faith in the real presence. They are an opportunity for the congregation to reflect more deeply on the meaning of its liturgical action and its ecclesial existence. As the document "Holy Communion and Worship of the Eucharist Outside Mass" puts it:

"The same piety which moves the faithful to eucharistic adoration attracts them to a deeper participation in the paschal mystery. It makes them respond gratefully to the gifts of Christ who by his humanity continues to pour divine life upon the members of his body. Living with Christ the Lord, they achieve a close familiarity with him and in his presence pour out their hearts for themselves and for those dear to them; they pray for peace and for the salvation of the world."[156]

In this text the renewal of the assembly, its "deeper participation in the paschal mystery," is clearly seen as the goal of eucharistic devotions. Personal and private devotion such as prayer before Christ the Lord sacramentally present is viewed in a similar fashion: "It [prayer before the Blessed Sacrament] renews the covenant which in turn moves them [the faithful] to maintain in their lives what they have received by faith and by sacraments."[157]

354

Renewal of the Christian assembly does not stop, however, with prayerful gratitude for what God gives the church in the eucharist. Nor does the assembly's action cease when it leaves the Lord's table after Sunday Mass. We do not leave the liturgy and go back into a secular world; rather, we leave the liturgy in order to enter more deeply into what Karl Rahner calls the "liturgy of the world, breathing of death and sacrifice, which God celebrates and causes to be celebrated in and through human history."[158] The sacraments are not a temple which we enter in order to divest ourselves of the messiness and grime of secular life; rather they are landmarks, signs that the entire world has been permeated with God's real presence and belongs to God. Rahner has stated this point beautifully in an essay, "The Person in the Sacramental Event":

" . . . the sacraments constitute the manifestation of the holiness and the redeemed state of the secular dimension of human life and of the world. Man does not enter a temple, a fane which encloses the holy and cuts off from a godless and secular world which remains outside. Rather in the free breadth of a divine world he erects a landmark, a sign of the fact that this entire world belongs to God. . . . The sacrament constitutes a small sign, necessary, reasonable and indispensable, within the infinitude of the world as permeated by God. It is the sign which reminds *us* of this limitlessness of the presence of divine grace, and in this sense and in no other . . . is intended to be an event of grace."[159]

The sacraments are not smug testimonies to the superiority of Christians over the godless world; they are, as Rahner says, small signs of the limitlessness of God's grace, landmarks that point to that larger liturgy of the world in which all human beings are celebrants. Our Christian liturgy takes place within this larger liturgy of birth and death, suffering and hope. Every Christian sacrament is thus an ikon of the world, a remembering (*anamnesis*) of the "grace of the world, which permeates the whole of history as judgement when it is denied, as a blessed future when it is accepted."[160]

Rahner's understanding of the relation between sacrament and world is extremely helpful. It shows that the sacraments do not turn us away from the world (where God is presumed dead or absent) toward the sacraments (where God is presumed alive and present), but rather the sacraments (where God is present) turn us toward the world (where God is limitlessly present in human flesh and history). The sacraments are events of grace for us precisely because they keep us from forgetting that God has embraced the entire world unconditionally, flooded it with presence and grace, said "yes" to its history, invited it to a blessed future.

Seen in this light, the Christian eucharist assumes even deeper meaning. It is not for nothing that the eucharistic prayer characteristically begins with a hymn of creation that invites all the powers of heaven and earth to "give thanks and praise, always and everywhere." This is not mere liturgical hyperbole; it is a factual recognition of that larger liturgy of the world (indeed, of the cosmos) within which the liturgy of eucharist occurs. We begin the sacrifice of praise and thanksgiving by acknowledging that God has indeed permeated history and the world with grace and presence. And we recognize, too, that the eucharist points not away from the world toward some abstract sphere of divine presence, but toward the world—its people and its history. That is why the eucharistic prayer names very specific persons, events, deed, needs and hopes: the history of Israel, Jesus, the Christian community living and dead, all men and women of good will. The eucharist points toward the concrete history of the world as the place where the God of Jesus Christ is met.

Celebrating the eucharistic liturgy means embracing the liturgy of the world with all its death and sacrifice, its hungers and hopes. It does not mean retreating into some sacred precinct distant from world history. All the hungers of the world, physical and spiritual, become the concern of the community that celebrates the Supper of the Lord just as they became God's concern in the life and ministry of Jesus. In a world where hunger is a paramount social problem Christians cannot eat their bread—especially their eucharistic bread—in the comfortable privacy of sacred places. Paul's stern warning to the Corinthian community rings especially true for us today: eating and drinking without regard for the needy brings judgment and condemnation.

SUMMARY
This chapter has explored the 1973 reforms of those liturgical devotions—exposition, Benediction, processions—that are associated with the cult of the eucharist outside Mass. Our historical notes examined the rise of eucharistic customs like the Forty Hours Devotion, now referred to simply as a period of "lengthy exposition." We also noted the origins of Eucharistic Congresses and the history of eucharistic devotions in the United States. In the theological and pastoral sections of the chapter, we saw that devotion to the eucharist begins and ends with the actions of the Christian assembly at Mass (praise and thanksgiving, eating and drinking). We saw, too, that the eucharist, whether celebrated as sacrament or venerated devotionally, invites us to participate in the larger "liturgy of the world," where God's presence and grace are available to all humankind.

The worship of the eucharist outside Mass is thus neither a retreat from the world nor a device for avoiding the Christian assembly and its liturgical action. Although such devotions always remain secondary both to the Mass and to the prime purpose of eucharistic reservation, which is viaticum, they can become, if handled wisely, a pastoral resource for renewal and for attention to the needs and hopes of all humanity.

1. See "Holy Communion and Worship of the Eucharist Outside Mass" in *The Rites* (2 vols.; New York: Pueblo Publishing Company, 1976–1980), I, p. 484. Hereafter, citations of this document and its contents will be made as follows: HCWE, I (the volume of *The Rites*), followed by the appropriate page references.

2. HCWE, 5; I, p. 456.

3. See Josef Jungmann, "Die Andacht der Vierzig Stunden und das heilige Grab," *Liturgisches Jahrbuch* 2 (1952), 184 (complete article: 184-198).

4. See ibid., 184. See also Herbert Thurston, "Forty Hours' Devotion," *Catholic Encyclopedia*, edited by Charles G. Herbermann et al. (15 vols.; New York: Appleton, 1907–), Vol. 6, p. 152.

5. See Jungmann, "Die Andacht der Vierzig Stunden," p. 184.

6. See Thurston, "Forty Hours' Devotion," p. 152.

7. Ibid.

8. Ibid., p. 151.

9. See the text of this bull in L. Cherubini *et al.*, eds., *Magnum Bullarium Romanum* (Rome and Luxemburg, 1742; 8 vols.), Vol. 2, pp. 34-37.

10. *Magnum Bullarium Romanum*, Vol. 2, p. 34.

11. On the importance of the principle of ceaseless prayer in the early church, see William G. Storey, "The Liturgy of the Hours: Cathedral versus Monastery," in *Christians at Prayer*, edited by John Gallen (Notre Dame, Ind.: University of Notre Dame Press, 1977), pp. 61-68.

12. *Magnum Bullarium Romanum*, Vol. 3, p. 25 (complete text: pp. 24-25).

13. Ibid., Vol. 3, p. 230.

14. For the text of the *Instructio Clementina* and a commentary on it, see Aloisio Gardellini and Wolfgang Muehlbauer, eds., *Decreta Authentica Congregationis Sacrorum Rituum* (3 vols.; Munich: J.J. Lentneriana, 1863), Vol. 1, pp. 709-893.

15. *Instructio Clementina*, III; ed. Gardellini/Muehlbauer, Vol. 1, p. 718.

16. *Instructio Clementina*, IV; ed. Gardellini/Muehlbauer, Vol. 1, p. 726.

17. *Instructio Clementina*, V, VI; ed. Gardellini/Muehlbauer, Vol. 1, pp. 730, 735.

18. *Instructio Clementina*, XII, XIII; ed. Gardellini/Meuhlbauer, Vol. 1, pp. 765-770.

19. *Instructio Clementina*, XVI, XVII; ed. Gardellini/ Muehlbauer, Vol. 1, pp. 775, 777.

20. See *Instructio Clementina*, XVIII, ed. Gardellini/ Muehlbauer, Vol. 1, p. 780.

21. See *Concilii Plenarii Baltimorensis II Acta et Decreta* (Baltimore: J. Murphy, 1868), p. 195.

22. See *Ceremonial for the Use of the Catholic Churches in the United States of America* (3rd edition; Baltimore: Kelly, Piet and Co., 1871), pp. 499-517.

23. See, for example, Walter Schmitz, ed., *Manual for Forty Hours* (New edition; Washington, D.C.: The Catholic University of America Press, 1960).

24. See Jungmann, "Die Andacht der Vierzig Stunden," 185-198.

25. See Blandine-Dominique Berger, *Le Drame liturgique de Pâques* (Théologie historique, 37; Paris: Beauchesne, 1976), pp. 57-84.

26. Augustine, *De Trinitate*, IV.6; PL 42: cols. 894-895.

27. See *Apostolic Tradition*, 20; in Geoffrey Cuming, *Hippolytus: A Text for Students* (Grove Liturgical Study, no. 8; Bramcote, Notts.: Grove Books, 1976), pp. 17-18. Hippolytus describes the fasting by candidates and community on the Friday and Saturday before Pascha.

28. See Emile Bertaud, "Dévotion eucharistique," *Dictionnaire de Spiritualité*, IV/2, col. 1633.

29. See *XIeme Congres Eucharistique International*; Bruxelles, 13-17 Juillet, 1898 (Brussels: Joseph Goemaere, 1899), pp. 98-108, 206-222, 289-291, 311-345.

359

30. Ibid., pp. 377-389.

31. Ibid., p. 385.

32. Ibid., pp. 405-434.

33. Ibid., pp. 406-407.

34. Ibid., pp. 407-408.

35. Ibid., p. 411.

36. Ibid., p. 415.

37. See C.F. Donovan, ed., *The Story of the Twenty-Eighth International Eucharistic Congress* (Chicago: Eucharistic Congress Committee, 1927), p. 478.

38. Ibid., p. 478.

39. Ibid., pp. 445, 450.

40. See James Talley, ed., *Jesus, The Living Bread. A Chronicle of the Forty-First International Eucharistic Congress* (Plainfield, N.J.: Logos International, 1976), pp. 34-68.

41. Ibid., pp. 55, 57.

42. See J.C. Willke, "Eucharistic Congresses," NCE, Vol. 5, pp. 617-618.

43. HCWE, 111; I, p. 495.

44. See J.C. Selner *et al.*, eds., *A Compilation of the Litanies, Vespers Hymns and Anthems as Sung in the Catholic Church*, by John Aitken (Philadelphia: 1787; facsimile edition: Philadelphia: Musical Americana (Harry Dichter), 1956).

45. Ibid., unnumbered page immediately before the title page in the facsimile edition.

46. John Aitken, *A Compilation*, ed. J.C. Selner, pp. 17-23; 119-121.

47. Ibid., pp. 4-8.

48. Ibid., pp. 28, 30. Aitken does not include the other hymn commonly used at Benediction, the *O Salutaris Hostia*.

49. See ibid., p. 8, n. 1; pp. 3, 5. Aitken himself was probably not a Catholic; he seems simply to have included material in

his *Compilation* that was actually being used in Catholic parishes.

50. See *Concilia Provincialia Baltimori Habita* (Baltimore: John Murphy, 1842), pp. 15-16.

51. Ibid., p. 77.

52. Ibid., p. 138, note.

53. See *A Manual of the Ceremonies used in the Catholic Church* (Boston: H.L. Devereux, 1833), p. v.

54. Ibid., pp. 82-87, 258.

55. Ibid., pp. 258-260.

56. See *Rituale Romanum Pauli V Pontificis Maximi Iussu Editum* (Rome: 1615), pp. 215-220.

57. See *Concilia Provincialia Blatimori*, p. 138.

58. Ibid., p. 140.

59. See the acts and decrees of the First Plenary Council of Baltimore (1852) in: *Acta et Decreta Sacrorum Conciliorum Recentiorum*. Collectio Lacensis, edited by the Jesuits (Freiburg: Herder, 1875), III, col. 145.

60. See *A Manual of Ceremonies* (1833), p. 85.

61. See *Ceremonial for the use of the Catholic Churches* (1871), p. 172, note.

62. See Robert Batastini, ed., *Worship. A Complete Hymnal and Mass Book for Parishes* (Chicago: G.I.A. Publications, 1971), no. 71.

63. See John Julian, ed., *A Dictionary of Hymnology* (Revised edition with new supplement; London: John Murray, 1907), p. 1723.

64. See *A Manual of Ceremonies* (1833), p. 172.

65. See Adrian Fortescue, *The Ceremonies of the Roman Rite* (5th revised edition; London: Burns, Oates and Washbourne, 1934), p. 245.

66. See Joseph Christopher and Charles Spence, eds., *The Raccolta or Prayers and Devotions Enriched with Indulgences* (New York: Benziger Brothers, 1943), pp. 527-528.

67. See Herbert Thurston, "The Divine Praises," *The Month* 131 (1918), 511 (complete article: 510-513).

68. Ibid., 512.

69. See *The Raccolta*, ed. Christopher/Spence, p. 527.

70. See E. Bertaud, "Dévotion eucharistique," col. 1631.

71. See the Introduction to Part Two of this book.

72. See *Ceremonial for the Use of the Catholic Churches in the United States of America* (Philadelphia: H.L. Kilner and Co., 1894), pp. 79-85.

73. See G. Burton, ed., *The Choir Manual for Cathedral and Parish Church* (New York: J. Fischer and Bro., 1914), p. 424.

74. See *Key of Heaven. The Vest-Pocket Manual of Catholic Devotions* (Philadelphia: H.L. Kilner and Co., 1909), pp. 195-211.

75. See Charles Callan and John McHugh, eds., *Blessed Be God. A Complete Catholic Prayer Book* (New York: P.J. Kenedy and Sons, 1925), pp. 194-195.

76. See, for example, *The Catholic's Vade Mecum. A Select Manual of Prayers for Daily Use* (London: Burns and Oates, New York: Catholic Publication Society, n.d.), pp. 305-306

77. For the prayers after Mass prescribed by Leo XIII see: I. Pizzoni, "De Precibus post Missam Imperatis," *Ephemerides Liturgicae* 69 (1955), 54-60, 287-289.

78. Ibid., pp. 58-59.

79. See "Divine Praises, The," in F.L. Cross, ed., *The Oxford Dictionary of the Christian Church* (2nd edition; New York: Oxford University Press, 1974), p. 412.

80. See HCWE, I, p. 492.

81. See Callan/McHugh, eds., *Blessed Be God*, pp. 191-195.

82. The 1791 diocesan synod of Baltimore had spoken of Benediction at the end of Sunday vespers, but not in connection with Mass. The custom of giving Benediction immediately after Mass, though widely tolerated, was never considered entirely appropriate.

83. See, for example, *Key of Heaven* (1909), pp. 175-195; *Blessed*

Be God (ed. Callan/McHugh, 1925), pp. 174-190; *The Catholic's Vade-Mecum* (n.d.; probably late nineteenth century), pp. 102-125.

84. In two of the three prayerbooks mentioned in the previous note, the section on Benediction follows immediately after the texts for vespers and/or compline: *Key of Heaven*, pp. 195-197; *Blessed Be God*, pp. 191-195.

85. See *Concilia Plenarii Baltimorensis II Acta et Decreta*, pp. 193-197.

86. See *A Manual of Ceremonies* (1833), pp. 241-260.

87. See *Ceremonial for the Use of the Catholic Churches* (1871), pp. 499-517; 1894 edition, pp. 406-421.

88. See *Concilia Plenarii Baltimorensis II Acta et Decreta*, p. 195.

89. Ibid.

90. Ibid., pp. 195-196.

91. Ibid., p. 196; see *Ceremonial for the Use of the Catholic Churches* (1871), pp. 499-517.

92. See *Key of Heaven* (1909), p. 206.

93. See *Concilia Plenarii Baltimorensis II Acta et Decreta*, p. 193.

94. Ibid., p. 136.

95. Ibid., p. 193.

96. Ibid., pp. 193-194.

97. Examples of such defiance through the use of symbols and verbal slogans abounded, for instance, among the "counter-cultural" activists of the 1960s in the United States: "Hell no, we won't go!"; "Black is beautiful!"; "Never trust anyone over thirty!"

98. See, for example, Andrew Greeley, *An Ugly Little Secret: Anti-Catholicism in North America* (Kansas City: Sheed, Andrews and McNeel, 1972).

99. See *Acta et Decreta Sacrocum Conciliorum Recentiorum (Collectio Lacensis)*, III, col. 48.

100. For the pertinent passages of Leo's letter, see DS 3340-3346.

101. See especially DS 3343-3346.

102. HCWE, I, pp. 490-492.

103. Ibid., pp. 493-494.

104. Ibid., pp. 496-497.

105. Ibid., p. 487.

106. Ibid., p. 486.

107. Ibid.

108. Ibid.

109. Ibid.

110. Ibid., pp. 486-487.

111. One recalls, for example, the custom that existed in many churches before the Council: two candles were lit during a low Mass at which there was neither music nor singing by the congregation; as soon as Mass ended, servers lit dozens of candles, clouds of incense arose, the organ played, the choir sang, and the sacrament was exposed for Benediction. These customs give the impression that Benediction was somehow more important than Mass.

112. HCWE, I, p. 487.

113. As we have noted earlier in this chapter, a similar provision was made for Forty Hours in American parishes during the nineteenth century.

114. See details in HCWE, 88; I, p. 487.

115. HCWE, 89; I, pp. 487-488.

116. Ibid., p. 488.

117. Ibid.

118. Ibid.

119. Ibid., pp. 488-489.

120. Ibid., p. 489.

121. Ibid., p. 489.

122. See HCWE 93-100; I, pp. 490-492.

123. Ibid., p. 490.

124. Ibid.

125. Alternative prayers may also be used: see HCWE, I, pp. 510-512.

126. HCWE, 100; I, pp. 491-492.

127. HCWE, 102; I, p. 493.

128. One could also speak of a "procession with the Blessed Sacrament" in the 1614 ritual for communion of the sick, but the purpose of this latter was, naturally, different. See *Rituale Romanum Pauli V* (1615), pp. 62-66 (communion of the sick); pp. 215-220 (procession on Corpus Christi).

129. HCWE, 104; I, p. 493.

130. HCWE, 108; I, p. 494.

131. HCWE, 101; I, p. 493.

132. HCWE, 112; I, p. 496.

133. HCWE, 110; I, p. 495.

134. Ibid.

135. HCWE, 111; I, pp. 495-496.

136. See *Constitution on the Liturgy*, 34; in James J. Megivern, ed., Worship and Liturgy (Official Catholic Teachings; Wilmington, N.C.: McGrath Publishing Company, 1978), p. 208.

137. Ibid., sections 80, 101, 109; Megivern, *Worship and Liturgy*, pp. 219-220, 224, 226-227.

138. See Karl Rahner, "The Theology of the Symbol," *Theological Investigations IV*, translated by Kevin Smyth (Baltimore: Helicon Press, 1966), pp. 221-252.

139. HCWE, 5; I, p. 456.

140. HCWE, 6; I, p. 456.

141. See Karl Rahner, "The Presence of the Lord in the Christian Community at Worship," *Theological Investigations* X, translated by David Bourke (New York: Herder and Herder, 1973), pp. 71-83.

142. See Karl Rahner, "Considerations on the Active Role of

the Person in the Sacramental Event," *Theological Investigations* XIV, translated by David Bourke (New York: Seabury Press, 1976), pp. 161-184.

143. Ibid., p. 166.

144. Ibid., p. 169.

145. HCWE, 80; I, p. 484.

146. HCWE, 1-4, 13-15, 79-81, 82-83; I, pp. 455-456, 459-460, 484-485, 486.

147. HCWE, 1; I, p. 455.

148. HCWE, 14; I, p. 459.

149. HCWE, 82; I, p. 486.

150. On the word as "efficacious event," see Karl Rahner, "What is a Sacrament?" *Theological Investigations* XIV, pp. 137-141.

151. See Leander Keck, *Paul and His Letters* (Proclamation Commentaries; Philadelphia: Fortress Press, 1979), p. 51.

152. Ibid.

153. Ibid.

154. See Rahner, "What is a Sacrament?" p. 141.

155. On this point see Pius XII's encyclical "Mediator Dei," 93; in Megivern, *Worship and Liturgy*, p. 93.

156. HCWE, 80; I, p. 484.

157. HCWE, 81; I, p. 485.

158. See Rahner, "Considerations on the Active Role of the Person in the Sacramental Event," *Theological Investigations* XIV, p. 169.

159. Ibid.

160. Ibid., p. 171.

Chapter Eight

Eucharistic Cult and Devotion:
An Assessment

INTRODUCTION

The previous chapters of this book have explored in detail the historical evolution and contemporary reform of the worship of the eucharist outside Mass. Two themes have consistently emerged in those chapters: 1) the cult of the eucharist outside Mass must be located, historically, within the evolution of the liturgy itself; and 2) the disengagement of holy communion from its immediate context in the assembly's worship began happening at a rather early period of Christian history. We have seen, however, that eucharistic devotions *per se* (exposition, processions, Benediction, visits) are virtually nonexistent during the first millenium of the church's life, and only begin to appear some time before the end of the eleventh century.

It could be argued that the burgeoning eucharistic cult of the twelfth and thirteenth centuries represents a deformity of the tradition, a pietistic excrescence produced at a period when Christian theology and education were at a low ebb. Such a thesis is difficult to maintain, however, especially when one considers that twelfth-century Europe enjoyed a notable renaissance, one that laid foundations for the important and influential university centers of the thirteenth century.[1] This renaissance touched nearly all aspects of medieval life: language and letters, through the revival of Latin classics and the translation of works from Arabic; law and jurisprudence, through the influence of centers like Bologna; art and architecture, through the impact of Gothic style on church buildings; the natural sciences (e.g., mathematics), especially through contact with the works of Arabic scholars.

In short, the centuries that saw the rapid rise and spread of eucharistic worship outside Mass can hardly be dismissed as unenlightened or utterly barbaric. Indeed, the contrary is true: the cult of the eucharist emerges in Europe during an era of remarkable awakening in the arts and sciences. Part of this awakening, it seems certain, was a direct outgrowth of those bellicose forays into the Middle East known as the Crusades. The First Crusade was launched by Pope Urban II in November of 1095, and however ill-fated the project appears to us today, it had the distinct advantage of putting Europeans into direct contact with centers that represented a more ancient and more sophisticated culture.[2] As a matter of fact, the First Crusade—an imperialist campaign of expansion waged under a veneer of religious motivations—was highly successful: Constantinople was invested in 1096 and Jerusalem fell in July of 1099. This breach into the Arab world gave Westerners access to elements of science, epecially geometry and mathematics, that had formerly been inaccessible. Euclid's *Elements of Geometry*, for example, reentered the West through an Arabic version discovered and translated by an English scholar, Adelard of Bath, sometime between 1114 and 1120.[3] Discoveries of this sort might not have been possible had not the First Crusade opened up contact with parts of Syria and Anatolia previously isolated from the West.[4]

It was upon architecture, however, that the influence of Arab skills and sciences had greatest impact. John Harvey has argued that western architects derived the pointed arch—central symbol and mark of Gothic style—from eastern sources.[5] He bases his argument on two factors: first, that examples of Moslem architecture using the pointed arch were not available to westerners prior to the invasion of new territories during the First Crusade; and secondly, that the technology needed to create this architectural form coincided with the rediscovery of Euclidian geometry through its Arabic ver-

368

sions.[6] While art historians would not all agree with Harvey's assessment of Moslem inspiration as a source for Gothic style, particularly the pointed arch, there can be little doubt that twelfth-century art and architecture in Europe benefited from contact with Arabic science.[7]

The principal point here is that at the turn of the eleventh century, a major shift occurred in European attitudes toward both art and science. Lynn White has summarized the change in this way: "the emergence of Gothic art reflects a fundamental change in the European attitude towards the natural environment. Things ceased to be merely symbols, rebuses, *Dei vestigia*, and became objects interesting and important in themselves, quite apart from man's spiritual needs."[8] In the world of late antiquity and the earlier middle ages, White contends, people lived "not in a world of visible facts but rather in a world of symbols."[9] Their concern focused not on nature as an object worthy of study in its own right, but on nature as a source of hidden meanings, symbolic references and allegorical interpretations. As White explains:

"the pelican, which was believed to nourish its young with its own blood, was the analogue of Christ, who feeds mankind with his blood. In such a world there was no thought of hiding behind a clump of reeds actually to observe the habits of a pelican. There would have been no point in it. Once one had grasped the spiritual meaning of the pelican, one lost interest in individual pelicans."[10]

Attitudes like the one just described began changing around the beginning of the twelfth century. Suddenly, it seemed, people were interested in individual pelicans, and this interest began to manifest itself in art and in the close observation of natural phenomena which we associate with the rise of modern science. As Adelard of Bath, the twelfth-century translator of Euclid's *Elements*, once quipped: "I'm not the sort who can be fed with a

369

picture of beefsteak!"[11] Clearly, something new was afoot; impatient with allegorical explanations of flora and fauna (such as those commonly found in medieval beastiaries and herbals), people began to acquire "a fresh sense of the immediacies of concrete experience, a new attachment to physical actualities."[12]

This new attitude toward the natural world made its impact felt especially in the visual arts. An example can be seen in the evolution of decoration used for capitals in twelfth-century churches. As the century progressed, the flowers and foliage on capitals carved by anonymous sculptors gradually lost their abstract, generalized quality and began to imitate, much more directly, the actual shape and motion of living plants. By the early thirteenth century, artists were quite consciously imitating the irregular design of grape leaves and eglantine (sweetbrier). "Thus from 1140 to 1240," Lynn White writes, "Gothic capitals changed from the barest reminiscence of nature to a naturalism which sacrificed design to exactitude of observation. The interpretation of forms ceased, and floral sculpture became botanizing."[13] A similar evolution can be discerned in Gothic art's treatment of the human face and figure. The rather more abstract, iconographic style of Romanesque artists (still visible, for example, in the sculpture of Giselbertus at Autun) gave way to human forms of astonishingly lifelike quality (e.g., the figure sculptures of Rouen and Chartres).

One is thus not surprised to hear Thomas Aquinas declare, in the middle of the thirteenth century, that "art imitates nature": *Ea quae sunt secundum artem imitantur ea quae sunt secundum naturam.*[14] This declaration could hardly have been made two centuries earlier! For the shift exhibited in the visual arts of the twelfth and thirteenth centuries reflects a more fundamental change of attitude toward the investigation of nature. One could perhaps distinguish attitudes before and after the renaissance of the twelfth century by speaking of a differ-

370

ence in critical method as it was applied to the realities of the natural world. Before, nature was important not because of what it revealed about itself, but because of what it disclosed about transcendent and eternal truths (God, faith, Christian doctrine). After, nature became important for its own sake and its own truth. The underlying question was: what sort of truth does one hope to derive from the natural world—the transcendent truth signaled by God's creation, or the immanent truth contained within God's creation? Despite its occasional extravagances, the earlier allegorical method provided a way into nature that led the mind toward mysteries surpassing nature. The newer scientific method that began emerging in the twelfth century, however, provided a more precise entry into the mysteries of nature itself.

Although generalized contrasts of this sort are severely limited in their usefulness, they can perhaps give us a glimpse of what was happening in culture and the arts at that point in history when the cult of the eucharist began to emerge. For the shift in attitude described above had a decisive impact on Christian worship and piety. As we saw in Chapters Two and Three, the allegorical method was a common form of liturgical hermeneutic during the late antique and early medieval periods. From Theodore of Mopsuestia to Amalarius of Metz, allegorial interpretations of worship were popular. Nor did these die with the advent of twelfth-century *art nouveau*. Allegorical and symbolic interpretations of the ritual drama continued to exist, but they took on a new factual and graphic quality. [15] Contemplative interest shifted toward the concrete events of Jesus' historical life: his birth, his earthly career, his passion. And this interest was reflected in the liturgical art of the period, particularly sculpture, painting, and drama.

Some examples will help illustrate this point. In Chapter Three we noted that elements of drama had crept into medieval worship during the tenth century. The *Regularis Concordia* (ca. 970) provides us with a very early

371

account of the "empty tomb drama" attached to the final responsory at the office of Easter matins (vigils). In the *Regularis*, the "visit to the tomb" is still a liturgical event carried out by liturgical ministers who are vested in liturgical garb (albs). But by the twelfth and thirteenth centuries, the drama had expanded significantly: props, costume, extended dialogue, and dramatic roles had transformed symbolic ritual into realistic theatre.[16] A similar movement toward realism can be detected in sculpture and painting. By the middle of the thirteenth century, realistic crucifixes appear that show the body of Christ beaten, bloodied, and contorted with pain.[17] The same century witnessed the introduction of the crèche at Christmas, probably under the influence of Franciscan piety.[18]

All these factors—the twelfth-century renaissance, the evolution of new forms in art and architecture, the shifting attitude toward nature and its scientific investigation—could hardly escape influencing Christian worship and piety. Two themes emerge that seem especially relevant to the question of eucharistic worship outside Mass: 1) the emphasis on visual realism evident in the desire to make art imitate nature; and 2) the increasing impatience with symbolism (a mediated form of encountering transcendent mystery), coupled with a hunger for the natural, the literal, and the real. This second theme may at first appear startling; we commonly view the Middle Ages as an era infatuated by symbols and their mediated meanings. In fact, however, there is evidence that during the twelfth and thirteenth centuries, with their surging interest in nature, attention turned from the symbolic and mystical to the literal and historical. This turning was especially evident in the interpretation of the Bible. During the twelfth century, the older "spiritual exposition" of the Bible commonly associated with the monastic schools and the practice of *lectio divina*, began declining. In its place, a newer "literal exposition," associated with the theological *quaestiones* and *disputationes* of the cathedral schools and the early universities, appeared.[19] This "literal exposition" should not be confused with what twentieth-century scholars call "fundamentalism"; twelfth-century "literalists" (like Andrew of St. Victor) were attempting to uncover the historical facts, the *veritas Hebraica* (Hebrew truth) of the scriptures, without falling into mystical fancy on the one hand or arid doctrinal speculation on the other.[20]

The literal expositors of the Bible, in short, were trying to treat the scriptures as an object of scientific investigation, striving to construct a science of exegesis. They were acutely attentive to biblical languages, especially Hebrew, to questions of authorship and literary style, to the correction of faulty texts, and to the verification of factual historical details.[21] In this the literal exegetes were not unlike those twelfth-century artists and sculptors who longed to depict with lifelike accuracy, flowers, vines, leaves, human faces, and figures. Here again we see an example of what Lynn White calls "natural science and naturalistic art," a shift of attitude toward the investigation of matter and its meaning.

What does all this have to do with understanding and assessing the cult of the eucharist outside Mass? It reveals that eucharistic cult arose and spread during an age intensely interested in "seeing things as they are," in "the immediacies of concrete experience."[22] As White has written:

". . . at the end of the twelfth century Catholic peity suddenly concentrated itself upon an effort to bring God down to earth and to see and touch him. It was as though Europe had become populated with doubting Thomases eager to thrust their fingers into the very wounds of Christ. To an extraordinary degree the new eucharistic cult was empirical in temper, permitting the constant seeing and handling of God. . . . Superficially the new piety might seem to be a development and expansion of the traditional sacramentalism, and as such a buttressing of the older symbolic and mediate view of nature. But, as the more conservative Eastern Church suspected, this was a sacramentalism of a new flavor, suffused with a spirit alien to that of the first Christian millenium. It seemed almost that the Latin Church, in centering its devotion upon the actual physical substance of its deity, had inadvertently deified matter."[23]

At its origins, the cult of the eucharist outside Mass thus reflected the shifting interests of the age—interests that affected art, architecture, science, and biblical exegesis as well. The cult arose not as a result of severe theological decline, but as part of a larger reaction within European culture. This reaction enfranchised scientific attitudes toward nature while it exhibited increasing impatience with the older symbolic or allegorical perceptions of the world characteristic of spiritual exegesis and mystagogic commentary on the liturgy. The desire to see, the drive to grasp things in their concrete immediacy and physical actuality, led to a kind of empiricism that touched even the hallowed symbolism of sacraments and worship. The questions raised about the eucharist during the twelfth century (discussed above in Chapter Four) betray a growing fascination with the eucharistic species as objects in nature open to scientific analysis. Exactly when does a change take place in bread and wine? Can a body (even a glorified one) exist without its blood? Is the entire Christ, in his human and divine actuality, present in each of the eucharistic species? Does each fragment of bread or droplet of wine contain the Lord's body and blood? Though questions like these had begun to appear as early as the ninth century (during another European renaissance, the Carolingian one), they were approached with new intensity in the twelfth, especially in the newer cathedral schools. Ninth-century monastic theologians like Paschasius Radbertus and Ratramnus had been more concerned about symbolism (sacramentalism) itself: about

374

the relation between images and symbols (*figurae*) and truth (*veritas*). But the schoolmen, having recovered Aristotelian thought through Arabic translations and commentaries of the twelfth and thirteenth centuries, seemed more preoccupied about the structure of nature and matter: about the relation between substance and accidents, actuation (*forma*) and potency (*materia*).

This emphasis on the empirical investigation of objects, coupled with the desire to "see things as they really are" rather than through the mediation of symbolic language and action, certainly contributed to the cult of the eucharist outside Mass. As material realities, as objects occurring in nature, the eucharistic bread and wine could be analyzed and reacted to quite independently of liturgical rites and gestures. After all, they can be seen; and what is visible is open to empirical inspection.

But sacramental empiricism of the sort that developed among the early scholastics cannot by itself explain the survival of eucharistic worship and devotion in later ages. How can one account for the continuing popularity of customs such as exposition, Benediction, and processions that make the eucharistic species an object of ocular communion? To answer this question, it is necessary to dig below the surface of historical data in order to raise the more fundamental issue of the relation between visual perception and ritual symbols. In the first section of this chapter, that relation will be explored with the help of Erik Erikson. The second section will dwell on a related issue: the manner in which symbols help us deal with simultaneous experiences of "presence" and "absence." Finally, in the third section, the relation between eucharistic liturgy and eucharistic devotions will be discussed.

THE PRIMACY OF VISION
From earliest times, vision has been a common metaphor for the Christian experience of world-transcending realities. From the Easter appearance

stories in the synoptics to the Johannine invitation to "come and see" (John 1.39), to the seer's Lord's Day vision on the isle of Patmos, to Augustine's illumination at Ostia, to St. Benedict's perception of the whole world in a ray of light, seeing has been identified with grace and mystical intuition. Even in a systematic theology such as Aquinas's, the ultimate condition of humanity in the presence of God is described as *visio beatifica*, the beatific vision.

Nor has this emphasis on vision been restricted to western Christianity. Orthodoxy too has insisted on the importance of visual symbolism, especially in its theology of icons. As Leonid Ouspensky has written: "It is absolutely impossible to imagine the smallest liturgical rite in the Orthodox Church without icons. The liturgical and sacramental life of the Church is inseparable from the image. . . . The icon is an object of worship embodying divine grace and forming an integral part of the liturgy."[24] The icon is not merely an object of visual perception or spiritual veneration, but a revealing source that corresponds to the word (an acoustic symbol) of scripture. "That which the word communicates by sound," wrote St. Basil, "the painting shows silently by representation."[25] Word and image together constitute the continuing sources of revelation for God's people. This is true, Orthodoxy asserts, because the "incarnation, the fact that God assumed human flesh, has sanctified . . . the entire terrestrial world. Thus matter itself gains an enormous significance."[26] As St. John Damascene put it, "I do not adore matter, but I adore the Creator of matter, who became matter for me, inhabiting matter and accomplishing my salvation through matter."[27] Essentially, the icon is a form of preaching, a visual proclamation of God's presence comparable to the preacher's breaking open the bread of the Word to nourish the assembly. Just as the Lord is truly present in the Word preached, heard and heeded, so the Lord who "sanctified the entire terrestrial world" by "inhabiting matter" is present in the icon.

376

The icon thus invites the believer to communion with the Lord whose coming in our flesh has forever blessed the colors, forms and textures of creation. Like all authentic symbols, icons do not merely represent something; they trigger a transaction (in this case, a *visual* one) that draws the beholder into the presence of the reality itself.[28] By gazing on the icon, I do not merely take it into myself through the power of visual ingestion; it takes me into itself, causing me to inhabit its world. The transaction is transforming: I leave the icon's world altered and perhaps shaken. It is less like seeing than like being for the first time seen, "knocked breathless by a powerful glance."[29]

Vision and Ritualization
It is probably not accidental that in both eastern and western Christianity visual symbols are paramount. If an underlying anthropological reason for this is sought, one may perhaps find it in the critical role vision plays in the psychological development of human beings. In his Godkin Lectures given at Harvard University in 1972, Erik Erikson cites a series of studies done by Dr. René Spitz and his colleagues at Denver. These studies reveal what a critical contribution vision makes to the development of a rudimentary sense of reality in the human infant.[30] As Spitz reports: "Vision introduces into the infant's world, in which so far contact perception predominated, the new and fateful distance perception. Because of distance perception the child begins to understand continuity in time and coherence in space."[31]

Commenting on these reports, Erikson notes that vision "becomes the leading perceptual as well as emotional modality for the organization of a sensory and sensual space as marked by the infant's interplay with the primal person [usually the mother]."[32] So vital is vision to the child's sense of reality that seeing may even outdistance the infant's need for food and comfort. This has been demonstrated in experiments involving a sucking mechanism to which a projector and screen have been connected. Infants linked up with the mechanism will suck with varying intensity and speed until the image projected on the screen becomes clear, providing a good visual stimulus.[33] The experiments indicated that the infants were more concerned about the clear visual image than about nourishment. Erikson sees in this infantile hunger for clear vision the indistinct rudiments of both consciousness ("I"/"not I") and religion, which "seeks for a vision of sanctioned centrality."[34]

Even if one is unwilling to accept Erikson's conclusions about the remote origins of consciousness and religion, there can be little doubt that vision plays an enormous part in one's development throughout a lifetime. As Joan Erikson has remarked: "We begin life with this relatedness to eyes. . . . It is with eyes that concern and love are communicated, and distance and anger, as well. Growing maturity does not alter this eye-centeredness, for all through life our social intercourse with others is eye-focussed: the eye that blesses and curses."[35]

This "eye-centeredness" characteristic of all social life begins in earliest infancy, Erik Erikson argues, with those eye-focused patterns of mutual recognition between parent and child. Vision is thus the first step in what Erikson calls the "ontogeny of ritualization."[36] Though the word is somewhat awkward, "ritualization" refers to a basic element of all human existence, for humans, unlike other species, need a prolonged childhood in which to be "familiarized by ritualization with a particular version of human existence."[37] Ritual is thus a primary way of becoming human, "a creative formalization which helps to avoid both impulsive excess and compulsive self-restriction, both social anomie and moralistic coercion."[38] The rituals through which we become human are not necessarily grand displays; they are often nothing more or less than the "minute patterns of daily interplay."[39] Nor are rituals always highly formalized; many of them are improvised playfully on a day-to-day basis. Erikson thus concludes that ritualization "is a mixture of formality and improvisation, a rhyming in time. It is closer to a *ritus* as a daily custom than to a rite as a periodical ceremony; although daily custom creates ritual needs which then find periodical fulfillment in grand rituals."[40]

Ritualization is thus our prime way of acquiring a distinctively *human* identity. And this process of acquisition begins in earliest infancy with the ritualized interactions between mother or maternal figure and infant. As we have noted, further, these ritual patterns are typically centered on the power of vision, both the infant's and the mother's. At the very outset of human life, therefore, a ritual pattern is established that will remain with the person throughout life:

"The human being which at the beginning wants, in addition to the fulfillment of oral and sensory needs, to be gazed upon by the primal parent and to respond to the gaze, to look up to the parental countenance and to be responded to, continues to look up, and to look for somebody to look up to, and that is somebody who will, in the very act of returning his glance, lift him up."[41]

The fundamental human ritual of seeing and being seen, of gazing and being gazed upon, lies at the root of all subsequent ritualization. Erikson suggests that this is so because of an inborn human need for "regular and mutual affirmation and certification."[42] "This need," Erikson notes, "will reassert itself in every stage of life as a demand for ever new, ever more formalized and more widely shared ritualizations . . . which repeat the face-to-face 'recognition' and the name-to-name correspondence of the hoped for."[43] The range of such "rituals of recognition" is enormous: they embrace everything from the exchange of greetings among friends (or among people at liturgy) to the carefully choreographed appearances of a political or religious leader with "charisma."

We thus purchase our humanity through rituals of mutual recognition, and we renegotiate the purchase throughout a lifetime. Like all rituals, these are crisscrossed by curious paradoxes. Often playful, they are also carefully structured, formally rehearsed and staged, surrounded by scores of written and unwritten rules. Intensely familiar because so often repeated, they can also provoke the shock and surprise of recognition. Whether one is engaged in a "microritual" with an unwelcome salesperson at the front door or a "macroritual" like Easter Mass in St. Peter's Square, the paradoxical combinations of structure and improvisation, surprise and familiarity, are in evidence.[44]

Vision and Symbolization

Erik Erikson's assessment of the primacy of vision at the origins of ritualization can be extended to include the process by which human beings discover symbols and their power. Symbols and rites are, after all, two sides of a single coin; to speak of the origins of the one is to speak of the origins of the other. Or to put the matter another way, symbols and rites are mutually implicating: each requires the presence of the other. Symbols are the always implied penumbra of rituals, and rituals are the always implied penumbra of symbols. This is true precisely because both rites and symbols are transactions, verbs rather than nouns. Language, for example, is a fundamental human ritual of mutual recognition; speakers imply hearers and together they imply discourse, conversation. As ritual, langauge bears the paradoxical characteristics noted earlier: playful improvisation and controlling structure, easy familiarity and unbidden surprise. At the same time, if we immerse ourselves in the ritual process of language we discover a mighty ambiguity. On the one hand, our words die by the thousands every day, thrown away like confetti. On the other hand, language survives, stubbornly refuses to die. Even after a conversation is ended and we withdraw into silence, language remains in a state of readi-

380

ness, waiting to be tapped like an inexhaustible reservoir. Indeed, language reveals itself to us as an eternal circle, without beginning or end; it has always been there and will continue to be even after our deaths.

Language is thus simultaneously a ritual process with a beginning and an ending and a symbolic signal without beginning or end. And since it is a common denominator among human experiences, language can serve as a useful example of the way rites and symbols imply one another. The question now is: do symbols arise from the same source as rituals? Are both of them rooted in the common experience of the mutual recognition, through vision, of infant and parent?

The question must be answered affirmatively. The power to perform ritually and the power to recognize symbols as they emerge within the ritual process are both rooted in the primal urge to see and be seen, to gaze and be gazed upon.[45] But more can be said. To borrow a metaphor from Urban T. Holmes, both rites and symbols arise in "the land east of the river."[46] Holmes's metaphor derives from his vision of the "landscape of reality": a land east and west of a "river" that bisects our human consciousness. The land west of the river is the territory of structure, order and control, predictability, clarity and precise expectations. East of the river is the land of antistructure, of metaphor, symbol, story and, I would add, ritual. At the very easternmost edge of this landscape lies the abyss, the deep floor of the ocean where the points of transformation between the finite and the infinite occur.[47] As Holmes remarks: "We never get rid of the abyss. It is within human history. Our personal consciousness arises from the infinite, dark void of our unknowing. Chaos is the source of our creativity. . . . Our consciousness—our reality, our meaning, and our truth—is made from and arises from the abyss, from chaos."[48]

Rites and symbols well up from the abyss; they glide into our consciousness as we journey through the "land east of the river"; they help us make passage across the river to the "west" and back again. In other words, both rites and symbols are concerned with passages and their successful negotiation—whether the passage is through a door (the microrituals of etiquette, courtesy, esteem, deference) or through death (the macrorituals of dying and burying). Ritual is the repeatable strategy for negotiating such passages; symbol is the repeatable "verb" that inexhaustibly energizes the passage, keeps it in motion, pulls it forward, gives it coherence and plausibility.

I have said that rites and symbols deal above all with passages, with daily and seasonal transitions in human life. And this fact reveals a breaking point within both ritualization and symbolism. As Erikson notes: "the earliest affirmation soon becomes much needed re-affirmation in the face of the fact that the very experiences which through ritualization give a measure of security also expose the growing being to a series of estrangements."[49] If we remember that rites and symbols well up from "the abyss," from a dark and unknowable chaos that borders the edges of human consciousness, then Erikson's admonitions become weightier. The visual patterns of mutual recognition that commence the process of ritualization in infancy also create the possibility of separation and abandonment (as every parent who has ever left a small child with a babysitter for the first time knows!). Rituals of recognition/presence imply, as their binary opposite, rituals of separation/abandonment/absence. And the same can be said of symbols. Every symbol that signals a hallowed presence has a shadow that simultaneously signals a menacing absence. A symbol is thus a kind of pivot, a point of exchange that permits people to confront an enormous range of ambiguous experiences: presence and absence, belonging and separation, acceptance and abandonment, and ultimately life or death. Our perception of symbols as something numinous derives precisely from their capacity to combine conflicting and ambiguous experiences into a coherent pattern of action in which we can participate.

An example of the symbol's power to perform as a pivot that permits the successful negotiation of ambiguous passages in human life can be seen in baptism. Christian initiation plays powerfully on the ambiguous ability of water both to bestow life and to deal death. The baptismal waters symbolize, simultaneously, presence and absense, belonging and separation. As a ritual bath, baptism signals the presence of life cleansed, renewed and refreshed; as a watery grave, baptism signals the extinction of life, destruction and death. By the same token, initiation ushers the person into a new community (belonging); it also separates one definitively from a former life with its loyalties and allegiances (separation).

Our ability to participate in ambiguous symbols such as those of Christian baptism is rooted, Erikson would argue, in the earliest experiences of infancy: the face-to-face rituals of recognition which imply, as their shadowy counterpart, rituals of separation, estrangement and abandonment. We learn this fundamental ritual strategy, and the symbols that keep the strategy in motion, through the games played between parent (maternal figure) and infant: "peekaboo," the regular rhythm of the parent's appearances and disappearances, the hide-and-seek quality of familiar faces that reveal, then conceal themselves.[50]

Visual and Acoustic Symbols
Given these remote origins of ritual and symbolic competence in the earliest stages of an infant's development, it is not surprising that most symbols fall into two categories: visual and acoustic. Parent and infant participate not only in reciprocal rituals of seeing and being seen, but also in rituals of naming and being named. Whether the name has been carefully selected and given in a tribal ceremony, as it is in some archaic cultures, or

whether it is assigned somewhat arbitrarily by the parents, it quickly becomes part of the meaning attached to the infant's life. As Erikson remarks:

". . . whatever procedures have given meaning to the name, that meaning now exerts a certain effect on the way in which the name is repeated during the greeting procedure—together with other emphases of caring attention which have a very special meaning for the maternal person(s) and eventually for the child. Thus, the mother also refers to herself with a special designation. This mutual assignment of a very special meaning is, I think, the ontogenetic source of one pervasive element in human ritualization, which is based on a mutuality of recognition, by face and by name."[51]

Seeing and naming (hearing and being heard) thus constitute the most primitive ways infants organize their world in space and time. This fact of human development assumes even greater significance when we place it in the context of explicitly religious symbols. The Hebrew and Christian scriptures regularly symbolize the relation between God and humankind through visual and acoustic image transactions. This relationship is, moreover, mutually defined as one that exists between parent and child:

Relationship: God = Parent (Father/Mother/Creator of life)

Symbols of
relationship: The face of God (simultaneously a source of life and a source of death; signal of presence and absence)

The word of God (calls forth life, judges the quality of life)

The name of God (unutterable yet revealing; surpasses human control and manipulation)

In the Bible, the primary symbols of the relationship between God and persons are thus visual and acoustic ones, and like all symbols these are inherently ambiguous. God's face may shine upon people, blessing them (symbol of recognition, assurance, approval); but the face may also be hidden, turned aside or withdrawn from view (symbol of rejection, estrangement, abandonment). Similarly, God's word utters a world and orders its life (symbol of creative power); but the word, like the face, may be withdrawn, the Speaker may choose not to speak (symbol of absence).

This same pattern of ambiguous visual and vocal symbolism continues in the New Testament. Paul, for example, is fond of the acoustic symbol, the Word heard and heeded in faith (Romans 10.17 ff.). Implicitly, Paul understands the relation between humankind and God as a conversation that reached its highest point of intensity in the life and death of Jesus. Message (proclamation) and obedience (response) thus loom large in Paul's theology of Christian faith and existence. John, in contrast, is fond of visual symbols: the Word has become flesh, visible and palpable. This flesh-taking Word reveals its power in water, light, and birth (John 3), in a bread that becomes life-giving flesh (John 6), in a body touched, held, sensed, seen and now gone away (1 John 1 and John 16, where Jesus must "go away" and no longer be seen). One must now search to see Jesus in the community of love, the *koinonia*, that believes in him and confesses that he truly came "in the flesh" (1 John 2). Implicitly, John understands the relation between humankind and God as a matter of flesh and blood, of eating and drinking, of life in a privileged community of witnesses.

The explicitly religious symbolism of the Hebrew and Christian testaments is thus intimately linked to what Erikson has described as the ontogenetic source of all ritual symbolism: seeing and naming. The presence of such fundamental visual and acoustic symbols (face, word, name) in the Bible suggests that Erikson is right when he argues that the beginnings of faith are closely bound up with the face-to-face rituals of recognition exchanged between parent and child. All religion, Erikson notes, seeks "a vision of sanctioned centrality," a center inhabited by a divine "I" and mediated through symbols of seeing and naming.[52] Discovery of such a center, which begins in earliest infancy and continues throughout life, makes a crucial difference. It is what allows people to perceive life as "active and effective, rather than inactivated and helpless; selectively aware rather than overwhelmed by or deprived of sensations; and above all, chosen and confirmed rather than bypassed and abandoned."[53]

The Desire to See the Host
The search for a vision of "sanctioned centrality," begun in the infant's hunger for the familiar maternal face and continued in the adult's quest for a "center that will hold," sheds light on what Edouard Dumoutet called "the desire to see the host." This desire has not been restricted to medieval Christianity; it has been implicit even in the twentieth-century reforms of Roman Catholic worship. One of the most obvious features of the liturgy since the Second Vatican Council is that the ritual actions and elements are plainly displayed so that all can see them. Presider and altar now face (an interesting metaphoric transference from noun to verb) the people. Bread and wine are visible throughout the liturgy of the table, from the preparation of gifts to the act of communion. Perhaps unconsciously, the recent reforms have cooperated with the primitive human instinct to see face-to-face, to gaze and be gazed upon, to participate in rituals of mutual recognition, seeing and naming.

It can be argued that the recent liturgical reforms (which intensify the congregation's ability to participate visually in the ritual elements and actions) and the medieval fascination with the host as an object of contemplation (ocular communion with the God "contained" in the eucharistic wafer) are both rooted in the same ontogenetic source: the search for a vision of sanctioned centrality. At first this may seem incongruous. Many liturgists today would argue that the conciliar reforms were aimed at weaning people away from devotional gazing at the host so that they could participate more fully in all the liturgical actions (songs, responses, gestures, roles, ministerial reception of communion). This is unquestionably true. At the same time, it must be pointed out that the reform did not abandon visual symbolism, but rather shifted its center. In the new liturgy, visual attention centers not on objects such as prayerbooks, statues, tabernacle, elaborately brocaded vestments that tell stories, or the host encased in a monstrance or hidden in a tabernacle, but on people and their actions. In short, the visual fulcrum of "sanctioned centrality" has shifted away from inert objects toward the ritual actions themselves of taking, blessing, breaking, and sharing.

Despite the many conservative criticisms directed against it, this shift does not violate the fundamental human need for a visual center. It does, however, make that center more difficult to isolate or define. Unlike the rather static centrality supplied by the host in the monstrance or in the ciborium or in the tabernacle, the visual center of the reformed liturgy is in motion and cannot easily be fixed on a single element or ritual gesture.

Neither of these two expressions of visual symbolism need necessarily exclude the other. Still, they are different, and the difference is important. The visual centrality associated with eucharistic piety outside Mass (exposition, Benediction, visits) is strongly reminiscent of the earliest stage of ritual development: the infant's desire to see and the parent's desire to be seen. That this stage of development is and remains important cannot be denied, for it provides that pervasive sense of security, familiarity, and mutuality without which a person may easily withdraw into narcissistic and psychotic isolation.[54] Nevertheless, ritualization does not stop at this first stage; as human beings develop through childhood, school age, adolescence, and adult maturity, they learn new ritual strategies for negotiating the inevitable passages of life (self-directed action, learning, sexual identity, marriage and vocation, generative action for others). At the adult level, a new and critical element is added to the person's ritual repertoire, what Erikson calls "the generational."[55] This element, which I prefer to label generative, is characteristic of persons who have satisfactorily integrated earlier stages of ritual negotiation—identity (adolescence) and intimacy (young adulthood). At the generative level of ritual expression, people are ready to take on the larger responsibilities of adult life, e.g., the intimacy shared by husband and wife expands to generate new life and personality in a child; the minister's personal intimacy with the Lord expands to embrace others by serving their needs and answering their call for help.

The reformed liturgy, with its emphasis on participation in ritual action rather than meditation upon ritual objects, invites us to generativity, to concern and responsibility for the larger world and its needs. Karl Rahner's comments about the "liturgy of the world," already mentioned in Chapter Seven, are apropos here as well. Christian worship is not an oasis of intimacy in an otherwise harsh and wicked world. It is a sacramental symbol that points toward the world as the place where God constantly celebrates, and causes to be celebrated, that vast liturgy of human life "breathing of death and sacrifice."[56] Sacramental symbols are neither a temple that enclose the holy nor a group-therapy session on identity and intimacy. Rather, they "constitute the manifestation of the holiness and the redeemed state of the secular dimension of human life and of the world."[57] As such, the symbols of Christian worship invite us not to "learn more about the liturgy" but to learn more about

388

life—about "this immense history of birth and death, complete superficiality, folly, inadequacy and hatred . . . on the one hand, and silent submission, responsibility even to death in dying and in joyfulness . . . on the other."[58] By focusing attention on ritual action rather than cultic object, the reformed liturgy invites us to a deeper participation in that mystery-laden liturgy of the world to which all our sacraments point.

This is not to deny the legitimacy or value of eucharistic devotions outside Mass or of personal prayer in the presence of the sacramental species. The need for seeing and being seen, for gazing and being gazed upon, for a numinous visual symbol of "sanctioned centrality," lasts throughout life. But mature adult development in faith as in the rest of human life demands that we integrate this legitimate need for security, familiarity and mutuality into generative modes of symbolic expression and ritual behavior. This means that one must mature beyond the point where worship is perceived merely as private prayer in a communal setting or as personal intimacy with God. Generativity requires that in celebrating the liturgy we also embrace the larger mission of the church: the mission to become bread broken in service for a hungering world.

THE LANGUAGE OF EUCHARISTIC SYMBOLISM

Erikson's work on the ontogeny of ritual is useful in assessing the relation between symbols and our developing human need for them. His work gives us, in effect, a psychology of ritual symbols, a systematic way to understand the linkage between stages of human growth and the types of ritualization which fuel those stages.[59] In the previous section we noted that Erikson's analysis implicitly points to a "shadow" attached to every rite or symbol; rituals of recognition imply rituals of separation and abandonment, symbols of presence imply symbols of absence. In the Hebrew Bible, for instance, God's "face" may symbolize a source of blessing, light and sustenance ("Let the light of your face shine upon us"), or it may signal death and abandonment ("No one can look on God's face and live"; "Why have you turned your face away from me?").

This double effect characteristic of symbols—every symbol also implies its opposite—invites us to take a closer look at symbolic structure, especially as it applies to the eucharist, for the eucharistic symbols imply that the Lord is simultaneously *present among* and *absent from* his people. Such an assertion seems absurd or even heterodox at first hearing. Yet the New Testament makes it clear that the historical Jesus of Nazareth, the Crucified One who was raised from death by God's power and who showed himself to believers, has gone away. The end of Luke's gospel and the beginning of Acts, for example, confront the reader with ascension symbolism: Jesus is "carried up into heaven," and the gaping disciples are gently chided for standing about looking dumbfounded (Acts 1.6-11; Luke 24.50-51). Similarly, John's gospel depicts a farewell meal punctuated by Jesus' extended discourses about why he must go away and about who will come to comfort the disciples ("another consoler, the Paraclete"; John 14–16). By proclaiming Jesus as the One who will come again, New Testament Christianity clearly implies that the Lord is somehow absent from the historical world as believers now experience it. He is "in heaven" or "with the Father" or "at God's right hand."

At the same time, the New Testament sources imply that Jesus the Risen One is present to his people. Eating and drinking the Lord's Supper proclaims the death of Jesus and gives believers a participation in his body and blood (1 Cor 10.16-17; 11.26). To be baptized is to be "clothed" with Christ (the implied metaphor in Gal 3.27). More astonishing still, the church itself is the "body of Christ" member for member (1 Cor 6.15; 10.17). The New Testament thus confronts us with symbols that connote both presence and absence, departure and meeting.

Absence	*Presence*
Empty tomb	Breaking of bread (Luke 24)
Ascension	
Stranger who appears,	Another consoler (John 16)
then vanishes (Luke 24)	Lord's Supper (1 Cor 10)
Waiting for a second coming	

Church as body of Christ

The New Testament literature plays on a paradox of magnificent proportions: Jesus is away yet present, with his people yet in heaven and thus no longer located in this world. More paradoxical yet is Paul's sentence in 1 Corinthians 11.26: "For as often as you eat this bread and drink the cup, you proclaim the Lord's death until he comes." The formula is so familiar that it no longer startles us, but if we inspect it closely we will find it disconcerting. First, the formula says nothing about Jesus' resurrection; it does not relate eucharist to Easter but rather to Jesus' death. Secondly, the formula points to Jesus' absence: he has died, i.e., departed from the world of the living and their history, and will come again, i.e., will return in a future that has not yet happened. The eucharist is an action suspended between two human symbols of absence: death and future, accomplished but not yet fulfilled. Paul says nothing in this formula about making an absent One present, nor about eucharist as "dining with the Risen Christ." At the same time, an earlier formula of Paul's found in 1 Corinthians 10.16, speaks of eating and drinking as establishing "communion" (*koinonia*, fellowship) with the Lord's body and blood. The word Paul uses to describe communion with Christ in this passage is the same word John uses to depict the fellowship (*koinonia*) that exists among believers (1 John 1.6). And the word Paul uses for Christ's body in 1 Corinthians 10.16 (*sōma*)

391

is the same word he uses in verse 17 to identify the united believers.

What is astonishing here is that Paul uses the same symbols—eating and drinking—to signal both absence and presence, actual communion and future consummation:

Eating and drinking (1 Cor. 11.26)	signals	Death of the Lord Future coming (symbols of absence)
Eating and drinking (1 Cor. 10.16)	signals	Communion, participation Fellowship (symbols of presence)

How is it possible for Paul to invoke the same symbols for apparently irreconcilable realities? How can one claim that eating and drinking simultaneously proclaim Jesus' death (his real absence from the world's continuing history) and offer communion with the Lord's body and blood (his real presence to believers)? How can Christians "wait" for someone who is already present, or have communion in the body and blood of One who has died and "gone away"? In order to answer these questions we need to examine the structure of symbols more closely. Specifically, we need to see how the symbol's double effect can put together realities that appear to be contradictory.

Language as Metaphor
It has long been assumed that language can be divided into two categories: the literal and the figurative. Precision, empirical verifiability, accuracy and controlled meanings characterize the literal ("proper") use of language, while poetic strategies (metaphor, simile, deliberate ambiguity) govern its figurative use. Today, however, philosphers of language like Paul Ricoeur have challenged this common assumption. Ricoeur argues that the distinction between "proper" and "figurative"

language is illusory and suggests further that at its origins all human language is metaphorical.[60] Other writers have adopted Ricoeur's position. W.V. Quine notes:

". . . it is a mistake . . . to think of linguistic usage as literalistic in its main body and metaphorical in its trimming. Metaphor, or something like it, governs both the growth of language and our acquisition of it. What comes as a subsequent refinement is rather cognitive discourse itself, at its most drably literal. The neatly worked out inner stretches of science are an open space in the tropical jungle, created by clearing tropes away."[61]

In the beginning was metaphor. Language neither begins nor develops as an exact science that captures what is and what is real; at the heart of all human speech lies an inexhaustible core of ambiguity that can never be eradicated by our efforts at exactitude. As John Dominic Crossan has commented: "It is not that our language is normally or intrinsically univalent and only the perversity of poets and the deviance of novelists render it polyvalent. Language, because of the act of arbitrary convention at its heart, is intrinsically polyvalent and only our careful endeavors or our most indifferent occasions render it univalent."[62] While it is true that we sometimes need or want to force language into literal, univalent meanings, language itself always resists our attempts at neatness. In short, we need to think of language not as a stern disciplinarian who orders ideas into neat logical rows, but as a rebellious animal that struggles to free itself.

The implications of this view of language are enormous. Language signals not the presence of exact fixed meanings, but the absence of such meanings. This absence, Crossan observes, "is the foundation and horizon of all language and of all thought."[63] At the heart of all our words and discourse lies not a precious box containing

exact meanings and precise definitions, but a "hole"—a
center that refuses to hold still or be filled. There is no
fixed center in language, and it is precisely for this reason that words can generate so many different meanings and so many conflicting interpretations. This is also
why writers like Ricoeur, Quine and Crossan contend
that "metaphoricity" characterizes all language, for by
its nature metaphor refuses to cooperate with our projects of linguistic exactitude and literal meaning. All
metaphor, and thus all language, points to a void of
meaning at its core, to the absence of a "fixed center"
which we can manipulate or control.[64] Or as Karsten
Harries has put it, "metaphor implies lack."[65] Far from
being a problem this lack gives language its power of
transcendence, its ability to gesture toward what lies
beyond itself (toward an "Other"). "Metaphors," Harries writes, "speak of what remains absent"; they call
attention to an "Other" who surpasses all our schemes
to control, manipulate, or dominate.[66]

We must think of metaphor as language caught in the
act of disintegrating, caught in the act of falling apart.
Or to use another set of images, metaphor is language
making fun of itself, clowning, devilishly whispering to
us that at the "center" lies not "something" but "nothing." By falling apart, language opens us to what tran-
scends it, gives us a glimpse of that "Other" who is
always absent (i.e., always beyond our power to seize
and control).[67] When one immerses oneself in the
metaphoricity of language, one comes face to face with
the void:

"Sentences fall apart into words, words congeal into
eyes that stare at the poet, the eyes force him to stare
back at them and become whirlpools that lead into the
void. And yet this disintegration of language does not
lead to silence. Against the background of silence the
presence of things manifests itself. As language falls
apart, contact with being is reestablished. Something as
simple as a half-filled pitcher, darkened by the shadow

of a nut tree, becomes an epiphany of transcendence. . .
Rendering language questionable, the poet's metaphor
succeeds in gesturing towards a language that shall
never be ours in which . . . things speak to us."[68]

Metaphor, long recognized as central to the poet's utterance, is now being understood as the common property
of all human language. Further, metaphor is coming to
be regarded not as a surplus of meaning in language
(the earlier Ricoeur), nor as a strange and thus improper
form of speech (Aristotle), but as a void, a cipher at the
heart of language. And precisely because metaphor
signals the lack of a fixed center in language, it can gesture toward that transcendent Other who is inevitably
"absent."

Metaphor and Symbol
These recent investigations by Ricoeur, Crossan, and
others into the aboriginal metaphoricity of language
have important repercussions for understanding symbols. As we have noted earlier in this chapter, symbols
have the paradoxical power to fuse apparently irreconcilable realities. Only by signaling what is genuinely absent can the symbol draw us toward something present.
Symbols work precisely by exposing us to the void, to
the absence of a fixed center that can be dominated by
sense perceptions or cognitive operations. Ironically,
symbols can mediate something to us only by forcing us
to recognize that the "something" is genuinely absent.

Symbolism is thus rooted in the inherent metaphoricity
of human language. What makes a symbol possible is
the hole, the cipher at the heart of language, to which
metaphor inevitably leads us. It makes little difference
whether the symbol is verbal (as in poetry) or gestural
(as in worship and sacraments). Language, after all, is
itself a gesture, a transaction implying speakers and
hearers, a ritual that incarnates itself in discourse, spoken or written. What metaphor is to language, symbol is
to those nonverbal transactions we call rituals.

Metaphor energizes language by leading it to the brink of disintegration; as it falls apart, "contact with being is reestablished."[69] Symbol energizes ritual by exposing participants to its empty center; as the ritual falls apart around that center, we are drawn into the presence of an Other who can never be held or captured.

In short symbols force us to recognize, simultaneously, real absence and real presence, the empty center and the transcendent Other. In a symbol we journey into the presence of the Other by passing through the desert, the empty center that holds nothing. That is why, as we noted earlier in this chapter, symbols have a double effect, they project a shadow. Far from being inert objects that contain something, symbols are ever in motion. Their motion takes three forms: 1) a movement from outside to inside; 2) a movement toward iconoclasm; 3) a movement between the poles of absence and presence. Each of these forms of symbolic motion needs a word of explanation.

Outside and inside: It has long been noticed that symbols have an outside and an inside, a sense-perceptible reality and a non-sense-perceptible one. The water of baptism, for example, embraces both a visual and an auditory element (water itself) and a hidden significance (immersion into Christ, entrance into a community). One can reach the hidden significance only by immersing oneself in the visible element. This happens not by thinking about the water or its meaning, but by washing in it. The act of washing triggers a movement toward the inside of the symbol. Paul Ricoeur speaks of this movement as the "double intentionality" of the symbol: literal and opaque.[70] The literal intention of the symbol is straightforward and obvious: bathing with water is a good way to remove dirt and grime. But the opaque intention of the symbol is not obvious at all: bathing causes one to "put on Christ" and become a member of a new community. As Ricoeur explains, "the first, literal, patent meaning analogously intends a second meaning which is not given otherwise than in the first."[71]

The relation between the outside (literal) and the inside (opaque) of symbols is important. Ricoeur describes the linkage between the two as analogous (A is to B as C is to D). But in the case of symbols, the analogous meaning that binds the second meaning to the first cannot be objectivized, i.e., cannot be grasped or controlled by the logical assaults of the human intellect. As Ricoeur puts it, "symbol is the very movement of the primary meaning that makes us share in the latent meaning and thereby assimilates us to the symbolized, without our being able intellectually to dominate the similarity."[72] It is the movement itself—from outside to inside—that constitutes the symbol's power to disclose meaning and make present the reality symbolized.

In baptism, for instance, the analogous meaning that links the symbol's literal significance to its opaque significance cannot readily be made the object of intellectual understanding. For one thing the analogy is freighted with ambiguity: water is both life-giving and death-dealing; washing both destroys something (dirt) and creates something (cleanliness). As in the case of metaphor, the symbol confronts us with the absence of a fixed center of meaning that can be controlled by rational investigation. We can arrive at baptism's opaque meaning only by "going through the ritual motions" of washing. It is not a matter of our grasping the symbol's ultimate meaning, but of the symbol's power to assimilate us to itself.

Like metaphor, symbol "speaks of what remains absent."[73] Christ and the community are not contained in the baptismal waters; literally, they are absent. Nor is the analogous linkage between the literal bath and the opaque significance (union with the Lord and his people) an "object" which we can control by thinking about it. We are united to Christ and the community in baptism only by submitting to a bath in which nothing appears to be present but us and the water. In symbols we discover presence through absence; we are assimilated to what is symbolized by moving from the outside to the inside.

A movement toward iconoclasm: A second type of motion is also characteristic of symbols: what may be called a movement toward iconoclasm. As Ricoeur notes, every symbol is the destroyer of a prior symbol; every symbol is an act of revolutionary iconoclasm.[74] At first this may seem absurd, for if every new symbol destroys its ancestor, how can ancient symbols survive? Ricoeur responds to this issue by drawing attention to the symbolism of sin. In its most archaic manifestations, sin is ordinarily symbolized by physical stain, dirt or filth—Lady Macbeth's "damned spot." Sin is regarded as a contagion, an alien power that lays hold on the sinner. But this very symbolism of staining triggers a further reflection: it is I, a human being, who am stained. Evil is not merely an external force that grips me unawares; it is something I intend and do. The symbolism of sin thus shifts from external to internal, from something "out there" to something "in me." The notion of sin as something done to me by another ("the devil made me do it!") is replaced by the notion of sin as a broken relationship for which I am at least in part responsible.

This iconoclastic movement of the symbol is not, however, entirely destructive. New symbols reappropriate older ones and thus effect a change in their meaning(s). For example, the internalized symbols of sin (I have broken a relationship, I have not kept faith with another) reappropriate the more archaic symbols (sin as grime, stain, filth), with the result that sin is now perceived as simultaneously internal and external. A good illustration of this may be found in Psalm 51:

Behold, I was brought forth in iniquity,
and in sin did my mother conceive me. . . .

Purge me with hyssop, and I shall be clean;
wash me, and I shall be whiter than snow.   (Ps 51.5, 7)

Against thee, thee only, have I sinned,
and done that which is evil in thy sight,
so that thou art justified in thy sentence
and blameless in thy judgment.   (Ps 51.4)

In the first of these passages, sin is symbolized as a condition that exists even before the sinner was born and as a stain that must be expunged. In the second, sin is perceived in terms of relationship with another who will render judgment on my personal action. The psalm thus projects an extremely complex portrait of sin. Sinfulness is recognized as both outside and inside, as something beyond my control yet as something conscious, personal, intentional.

Symbols thus react iconoclastically upon one another. Even within the same pattern of symbolism (e.g., sin), such a reaction takes place, with the result that symbols become increasingly dense and ambiguous. As they evolve, symbols absorb new and often conflicting meanings that cannot be reconciled or controlled by the usual strategies of intellect. Resisting all our efforts to domesticate them, symbols assimilate us to themselves rather than vice versa.

Poles of absence and presence: The two types of symbolic motion described above help explain why symbols can point simultaneously to absence and presence, to what is there and not there. A symbol has no fixed center of meaning, nor has it any core that ensnares objects and holds them in place. Perhaps one could best describe the structure of a symbol by comparing it to the structure of a molecule. While molecules may be stable units, they are best thought of as bundles of energy and motion. And while molecules display the characteristic properties of physical elements (e.g., oxygen or hydrogen), they cannot be said to contain those elements. Rather, the element is what results from the configuration and

399

interaction of atoms in the molecules and from the energy generated and released by that interaction.

Something similar may be said about symbols: they are bundles of energy and motion that exhibit the characteristic properties of something without containing or capturing that something. Sin, to continue the example given earlier, is not somehow contained in either the symbols of stain and dirt or the symbols of broken relationship and judgment. Yet the power of sin touches us only through those symbols; we recognize ourselves as sinners only by contacting the ambiguous language of contamination (alien external power) and judgment (broken faith, personal responsibility).[75] Sin makes itself present to our experience precisely in and through what Ricoeur calls the "primal language" of avowal and confession.[76] This language, ritual and symbolic, signals both presence and absence; for at the same moment one is exposed to both estrangement (absence of purity, fidelity, integrity) and holiness (presence of a Holy One who judges us). The language of avowal thus empowers us both to recognize the condition of sin and to move toward reconciliation. Communion with the Holy One who judges is revealed, paradoxically, through the negative symbols of estrangement and guilt. Every symbol implies its shadow, its reverse image.

All three types of symbolic motion—inside and outside, iconoclastic conflict, absence and presence—are important for understanding the nature of symbols generally and the structure of eucharistic symbolism specifically.

Eucharistic Symbolism
Theologians have long recognized that the structure of eucharistic symbolism is complex, compounded of real presence and real absence. Thomas Aquinas, for example, affirmed that the Lord's body is not present in this sacrament "as in a place" (*sicut in loco*).[77] The quantitative dimensions of Christ's risen body and blood are not somehow crammed into the physical dimensions of

bread and wine. That is why Aquinas insisted that the proper way to understand Christ's presence in the eucharist is according to the category of "substance," since substance "cannot be seen by the bodily eye, nor is it the object of any sense, nor can it be imagined."[78] From a local, sensate or quantitative point of view, Christ's body and blood are absent from the eucharistic species; they are present, instead, substantially and symbolically (*per modum sacramenti*, "sacramentally"). For Aquinas there could be no possibility of Christ's being imprisoned in bread and wine or contained in them like flowers in a vase.

Through his sophisticated use of the Aristotelian category of substance, Aquinas was able to deal with the ambivalent Christian conviction, noted above in Paul's writings, that Christ is simultaneously absent and present in the celebration of the Lord's Supper. Locally and quantitatively, Jesus is absent; "substantially" he is present. Though Aquinas and Paul were asking different questions, each was dealing with a similar problem: how can Christ be present (offering us communion with himself) and "yet to come" (thus really absent in some way)? How can a glorified body, no longer located in ordinary space and time, be somehow present in bread eaten and wine drunk? Paul resolves the absence/ presence problem by appealing to the expiatory significance of Jesus' death (an event in time whose effects transcend time) and to the gathering of the church itself as the "body of Christ." Aquinas resolves the problem by examining, philosophically, the nature of change that happens by God's power at the deepest metaphysical level of reality (the level of "substance").

Our examination of the structure and function of symbols offers still another way to understand the real presence and real absence of Christ in the eucharist. Both metaphor and symbol reveal the absence of a fixed center that can be controlled by speech or thought (language) or manipulated by human action (ritual). For this

401

reason both metaphor and symbol shove us toward transcendence, toward that Other One who never submits to control or manipulation, and who may be signaled but never imprisoned by our thought and action. Symbols have shadows: they affirm presence while signaling absence, and affirm absence while signaling presence. This is precisely what gives symbols their inexhaustible vitality, their ability to draw us ever more deeply into themselves and their mysterious power to bestow and withold.

These ambiguous characteristics of the symbols are crucial for understanding the eucharist as both a liturgical action and a permanent sacrament that can be venerated apart from Mass. There is always danger, as Paul Ricoeur warns, of allowing symbols to harden into idolatry.[79] This happens, for example, when the Lord is regarded as a prisoner in the tabernacle, quantitatively trapped in bread and wine and locked away behind golden doors. It is in danger of happening, too, whenever the symbolic pattern of action (community praise and thanksgiving)–object (sanctified bread and wine)–action (eating and drinking) is interrupted through excessive attention to the eucharistic species as things to be looked at. In short, eucharistic symbolism is impoverished whenever we attempt to give the symbols of bread and wine a fixed center that can be controlled or manipulated by human thought or activity.

As both liturgical action and permanent sacrament, therefore, the eucharist speaks powerfully of the Lord who is present and absent, with his people always yet destined to come again. Perhaps the easiest way to grasp the intensely ambiguous symbolism of the eucharist is to reflect on this: we sinners eat and drink the Supper of the Lord. This apparently simple statement bristles with contradictions that can only be reconciled symbolically. To be a sinner, after all, is to be estranged from God and from one's authentic self; sin is symbolized by the ineradicable stain, the branded mark of the alien, the broken relationship. The symbolism of sin cries absence, even as it implies the presence of a Holy One who judges without malice or compromise. At the same time, eating and drinking always implies presence, communion, relationship renewed. If sinners dine with the Holy Lord, then we are confronted with a contradiction of uncontrollable proportions. The two realities—sinfulness and holiness—can be put together only through a symbol that embraces both presence and absence.

LITURGY AND DEVOTIONS
The first two sections of this chapter have helped to demonstrate how extraordinarily complex the eucharistic symbolism is. Erik Erikson's work aids us in understanding the remote psychological roots of the human need to gaze upon objects of ultimate value ("sanctioned centrality"). Recent investigations into the structure of language, metaphor, and symbol help us perceive the eucharist's power to signal, simultaneously, both presence and absence. In this final section of the chapter we need to explore the relation between eucharistic liturgy and eucharistic devotions, between the sacrament as action of God's gathered people and the sacrament as an object that can be reserved, venerated, visited, and adored.

Folk Religion
In his classic study of early Christian worship Josef Jungmann cautioned against the impulse to romanticize the liturgical life of those formative centuries. The life of the earliest Christians, Jungmann observed, did not revolve exclusively around public worship.[80] Devotional prayer of a private or domestic sort was recommended to Christians from the beginning. The *Didache*, for example, encourages the recitation of the Lord's Prayer three times a day.[81] The *Apostolic Tradition* of Hippolytus speaks of a variety of devotional practices: prayer at midnight, upon waking, as well as at the third, sixth,

and ninth hours of the day; the sign of the cross; the domestic reception of the reserved eucharist on weekdays.[82] None of these practices involved a public assembly for worship; all took place within the domestic privacy of the household. Later, of course, some of these devotional patterns were formalized; prayer in the morning and evening developed into the public liturgies of lauds and vespers; the custom of praying in the middle of the night was institutionalized in the monastic pattern of daily vigils.[83] Despite such liturgical developments, especially after the fourth century, it is probably true to say that in all ages Christians have done more praying outside of churches than in them.

From the beginning, therefore, popular piety has played a visible role in the daily life and consciousness of Christians. But it is not easy to identify exactly what constitutes this popular piety; the phenomenon varies so greatly from culture to culture and from age to age that generalizations about it are never very accurate. Nevertheless, sociologists of religion have attempted to outline some common features of folk religion, and a review of these may be useful in our effort to understand the place of eucharistic devotions in Roman Catholic life.

In his recent book *Popular Religion in America*, Peter Williams describes folk religion as the "Little Tradition," a syncretistic mixture that blends "elements from the great tradition into a body of pre-existent beliefs and practices which have been handed down for countless generations."[84] This rough definition is especially applicable to peoples who have remained physically or psychologically isolated from major urban centers. In such situations (Williams cites the example of certain mountain villages in Mexico), the Great Tradition of a religion like Christianity became a veneer adapted to traditional customs, "to be invoked when pressures for conformity ran high or when invocation of the old gods proved inefficacious."[85] Folk religion acts as a conservative influence in cases like these; it may even stimulate resistance against the "new ways" of the Great Tradition.

But there is another aspect of folk religion that is probably more basic and more important than its potentially conservative instinct. Williams notes that folk religion is a process that helps people deal symbolically with the problems of daily life "for which the great tradition provides no immediately compelling solution."[86] In this sense popular religion is more creative than conservative; it deals with the practical immediacies of daily living, while the Great Tradition concerns itself with more universal matters of official doctrine and public cult. As a symbolic process, folk religion will often reinterpret or manipulate symbols derived from the Great Tradition. In some cases—for example, when representatives of the official religion protest such reinterpretations—folk religionists may return to elements of a more archaic religious system (magical charms, folk cures, superstitions). This may help to explain, for instance, why the eucharist has sometimes been used by people of varying ages and cultures for such diverse things as warding off evil spirits, insuring the fertility of fields, increasing one's potency in sexual love, healing the body's wounds.[87] The Great Tradition has viewed these practices with suspicion, not to say horror; but in the context of folk religion—the manipulation of symbols to deal with the immediacies of daily life—such customs have a logic.

It is important to notice that folk religion asserts its place sometimes creatively, sometimes conservatively, in precisely those situations where the Great Tradition has provided no compelling solution. For this reason folk religion is most powerful when it touches basic human activities or crises. Williams identifies six of these in his effort to construct a rough typology of folk beliefs and practices.[88]

Food: As an element essential for human survival, food in all its aspects—planting and harvesting, gathering and preparing, serving—provides a basic occasion for folk customs. Some of these customs survive even in cultures that consider themselves technologically advanced: e.g., planting garden vegetables according to the phases of the moon.

Health and illness: Even in an era of modern medicine, folk beliefs may survive: e.g., it is dangerous to eat oysters in months that do not have an "r" in their name. Again, whereas ancient cultures often intertwined the arts of healing and priesthood, modern societies may transfer the sacral qualities of the priest onto the medical profession (the doctor or surgeon as a kind of secular high priest).

Life cycle: All the important transitions in human life—birth, puberty, adult vocation, death—are susceptible to interpretation by the symbolic process of folk religion. Marriage customs provide a good example: many a June bride still wears "something old, something new, something borrowed, and something blue."

The dead: As the ultimately mysterious crisis that concludes human life, death is a particularly rich occasion for folk beliefs and practices. Ritual keening, ghost stories, the food and drink served at wakes, may all reflect attitudes toward death shaped by archaic notions of the soul's final perilous journey.

The future: The only language humans have for speaking about the future is a symbolic one. Ironically, however, the future can be discussed only by collecting images from our human past: paradise, fiery conflagrations, frontiers, bountiful harvests, floods and quakes. Even though industrialized cultures speak of a "science" of the future, few believe that such predictions are very accurate. And toward the end of every year, newspaper readers devour the prophecies of seers who claim to have one leg up on the future.

Evil and misfortune: Finally, folk religion offers people a way to deal with an experience no theology has ever adequately explained: the problem of evil. Responses to this problem vary, but nearly every culture has devised some way to react to evil actual or threatened: through active cooperation with malevolent powers ("black magic," as in witchcraft) or through magical modes of resistance ("white magic," as in charms, amulets, spells, and incantations). Even advanced cultures occasionally engage in witch hunts, exercises in exorcism, as the United States did during the McCarthy era.

Three points about this typological list should be noted. First, all the items enumerated in it transcend cultural, geographical and temporal boundaries. In short, these are universal human concerns that touch people of all times and places. Secondly, the list reflects concern for daily immediacies of life: food, health, birth and dying, marriage and family, sickness and evil, the future. Thirdly, the list embraces events and crises for which the symbols of the Great Tradition offer no compelling solution. A word about this last point is in order.

Persons familiar with the Christian symbol system might well argue that all the items included in Williams's typological list are dealt with in the sacramental economy:

Food: eucharist, symbol of human hunger's satisfaction
Health and illness: anointing the sick, symbol of health restored or ultimate healing ("in glory") achieved
Life cycle: initiation, marriage, order: symbols of Christian maturity and adult vocation
Death: initiation, the true death to sin, the beginning of everlasting life
Future: eucharist, symbol of eschatological banqueting in God's kingdom and the ultimate unity of humankind
Evil and misfortune: reconciliation, symbol of ultimate victory over sin, alienation, evil

Although few would deny that the sacraments respond to life-crisis moments, there are some problems which the symbols of the Great Tradition do not address, at least not in any immediate or compelling way. The eucharist, for example, may well be the symbol of hunger's satisfaction and humankind's ultimate unity, but the symbol does not supply an immediate response to the empty cupboard or the inflated prices at the supermarket. Similarly, the sacrament of reconciliation may signal Christ' ultimate power over sin and evil; but it does not prevent an x-ray from revealing cancer of the pancreas, nor does it exclude the possibility that a DC 10 carrying three hundred people may crash on take-off. In short, while the sacramental symbols of the Great Tradition respond to the ultimate questions of meaning and destiny, they do not provide solutions to the *ad hoc* immediacies of daily life. And this is precisely where folk religion enters the picture: it supplies a symbolic way of negotiating the daily traumas that press on human beings and threaten their existence.

Folk religion thus arms people with micro-rituals and symbols that help them survive the aggravations of everyday life. St. Anthony will help me find the gloves I lost while walking to the subway; a novena to St. Jude may aid my alcoholic brother in facing his problem and asking for help; a pilgrimage to Lourdes may strengthen my wife in her battle against multiple sclerosis; a visit to the Blessed Sacrament on All Soul's Day may release my father from purgatory. These are not mere superstitious actions or beliefs. They allow the believer to act concretely in behalf of someone, and they imply that one person's faith may become another's boon. Further, the rituals of folk religion enable a person to respond to immediate crises in a manner that is personal, direct, and unencumbered by the refinements of official doctrine or cultic paraphenalia.

Popular religion has the distinct advantage of offering people an immediate and personal course of action in daily situations were the action of the liturgical assembly is either inappropriate or impossible. I cannot convene the eucharistic assembly while I am sitting up at three in the morning with a sick child, but I can say a rosary, recite the Litany of Loretto, or light a votive candle. The informal pieties of folk religion permit believers to adapt or alter the symbolism of the Great Tradition in order to "fill in the gaps."[89]

Personal Presence

The power of folk religion to adapt the symbolism of the Great Tradition may help us understand why the eucharist became the focus of so many devotional needs. In the first section of this chapter we have already noted the primacy of vision (seeing and being seen) in the development of human capacity for ritual and symbolic behavior. As Erik Erikson observes, humans seek a "vision of sanctioned centrality"[90] from the very beginning of their lives. This visual center, first expressed in the rituals of mutual recognition between parent and child, provides a fundamental sense of security, belonging, identity. Nor does the search for a vision of sanctioned centrality cease with childhood. It continues, in different symbolic modes, throughout life.

We have also seen, however, that the eucharistic symbols, like all symbols, do not provide a "fixed center" of meaning that can be controlled by human thought or action. This very lack of a fixed center cuts two ways: it gives symbols their inexhaustible vitality and power, and at the same time it causes frustration. Humans want to cling to a secure center of meaning and value, yet symbols push us off center, force us to deal with an Other who is limitless. Every symbol has a shadow and thus confronts us with simultaneous presence and absence.

These two factors—the human search for a vision of sanctioned centrality and the ambiguous presence/absence of symbols—create something of a dilemma.

409

Psychologically, and often unconsciously, we want the eucharist to provide us with that primordial sense of mutual recognition (gazing and being gazed upon lovingly) which was present at the earliest stages of our human development. At the same time, the eucharistic symbols resist our infantile impulse to manipulate and control. This conflict may help explain why, in the customs and beliefs of folk religion, the eucharist has sometimes been adapted for purposes other than nourishment and communion—as a good-luck charm, a medicinal poultice, a visual center of prayer and adoration, a device to settle legal claims, and so forth.

Underlying all these factors, however, is a deeper insight shared by the Great Tradition and folk religion alike. Although the modes of Christ's real presence among Christians are many, the eucharist has been perceived both popularly and theologically as unique. No matter how one struggles to interpret it, the uniqueness of Christ's eucharistic presence is somehow linked to the elements of bread and wine. As theologian John Macquarrie has observed, "A real presence is not simply a genuine presence, but an embodied, even a thingly presence."[91] Commenting on various models of presence—temporal, local/spatial, personal— Macquarrie notes that the personal model is perhaps the best one for expressing the uniqueness of the eucharistic symbols. It may thus be helpful to explore more fully what is meant by "personal presence" in the eucharist.

Personal presence, at least as we know it in the world of human realities, includes both spiritual and physical aspects. That is one of the reasons why Christian faith affirms the holiness of the body, for in a profound sense the body is the sacrament of human personality, the prime symbol that mediates who we are to others. At the same time, we recognize that the mystery of personal presence cannot be restricted to empirical phenomena.[92] In the case of the eucharist, Christ's personal presence is, as Macquarrie remarks, "focussed in the consecrated elements as its center, but . . . not re-stricted to them."[93] In the language of Aquinas, the personal presence of Christ is not "local" in the sense of quantitative restriction to the physical objects of bread and wine.

Two other points about personal presence deserve attention: the relationship between person and world, and the reciprocity implied by the presence of one human being to another. Working off Martin Heidegger's notion of world as a "nexus of significations" that build up a universe of meaning, Macquarrie notes that two things are essential for any adequate definition of world: there must be a unified structure of meaning, and there must be humans who can and do participate in that structure.[94] The things one encounters in this world are constituted by their "signification," i.e., "by the way they are incorporated into the personal, historical world of mankind."[95] Take fire as an example. As a thing observed by people living in the world, fire may simply be described as a chemical reaction involving the rapid oxidation of materials with concomitant release of heat, light, water, energy. But as part of an actual world related to human history, fire means more: warmth, survival, danger, the family hearth, security. These personal and historical meanings of fire are not merely tacked on to the "proper meaning"; they are an essential part of what fire is, they belong to its "ontological structure."[96]

Something similar can be said about bread and wine: these are not merely products of nature and labor, they are also linked, in their very being, to the history and life of humankind, to a world that has been shaped by persons. As a result, the full ontological significance of bread and wine can be discerned only when we relate them to a human history that continues to unfold, to a world still in process of becoming. When Christians say that in the eucharist the body and blood of Jesus are somehow identified with bread and wine, they are

411

speaking of a reality charged with ontological significance. The world of meanings linked to bread and wine are "transignified," i.e., transformed at the deepest level of their sign reality, as they receive the unique meaning of Christ's body and blood.[97] This is why some theologians today speak of "transignification" as a way to understand the uniqueness of Jesus' presence in the eucharist.

But the Lord's personal presence in the eucharist means something more still. A meeting of persons is not the coming together of two objects; it signifies reciprocity, mutuality. In a human meeting, Macquarrie comments, "my friend is not there as an object over against me; he is there with me in a reciprocal relationship."[99] At the same time, a friend's presence is not merely subjective; my friend is not the product of my imagination, he or she is really there. In the eucharist, the reciprocity of personal presence is initiated by Christ, not by human strategies of manipulation. Macquarrie summarizes this point with finesse:

"The initiative is Christ's and he is . . . the *minister principalis* of the Eucharist. He enables us to have faith and, indeed, to be persons capable of knowing his presence. Our personhood is not something we already possess, but something that comes into being in relation to other persons; and in the Eucharist above all our personhood is enhanced, even created, through the presence of the person of Christ. He is there before we are. Our presence to one another in the Eucharist, the so-called horizontal dimension, is made possible only through Christ's already being present and communing with us."[100]

The personal presence of Christ in the eucharist—focused in the elements but not restricted to them—is encountered by Christians in both the assembly's action and in the reserved sacrament. Even after the eucharistic action has ended, bread and wine continue to project a world of meanings transignified now by the unique meaning of the Lord's body and blood. One can thus still speak of a real personal meeting between the believer and Christ in such customs as visits and prayer before the Blessed Sacrament. This presence is not a subjective projection of my imagination, nor is it a mere object existing "out there." Personal presence signifies mutuality, a meeting of people that renders the subject/object distinction "irrelevant and misleading."[101]

Devotions
Our brief analysis of folk religion and personal presence can help us assess more adequately the role of eucharistic devotions in Christian life. These devotions seem to stress two things: first, there is a legitimate human need, recognizable in all forms of folk religion, to adapt symbols to the concrete immediacies of daily life, especially in situations where the Great Tradition offers no compelling solution; secondly, Christians have sensed, almost from the beginning, that there is a unique connection between the Lord's presence and the eucharistic elements. As we have seen in Chapter One, the very transmission of the eucharistic traditions in the New Testament texts seems to point toward an early linkage between the presence of Christ and the bread and wine of the Supper.[102]

Eucharistic devotions are perhaps best understood as adaptations of traditional symbols in the style of folk religion. In an illuminating essay on popular devotions, Carl Dehne outlines some of the prominent characteristics of Catholic devotional life.[103] Although these characteristics are not restricted to the cult of the eucharist outside Mass, they are clearly applicable to it.

Privileged intercession: One is often struck by the attitude of easy familiarity displayed in popular devotions. Saints are not only spoken to but sometimes scolded or reminded of obligations to their clients. Devotional language and gesture are often extravagant: Jesus is ad-

413

dressed with the intimate words of human love, comforted in his bitter passion, lullabied as a tiny infant. The freedom and expressiveness of popular devotion reveal the consciousness of a privileged relationship: "the worshiper," Dehne explains, "is a privileged person—a chosen and choosing one."[104] As special clients of God and the saints, worshipers are also conscious of a privileged power of intercession, one that permits them to take liberties prohibited by the prayers and rituals of official cult. Josef Jungmann once observed that the notion of client and patron, common in many popular devotions, is rooted in Roman law.[105] As early as the fourth century legal terminology (*patronus–clientela*) was applied to the relation between a martyred saint and the community that cared for the saint's tomb. The saintly patron was regarded as a living person with legal rights, and the community was the saint's privileged *familia*. With the passage of time, the patron–client relationship was extended to include the relation between a community or individual and other popular saints whose veneration was cultivated. Just as the patron had rights to gifts and endowments, so the *familia* could expect certain favors in return: protection, the saint's powerful intercession with God. The privileged intimacy characteristic of the patron–client relationship eventually shaped large areas of Catholic devotional life.

Person-centered: Popular devotions focus on persons and their needs rather than upon major themes of doctrine or revelation. As Dehne puts it, "The devotions are designed for the kind of person who would rather visit a tomb or touch a cross than read a really good paragraph on the Paschal Mystery."[106]

Christocentric: In Roman Catholic life, popular devotions became closely associated with the reserved eucharist. Novenas, Stations of the Cross, and Marian devotions during May or October were often conducted in the presence of the Blessed Sacrament and concluded with an explicitly eucharistic exercise like Benediction. Im-

414

plicitly, the devotions provided people with an opportunity to ritualize the Lord's presence among his people in ways that were more informal, less supervised, and more directly attached to daily concerns than were the patterns of official liturgy. Even if the devotion emphasized a theme distant from the central core of Catholic teaching (e.g., Miraculous Medal Novenas), the presence of the reserved sacrament provided a pervasive Christocentric atmosphere.

Clarity of expression: Despite their frequently inflated language, popular devotions left little doubt about their intent. Supplication, praise, intercession were direct and obvious. Even the elaborate ritual of an event like Benediction failed to conceal its purpose: affirmation of the Lord's personal nearness in the eucharist, praise of his presence and his daily gifts to the faithful.[107]

Spiral structure: Dehne observes that the structure of popular devotions was not linear but "circular or spiral."[108] The model for these pious exercises was neither the logical development of a classroom lecture nor the rather coherent unfolding of events we see in liturgies like those of Holy Week. Repetitions, starts and stops, dramatic rather than logical climaxes abound. The model seems to have been the personal conversation rather than the lecture or the sermon.

Ceremonial: Devotions provided an occasion for ceremonial gesture and vernacular singing that were impossible in the liturgy prior to the Second Vatican Council. One need only think of the contrast between a Latin low Mass and the exuberant stage effects, including lights, smoke, and singing that accompanied Benediction. One may certainly criticize the theology implied by such contrast, but one has to admit that the eucharistic devotions exerted a more direct appeal to the human senses. Even today's vernacular liturgies often seem to lack the sustained praise and dramatic color of the Benediction service. "It is sobering to reflect," Dehne writes, "that in the majority of parochial settings, there is no such thing as an extended, splendid, non-functional moment of communal praise. The Gloria of the eucharistic liturgy is the business of a mumbled half-minute; the Sanctus takes less than fifteen seconds. Hymns of praise, when they do occur, are almost always . . . subordinated to the relatively insignificant activities they accompany, like coming or going."[109]

Repetition: The pattern of popular devotions is nearly always unvarying; repetitions are common and worshipers often know all the prayers and music by heart.[110] This allows ease in participating and also frees worshipers for prayer instead of for flipping confusedly through the pages of printed worship aids.

These characteristics of popular devotions link up rather well with the features of folk religion discussed earlier. It is important to recognize that the macro-rituals of public worship, for all their value and importance, cannot be expected to meet the devotional needs of all Christians all the time. Popular piety is a legitimate and, one suspects, inevitable response to the gaps in religious experience where the powerful macro-symbols of official cult seem inapplicable or irrelevant. The eucharist provides a good illustration of this point. The liturgical action, with its climax in the sharing of hallowed food and drink, speaks strongly of a people's identity, of its search for communion with God and others, of its hope for the eschatological unity of humankind at the Supper of the Lamb. But there are other human impulses which the liturgical action, as such, does not intend to satisfy. A Christian's desire simply to "be near" the Lord, to savor his personal presence, to look with love upon a gift of ultimate value: these longings often find fulfillment in popular eucharistic devotions like Benediction or exposition.

Eucharistic devotions thus respond to a genuine human need that originates in earliest infancy (Erikson's

416

"search for a vision of sanctioned centrality") and continues throughout life. Not everyone will experience this need with equal intensity, and thus one must be cautious in using devotions as the gauge of an individual's faith in the eucharist. One must remember, too, that we come to know Christ's presence among his people above all in the eucharistic liturgy. With those qualifications in mind, however, we can admit that many (perhaps most) people need, at some point in their religious development, a concrete manifestation of divine reality that is visible and tangible. In religion, sense and spirit go together, and this is especially true in Christianity, which has traditionally defended the capacity of material things to mediate spiritual and divine realities. The material elements of the eucharist, venerated both in the liturgy and in popular devotions, are the privileged focus of that wider presence of Christ which Christians experience in the assembly, the Word, the ministry and the other sacraments. John Macquarrie says it well when he notes that the material elements of the eucharist

". . . become for Christians the focus of a wider presence. It is in terms of this focusing of our Lord's presence that the service of Benediction is to be understood. . . . Psychologically speaking, we need some concrete visible manifestation toward which to direct our devotion; while theologically speaking, this is already provided for us by our Lord's gracious manifestation of his presence in the Blessed Sacrament."[111]

SUMMARY
In this chapter we have attempted to assess eucharistic cult and devotions from three different angles: psychological, symbolic, and sociological. Erik Erikson's understanding of the origins of ritualization has helped us see the importance of visual symbols in the psychological and religious development of human beings. Modern research into the complex structure of symbols has aided us in identifying both presence and absence in

417

the eucharistic elements. Finally, our brief examination of folk religion, its customs and concerns, has given us a way to assess the importance of popular devotions in Christian life. None of these angles, taken alone or together, can provide a full explanation of the significance believers have attached through the centuries to such customs as eucharistic processions, exposition, visits and Benediction. But they can help us to understand the complex phenomenon of eucharistic piety and lead others to grasp some of its richness.

NOTES

1. See the classic work of Charles Haskins, *The Renaissance of the Twelfth Century* (Cambridge: Harvard University Press, 1927). See also: Christopher Brooke, *The Twelfth Century Renaissance* (History of European Civilization Library; New York: Harcourt, Brace and World, 1969).

2. See John Harvey, *The Master Builders. Architecture in the Middle Ages* (Library of Medieval Civilization; New York: McGraw-Hill, 1971), p. 27.

3. See Brooke, *The Twelfth Century*, p. 103.

4. Ibid., p. 102.

5. See Harvey, *The Master Builders*, p. 28.

6. See ibid., pp. 27-39; see also Brooke, *The Twelfth Century*, pp. 102-103.

7. See the discussion in Paul Frankl, *Gothic Architecture*, translated by Dieter Pevsner (The Pelican History of Art; Baltimore: Penguin Books, 1962), pp. 17-30.

8. Lynn White, Jr., "Natural Science and Naturalistic Art in the Middle Ages," in *Medieval Religion and Technology. Collected Essays* (Berkeley: University of California Press, 1978), p. 33.

9. Ibid., p. 27.

10. Ibid.

11. Cited ibid., p. 29, n. 10.

12. Ibid., p. 28.

13. Ibid., pp. 30-31.

14. Cited ibid., p. 32, n. 16.

15. Ibid., p. 33.

16. For further discussion see Blandine-Dominique Berger, *Le Drame Liturgique de Pâques* (Théologie historique, no. 37; Paris: Beauchesne, 1976), pp. 247-256 for a listing of sources that indicate roles assigned to the *dramatis personae* of the liturgical plays associated with Holy Week.

17. See White, "Natural Science and Naturalistic Art," p. 36.

18. See ibid., pp. 37-38.

19. See Beryl Smalley, *The Study of the Bible in the Middle Ages* (2nd edition; New York: Philosophical Library, 1952), pp. 83-111, 281-292.

20. See ibid., pp, 118-119. See also: Henri de Lubac, *Exégèse Médiévale* (4 vols.; "Théologie," vols. 41, 42, 59; Paris: Aubier, 1959–1963), III, pp. 361-372.

21. See de Lubac, *Exégèse Médiévale*, III, pp. 361-363.

22. See White, "Natural Science and Naturalistic Art," p. 28.

23. Ibid., pp. 33-34.

24. Leonid Ouspensky, *Theology of the Icon*, translated by Elizabeth Meyendorff (Crestwood, N.Y.: Saint Vladimir's Seminary Press, 1978), p. 10.

25. Cited ibid., p. 10. The reference is to Basil, *Homily 19* on the Forty Martyrs: PG 31: 509A.

26. Ouspensky, *Theology of the Icon*, p. 55.

27. Cited ibid., p. 55. The reference is to John Damascene, *First Treatise*, chap. 16: PG 94: 1245.

28. On the transactional character of symbols, see Nathan Mitchell, "Symbols are Actions, Not Objects—New Directions for an Old Problem," *Living Worship* 13 (February, 1977), 1-4.

29. See Annie Dillard, *Pilgrim at Tinker Creek* (New York: Bantam Books, paper; 1975), pp. 35-36.

30. See Erik Erikson, *Toys and Reasons. Stages in the Ritualization of Experience* (New York: W.W. Norton and Company, 1977).

31. Cited ibid., p. 46.

32. See ibid., p. 47.

33. See ibid., p. 48.

34. Ibid., p. 49.

35. Cited ibid., p. 47.

36. See ibid., pp. 67-118.

37. Ibid., p. 79.

38. Ibid., p. 82.

39. Ibid., p. 79.

40. Ibid., p. 79.

41. Ibid., p. 91.

42. Ibid., p. 88.

43. Ibid.

44. See ibid., pp. 88-89.

45. Erikson also implies this; see *Toys and Reasons*, p. 89.

46. See Urban T. Holmes, *The Priest in Community* (New York: Seabury Press, 1978), pp. 9-34.

47. See ibid., pp. 17-20.

48. Ibid., pp. 18-19.

49. Erikson, *Toys and Reasons*, p. 89.

50. See ibid., pp. 85-92.

51. Ibid., p. 87.

52. Ibid., pp. 49-50.

53. Ibid., p. 49.

54. See Erikson, *Toys and Reasons*, p. 89.

55. Ibid., p. 111.

56. See Karl Rahner, "Considerations on the Active Role of the Person in the Sacramental Event," in *Theological Investigations*, XIV, translated by David Bourke (New York: Seabury Press, 1976), p. 169.

57. Ibid.

58. Ibid.

59. See Erikson, *Toys and Reasons*, p. 114, for a summary chart of the connections between stages of growth and ritualization.

60. See Paul Ricoeur, *The Rule of Metaphor. Multi-disciplinary Studies of the Creation of Meaning in Language*, translated by Robert Czerny *et al*. (Toronto: University of Toronto Press, 1977), pp. 22-23.

61. See W.V. Quine, "A Postscript on Metaphor," in Sheldon Sacks, ed., *On Metaphor* (Chicago: University of Chicago Press, 1979), p. 160.

62. John Dominic Crossan, *Cliffs of Fall. Paradox and Polyvalence in the Parables of Jesus* (New York: Seabury Press, 1980), pp. 8-9.

63. Ibid., p. 10.

64. Ibid.

65. See Karsten Harries, "Metaphor and Transcendence," in Sacks, ed., *On Metaphor*, p. 82.

66. Ibid.

67. See ibid., p. 88.

68. Ibid.

69. Ibid.

70. See Paul Ricoeur, "The Hermeneutics of Symbols and Philosophical Reflection," *International Philosophical Quarterly* 2 (1962), 194.

71. Ibid., p. 194.

72. Ibid. ·

73. See Karsten Harries, "Metaphor and Transcendence," in Sacks, ed., *On Metaphor*, p. 82.

74. See Ricoeur, "The Hermeneutics of Symbols," p. 196.

75. See ibid., pp. 193-194 for a discussion of the inevitably symbolic language of sin and guilt.

76. See ibid., p. 193.

77. See Thomas Aquinas, *Summa Theologiae*, IIIa, 76, 5.

78. *Summa Theologiae*, IIIa, 76, 7.

79. See Ricoeur, "The Hermeneuties of Symbols," p. 198.

80. See Josef Jungmann, *The Early Liturgy*, translated by Francis Brunner (Liturgical Studies, VI; Notre Dame, Ind.: University of Notre Dame Press, 1959), p. 97.

81. *Didache* 8.2-3.

82. *Apostolic Tradition*, nos. 35-43, in the translation of Geoffrey J. Cuming, *Hippolytus: A Text for Students* (Grove Liturgical Study, no. 8; Bramcote, Notts.: Grove Books, 1976), pp. 27-31.

83. On these and related developments, see William G. Storey, "The Liturgy of the Hours: Cathedral versus Monastery," in John Gallen, ed., *Christians at Prayer* (Notre Dame, Ind.: University of Notre Dame Press, 1977), pp. 61-82.

84. See Peter W. Williams, *Popular Religion in America* (Prentice-Hall Studies in Religion Series; Englewood Cliffs, N.J.: Prentice-Hall, 1980), p. 60.

85. Ibid., p. 60.

86. Ibid., p. 65.

87. Numerous examples of such practices may be found in Adolf Franz, *Die Messe im deutschen Mittelalter* (Freiburg im Breisgau/St. Louis: Herder, 1902).

88. Williams, *Popular Religion in America*, pp. 65-66.

89. Ibid., p. 65.

90. See Erikson, *Toys and Reasons*, p. 49.

91. John Macquarrie, "Eucharistic Presence," in *Paths in Spirituality* (New York: Harper and Row, 1972), p. 86.

92. See ibid., p. 87.

93. Ibid.

94. Ibid., p. 89.

95. Ibid.

96. Ibid., p. 90.

97. Ibid.

98. See Edward Schillebeeckx, "Transubstantiation, Transfinalization, Transignification," *Worship* 40 (1966), 324-338.

99. Macquarrie, "Eucharistic Presence," p. 91.

100. Ibid.

101. Ibid.

102. See the section of Chapter One entitled "Stage Three: Eucharist as an Independent Rite."

103. See Carl Dehne, "Roman Catholic Popular Devotions," in Gallen, ed., *Christians at Prayer*, pp. 83-99.

104. Ibid., p. 93.

105. See Josef Jungmann, "From Patrocinium to the Act of Consecration," in *Pastoral Liturgy*, translated anonymously (New York: Herder and Herder, 1962), pp. 296-297.

106. Dehne, "Roman Catholic Popular Devotions," p. 94.

107. Ibid., pp. 94-95.

108. Ibid., p. 95.

109. Ibid.

110. Ibid., pp. 95-96.

111. John Macquarrie, "Benediction of the Blessed Sacrament," in *Paths in Spirituality*, p. 99.

Conclusion

In the opinion of some critics, T.S. Eliot's last major
poetic work, *Four Quartets*, celebrates the elemental
forces that engender and shape human life: earth, air,
fire and water.[1] There is reason to believe that this is so.
The imagery of each poem plays with these elements,
and Eliot quoted Heraclitus, a proponent of the "all is
fire" theory, at the beginning of the *Quartets*. Eliot's intentions are perhaps irrelevant; the poems speak for
themselves. In the Good Friday lyric contained in "East
Coker," the poet's attention turns to the earth, a
"hospital/Endowed by the ruined millionaire."[2] The
poem is not especially optimistic, and it hints darkly that
the healing of humankind will not happen until "our
sickness . . . grows worse."[3] The final two stanzas of the
lyric continue the theme of illness and restoration:

The chill ascends from feet to knees,
The fever sings in mental wires.
If to be warmed, then I must freeze
And quake in frigid purgatorial fires
Of which the flame is roses, and the smoke is briars.

The dripping blood our only drink,
The bloody flesh our only food:
In spite of which we like to think
That we are sound, substantial flesh and blood—
Again, in spite of that, we call this Friday good.[4]

The eucharistic reference in the final stanza is almost
savage in its realism and its irony. We hospitalized
people, the poet claims, delude ourselves into thinking
that we are healthy, "sound, substantial." But the
eucharist calls our bluff: there we feed on the flesh and

blood of One who was torn, broken—and we call that Friday good. In this lyric the eucharist is elevated beyond its ordinary significance as a Christian sacrament; it becomes an ironic comment on a culture that cannot be healed unless it recognizes its moribund nature.

Eliot's use of eucharistic images to comment on his times illustrates a theme that has unfolded throughout this book. From the first century to the twentieth, the eucharist has not only survived as the central act of Christian worship; it has stubbornly resisted any single interpretation of its meaning. From Paul's ecclesiological understanding (the meal that seals a new covenant for a new people of God) to Paschasius's staunch realism (the eucharistic body is the historical body of Christ) to Aquinas's sophisticated sacramentalism (the eucharist offers the substance of Christ's glorified body and blood), pastors and theologians have struggled to understand the words and deeds of Jesus at that farewell meal with his friends. And while theologians argued, ordinary Christians continued to find ways of ritualizing what faith told them was true: Christ is present in the bread and wine of the Supper. As we have seen, these popular ritualizations took many forms: processions, exposition, Benediction, visits, the reception of the sacrament outside Mass. Like the theories of change and presence propounded by theologians, these devotions were sometimes fruitful, sometimes not. But it is important to recognize that the theological hermeneutics of the scholars, and the folk hermeneutics of popular piety, pointed in the same direction: to discover what it means to say that Jesus Christ, dead and rising, continues to eat and drink with his people.

The purpose of this book has been neither to defend nor to deny the multitudinous theologies and popular customs that have attached themselves to the eucharist over the centuries, but simply to understand them and thus to enrich our perception of a many-faceted mystery. For the eucharist remains in sum a mystery profound in its utter simplicity. The earthly Jesus took the earthly elements of bread and wine, blessed God for them, identified himself with them. As Gregory Dix observed: "At the heart of it all is the eucharistic action, a thing of an absolute simplicity—the taking, blessing, breaking and giving of bread and the taking, blessing, and giving of a cup of wine and water, as these were first done with their new meaning by a young Jew before and after supper with His friends on the night before He died . . ."[5]

Our study of the cult of the eucharist outside Mass ends where it began, with the profoundly human gestures of a meal. For twenty centuries these gestures have been an inexhaustible source of nourishment for Christians. As both liturgical action and permanent sacrament, the eucharist has led believers to the conviction that the Lord continues to be available, present, interested in the variegated textures of human life and history. The story, the action, and the mystery continue to unfold.

NOTES

1. See Elizabeth Schneider, *T.S. Eliot. The Pattern in the Carpet* (Berkeley: University of California Press, 1975).

2. T.S. Eliot, *Four Quartets* (New York: Harcourt, Brace and World, paper, 1943), p. 30.

3. Eliot, *Four Quartets*, p. 29.

4. Ibid., p. 30.

5. Gregory Dix, *The Shape of the Liturgy* (Westminster: Dacre Press, 1945), pp. 743-744.

Bibliography

I. SOURCES

A. *Ancient, Medieval and Reformation (to 1600 A.D.)*

Amalarius of Metz, *Codex Expositionis*. Critical Latin text in J.M. Hanssens, ed., *Amalarii Episcopi Opera Liturgica Omnia*. Studi e Testi 138-140; 3 Vols.; Città del Vaticano: Biblioteca Apostolica Vaticana, 1948.

――――. *Epistola ad Hilduinum Abbatem*. Critical Latin text in J.M. Hanssens (see entry above).

――――. *Liber Officialis*. Critical Latin text in J.M. Hanssens (see first entry).

――――. *Liber Officiorum*. Critical Latin text in J.M. Hanssens (see first entry).

――――. *Ordinis Missae Expositio*. Critical Latin text in J.M. Hanssens (see first entry).

Ambrose of Milan. *Funeral Oration for Satyrus*. English translation in Leo P. McCauley *et al*. *Funeral Orations by Saint Gregory Nazianzen and Saint Ambrose*. Fathers of the Church, Vol. 22; New York: Fathers of the Church, 1953, pp. 161-259.

――――. *On the Sacraments*. English translation in Edward Yarnold, *The Awe-Inspiring Rites of Initiation*. Slough: St. Paul Publications, 1971, pp. 99-153.

The Ancrene Riwle. Text in M.B. Salu, ed., *The Ancrene Riwle*. London: Burns and Oates, 1955.

Angilbert of St. Riquier. *Institutio de diuersitate Officiorum*. Critical Latin text in Kassius Hallinger, ed., *Corpus Consuetudinum Monasticarum*, Tomus I: *Initia Consuetudinis Benedictinae*. Siegburg: F. Schmitt, 1963, pp. 283-303.

Apostolic Tradition of Hippolytus. English translation with notes in Geoffrey J. Cuming, *Hippolytus: A Text for Students*. Grove Liturgical Study No. 8; Bramcote, Notts.: Grove Books, 1976.

Augustine of Hippo. *Confessions*. English translation in John K. Ryan, *Confessions of St. Augustine*. New York: Doubleday Image Books, 1960.

427

————. *Enarrationes in Psalmos*. Critical Latin text in Eligius Dekkers and Johannes Fraipont, eds., *Sancti Aurelii Augustini Enarrationes in Psalmos*. 3 Vols.; *Corpus Christianorum* 38-40; Turnholt: Brepols, 1956.

Bede the Venerable. *A History of the English Church and People*. English translation in Leo Sherley-Price, *Bede: A History of the English Church and People*. Baltimore: Penguin Books, 1960.

Berengarius of Tours. *De Sacra Coena*. Critical Latin text in W.H. Beekenkamp, ed., *Berengarii Turonensis de sacra coena adversus Lanfrancum*. Kerkhistorische Studien, Vol. II; Le Haye: 1941.

————. *Letter to Adelman of Liege*. Critical Latin text in Jean de Montclos. *Lanfranc et Bérengar*. La Controverse eucharistique du xie siècle. Spicilegium Sacrum Lovaniense. Études et Documents, 37; Louvain: 1971; Appendix II, pp. 531-538.

Brightman, F.E. *Liturgies Eastern and Western*. Oxford: Clarendon Press, 1896; reprinted,1965.

Caesarius of Arles. *Sermons*. Critical Latin text in G. Morin, ed., *Sancti Caesarii Arelatensis Sermones*. 2 Vols.; Editio altera; *Corpus Christianorum* 103-104; Turnholt: Brepols, 1953.

Councils and Synods, with Other Documents Relating to the English Church. Edited by Frederick Maurice Powicke and C.R. Cheney. 2 Vols.; Oxford: Clarendon Press, 1964.

Cyprian of Carthage. *The Lapsed*. English translation in Maurice Bevenot, *St. Cyprian: The Lapsed; The Unity of the Catholic Church*. Ancient Christian Writers, No. 25; Westminster, Md.: The Newman Press, 1957.

————. *Letters*. English translation in Rose Bernard Donna, *St. Cyprian: Letters 1-81*. Fathers of the Church, Vol. 51; Washington, D.C.: The Catholic University of America Press, 1964.

Cyril of Jerusalem. *Catecheses (Baptismal Homilies)*. English translation in Edward Yarnold, *The Awe-Inspiring Rites of Initiation*. Slough: St. Paul Publications, 1971, pp. 68-95.

Decreta Lanfranci. Critical Latin text and English translation in David Knowles, ed., *The Monastic Constitutions of Lanfranc*. New York: Oxford University Press, 1951.

Doudha. *Liber manualis*. PL 106: cols. 109-118. Critical Latin text in Pierre Riché, ed., *Doudha: Manuel pour mon Fils*. Translated by Bernard de Vregille and Claude Mondésert. Sources chrétiennes, 225; Paris: Cerf, 1975.

Didache. English translation in Maxwell Staniforth, *Early Christian Writings*. Baltimore: Penguin Books, 1968, pp. 227-235.

Disputatio Puerorum. PL 101: cols. 1099-1144.

Divina disponente clementia (Bull of Pius IV, 1560). Latin text in L. Cherubini *et al.*, eds., *Magnum Bullarium Romanum*. 8 Vols.; Rome and Luxemburg: 1742, II, pp. 34-37.

Egeria's Travels (Peregrinatio Egeriae)..English translation with notes and commentary in John Wilkinson, *Egeria's Travels*. London: SPCK, 1971.

Epigrammata Damasiana. Texts and commentary in Antonius Ferrua, ed., *Epigrammata Damasiana*. Sussidi allo Studio delle Antichità Cristiane, II; Città del Vaticano: Pontifico Istituto di Archeologia Cristiana, 1942.

Eusebius of Caesarea. *The History of the Church*. English translation in G.A. Williamson, *Eusebius: The History of the Church*. Baltimore: Penguin Books, 1965.

Expositio Antiquae Liturgiae Gallicanae. Critical Latin text in E.C. Ratcliff, ed., *Expositio Antiquae Liturgiae Gallicanae*. Henry Bradshaw Society, Vol. 98. London: HBS, 1971.

The Gilbertine Rite. Edited by R.M. Woolley. 2 Vols. Henry Bradshaw Society, 59-60; London: HBS, 1921.

Graves et diuturnae (Bull of Clement VIII, 1592). Latin text in L. Cherubini *et al.*, eds., *Magnum Bullarium Romanum*. 8 Vols.; Rome and Luxemburg: 1742, III, pp. 24-25.

Gregory the Great, *Dialogues, Book II*. English translation in Myra Uhlfelder, *Gregory the Great: Dialogues, Book II*. The Library of Liberal Arts; Indianapolis: Bobbs-Merrill, 1967.

Grimlac. *Regula Solitariorum*. PL 103: cols. 575-664.

The Hereford Breviary. Latin text edited by Walter Howard Frere and Langton E.G. Brown. 3 Vols.; Henry Bradshaw Society, 26, 40, 46; London: Harrison and Sons, 1904–1915.

Ignatius of Antioch. *Letters*. English translation in Maxwell Staniforth, *Early Christian Writings*. New York: Penguin Books, 1968, pp. 75-131.

Innocent I. *Letter to Decentius of Gubbio*. Latin text in PL 20: cols. 556-557.

Jerome. *Letters*. Critical Latin text in Isidore Hilberg, ed., *Sancti Eusebii Hieronymi Epistulae*. CSEL Vol. 54; Vienna: F. Tempsky, 1910.

St. John Chrysostom. *Baptismal Instructions*. English translation in Paul W. Harkins; Ancient Christian Writers, Vol. 31; Westminster, Md.: The Newman Press, 1963.

John Myrc's Instructions for Parish Priests. Edited by Edward Peacock. Early English Text Society, 31; London: Truebner and Co., 1868.

Jonas of Orleans. *De Institutione Laicali*. Latin text in PL 106: cols. 121-278.

Justin Martyr. *First Apology*. English translation (partial) in Willi Rordorf *et al.*, *The Eucharist of the Early Christians*. Translated by Matthew J. O'Connell. New York: Pueblo Publishing Company, 1978, pp. 71-73.

Lanfranc of Bec. *Liber de Corpore et Sanguine Domini*. Latin text in PL 150: cols. 407-442.

The Lay Folks Mass Book. Edited by Thomas F. Simmons; Early English Text Society, 71; London: N. Truebner and Co., 1899.

Leo the Great. *Letters*. Translated by Edmund Hunt. Fathers of the Church, Vol. 34; New York: Fathers of the Church, 1957.

Libelli Precum Quattipr Aevi Karolini. Edited by Andre Wilmart. Rome: Ephemerides Liturgicae, 1940.

Libelli Precum Quattuor Aevi Karolini. Edited by Andre Wilmart. by Leo Cunibert Mohlberg. Rerum Ecclesiasticarum Documenta, Series Major. Fontes IV; Rome: Herder, 1960.

Medieval Handbooks of Penance. Edited and translated by John T. McNeil and Helena M. Gamber. Records of Civilization, Sources and Studies, XXIX; New York: Columbia University Press, 1938.

Missale ad usum insignis et praeclarae ecclesiae Sarum. Edited by F.H. Dickinson. London: J. Parker and Co., 1861–1883; reprint: Gregg International Publishers, 1969.

Missale ad usum percelebris ecclesiae Herfordensis. Edited by W.G.

Henderson. London: 1874; reprint: Gregg International Publishers, 1969.

Missale Francorum. Edited by Leo Cunibert Mohlberg. Rerum Ecclesiasticarum Documenta, Series Major. Fontes II; Rome: Herder, 1957.

Missale Romanum. Edited by Robert Lippe. Henry Bradshaw Society, 17; London: 1899 (edition of the 1474 Missal).

Les Ordines Romani du haut moyen âge. Edited by Michel Andrieu. 5 Vols.; Spicilegium Sacrum Lovaniense 11, 23, 24, 28, 29; Louvain: 1931–1961.

Ordo Romanus Primus. English translation by E.G. Cuthbert and F. Atchley. London: The De La More Press, 1905.

Paschasius Radbertus. *De Corpore et Sanguine Domini*. Edited by Beda Paulus. Corpus Christianorum, continuatio mediaevalis 16; Turnholt: Brepols, 1969.

Le Pontificale romain au Moyen-Age. Edited by Michel Andrieu. Studi e Testi 86-88; 99; 4 Vols.; Città del Vaticano: Biblioteca Apostolica Vaticana, 1938–1941.

Le Pontificale romano-germanique du dixième siècle. Edited by Cyrille Vogel. Studi e Testi 226-227; 2 Vols.; Città del Vaticano: Biblioteca Apostolica Vaticana, 1963.

Processionale ad usum insignis ac praeclarae ecclesiae Sarum. Edited by W.G. Henderson. Leeds: M'Corquodale and Co., 1882; reprint: Gregg International Publishers, 1969.

Ratramnus. *De Corpore et Sanguine Domini*. Latin text in PL 121: cols. 125-170.

Regino of Prüm. *De Ecclesiasticis Disciplinis Libri Duo*. Latin text in PL 132: cols. 185-400.

Regularis Concordia. Edited and translated by Thomas Symons. New York: Oxford University Press, 1953.

Ritus Orientalium. Edited by H. Denziger. Wurzburg: 1864.

The Rule of the Master. Translated by Luke Eberle. Kalamazoo: Cistercian Publications, 1977.

Sacramentarium Veronense. Edited by Leo Cunibert Mohlberg. Rerum Ecclesiasticarum Documenta, Series Major. Fontes I; Rome: Herder, 1956.

Socrates. *Ecclesiastical History*. Translated anonymously. The Greek Ecclesiastical Historians, Vol. 3; London: Samuel Bagster, 1844.

Statuta Ecclesiae Antiquae. Edited by Charles Munier. Bibliothèque de l'Institut de Droit canonique de l'Université de Strasbourg, Vol. 5; Strasbourg: Presses Universitaires de France, 1960.

Tertullian. *On Monogamy*. Translated by William P. Le Saint. *Treatises on Marriage and Remarriage*. Ancient Christian Writers, Vol. 13; Westminster, Md.: The Newman Press, 1951.

————. *On Prayer*. Translated by Rudolph Arbesmann *et al.*, *Disciplinary, Moral and Ascetical Works*. Fathers of the Church, Vol. 40; New York: Fathers of the Church, 1959.

Theodore of Mopsuestia. *Baptismal Homilies*. English translation in Edward Yarnold, *The Awe-Inspiring Rites of Initiation*. Slough: St. Paul Publications, 1971, pp. 176-263.

Theodulph of Orleans. *Capitulare*. Latin text in PL 105: cols. 207-224.

Thomas Aquinas. *Summa Theologiae*. Edited by Petrus Caramello. 4 Vols.; Rome: Marietti, 1956.

Vitae Sanctorum Hiberniae. Edited by Charles Plummer. 2 Vols.; Oxford: Oxford University Press, 1968.

B. *Modern (1600 to the present)*
Acta et Decreta Sacrorum Conciliorum Recentiorum. Collectio Lacensis. Edited by presbyters of the Society of Jesus. Freiburg: Herder, 1875, III, cols. 129-154 (for acts of the First Plenary Council of Baltimore, 1852).

Blessed Be God. A Complete Catholic Prayer Book. New York: P.J. Kenedy and Sons, 1925.

The Catholic's Vade Mecum. A Select Manual of Prayers for Daily Use. London: Burns and Oates; New York: Catholic Publication Society, n.d.

Ceremonial for the Use of the Catholic Churches in the United States of America. Third edition; Baltimore: Kelly, Piet and Co., 1871.

The Choir Manual for Cathedral and Parish Church. Edited by G. Burton. New York: J. Fischer and Bro., 1914.

A Compilation of the Litanies, Vespers, Hymns and Anthems as Sung in the Catholic Church. Compiled by John Aitken. Philadelphia: 1787. Facsimile edition by J.C. Selner et al. Philadelphia: Musical Americana (Harry Dichter), 1956.

Concilii Plenarii Baltimorensis II Acta et Decreta. Baltimore: J. Murphy, 1868.

Concilii Provincialia Baltimori Habita. Baltimore: John Murphy, 1842.

Constitution on the Sacred Liturgy. English translation in James J. Megivern, ed., Worship and Liturgy. Official Catholic Teachings; Wilmington, N.C.: McGrath Publishing Company, 1978, pp. 197-234.

Denziger, H. and Schönmetzer, A., eds. Enchiridion Symbolorum. Definitionum et Declarationum, 35th ed. Fribourg, 1967.

General Instruction on the Liturgy of the Hours. English translation and commentary in A.-M. Roguet, The Liturgy of the Hours. The General Instruction with Commentary. Translated by Peter Coughlan and Peter Purdue; Collegeville, Minn.: The Liturgical Press, 1971.

Immensae Caritatis (1973). English translation, with commentary, in Bishops' Committee on the Liturgy, Study Text 1: Holy Communion. Washington, D.C.: Publications Office, USCC, 1973.

Instructio Clementina (Clement XI, 1705). Latin text and commentary in Aloisio Gardellini and Wolfgang Muehlbauer, eds., Decreta Authentica Congregationis Sacrorum Rituum. 3 Vols.; Munich: J.J. Lentneriana, 1863, I, pp. 709-893.

Key of Heaven. The Vest-Pocket Manual of Catholic Devotions. Philadelphia: H.L. Kilner and Co., 1909.

Lumen Gentium (Dogmatic Constitution on the Church.) English translation with notes in Austin Flannery, ed., Vatican Council II: The Conciliar and Post Conciliar Documents. Collegeville, Minn.: The Liturgical Press, 1975, pp. 350-423.

McNeiry, C. Thursdays with the Blessed Sacrament. New York: Benziger Brothers, 1917.

Manual for Forty Hours. Edited by Walter Schmitz. New edition; Washington, D.C.: The Catholic University of America Press, 1960.

433

A Manual of the Ceremonies used in the Catholic Church. Boston: H.L. Devereux, 1833.

Mediator Dei. Encyclical Letter of Pius XII on the Sacred Liturgy. Latin text in *Acta Apostolicae Sedis* 39 (1947), 521-600.

Megivern, James J., ed. *Worship and Liturgy*. Official Catholic Teachings; Wilmington, N.C.: McGrath Publishing Company, 1978.

Ministeria Quaedam (1972). English translation in *The Rites*. 2 Vols.; New York: Pueblo Publishing Company, 1976–1980, I, pp. 726-731.

"De Musica Sacra et Sacra Liturgia ad Mentem Litterarum Encyclicarum Pii Papae XII." Decree of the Sacred Congregation of Rites, 3 September 1958. Latin text in *Acta Apostolicae Sedis* 50 (1958), 630-663.

The Raccolta or Prayers and Devotions Enriched with Indulgences. Edited by Joseph Christopher and Charles Spence. New York: Benziger Brothers, 1943.

The Rites. 2 Vols. New York: Pueblo Publishing Company, 1976–1980.

Rite of Institution of Readers and Acolytes, Admission to Candidacy for Ordination as Deacons and Priests. English translation in *The Rites* (see previous entry), I, pp. 740-756.

Rituale Romanum. Editio Prima juxta typicam Vaticanam. New York: Benziger Brothers, 1953.

Rituale Romanum Pauli V Pontificis Maximi iussu editum. Rome: 1615.

Romanus Pontifex (Bull of Paul V, 1606). Latin text in L. Cherubini *et al.*, eds., *Magnum Bullarium Romanum*. 8 Vols.; Rome and Luxemburg: 1742, III, p. 230.

II. LITERATURE

Achtemeier, Paul. *Mark*. Proclamation Commentaries. Philadelphia: Fortress Press, 1975.

Beauduin, Lambert. *Mélanges liturgiques*. Louvain: Abbaye du Mont César, Centre liturgique, 1954.

Berger, Blandine-Dominique. *Le Drame liturgique de Pâques*. Théologie historique, No. 37. Paris: Beauchesne, 1976.

Bertaud, Emile. "Dévotion eucharistique." *Dictionnaire de Spiritualité* IV/2, cols. 1621-1637.

Bishops' Committee on the Liturgy. *The Body of Christ*. Washington, D.C.: NCCB, 1977.

──────. *Study Text 3: Ministries in the Church*. Washington, D.C.: Publications Office, USCC, 1974.

Boudurand, E. *L'Education carolingienne. Le Manuel de Dhouda*. Paris: Picard, 1887.

Brooke, Christopher. *The Twelfth Century Renaissance*. History of European Civilization Library. New York: Harcourt, Brace and World, 1969.

Browe, Peter. *Die Verehrung der Eucharistie im Mittelalter*. Rome: Herder, 1967; reprint of the 1933 edition.

Cabrol, Fernand. "Elevation." DACL IV/2, cols. 2662-2670.

──────. *Le Livre de la Prière antique*. Paris: Librarie Religieuse H. Oudin, 1900.

Canadian Conference of Catholic Bishops. "Rites for the Sick and Dying." *National Bulletin on Liturgy*, No. 57 (Vol. 10; January–February, 1977).

Capon, Robert. *Party Spirit*. New York: William Morrow and Company, 1979.

Cohn, Norman. *The Pursuit of the Millenium*. Second edition. New York: Harper and Row, 1961.

Corish, Patrick J. "The Christian Mission." In *idem*, general editor, *A History of Irish Catholicism*, Vol. 1. Dublin: Gill and Macmillan, 1971.

Crehan, Joseph. "The Seven Orders of Christ." *Theological Studies* 19 (1958), 81-93.

Crossan, John Dominic. *Cliffs of Fall. Paradox and Polyvalence in the Parables of Jesus*. New York: The Seabury Press, 1980.

──────. *The Dark Interval*. Niles, Ill.: Argus Communications, 1975.

Day, E. "Tarsicius, St." NCE 13, p. 940.

Dehne, Carl. "Roman Catholic Popular Devotions." In John Gallen, ed., *Christians at Prayer*. Notre Dame, Ind.: University of Notre Dame Press, 1977, pp. 83-99.

Dix, Gregory. *A Detection of Aumbries*. Westminster: Dacre Press, 1954.

———. *The Shape of the Liturgy*. Westminster: Dacre Press, 1945.

Donovan, C.F., ed. *The Story of the Twenty-Eighth International Eucharistic Congress*. Chicago: Eucharistic Congress Committee, 1927.

Dumoutet, E. *Le Desir de Voir l'Hostie*. Paris: Gabriel Beauchesne, 1926.

Empie, Paul C. and Murphy, T. Austin, eds. *Lutherans and Catholics in Dialogue*, I-III. Minneapolis: Augsburg Publishing House, 1967.

Erikson, Erik. *Toys and Reasons. Stages in the Ritualization of Experience*. New York: W.W. Norton and Company, 1977.

Fortescue, Adrian. *The Ceremonies of the Roman Rite*. Fifth revised edition. London: Burns, Oates and Washbourne, 1934.

Frankl, Paul. *Gothic Architecture*. Translated by Dieter Pevsner. The Pelican History of Art. Baltimore: Penguin Books, 1962.

Franz, Adolf. *Die kirchlichen Benediktionen im Mittelalter*. 2 Vols. Freiburg im Breisgau: Herdersche Verlagshandlung, 1909.

———. *Die Messe im deutschen Mittelalter*. Freiburg im Breisgau/St. Louis: Herder, 1902.

Freestone, W.H. *The Sacrament Reserved*. Alcuin Club Collections, XXI. London: A.R. Mowbray and Co., 1917.

Fuller, Reginald. *The Formation of the Resurrection Narratives*. New York: Macmillan, 1971.

Funk, Robert. *Language, Hermeneutic, and Word of God*. New York: Harper and Row, 1966.

Gibson, Margaret. *Lanfranc of Bec*. Oxford: Clarendon Press, 1978.

436

Gougaud, Louis. *Devotional and Ascetic Practices in the Middle Ages*. Translated by C.C. Bateman. London: Burns, Oates and Washbourne, 1927.

Greeley, Andrew. *An Ugly Little Secret. Anti-Catholicism in North America*. Kansas City: Sheed, Andrews and McNeel, 1972.

Häussling, Angelus. *Mönchskonvent und Eucharistiefeier*. Liturgiegeschichtliche Quellen und Forschungen, 58. Münster: Aschendorffsche Verlagsbuchhandlung, 1973.

Hall, Donald. *Remembering Poets*. New York: Harper Colophon Books, 1978.

Hanssens, Jean Micheal. *La Liturgie d'Hippolyte*. 2 Vols. Rome: Pontificium Institutum Orientalium Studiorum, 1959.

Harries, Karsten. "Metaphor and Transcendence." In Sheldon Sacks, ed., *On Metaphor*. Chicago: The University of Chicago Press, 1979.

Harvey, John. *The Master Builders. Architecture in the Middle Ages*. Library of Medieval Civilization. New York: McGraw-Hill, 1971.

Haskins, Charles. *The Renaissance of the Twelfth Century*. Cambridge: Harvard University Press, 1927.

Hater, Robert J. *The Ministry Explosion. A New Awareness of Every Christian's Call to Minister*. Dubuque, Iowa: William C. Brown, 1979.

Hefele, Charles Joseph and Leclercq, Henri. *Histoire des Conciles*. 11 Vols. Paris: Letouzey et Ané, 1907–1952.

Heidegger, Martin. *Existence and Being*. Translated by Douglas Scott. Chicago: Henry Regnery Co., 1949.

———. *Poetry, Language, Thought*. Translated by Albert Hofstadter. New York: Harper Colophon Books, 1971.

Holmes, Urban T. *The Priest in Community*. New York: The Seabury Press, 1978.

Julian, John, ed. *A Dictionary of Hymnology*. Revised edition with new supplement. London: John Murray, 1907.

Jungmann, Josef. "Die Andacht der Vierzig Stunden und das

heilige Grab." *Liturgisches Jahrbuch* 2 (1952), 184-198.

―――. *The Early Liturgy*. Translated by Francis Brunner. Liturgical Studies, VI. Notre Dame, Ind.: University of Notre Dame Press, 1959.

―――. "From Patrocinium to the Act of Consecration." In *idem, Pastoral Liturgy*. Translated anonymously. New York: Herder and Herder, 1962, pp. 295-314.

―――. *Missarum Solemnia*. 2 Vols. New York: Benziger, 1955; fifth edition, Vienna: Herder, 1962.

Keck, Leander. *Paul and His Letters. Proclamation Commentaries*. Philadelphia: Fortress Press, 1979.

Kennedy, V.L. "The Date of the Parisian Decree on the Elevation of the Host." *Medieval Studies 8* (1946), 87-96.

―――. "The Moment of Consecration and the Elevation of the Host." *Medieval Studies* 6 (1944), 121-150.

King, Archdale and Pocknee, Cyril. *Eucharistic Reservation in the Western Church*. London: 1965.

Klauser, Theodor. *A Short History of the Western Liturgy*. Translated by John Halliburton. Second edition. New York: Oxford University Press, 1979.

Kleinheyer, Bruno. *Die Priesterweihe im römischen Ritus*. Trierer Theologische Studien, Bd. 12. Trier: Paulinus-Verlag, 1962.

Leclercq, Henri. "Reliques et Reliquaires." DACL XIV/2, cols. 2294-2359.

Leclerq, J., Vandenbroucke, F., and Bouyer, L. *A History of Christian Spirituality*, Vol. II. Translated by the Benedictines of Holme Eden Abbey. London: Burns and Oates, 1968.

Leroquais, Victor. "L'Ordo Missae du sacramentaire d'Amiens." *Ephemerides Liturgicae* 41 (1927), 435-445.

Lubac, Henri de. *Corpus Mysticum*. L'Eucharistie et l'Eglise au Moyen Age; Etude historique. Second edition revised and enlarged. Paris: Aubier, 1949.

―――. *Exégès Médiévale*. 4 Vols. Théologie, Vols. 41, 42, 59. Paris: Aubier, 1959–1963.

McBrien, Richard. *Catholicism*. 2 Vols. Minneapolis: Winston

Press, 1980.

————. *Church. The Continuing Quest*. Paramus, N.J.: Newman Press, 1970.

McDonnell, Ernest W. *The Beguines and Beghards in Medieval Culture*. New Jersey: Rutgers University Press, 1954.

Macquarrie, John. "Benediction of the Blessed Sacrament." In *idem, Paths in Spirituality*. New York: Harper and Row, 1972, pp. 94-102.

————. "Eucharistic Presence." In *idem, Paths in Spirituality*. New York: Harper and Row, 1972, pp. 82-93.

Martimort, A.-G., ed. *The Church at Prayer: The Eucharist*. Translated by Damian Smyth *et al*. New York: Herder and Herder, 1973.

Marxsen, Willi. *The Beginnings of Christology*. Translated by Paul Achtemeier and Lorenz Nieting. Philadelphia: Fortress Press, 1979.

Mateos, Juan. "El Nuevo Testamento y su Mensaje." In *Nuevo Testamento*. Translated and edited by Juan Mateos, Luis Alonso Schokel *et al*. Huntington, Ind.: Our Sunday Visitor, 1975, pp. 13-44.

Maurice, V. "Acolyte." DTC I/1, cols. 312-316.

Mitchell, Nathan, ed. *The Rite of Penance*. Commentaries, Vol. III: Background and Directions. Washington, D.C.: The Liturgical Conference, 1978.

————. "Symbols are Actions, not Objects—New Directions for an Old Problem." *Living Worship* 13 (February, 1977), 1-4.

Montague, George. *The Holy Spirit. Growth of a Biblical Tradition*. New York: Paulist Press, 1976.

Montclos, Jean de. *Lanfranc et Bérengar. La Controverse eucharistique du xie siècle*. Spicilegium Sacrum Lovaniense. Etudes et Documents, 37. Louvain: 1971.

Nocent, Adrian. *The Liturgical Year*. Translated by Matthew J. O'Connell. 4 Vols., Collegeville, Minn.: The Liturgical Press, 1977.

Nussbaum, Otto. *Die Aufbewahrung der Eucharistie*. Theophaneia, 29. Bonn: Hanstein, 1979.

————. *Kloster, Priestermönch und Privatmesse*. Theophaneia, 14. Bonn: Hanstein, 1961.

XIeme *Congres Eucharistique International*. Bruxelles, 13-17 Juillet 1898. Brussels: Joseph Goemaere, 1899.

Ouspensky, Leonid. *Theology of the Icon*. Translated by Elizabeth Meyendorff. Crestwood, N.Y.: Saint Vladimir's Seminary Press, 1978.

Perrin, Norman. *Jesus and the Language of the Kingdom*. Philadelphia: Fortress Press, 1976.

————. *Rediscovering the Teaching of Jesus*. New York: Harper and Row, 1967.

Pizzoni, I. "De Precibus post Missam Imperatis." *Ephemerides Liturgicae* 69 (1955), 54-60; 287-289.

Quine, W.V. "A Postscript on Metaphor." In Sheldon Sacks, ed., *On Metaphor*. Chicago: The University of Chicago Press, 1979.

Rahner, Karl. *The Church and the Sacraments*. Translated by W.J. O'Hara. Quaestiones Disputatae, 9. New York: Herder and Herder, 1963.

————. "Considerations on the Active Role of the Person in the Sacramental Event." *Theological Investigations*, XIV. Translated by David Bourke. New York: The Seabury Press, 1976, pp. 161-184.

————. "The Presence of the Lord in the Christian Community at Worship." *Theological Investigations*, X. Translated by David Bourke. New York: Herder and Herder, 1973, pp. 71-83.

————. "The Theology of the Symbol." In *Theological Investigations*, IV. Translated by Kevin Smyth. Baltimore: Helicon Press, 1966, pp. 221-252.

————. "What is a Sacrament?" In *Theological Investigations*, XIV. Translated by David Bourke. New York: The Seabury Press, 1976, pp. 135-148.

————. "The Word and the Eucharist." In *Theological Investigations*, IV. Translated by Kevin Smyth. Baltimore: Helicon Press, 1966, pp. 253-286.

Ricoeur, Paul. "The Hermeneutics of Symbols and Philosophical Reflection." *International Philosophical Quarterly* 2 (1962), 191-218.

———. *The Rule of Metaphor*. Multi-disciplinary Studies in the Creation of Meaning in Language. Translated by Robert Czerny *et al*. Toronto: University of Toronto Press, 1977.

———. *The Symbolism of Evil*. Translated by Emerson Buchanan. Boston: Beacon Press, 1967; paperback edition, 1969.

Righetti, Mario. *Manuale di Storia liturgica*. 4 Vols. Milan: Editrice Ancora, 1946–1953.

Rordorf, Willi, *et al*. *The Eucharist of the Early Christians*. Translated by Matthew J. O'Connell. New York: Pueblo Publishing Company, 1978.

Rowell, Geoffrey. *The Liturgy of Christian Burial*. Alcuin Club Collections, No. 59. London: SPCK, 1977.

Rush, Alfred C. *Death and Burial in Christian Antiquity*. The Catholic University of America Studies in Christian Antiquity, 1. Washington, D.C.: The Catholic University of America Press, 1941.

———. "The Eucharist, the Sacrament of the Dying in Christian Antiquity." *The Jurist* 34 (1974), 10-35.

Russell, Jeffrey Burton. *Dissent and Reform in the Early Middle Ages*. Los Angeles: University of California Press, 1965.

———. *A History of Medieval Christianity. Prophecy and Order*. New York: Crowell, 1968.

Rutherford, Richard. *The Death of a Christian. The Rite of Funerals*. New York: Pueblo Publishing Company, 1980.

Schillebeeckx, Edward. *Christ*. Translated by John Bowden. New York: The Seabury Press, 1980.

———. *Christ, the Sacrament of the Encounter with God*. Translated by Paul Barrett *et al*. New York: Sheed and Ward, 1963.

———. *Jesus*. Translated by H. Hoskins. New York: The Seabury Press, 1979.

———. "Transubstantiation, Transfinalization, Transignification." *Worship* 40 (1966), 324-338.

Sheppard, Lancelot. *The Liturgical Books*. Twentieth Century

Encyclopedia of Catholicism, 109; New York: Hawthorn Books, 1962.

Sitwell, Gerard. "Private Devotions in the *Ancrene Riwle*." In M.B. Salu, ed., *The Ancrene Riwle*. London: Burns and Oates, 1955, pp. 193-196.

Smalley, Beryl. *The Study of the Bible in the Middle Ages*. Second edition. New York: Philosophical Library, 1952.

Staniforth, Maxwell, trans. *Early Christian Writings*. Baltimore: Penguin Books, 1968.

Storey, William G. "The Liturgy of the Hours: Cathedral versus Monastery." In *Christians at Prayer*. Edited by John Gallen. Notre Dame, Ind.: University of Notre Dame Press, 1977, pp. 61-82.

Talley, James, ed. *Jesus, the Living Bread*. A Chronicle of the Forty-First Eucharistic Congress. Plainfield, N.J.: Logos International, 1976.

Thurston, Herbert. "Benediction of the Blessed Sacrament." *The Month* 98 (1901), 58-69; 186-193; 264-276.

———. "The Divine Praises." *The Month* 131 (1918), 510-513.

———. "Forty Hours' Devotion." *Catholic Encyclopedia*. Edited by Charles G. Herbermann *et al*. 15 Vols. New York: Appleton, 1907; Vol. 6, pp. 151-152.

———. "Our English Benediction Service." *The Month* 106 (1905), 396-402.

Turner, Victor. *Dramas, Fields, and Metaphors. Symbolic Action in Human Society*. Ithaca, N.Y.: Cornell Univeristy Press, 1974.

Vogel, Cyrille. *Le Pécheur et la pénitence au Moyen Age*. Chrétiens de tous les temps, 30. Paris: Cerf, 1969.

Wakefield, Walter and Evans, Austin. *Heresies of the High Middle Ages*. Records of Civilization; Sources and Studies. New York: Columbia University Press, 1969.

Weaver, F. Ellen. *The Evolution of the Reform of Port-Royal*. Paris: Beauchesne, 1978.

White, James. *Introduction to Christian Worship*. Nashville: Abingdon, 1980.

White, Lynn. "Natural Science and Naturalistic Art in the Middle Ages." In *idem, Medieval Religion and Technology*. Collected Essays. Berkeley: University of California Press, 1978.

Williams, Peter. *Popular Religion in America*. Prentice-Hall Studies in Religion Series. Englewood Cliffs, N.J.: Prentice-Hall, 1980.

Willke, J.C. "Eucharistic Congresses." NCE 5, 617-618.

Wilmart, Andre. *Auteurs spirituels et Textes dévots du Moyen âge*. Etudes d'Histoire littéraire. Paris: Etudes Augustiniennes, 1971; reprint of the 1932 edition.

Wolff, Renata. "Patterns of Medieval Monastic Reform." *The American Benedictine Reivew* 18 (1967), 375-384.

Young, Karl. *The Drama of the Medieval Church*. 2 Vols. Oxford: Clarendon Press, 1933.

Index

454

O

Odilia, Saint, 275

Offertory rite, 46, 48, 49, 50, 51

Olivetan Benedictines, 207

On Frequent Communion, 207–208, 210

On Monogamy, 30

On Prayer, 15

Order of the Incarnate Word and of the Blessed Sacrament, 207

Ordinale Gilbertinum, 226–227, 228, 229, 230

Ordinary Rite of Communion of the Sick, 268ff.

Ordo Ecclesiae Lateranensis, 226

Ordo of Angilbert of St. Riquier, 91, 92, 226, 228, 229

Ordo Romanus Primus, 48, 56–57, 59, 68, 93, 100, 288, 289, 291

Ordo Romanus XXIII, 94–95, 222, 224, 225

Ordo Romanus XXXIV, 289

Ordo Romanus XXXV, 290

Ordo Romanus, XLII, 108–109

Ordo Romanus XLIX, 112f.

Ottaviani, Cardinal, 294

Ouspensky, Leonid, 376

P

Palm Sunday, liturgy of, 129–131, 170–171, 224

Pantaleon, Jacques, 175

Parable, nature of, 53

Paris, Synod of, 155f., 163

Pars Oculi, see "Instructions for parish priests, 203

Paschasius Radbertus, 5, 6, 46, 67, 73, 90, 100, 106, 116, 138, 150, 160, 197, 374

Passio sancti, Stephani papae, 285–286, 288

Pastorale (ritual), 202

Paul III, Pope, 206, 312–313, 314, 317

Paul V, Pope, 203, 314

Peckham, Archbishop of Canterbury, 168

Penance, sacrament of, and eucharistic, 70, 109–112

Perpetual adoration, 208, 340

Perrin, Norman, 19–21

Peter the Eater (Comester) *see* Peter of Troyes

456

Real presence of Christ in eucharist, 140ff., 146–147

Readers, 285

Reed, used at communion, 92

Regius (Regino) of Prüm, 93, 94, 167, 279

Regula Solitariorum, 71–72

Regularis Concordia, 115, 116, 129, 132, 133, 135, 371–372

Religion, folk, 403, 403–409

Reposition of eucharist, 339

Rerum Novarum, Encyclical, 320

Reservation of eucharist, 7, 11–13, 15, 16, 95, 108–109, 164ff., 224, 277–278, 310, 348
private, 11–12

Ricoeur, Paul, 392–393, 394, 395, 396–397, 398, 400, 403

Rite of Anointing, and Pastoral Care of the Sick, 269ff., 293

Rites, and ritual, 379–383, 389ff.

Ritual of 1973, 235ff., 292ff.

Rituale Romanum (1614), 201, 202, 203f., 210, 217–218, 231ff., 250, 253, 292, 326

Ritualization, 377ff., 389

Rituals, 202f.

Robert of Liège, Bishop, 175

Robert of Rheims, Archbishop, 179

Roguet, A.M., 295–296

Romanus Pontifex, bull, 314

Rudolf, Archpriest of Augsburg, 184

Rule of the Master, 219, 229, 251, 274, 275

Rush, Alfred, 277

S

Sacerdotale (ritual), 202

Sacrament houses, 168

Sacramentary of Amiens, 104f.
of Verona, 112, 233, 286

Sacrament, in theology of K. Rahner, 247f.

Sacred Congregation of Rites, 205–206, 211

Sacred Heart, devotion to, 235f.

Sacram Communionem, motu proprio, 237

Sacred music, motu proprio of Pius X on, 329

Sacrifice, nature of, 55f.

457

458

460